Coward

Also by Tim Clare

Fiction
The Honours
The Ice House

Non-fiction
We Can't All Be Astronauts

Coward

Why We Get
Anxious &
What We Can
Do About It

Tim Clare

CANONGATE

First published in Great Britain, the USA and Canada in 2022
by Canongate Books Ltd, 14 High Street, Edinburgh EH1 1TE

Distributed in the USA by Publishers Group West
and in Canada by Publishers Group Canada

canongate.co.uk

1

British Library Cataloguing-in-Publication Data
A catalogue record for this book is available on
request from the British Library

ISBN 978 1 83885 310 5

Typeset in Garamond by Palimpsest Book Production Ltd,
Falkirk, Stirlingshire

Printed and bound in Great Britain by Clays Ltd, Elcograf S.p.A.

For Suki

CONTENTS

HOW TO READ THIS BOOK

This is not a self-help book.

I'm barely qualified to dress myself, let alone coach someone I've never met through overcoming the most widespread mental illness in the world. It'd be like asking a goat to operate a lathe.

This is not a polemic.

It's not an urgent broadside against a pervasive scourge, an exploding of widespread myths, nor a profound meditation on the malady of our modern age.

This is not a manifesto. It's not a call-to-arms. It is not a spirited *cri de coeur*. I've done my best to present the strongest arguments of everyone I consulted – even if, ultimately, I disagreed with them.

This is not science. It includes science, and many scientists, but more than anything else it's a story. And the lab monkey is the author. Hi.

In this book, I'm going to act as a kind of medical skeleton of cowardice. I'm here with all my bones on display.

If you're skilled at avoiding things that make you uncomfortable, you might never consider yourself anxious. I didn't for years. Many adults unconsciously construct their lives around never putting themselves in a situation where they feel out of place, afraid, or like a beginner. They have a slew of rationalisations – I'm too busy, it looks boring, ugh, I can't think of anything *worse* – but the motivating prod is anxiety. They don't *feel* afraid, but fear controls their lives.

COWARD

I am a coward.

You are too.

This is a book about learning to face that.

—

My grandmother was a member of the Hitler Youth. One Boxing Day, our family was slumped in a post-turkey stupor when my dad asked why she and the people she knew hadn't done anything to stop the Holocaust.

Sat in her rocking chair, she paused to consider. 'We didn't know.'

But, my dad said, people must have had suspicions.

She recalled passing Auschwitz on a school trip. She said people used to ask: 'Why are there so many empty prams on Auschwitz station?' She remembered the policeman who lived at the end of her street, who had gone to work in the camp, and when he came back his hair had turned white. He locked himself in an attic room and shot himself.

'But,' she said, 'you have to understand: bombs were falling from the sky. We had no reason to question. We thought we knew who our enemies were.'

—

It's hard to remain open-minded while you're terrified.

Anxiety submits to authority. One of the gentle theses of this book – a suggestion, that you're free to weigh and reject – is that while anxiety makes us crave answers, a better way to live is to seek good questions. It's hard to be brutal and callous and cruel while also being curious.

Some people don't – can't – see themselves as anxious. Yet they're obsessed with immigrants swarming over the borders. With foreign or domestic powers plotting to destroy the country. With conspiracies or disturbing new trends.

They're not anxious; the world is threatening.

When we can't admit our anxiety and paranoia, we're vulnerable to misinformation, and manipulation by those who promise to make us feel safe.[1] We escape our uncomfortable anxiety by turning it into righteous anger. We turn our fellow humans into the Other. We stop noticing information that doesn't fit our model. We get locked in a single story. All we can see is the threat.

—

It's easy to be sceptical of things that don't fit your worldview. Most of us imagine that's all scepticism is. It's much harder, I've found, to maintain that scepticism when you're presented with exciting, counterintuitive answers that promise to transform your life. A lot of classic psychology experiments make for cool little stories. It feels almost mean-spirited to point out their flaws.

The sociologist Murray S. Davis wrote a terrific paper in the 1970s called 'That's Interesting!' in which he argued: 'It has long been thought that a theorist is considered great because his theories are true, but this is false. A theorist is considered great, not because his theories are true, but because they are *interesting*.'

For a theory to be interesting, Davis argues, it must overturn our weakly held assumptions while confirming our strongly held assumptions. If it fails to do the former, we think *Well, that's obvious*. If it fails to do the latter, we think *Well, that's absurd*. If it does both, we experience a pleasurable jolt of surprise – a prediction error – without threatening our overall model of the world. The theory feels intuitively right – it 'makes sense' – but it's also telling us something new – 'what seems to be X is, in fact, non-X' – and we feel smarter and better informed.

This principle applies to articles and videos we share on social media, to opinion pieces and conspiracy theories. As humans, our attention is drawn to difference, so – given huge data sets – what looks most anomalous looks most like a signal.

We see this tendency in popular science, especially in the realms of mental health and wellbeing – a desire not to let the facts get in the way of a good story. We've come to view the scientific method as mere pedantry, rather than an essential bulwark against human biases. TED Talks' slogan is 'Ideas worth spreading',[2] but truly worthwhile ideas are worth criticising.

Where relevant, I've included endnotes with references to studies. If I have reservations about the study design or reasons why I think we should be cautious about the authors' conclusions, I've mostly saved those for the endnotes too. Remember, in research a 'significant' difference isn't necessarily a large one. Significant means 'less than 5 per cent likely to have happened by chance'. Also, just because a study is peer-reviewed doesn't mean it's not shite.

Not everything I experienced is generalisable. People vary. In a couple of cases, I've changed people's names to protect their privacy. I did some really dumb shit. I'm allowed to because it's my life and I get to write my own risk assessments. Please don't copy me. Apply wisdom.

I.

TAIL

How I became anxious

Some years ago I grew a tail. It was about a sixth of my body length, a mix of cartilage and bone.

'Coward' comes from the Old French *coart*, meaning 'one with a tail'. It may have been intended to evoke a dog with its tail between its legs in the instinctive gesture of submission. In old descriptions of heraldry, a 'lion coward' is a coat of arms depicting a lion with its tail between its legs.

There are fewer than sixty cases of humans born with tails in medical literature. Some estimates put the number as low as twenty. The difference is accounted for by a distinction between a 'true tail', which contains muscle, can grow as long as 18cm and can move, and a 'pseudotail', a growth that superficially resembles a tail, but turns out to be a projecting bone, a tumour, or, in one macabre case, 'a thin, elongated parasitic fetus'.[1]

A human with a tail feels like a contradiction in terms. Perhaps we find such births unsettling because we think of evolution as an event in our distant past, not a journey that continues. Labels like 'human' and 'animal' imply a comforting permanence.

My tail lasted about four weeks before being reabsorbed into my body. As did yours. We all grow a tail inside the womb. It peaks around week five then retreats inside us. Its column of vertebrae becomes the main supporting structure for our developing skeleton. Our tail becomes our spine.

We never lost our tail. It hides within us.

———

When I first held my daughter, Suki, seconds after her birth, my sleep-deprived brain refused to process her as real. My wife's labour had lasted three days and nights. It had been so gruelling that, at points, we genuinely forgot a child was on the way.

The thing gazing up at me seemed like a sophisticated movie prop. Her hair was red with blood. We stared at each other, stunned.

I never felt I deserved to be a father, nor that I would be any good at it. All the same, I had longed for it. I had held my wife's hand in the hospital when, over a year earlier, the nurses told us she had miscarried. When they showed us the scan, with the empty space where a foetus ought to have been, I pawed at the air between me and the screen, as if I could reach inside the image and fix it.

I have heard people say that mentally ill people who have children are selfish. Perhaps I am.

Over the past fifteen years I have been diagnosed variously with generalised anxiety disorder, panic disorder, acute anxiety, panic attacks and depression. I've been called anxious, uptight, stressed, paranoid, hysterical and unhinged. A worrier. A pessimist. A neurotic.

All with some justification, I might add. I am not easy to be around. Most of my life has been shaped by fear – anticipating it, reducing it, blocking it out. But none of those labels ever quite felt like they fitted.

———

In English, we have many words to describe someone who is habitually afraid. We might call a person 'shy', which in some circles is almost complimentary, a near-synonym for 'modest'. If we think their fear serves a purpose we might call them 'concerned' or 'vigilant'. Drop their status a few notches and we have 'cautious', 'wary'. Drop it further and we hit ostensibly neutral terms: 'anxious', 'worried', 'fearful', 'nervous'. Want to imply a minor, vaguely comic failure of character? Call them 'jumpy', 'paranoid', 'panicked'. Our most critical terms make anxiety their whole identity. We might dub someone a 'wimp', or transform them into a 'baby', 'chicken', or 'pussy'. (The fearful undergo similar mutations in German: from the evocative *Angsthase* or 'fear-hare', and *Weichei*, a 'soft egg', to the chimeric *Duckmäuser*, literally 'duck mouse', a moral hypocrite too scared to voice their true opinion.)

At the bottom of the heap is 'coward' – a word which carries such odium that at many points in history being labelled one has been grounds for execution.

Most of our words for bravery are somatic – located within the body. We say someone has 'guts', 'heart', 'spine', 'balls', 'nerve' or, if we wish they were a bit less liberated, 'cheek'. To call someone a coward is to point out our shameful ancestral stowaway and imply it still controls them. Humanity's dirty little secret.

Hey you. Your tail is showing.

—

I wasn't always a coward.

My mum tells me that as a young child I was 'fearless', running off down the beach towards the ocean without looking back, toppling into the duck pond (I remember being underwater, the greeny-brown murk, the peace), shouting out in class and performing to an audience whenever I had the chance.

The change was gradual. Increased self-awareness, social intelligence and inhibition are, after all, natural and healthy parts of our development, as are the acquisition and generalisation of fears.[2] You burn your hand on a hot stove, you learn to be wary of touching any stove. You gauge the mood in the room before launching into that fifth rendition of 'Frère Jacques'.

When I was seven, my granddad died while we were on holiday together. One moment he was alive, the next my little brother ran in, wide-eyed, announcing: 'Pop's gone to Heaven!' My mum and nan were crying. A policeman came. I remember Nan with her head in her hands, saying, 'It's just a shell, it's just a shell'; *Pigeon Street* on the TV; standing in the corner of the kitchen, a box of Sugar Puffs at my head height; Dad drawing a multicoloured potato for my brother while Mum wept in the next room; the alien weirdness of a world where someone could be *deleted*, and what seemed like minutes later we were doing colouring-in and pointedly not mentioning it. We drove home that night.

I was relieved when I learned I was not invited to the funeral. Over the months that followed, I glimpsed the adults in my life naked with grief – the shock and raw boredom of death's aftermath. I learned never to speak of what had happened, or my feelings. I was spared the pain – and the catharsis – of saying goodbye. As far as I was concerned, Pop had been buried alive.

—

My first memory of deep, grinding worry comes from when I was fourteen, when the bullying started.

I had been to the dentist to get my braces checked. Walking home afterwards, I decided to pop into the local electronics shop to buy a birthday present for my brother. It was the closest thing our small town had to a record store. They had the entire Top 50 chart as CD singles. I loved music and would listen to hours of radio and albums every night. I was flicking through the charts when two boys from two years below came in and, after looking around for a bit, started teasing me.

I ignored them. I got teased a lot: about my weight, my glasses, my hair, my braces – nerd insignia that TV, movies and comics said meant you deserved abuse. I was kind of numb to it. It wasn't nice but it rarely felt personal. 'They're trying to get a reaction,' I was always told. 'Don't let them see they're getting to you and they'll leave you alone.'

Bullying moved like a storm front. Most of the time, all you had to do was hunker down, and it passed.

Eventually the boys wandered out. As they left, one of them glanced back through the window. Maybe I'd finally had enough, or maybe, with glass between us, I felt a rush of bravado. As he looked at me, I pulled a face.

They turned around and came back in. Standing either side of me, they started shouting, 'Pull us a face!' They called me 'Henry'. They kept shouting the name, over and over. They called to the shop assistant to say, 'Hello, Henry' to me, which he did, rolling his eyes as if reluctantly humouring them, but complying all the same. I stood there, staring down at the CDs in their clear plastic jewel cases, in silence, my cheeks burning, my hands shaking.

Don't let them see they're getting to you.

It can't have lasted longer than five minutes, but it felt like hours. Finally, they left.

It might not sound like the most traumatic experience, but to give you a sense of how excruciating recounting this incident is for me (I've never written it down, never told it in detail to anyone, even my wife) it took me days to write those few short paragraphs. I procrastinated. I ran miles. My sleep was patchy. In the middle of mundane tasks I found myself bursting into tears. When I finished, I came down with a heavy cold.

It's to do with what came afterwards. Every time those boys saw me at school, they would shout the name – even now, I instinctively call it 'the name' rather than exposing myself to the chest pains that come on when I type 'Henry' – circling me, yelling 'Pull us a face!', laughing. They snatched my pencil case and wouldn't give it back until I'd pulled a face. They hung around the entrance to school at the start and end of the day. I lived literally next door to my secondary school, so I ended up climbing through the hedge each morning rather than face them. They knew where I lived. My house got egged. We got prank calls where the person on the other end mocked my grandfather's voice (he had survived a tracheotomy and spoke in croaks). Once, when I didn't have any lessons in the morning, I woke up to find one of them in my house, climbing the stairs.

This was every day for an entire school year. My friends didn't do anything to help. Sometimes they joined in. I was scared to tell my parents – who assumed the egging was random pranksters – or teachers in case it made things worse. More than that, I felt ashamed. I still do. It was my fault. They had latched on to something defective and ugly in me. I felt helpless and humiliated and worthless. At night, I would lie on my bed and stare at the ceiling, my stomach churning, my head and hands clammy.

For years, I relived the incident, wishing I hadn't provoked them, wishing I hadn't left the house at all.

Wishing I'd had the sense to be a coward.

———

Self-blame seems perverse to those who haven't found themselves on the receiving end of something horrible and apparently random. But many of us would rather blame victims – including ourselves – than believe the world is unfair and out of our control.

In 1966 psychologist Melvin J. Lerner conducted a follow-up[3] to Stanley Milgram's famous experiments on obedience.[4] Students observed another student receiving electric shocks for making mistakes on a learning task. They were told they were taking part in research for the military about performing well under pressure. Their job was to watch the other participant for emotional cues. They were also asked to rate the participant's 'likeability'. They answered questions like: 'How easily would this person fit in with your friends?'

In reality, the other participant was an actor and the electric shocks were fake. Lerner found that when participants believed they were powerless to intervene in the fake student's suffering, they responded by rejecting and devaluing her. Lerner came to explain this through his 'Just-World Hypothesis'.[5] It's frightening to admit parts of life are out of our control, so, Lerner argued, we find ways to blame victims for their misfortune. 'Most people cannot afford,' he said, 'for the sake of their own sanity, to believe in a world governed by a schedule of random reinforcements.'

When Pop died, I acquired a dark secret. I had not wanted to go on holiday. Through some eerie, sympathetic magic, I had caused his heart attack.

When I was being bullied, I knew it was because of my own stupidity.

But there was an upside. If I had caused these bad things, it stood to reason I could stop them. If I could fix myself, I could make myself safe.

—

Cowardice is one explanation for why humans have survived so long. How we've morphed and bulked out and elaborated ourselves from protozoa, to fish flop-wheezing onto land, to tool-using chimps, to sad bipeds with Fitbits and sarcasm. Evolution rewards survival over satisfaction. It may be deeply pleasurable to notice how light bends when it strikes the dew drops beading on a waxy leaf, to appreciate the sweetness of dark berries plucked from the bush, but if you want to pass on your genes to the next generation it's preferable to spot the wolf approaching through the undergrowth, or the looming cliff edge.

Fear wants to keep us safe. Better stressed than dead.

—

Suki had a tricky start to life. She got an infection and had to return to hospital. The doctors weren't sure if she had meningitis.

Gazing down at Suki, a cannula in her wrist, her tiny chubby toes scrunched above the heart monitor strapped to her ankle, I feared for her. I loved her more than I knew how to deal with. I felt powerless. My wife was surviving on minutes of sleep, staying in the hospital for endless rounds of feeding, tests and medication. I was ragged and frightened. I have never felt more like a little boy dressed up as a man.

———

When Suki was about eight months old I had a severe panic attack. I was sprawled on the floor, screaming until my throat burned, delirious with terror. I can't remember the trigger but I still feel the gut-deep dread, the barrelling disorientation, the unreality, the conviction that my life was over, that I was going to lose my family and please mummy daddy jesus won't somebody HELP. My wife had closed the doors between us. I could hear her playing YouTube nursery rhymes to drown me out so our daughter wouldn't hear her daddy screaming, begging.

Just writing it down fills me with curdling shame. To be so scared that I couldn't stop myself from shrieking, even though I knew the noise might frighten my baby. So scared – of *nothing* – that I couldn't breathe, that my muscles cramped and my heart pounded and sweat poured from my prone, flailing body. That my wife had to act to protect my daughter from being scared by her own daddy. Like I was some kind of monster.

The more I suffered, the more contemptible I found myself.

———

For years before Suki was born, I managed my anxiety with alcohol and self-harm – drinking until I vomited or passed out, or punching myself repeatedly in the head. It was around then I had my first panic attacks, frightening episodes where I felt like I couldn't breathe or I was going insane. I thought the way I was treating my body was to blame, so I quit alcohol and stopped self-harming. But they had been my coping mechanisms. The anxiety and panic attacks got worse.

When my panic attacks were bad, I'd have several a day, three or four days in a row, each lasting between twenty minutes and an hour. When I was having a good spell, I might go as long as ten days without one.

I saw the doctor, got prescribed medication, got put on the long waiting list for cognitive behavioural therapy, did a stress-reduction course with handouts, paid for private therapy, changed medication, exercised, did meditation classes, yoga, and read book after book after book that promised to teach me how to get calm, de-stress, and beat anxiety.

For the longest time I didn't think of myself as having an anxiety or panic disorder. Because life has stressful bits, right? You move house, you change jobs, people you love get sick or die.

I could always point to some specific event, past or incoming, and say look, this is what's stressing me out right now. Either I need to get it out the way, or recover from it. Then I'll be fine. Sometimes my panic attacks would go away for as long as a month, maybe two.

But they always came back. Nothing I tried worked, until even the quiet times seemed like a lull while the enemy guns reloaded.

—

Anxiety is, by its nature, a disorder of avoidance.[6] Like a proximity sensor on a car, it warns of impending collisions. The shrill beeping gets louder and faster. You take evasive action.

It took me ages to admit I needed to tackle my cowardice head-on. Thinking about anxiety triggered anxiety. Feeling anxious had always been my signal to pull away, to retreat.

I was terrified of making things worse. It was like being stuck in a bad relationship, but you've become quite good at hiding from each other in different rooms, and maybe if you can just get through Christmas things will get better.

No one has ever greeted the dawn thinking: *Ah, what a perfect day for performing a painstaking emotional inventory that will bring me face to face with my darkest fears!*

And I might never have set off on that journey had I not met the guinea pigs.

II.

SHIFT HAPPENS
The moment I realised I couldn't go on like this

When Suki was two we visited a petting zoo, and I sneezed. We were looking down at the long-haired guinea pigs, and at my 'Achoo!' they stampeded.

The sign on the hutch said that guinea pigs have a 'strong startle reflex'. My panic attacks and anxiety had been plaguing me for over a decade, and on reading this I felt stirrings of kinship. I had found my tribe.

At a sudden noise or movement, a guinea pig either freezes or pegs it in a series of short zigzagging sprints. You've probably heard this referred to as the 'fight or flight response', though nowadays it's more often called 'fight, flight or freeze', 'the acute stress response' or, more suggestively, 'hyperarousal'. We have a similar hardwired reaction – a kind of evolutionary intruder alarm.

We have something else in common with guinea pigs. Early on, we learned to make our fear infectious.

Imagine you were strolling through central Tokyo and a load of pedestrians came running towards you yelling *Gojira!* Your heart rate would increase and adrenaline would flood your bloodstream, preparing you to run, even before you looked up to espy a 160-foot lizard tail-slapping a skyscraper. You understand – and a primitive part of your brain knows instinctively – that frightened faces, cries of alarm and fleeing humans probably equal danger.

This is the kind of thrift that natural selection does so well. Instead of relying on every member of the herd to be independently vigilant at all times, only one guinea pig needs to startle in response to some sensory cue – an aversive stimulus like a loud noise or pain, or a cue the guinea pig has learned to associate with a loud noise or pain – and the whole community startles. For wild cavies – ancestors of the guinea pigs we first domesticated 7,000 years ago – the stampede was a highly adaptive behaviour that maximised the group's chances of survival.

Another advantage of being a social species is you get to have specialists. If one member of the group is very anxious and her increased vigilance catches something her calmer pals miss, her triggered startle reflex warns everyone else. Gloria's pegging it, lads. Shit, Code Hawk, Code Hawk.

It's adaptive that Gloria is the only member of the herd to pass her days in this anxious, hypervigilant state. Maintaining high anxiety costs calories, depletes the immune system, impairs digestion and probably makes her pretty miserable.[2] For cavies, having at least one Gloria in the herd was an advantage. Her anxiety increased everyone else's chances of surviving to have litters of pups, while isolating the physiological burden in a single member.

Anxiety can be an individual curse and a community blessing. If the price of peace is eternal vigilance, the price of eternal vigilance is anxiety.

Gloria, like most of evolutionary psychology, is a work of fiction.[3] We don't know for certain that evolution differentially selects for some members of a group to be especially anxious, although some researchers have theorised that this is the case.[4] Gloria the anxious guinea pig is less scientific case study, more mythic archetype. We might think of her as a kind of guinea-pig shaman. She's a figure who spans cultures, species. Reviled and pitied and yet, in her own neurotic way, a sentinel. Keeper of the hidden backbone. Avatar of all that is gentle, vulnerable and fluffy.

Gloria is a coward.

This book is the story of how I became like Gloria in another way. How for years anxiety and panic ruled my life. And how, for the sake of my daughter, I decided to transform.

This is the story of how I became a guinea pig.

———

In this book, I'm mostly using 'anxiety' as shorthand for disordered, dysfunctional anxiety – long-term, destructive, intense fear and worry. Instead of providing useful prods – e.g. you should probably get up now if you want to be on time for work – disordered anxiety is a never-ending opera of alarm bells, warning lights and pop-up messages.

My anxiety was eclectic, agnostic with regards to scale. Global warming and the likelihood that human consciousness does not survive death were just as likely to keep me rocking in a nauseous daze as an upcoming train journey, or worrying that my wife was secretly annoyed at me.

I would get into spirals where I was crabby and couldn't concentrate. I'd binge on sweet snacks and caffeine to keep awake. I struggled to get the smallest things done. What was the point when the world was ending?

Soon I'd be frazzled, behind on tasks, and convinced of my own uselessness. I'd start monitoring friends and family for signs they were fed up with me.

'Are you annoyed with me?'

'No.'

'Are you sure?'

'Yes.'

'Why are you rolling your eyes, then?'

This strategy, sustained over several days, is quite annoying.

It would become hard to remember words. My stammer would emerge, until it was so bad I couldn't get sentences out. Loud noises would startle me. At night I'd lie awake, listening for voices in the street outside. When a friend spoke, I'd struggle to concentrate long enough to hear a full sentence. I'd start saying 'What? I can't hear you.' With each repetition, my pulse would accelerate. 'I feel anxious,' I'd say. 'It's coming back.' Realising I was sliding towards panic would frighten me, which made me slide faster.

I knew, of course, about fight, flight or freeze. I'd read dozens of books explaining that fear is 'just' a physiological response. Sometimes the build-up took days. Sometimes I'd wake up one morning, after weeks of feeling fine, and without explanation the symptoms were back. Eventually I'd have a full-blown panic attack. Usually several, chained together, with groggy comedowns in between.

It's hard to convey the experience of a panic attack to someone who hasn't had one. Even talking to other sufferers, I've realised they vary hugely from person to person. For now, if you want a sense of mine: Imagine you're late for an important appointment. You keep checking to see if the bus is coming. It keeps refusing to appear. You start cursing yourself for having left home so late, for not having been more prepared. You picture whoever it is you're meant to be meeting growing angrier and angrier. Your heart rate increases. You hop from foot to foot. Time is moving on. Fuck. You're such an idiot. Where's that bus?

Now take those thoughts, that rising discomfort, that itchy, twitchy feeling, and accelerate it past normal. Double it. Cube it. Crank up the volume. The speed. Turn the voice in your head to a cacophony of yells. The fidgety tremor to tightening muscles, crushing chest pain, a windpipe that's squeezing shut. Make the road and the bus stop and the sky seem unreal, like you're on TV, like you foresaw this in a dream.

Everyone's staring at you. You're a freak. You're a crazy person. You're going to vomit. You're going to have a heart attack and die.

A panic attack is a million sirens going off at once. It's the florid madness you always feared descending on you like a flock of burning crows. It's trying to do long division in your head against a timer during a firework display and for every answer you get wrong they shoot a member of your family.

Panic attacks hit me again and again until I was dog-tired, stunned and demoralised. Ashamed to leave the house in case people saw I'd been sobbing. In case I had an attack in public.

This went on for more than a decade. The more the panic cycle happens, the more automatic it becomes, until it feels inevitable. You know what's coming, which adds to your fear, which makes it worse. You try interventions like deep breathing, reasoning with yourself, repeating positive slogans, but it feels like trying to soak up rising floodwaters with a nappy. If you've ever fucked-up frying an egg or put your trousers on backwards after two hours' sleep, you'll know how difficult theoretically simple things can be when you're exhausted.

When the panic leaves, your limbs sag. Your thinking is sluggish. You have work to catch up on. Relationships to repair. Frankly, you feel like you deserve a break. So you sleep and comfort-eat. You kid yourself maybe it's gone for good now. Who, after all, wants a life devoted entirely to the War Against Panic? You want distractions, to make a decision without reflexively asking 'What if it makes me anxious?' I was married, I had a home. Sometimes I would hear my wife, Lisa, downstairs, singing, and feel a peace and belonging I never believed someone like me would get to experience.

But with every failed course of meds, every self-help book that led to nothing, I grew a little more pessimistic. Joy became a little harder. How can you close your eyes for a kiss when you're forever expecting a punch?

———

One day after a panic attack I did something which, in retrospect, feels like quite an achievement. I managed to make myself even more frightened.

As my terror settled down into the familiar ruminative, roiling boil of worry, I thought of all the articles I'd read – if I'm honest, skimmed – on the effects of parental mental illness on children. Studies linking parental mental illness to impaired academic achievement and resilience,[5] a higher risk of developing severe mental illness,[6] even a child's chance of getting asthma.[7] I was putting Suki at risk simply by existing.

I sat with that for a long time – the threat of passing this dark inheritance to my astonishing, hilarious, unrepeatable daughter. The cold reality of it cut through layers of despondency and self-pity.

Deep down, I didn't feel I deserved to be happy. But if I didn't love myself, did I at least love her? Children, in my experience, are pretty good at spotting discrepancies between what adults say and how they behave. After Pop died, there was a huge gap between what my parents said – *everything's okay, everything's fine* – and how they obviously felt. Children learn less from the verbal instructions we give, and more from the behaviour we model.

I imagined Suki seeing how I treat myself. I imagined her learning from me. I imagined her treating herself the same way.

In that moment, something shifted. I still had no idea what to do, no confidence in my ability to find a cure, but failure was unacceptable. If Suki could fight through infection to be with us, if my wife could fight through a changing body, seventy-two hours of labour and the months of sleep deprivation that followed, I could try one last time to beat anxiety.

We had just enrolled Suki in a research programme tracking the development of visual working memory in children. I went with her to the hospital and watched as scientists slid her sleeping body into an MRI scanner. On another occasion we visited the lab, where they strapped a huge Medusa-like fright-wig to her head called an fNIRS – functional near-infrared spectroscopy – scanner (pronounced 'eff-neers'). It measured the movement of blood through her brain as her eyes tracked coloured shapes on a screen. She enjoyed being the centre of attention and took her work as a young scientist very seriously.

Gazing at the map of Suki's brain on the computer screen, I was struck by the incredible advances we've made in psychology. The shifting oranges and reds represented concentrations of haemoglobin, carrying oxygen to areas demanding it most. I was watching her think.

I'd read articles about studies where scientists scanned the brains of anxious people or monitored the sweat glands of monks. I'd read about anxious genes, anxious gut bacteria, anxious robots, curing anxiety using extreme cold or fasting or forest walks or psychedelic drugs. If the newspapers were to be believed, break-throughs in anxiety research were coming thick and fast, across multiple disciplines.

None of these cutting-edge treatments was likely to be offered by my local GP. They were being tested round the world, in labs like this. Surely the answer's out there, I thought. Surely *someone* knows.

Over the next few weeks, I stayed up late into the night googling 'anxiety treatment' this and 'panic research' that. I kept reading that various new treatments looked 'promising' but 'more research was needed'. That in five, ten, perhaps twenty years they might be made available to the public.

Anxiety creates a state of emergency. It yells: deal with this problem *now*. So I decided: rather than waiting for innumerable rounds of clinical trials, for approval from regulatory bodies, for the political climate to shift so these treatments got funded, I would go direct to the researchers. I would hunt down people who had given their lives to studying anxiety and panic, and I would find out their secrets. Then I would test the treatments on myself.

I would make myself a guinea pig.

—

The terms of my challenge were simple. I would give myself a year. My fortieth birthday was approaching, which felt like a satisfying – if slightly ominous – cut-off point. I would approach every researcher I could find in any field whose work was even tangentially related to anxiety. I would ask them what they had learned. Then, as far as possible, I would apply their findings to my own life.

Giving myself a deadline was a way of making myself commit. There was no going into this half-heartedly, no making a change on Monday and giving up by Wednesday.

Of course, I really was on a deadline. Every day I remained unwell was another day of my daughter's childhood I was missing. It was another day I was failing to turn up as a father.

I had two more rules. First, everything had to be evidence-based. Naturally, new treatments would have less research behind them than established ones, but I wanted peer-reviewed studies, and at least some 'face plausibility' before I gave them my time.

Second, nothing expensive. I was a parent on a part-time writer's wage. I couldn't afford boutique cures, no matter how brilliant.

Aside from that, everything was on the table. In a kind of mania, I began banging out emails to researchers around the globe. All right, folks, I thought, let's see what you've got.

III.

THE EXERCIST

Exercise; the fight, flight or freeze response;
and neurotransmitters

Starting out, I felt bewildered. I borrowed psychology and neuro-science textbooks from the library to bone up on the basics. I barely understood a word. I might as well have been reading a potato.

I needed expert help. While I waited – anxiously, natch – for responses to my emails, I tried to think where to begin.

Like a lot of parents, in the face of patchy sleep and limited free time I'd let my physical activity and eating habits not so much slide as implode. I fought off exhaustion with caffeine and sugar. When my daughter finally fell asleep, it was all too easy to order takeaway on my phone: pizzas, kebabs, cheesy chips. They'd leave me feeling gross and bloated, a film of grease on my lips. What was I doing? Why couldn't I control myself? Whole days would pass without my eating a single piece of fresh fruit or vegetable.

I'd read articles about how the gut was a new frontier in mental health. How inflammation had been linked to depression and anxiety, and that inflammation increased if you were overweight or if you ate a lot of sugary, fatty food.

Friends and family had often told me I needed to do more exer-cise. That I had to 'get out the house'. Lots of newspaper articles claimed 'research shows' or 'science tells us that' exercise reduces anxiety.

Out of all the options open to me, changing my diet and exercising more seemed the least controversial. Even if they weren't enough on their own, surely they would help. But where was this research I'd heard so much about? When was it done? On whom? And what had it found?

—

It was late November 1913, just hours before Harvard University's football squad, the Harvard Crimson, were to play their final game of the season against their arch-rivals, Yale. Victory would mean a double triumph: satisfaction in a legendarily vicious match-up (the contest was suspended for three years after an 1894 game known as the 'Hampden Park Bloodbath', where four players received crippling injuries), and a perfect season. The second perfect season in a row, in fact – two straight years where Harvard had neither lost nor tied a game. Harvard Stadium, a great U-shaped amphitheatre of reinforced concrete, would soon reverberate with roaring fans. In light of the occasion, a bespectacled forty-something professor of physiology called Walter B. Cannon approached twenty-five members of the squad and asked if he could sample their urine.

Cannon wanted to see if – as with the dogs, cats and rabbits he had studied in his laboratory – emotional excitement produced a temporary rise in the players' blood sugar. He took samples before and after the game and found sugar in 12 cases post-match, including in 5 substitutes who had not been called upon to play.[1] He also took samples from an 'excited spectator of the Harvard victory' (the Crimson won 15–5) and found 'a marked glycosuria' (secretion of glucose into the urine) that was not present in a sample taken from the same person the following day.

Through this and many other experiments, Cannon came to formulate his theory of what he termed the 'fight or flight response'.[2] He argued that, when an animal faces a threat, its body responds by preparing either to run away or fight.

Cannon showed how pain or threatening situations trigger the release of adrenaline and an increase in blood sugar. These reflexes seemed to be associated with particular emotions like fear and rage, and, he reasoned, 'because reflexes as a rule are useful responses, we are justified in the surmise that under these circumstances these reactions may be useful. What, then, is their possible value?'[3]

Much research has built upon the work Cannon originally published in his 1915 book, *Bodily Changes In Pain, Hunger, Fear and Rage*, but the core principles remain the same. In the presence of pain or a perceived threat, our body stimulates the production of hormones like adrenaline, cortisol and noradrenaline which get us ready for action. Heart rate increases to pump additional blood to the muscles. Muscle tension increases to improve speed and strength. Blood clotting speeds up in case of injury. Blood sugar levels rise to provide the muscles with more energy. Breathing increases to flush out carbon dioxide in anticipation of an increase in waste CO_2 as muscles begin working harder. Some blood vessels constrict while others dilate, to redirect blood flow to where it's most needed. Digestion slows or stops. Vision narrows. Bladder and sphincter muscles loosen.[4]

All of this is in service of a term which Cannon invented: homeostasis (*homeo*, 'same', *stasis*, 'not moving'), referring to the processes by which our bodies maintain an internal balance when external conditions change. In the case of the fight, flight or freeze response, these physiological reactions assume you're about to engage in strenuous physical activity – either fighting or running for your life. High activity means your muscles need additional sugar, absorb more oxygen and expel more CO_2 from the cells (up to twenty times more than at rest, according to Cannon).

Since CO_2 is mildly acidic, less of it makes your blood more alkaline. If you don't vigorously fight or run away, heightened blood sugar and pH throw your body into temporary disequilibrium. Your ears ring. Your hands shake. You feel lightheaded. Fight or flight *disrupts* homeostasis when it's not followed by action.

Cannon argued that for these reactions to be of use, they had to happen quickly. No sense in diverting all that blood to the leg muscles unless it gets there fast enough to save you. He also argued that some results of strenuous activity – like breathlessness – themselves release adrenaline and raise blood sugar, accounting perhaps for the phenomenon of a 'second wind', but also meaning that, once an animal is in this state of high arousal, it's easier for the response to be retriggered.

The fight, flight or freeze response was honed over millions of years to protect predator and prey alike. As varied selection pressures meant successive generations shapeshifted to fit a vast range of habitats, as limbs elongated, as teeth sharpened or flattened, as skull capacity increased to accommodate burgeoning brains, this response was preserved. It's that essential.

And now, we are its heirs.

———

If you don't have an anxiety disorder, you might be mystified as to why someone suffering from the condition – especially if they've been suffering for *years* – wouldn't just whip on the spandex and hightail it down to the gym at the first opportunity. Why on earth would anyone resort to psychiatric medication or a long course of therapy when they could just hop on an exercise bike and pedal the screaming fantods away?

To begin to answer that, let's disappear up our own backsides.

Consider the humble bacterium E. coli. It's typically a little rod-shaped cell, 2 microns long and half a micron thick (or 0.002mm by 0.0005mm). E. coli likes to maintain an internal pH of 7.2 to 7.8 – marginally alkaline. However, when colonising the human gastrointestinal tract – which includes the large and small intestine, the stomach and the oesophagus – it faces an environment ranging from pH 4.5 to pH 9.[5] Therefore, to survive and reproduce, an E. coli bacterium needs to detect and respond to pH levels in its surroundings and within its own cells. This lets it figure out: *Are my surroundings too acid or alkali?* and *Am I too acid or alkali?* It does this through sensors that directly detect external or internal pH, and sensors that detect secondary changes that reliably signal a shift in pH. For example, when E. coli detects trimethylamine *N*-oxide (which decomposes into trimethylamine, a highly alkaline compound), it stimulates an enzyme which produces acid.[6] In this way, it maintains its internal balance, or homeostasis.

Systems like this are present in every organism that lives today or that has ever lived. They've shaped life itself. Something as simple as a bacterial cell can sense and respond to danger.

But crucially, its reactions happen in the moment. E. coli doesn't have much control over where it ends up. It has a little tail or 'flagellum' it can rotate counterclockwise in order to swim – after a fashion – but mostly it just has to go with the flow, trying to survive wherever it finds itself. It would be pointless for an E. coli bacterium to be able to predict that, in an hour, it's likely to wash up in the highly acidic environment of a human stomach. It can't act on that information.

Humans, by contrast, have lots of options for influencing the external world. We have limbs. We have language. All those chemo-receptors and homeostatic systems enjoyed by E. coli are still working away inside us, but we can go one better. Not only can we adjust if our surroundings are too hot or too cold – by sweating or shivering – we can take steps to avoid hostile environments altogether. We don't just have to think: *Ouch, this stove is burning me – I'll move my hand away.* We can see it and think: *That stove is likely to burn me – I won't touch it.*

We can detect and respond to dangers *before they happen.*

This is anxiety.

Anxiety works by anticipating and inhibiting. It says: *Don't do that, you'll get hurt. Don't do that, you'll be disappointed. Don't do that, you'll embarrass yourself.*

Anxiety likes routine. It likes predictability. It likes knowing outcomes.

Anxiety hates uncertainty. It hates change. Most of all, it hates any situation where you might, possibly, be out of your depth. Where the emotional pH of your environment might be beyond what you can adjust for.

Anxiety discourages you from taking any action that – from its perspective – might cause you physical or psychological harm. At a fundamental level, it wants to help you avoid anything that might upset your internal balance – anything that might disrupt homeostasis. It might do this with a voice in your head: *That'll turn out badly*. It might show you a mental image of a possible stressful event: the overcrowded restaurant, your boss looking disappointed. It might punish you with an unpleasant bodily sensation – a tight chest, a churning stomach, choking. Often, it hits you with thoughts, images and sensations simultaneously.

Anxiety makes you sensitive to mistakes – they *hurt* – so you remember and watch out for them next time. But it's not doing this out of spite. It's just trying to get your attention, to warn you, to keep you from greater danger. The world is nasty, unpredictable, and you, you poor thing, are so very fragile. It's not an insult, just reality. I wouldn't let my daughter, a preschooler, behind the controls of a helicopter mid-flight – not because I want to deny her new, enriching experiences, but because I want to keep her safe. In the same way, anxiety doesn't want to let you behind the controls of your own life, because you might crash.

Anxiety prefers the sure thing over the gamble. The now over the uncertain tomorrow. Limiting pain over chasing pleasure.

And anxiety *knows* – oh, if anything is truly knowable in this hellishly uncertain world, it knows this – if you attempt something new, you will fail.

You have the thought: *I should start a new exercise regime.*

Anxiety lowers its newspaper and glances at you doubtfully over its spectacles. *And how long's that going to last?*

The honest truth is, you don't know. But you feel like you ought to at least try.

You've failed every other time you've tried it, says anxiety.

Well, this time's going to be different, you think. I really need this.

You don't have the self-discipline. You haven't even got any running shoes.

I'll buy some.

Save your money. They'll sit in the shoe rack for the rest of the year, mocking you every time you see them. People waste small fortunes on gym memberships they never use. You're better off sparing yourself the disappointment.

But I'm miserable. I can't go on like this.

You're fundamentally broken. You can't fix yourself by jogging round the block.

Already you're feeling that crushing sensation round your heart, that dragging fatigue. It's true. You've literally never managed to do this before now. Why should today be any different?

Just fix yourself a peanut butter sandwich, anxiety says, turning its attention back to the obituary columns. *Eat some Pringles. Stop torturing yourself with all this aspirational rubbish. It's not for you.*

And you hang your head. Of course it's not. You? A runner? You're not sure what came over you.

———

People joke about being picked last for football or coming last in the cross-country. At school, I was literally picked last for football and I literally came dead-last in the cross-country. I have flat feet. I like indoor pursuits, like sleep. My commute to work is three metres.

I'd tried to change my diet before. I'd met up with friends to do workouts. The new routine only ever lasted a few weeks before something got in the way. Feeling like I'd earned a break, I'd return to old vices with the frenzied abandon of a just-bathed spaniel rolling in fox shit. If I didn't eat every couple of hours, I'd struggle to concentrate. My anxiety would spike. I'd stammer. My hands would become shaky. It became so bad my doctor sent me for a blood test to see if I was prediabetic. The test came back negative, but it was a wake-up call.

I couldn't go on with this cycle of peaks and crashes. But how was I supposed to magically attain the iron discipline to overhaul my diet and start exercising? I needed an expert. After a couple of emails, I headed to London to meet Dave Thomas, co-founder of the Foundry gym and a personal trainer with over 20,000 hours of training sessions under his belt.

———

'From a biochemical perspective, nothing has changed for our bodies from when we were hunter-gatherers.' I met Dave at his gym in London, and we got talking about Cannon's fight, flight or freeze response. Once, it helped us survive bears, wolves and sabre-toothed tigers – but we don't have those any more. 'What we do have is fucking annoying co-workers, we have stressful commutes, we have fast food, we have constant caffeine.'

In the face of these psychological, physiological and dietary stressors, our bodies react as if we're facing a physical threat. The stressful commute doesn't even need to happen – just the anticipation that it *might* is enough to trigger the response. One working definition of 'stress' within medical and psychological literature is 'a threat to homeostasis'.

The main trigger within the body is the hypothalamus, a cone-shaped structure near the base of your brain.* The hypothalamus can marshal all sorts of physiological responses throughout your body via the autonomic nervous system, which governs functions like breathing,

———

* 'Hypo' in this case meaning 'under', and 'thalamus', the part of the brain it sits beneath.

blood pressure and heart rate. The autonomic nervous system has two branches – the sympathetic and the parasympathetic. The sympathetic nervous system is what gets us pumped up, energised, and ready for action. The parasympathetic nervous system helps settle us down afterwards. If the sympathetic nervous system is responsible for 'fight or flight', the parasympathetic deals with 'rest and digest' – healing, recovering and refuelling, all essential parts of survival too.

Current models of the stress response go like this: the hypothalamus receives a signal from the amygdala that there's a threat (you actually have two amygdalae, one in either hemisphere, but they tend to be referred to in the singular). First, the hypothalamus triggers the sympathetic nervous system, relaying a message to the adrenal glands* way down beside your kidneys to start pumping out adrenaline. Adrenaline speeds up your heart rate, releases stored glucose – thus raising your blood sugar – dilates small airways in your lungs and stimulates your desire to breathe. This process is near-instantaneous, giving us a sudden burst of energy and speed to deal with whatever the danger is.[7]

The second part of the response is driven by a collaboration between the hypothalamus, the pituitary gland, and the adrenal gland – together known as the hypothalamic-pituitary-adrenal axis or HPA axis. Stress triggers a hormonal cascade – like a series of molecular dominoes. The hypothalamus releases vasopressin and corticotropin-releasing factor (CRF). CRF then stimulates the pituitary gland to release adrenocorticotropic hormone (or ACTH). ACTH stimulates the adrenal gland to produce glucocorticoids – one of which is cortisol.[8]

For our purposes, it's enough to remember: 'Stress in – adrenaline and cortisol out'.

Our heart rate increases. Our muscles tense. Our blood sugar rises. But unless strenuous physical activity follows quickly, these changes

---

* 'Ad' meaning 'next to', and 'renal', 'kidney'.

feel very uncomfortable. It's like turning up the heating on an already hot day.

Dave explained to me how, in the case of raised blood sugar, the pancreas responds by producing insulin, which promotes the re-absorption of sugar back into the cells. If you have a big spike in blood sugar – either from stress, or from consuming sugary foods – you get a corresponding spike in insulin, the sugar in your blood gets reabsorbed all at once, and you become hypoglycaemic.* Since glucose is the brain's primary fuel, this leads to trouble concentrating, irritability and fatigue.

Anxious people can get into horrible cycles where something frightens us, the fight, flight or freeze response triggers, we get a brief, twitchy hyperglycaemic high as our blood sugar peaks, then an insulin spike that reabsorbs it, leaving us shaky, exhausted and confused. So we neck a sugary energy drink to boost our blood sugar, only to trigger another insulin spike that sees us crashing back down an hour later.

Over time, elevated levels of insulin can cause the body to become insulin resistant, which might not sound so bad – fewer of those spikes and crashes, right – but leads to all sorts of problems like weight gain, muscle loss, and the onset of type 2 diabetes.

And it gets worse.

———

In 1950, the *British Medical Journal* published the text of a wonder-fully grandiloquent talk given by endocrinologist Hans Selye on a condition he called 'the General Adaptation Syndrome' (GAS). Though his subject was chronic stress, he spoke in the lofty tones of a prime minister rallying his nation to war. 'We shall never truly "understand" this phenomenon,' he warned, 'since the complete

---

* 'Hypo' meaning 'low', and 'glycaemic' relating to sugar.

comprehension of life is beyond the human mind.' It would, he said, take 'many generations' to elucidate the details. But the fog had 'sufficiently dispersed' to view general adaptation syndrome 'through that measure of "twilight" which permits us to discern the grandeur of its outlines but fills us with the insatiable desire to see more.'[9]

Selye subjected mice to conditions like chronic cold or repeated surgical injuries. He built upon Cannon's work to argue that when the fight or flight response – which he termed 'the Alarm Reaction' – gets repeatedly triggered, eventually it passes into a second stage, 'the Stage of Resistance'. Here, some reactions begin to normalise: blood thickening reduces, adrenaline and cortisol levels drop. However, unless the stressor goes away, things like heart rate and blood pressure remain elevated compared to baseline, keeping the animal on high alert. In the final stage, 'the Stage of Exhaustion', the body is depleted of hormones and resources, and the animal becomes exhausted and vulnerable to disease.

In rodent studies, animals that are subjected to prolonged, unpredictable stressors like cold, tail shocks or restraints, produce more cortisol when they're exposed to a new stressor. They become hyper-reactive to stress.

Selye – sometimes called 'the father of stress' – would go on to argue that chronic, systemic stress could cause conditions like rheumatoid arthritis, diabetes and hypertension. Selye and those who built on his theory found that prolonged stress led to the breakdown of muscle, inflammation, a suppressed immune system, poor sleep, and even things like impaired memory from suppressed neuron growth in the hippocampus,* part of the brain associated with the consolidation of short-term memories into long-term ones, and spatial memory).[10] In the short-term, chronically elevated cortisol

---

* *Hippos*, 'horse', and *kampos*, 'sea monster', as in *hippokampos*, the giant sea horse from classical Greek mythology which pulled Poseidon's chariot. We have two hippocampi, so named for their creepy resemblance to sea horses.

and adrenaline caused fatigue, irritability and anxiety. In the long-term, they led to burn-out, breakdown and collapse.[11]

Later refinements of Selye's model introduce the term 'allostasis' to refer to the processes and chemical messengers that maintain homeostasis.[12] Acute allostasis is normal, healthy and prompts adaptation. Allostatic overload comes when, for example, emotional threats mean our blood pressure is raised all the time. Stress is a regular part of everyday life, and includes positive experiences like excitement. Researchers use terms like allostatic overload to distinguish between stress, and being 'stressed out'.

Dave did a lot of work with executives from chronically stressful corporate environments. I asked if exercise was the answer to all of this – a way to 'burn off' unhelpful stress hormones.

First he urged caution. If you're already stressed in everyday life, 'suddenly heading out and trying to run marathons is just going to add to that. Suddenly putting yourself in a calorie deficit is just going to add to that.' Weight-training and circuit-training raise cortisol and adrenaline levels, at least during the exercise. 'That's not scary in itself. You need to elevate cortisol and adrenaline sometimes. You need that little bit of aggro – try to box without any stress hormones, you won't be a very good boxer. Straining your body sometimes is a good thing, as long as you're giving yourself time for recovery.'

The important thing for Dave was 'cortisol-conscious training' – not demonising stress hormones like cortisol, but being aware of their effects. 'Cortisol in itself is really important. It's kind of what gets you out of bed in the morning. But you should have a natural variance throughout the day.' Ideally, cortisol levels should peak in the morning and gradually taper off. Under chronic stress conditions, your cortisol levels flatten out, meaning you're continually tired, yet you struggle to sleep. A new high-impact exercise regime, he warned, can interfere with sleep.

There was one form of exercise, however, that he recommended unreservedly. 'I've been doing this for fifteen years – I know for a fact walking *hugely* improves people's mental health.' It was a great way, he said, to get my joints moving, keep my mind active, burn some calories and lower my adrenaline and cortisol levels. 'We're not talking about speed walking, but just going for a stroll.'

He recommended building up my 'non-exercise activity thermogenesis', or NEAT – that is, all the little daily activities that aren't exercise per se but add up, like taking the stairs instead of the lift, walking to the shops, or getting up from my chair every hour to do a five-minute lap of the garden. But especially relaxing, providing I made time for it, was walking in nature.

Research into the now well-known Japanese practice of *shinrin-yoku* or 'forest bathing' found that sitting or walking in the forest significantly reduced cortisol levels in the saliva. Reviewing research across twenty-four forests in Japan, the authors also found that forests promote 'lower pulse rate, lower blood pressure, greater parasympathetic nerve activity, and lower sympathetic nerve activity than do city environments'.[13] One study found that diabetic patients' blood glucose levels dropped when they walked 3–6km in a forest.[14] Another found that a single day's session of walking in the forest significantly lowered blood pressure and pulse rate while improving mood – particularly in participants with depressive tendencies.[15]

However, forest-bathing studies with control conditions show that walking or sitting in a city *also* lowers cortisol levels, blood pressure and pulse rate – just not quite as much. One would expect blood glucose levels to drop over the course of *any* gentle walk, since muscle activity uses up sugar. Mild exercise and rest help on their own.

There's other evidence that time spent in green, rural spaces improves mental health. One study found that people who spent more than two hours in nature per week reported significantly better health and wellbeing than people who didn't. The sample size was substantial – nearly 20,000 – but finding a correlation isn't the same as finding a cause. As the authors admitted: 'We are unable to rule out the possibility that the association is, at least in part, due to healthier, happier people spending more time in nature.'[16] Anxious or depressed people may feel less able or motivated to get out of the house.

Walking – in nature or otherwise – indisputably promotes general fitness. It's less likely to cause injury than weight-lifting or distance running, and it can help ease some of those physiological reactions seen in Selye's 'Resistance Stage' of stress. But these benefits may be mild, and seem to be more pronounced for depression sufferers than anxiety sufferers.

Dave also recommended weight-lifting – building strength, gaining lean mass, and developing my capacity for basic movements that, not so long ago, most humans could perform with little thought. He reckoned it would help my confidence and self-image.

In the end, he said, the evidence for exercise as a treatment for anxiety is mixed. But the worst that could happen was I got fitter, healthier, and reduced my risk factors for all sorts of illnesses.

'Does lifting weights make you feel good? Does it improve how you look? Does it improve certain hormonal profiles in the body? Yes, yes and yes.'

——

I'd expected Dave, as a gym owner, to claim exercise could do everything short of raise the dead. But when I dug into the literature, I discovered he was right about anxiety.

Many studies claim to show exercise reduces anxiety, but first we need to ask: What kind of anxiety, and what kind of exercise?

In a comprehensive review of the available research into anxiety and exercise, psychologist Peter Salmon of the University of Liverpool identified several problems.[17] Strenuous exercise has often been found to increase negative mood and decrease positive mood among people who don't exercise regularly. This shouldn't be surprising to anyone who's tried running for a bus after months of lying on the sofa eating

Rice Krispies squares and smoking blunts. It's knackering and humiliating. You don't stand there winded as the bus disappears, the coppery taste of blood in your mouth, thinking: *Wow, I feel so at peace.*

These unpleasant effects are likely underestimated in the research, because people who've had negative experiences with exercise are unlikely to sign up for studies that require it. This is a problem called selection bias. If the people you're studying aren't a representative sample of the people you ultimately hope to treat – because they're younger, richer, less ill, or whatever – your results may not generalise very well.

Another problem is deciding what counts as exercise. Is walking the same as sprinting? Is swimming the same as weight-training? How long did participants do the activity for? Does absolute intensity matter, or just intensity relative to the person's current level of fitness?

Judging whether exercise lifts someone's mood might depend on when you ask them – some forms of exercise reliably lower mood during the activity, but result in boosted mood later. Others boost mood temporarily, but it doesn't last.

Most importantly, how anxious were participants in the first place? Most studies of exercise's effects on anxiety, Salmon argued, don't use people with actual anxiety disorders (a problem across all anxiety research). The result is a body of literature focused on reducing stress in people who weren't anxious to begin with. 'Too many studies demonstrate antidepressant, anxiolytic, or stress-reducing effects in people who have not asked for these benefits.'

This lack of rigour – or, at least, consistency – is reflected in muddled, contradictory findings. One systematic review of eight randomised controlled trials studying exercise as a treatment for anxiety disorders found it appeared to reduce anxiety symptoms, but was less effective than antidepressants. Considering that antidepressants are, on average, only slightly better at treating anxiety symptoms than a placebo, this is a less than stellar outcome. The authors found no difference between high-intensity anaerobic exercise like sprinting, and low-intensity aerobic exercise, like walking.[18] Another systematic review, looking at data from fifteen studies, found high-intensity regimes were more effective than low-intensity ones.[19] Another, analysing 104 studies, found the opposite.[20]

One meta-analysis of 73 studies found that fitter people were actually slightly *more* sensitive to stress, in terms of changes in heart rate, blood pressure and cortisol levels, but that they recovered better than less fit people.[21] In other words, their fight, flight or freeze response was a little stronger than most people's, but didn't last as long – they returned to a relaxed state quicker.

And get this: whether a study finds positive results might depend on the *time of day it took place*. Remember how Dave said, in a normal, healthy person, cortisol levels follow a natural curve, peaking in the morning then tapering off over the rest of the day? Well, one meta-analysis of 208 laboratory studies of acute stressors like intense exercise, electric shocks, or social stressors like public speaking, found that *when* the experiments took place made a big difference to the results. Studies conducted in the morning – when cortisol levels are typically elevated – consistently found it harder to detect changes in cortisol levels than ones conducted in the afternoon. The average 'effect size' of studies conducted in the afternoon was over three times larger.[22]

Glucocorticoids are a class of hormone that includes cortisol, released at the end of the HPA-axis hormonal cascade. In chronic stress, glucocorticoid receptors – the little docking stations for cortisol – are 'upregulated', meaning they're much more sensitive and trigger more easily. As Dave pointed out, exercise raises cortisol levels acutely – meaning during the exercise – and regular exercise raises 'basal', or baseline, cortisol levels. For years, this presented a seeming paradox. Surely this should make people more anxious, not less.

The first answer is the most obvious. For many anxiety sufferers, exercise *does* increase anxiety. It's difficult, tiring, painful, and it ups production of stress hormones. No paradox there. But – as noted by one of the studies above – there's some evidence that exercise promotes a quicker 'return to baseline' from very high stress responses. Studies in mice and rats have found regular exercise leads to a reduction in the two hormonal precursors to cortisol release – two dominoes in that hormonal cascade – corticotropin-releasing factor (CRF) and adrenocorticotropic hormone (ACTH).

In addition, exercise may promote the production and release of neurotransmitters like dopamine and serotonin.[23] In the public imagination, dopamine is the 'motivation' hormone, and serotonin is the 'feel-good' hormone – a huge oversimplification in either case. Since antidepressants commonly prescribed for anxiety disorders increase the availability of serotonin in the brain, exercise may act in a similar way (though, as I later discovered, the link between serotonin levels and anxiety is a complex and highly charged source of debate).

Exercise also promotes the production and release of a protein called brain-derived neurotrophic factor, or BDNF.* This excites neurons, promoting activity and growth. Studies of chronically stressed rats have shown reduced levels of BDNF, and deficiencies have been repeatedly implicated in post-traumatic stress disorder (PTSD). It's a key protein behind neuroplasticity, or the brain's capacity to change and build new pathways. Though increased plasticity means that the brain is more efficient at encoding new fears and traumas,[24] it also means the brain might be better at *unlearning* responses to these fears.[25]

Another study in rats found that intense exercise prompted the release of a peptide called neuropeptide Y,[26] which in the brain – amongst other things – stimulates appetite and reduces anxiety. Some researchers characterise it as the counterbalance to CRF, the hormone that kicks off the fight, flight or freeze response. Emerging research suggests neuropeptide Y has 'unique stress-relieving, anxiolytic and neuroprotective properties' and may have a role in resilience and our

---

* 'Neuro' meaning 'related to the nervous system', and 'trophic', 'related to growth'.

ability to cope with stress.[27] Studies in humans have found that patients with anxiety disorders have reduced levels of neuropeptide Y,[28] and that lower levels are associated with worse PTSD symptoms and panic.[29] Some animal studies suggest low neuropeptide Y levels lead to a higher risk of alcoholism,[30] perhaps as a substitute for its anxiety-reducing effects.

Other rodent studies suggest sustained voluntary exercise increases the production of a neuropeptide called galanin, which may help control the release of noradrenaline, a hormone and neurotransmitter released during fight or flight.[31] In the brain, it raises alertness and is involved with the formation and retrieval of memories. In the body, it contributes to raised heart rate and blood pressure, the release of stored glucose (thus increasing your blood sugar) and inhibiting your ability to pee.

Noradrenaline's relationship to anxiety is complicated (two commonly prescribed medications for anxiety, SNRIs and propranolol, increase and decrease neural noradrenaline levels respectively). Researchers have tried to thread the noradrenergic needle by suggesting that improved regulation – the right amount at the right time – is part of the reason runners may be better able to withstand moderate stress.

Exercise also prompts the release of beta-endorphins.* Endorphins are popularly known as 'pleasure hormones' – again, an oversimplification. The body releases them in response to pain, during sex, or while laughing or eating chocolate. Endorphins are responsible for something that's been called 'the runner's high' – euphoria during vigorous exercise.

This last effect is not without dangers: endorphins are partly responsible for exercise addiction. Dave told me about people he saw

---

* 'Endorphin' is a portmanteau of 'endogenous' ('made from within') and 'morphine', a pain-blocking medication of the opiate family named after Morpheus, the Greek god of dreams.

'sprinting on a treadmill, six or seven days a week'. If you do intense regular exercise, or long periods of daily aerobic exercise, your brain may produce fewer endorphins during periods of rest to maintain a balance – homeostasis again. This can lead to low mood – even physical pain – if you stop exercising.

Another possibility is that, during intense exercise, parts of your brain responsible for worry shut down. I spoke with neuroscientist Arne Dietrich at the American University of Beirut in Lebanon, who proposed something he calls the Transient Hypofrontality Theory.[32] 'The idea is basically that your brain has to manage its resources, and so when you do something you constantly have to shift resources to what the brain currently needs. You can't run your entire brain the entire time, so there's always a budget that has to be allocated – in this case, oxygen, glucose and so on.' When we do demanding, aerobic exercise, our brains' priorities change. 'Your brain needs to shift resources to the areas that do your motion. The consequence of that is transient downregulation of prefrontal cortex activity. That causes a short-term decrease in anxiety and stress.' Parts of the prefrontal cortex are recruited when we worry and ruminate about the future.[33] 'This is actually a very complicated computation. No animal does this. Only we do.' Hence commonly reported feelings of time distortion during intense, prolonged exercise, and a reduced capacity for engaging in the sophisticated business of worry.

Another mechanism may be exposure.

Physical exercise can be unpleasant. You get out of breath, your heart races, you feel overwhelmed. These were the precise symptoms I had spent most of my life watching for and trying to avoid. Several studies have found that exercise can reduce 'anxiety sensitivity' – the degree to which you're constantly watching for physical symptoms of anxiety 'based on the belief that they will result in disastrous physical, psychological, and/or social outcomes'.[34] Exercise helps you get used to feelings of breathlessness, a racing heart and tense muscles without interpreting those sensations as signs of impending doom.

This is one reason why I think intense anaerobic exercise – activity that makes your body work so hard it starts breaking down glucose for energy without using oxygen – can be particularly beneficial for people who suffer from panic attacks. We spend our whole lives running and hiding from these horrible sensations, this curse that feels like dying. It's exhausting. Far more tiring than lacing up a pair of running shoes. There is something profoundly healing about voluntarily meeting those sensations, that feeling, head on. It's like finally standing up to your bullies.

Another potential benefit of exercise for anxiety sufferers is developing 'self-efficacy' – your sense of control. Those of us with high anxiety don't feel like we have much control over our lives. We don't feel confident in our ability to make changes or cope with challenges. 'You forget how many of the population can't do fairly basic movements,' Dave told me. Many of us struggle with press-ups, squats, touching our toes or just reaching the top of the stairs without getting out of breath. 'For a lot of people with anxiety, those are fairly big achievements. It sounds flippant but I've seen people literally bouncing round the room the first time they do a chin-up.' Dave said people often come into the gym focused on what they can't do, weights they can't lift. 'And when they do it, they prove themselves wrong. Once they do it, it starts to change their mental processes.'

I didn't know it then, but Dave had just started to pull on a thread woven through the whole moth-eaten sweater of anxiety. Something I'd encounter again in a locked cleaning cupboard, a freezing river, and neurotic robots.

IV.

EAT SHIT AND DIET

*The gut–brain connection, microbiota
and inflammation*

After my chat with Dave, I felt a responsibility to go through the motions of trying to get fit – if only so I could say 'Look, I tried, but I am constitutionally incapable of moving faster than a fully laden wheelie bin.'

Sure enough, I found resistance training painful, dull and dispiriting. I wasn't sure which exercises I should do, or how many, or whether I was doing them right. Lifting weights hurt my hands. I felt silly and out of my depth. It was the same story with running. My first few jogs were crap. For days after, I could barely get up and down the stairs. So why did I keep going?

Approaching researchers for advice had become, ironically, a source of huge anxiety. Every time I clicked 'send' I felt like I'd jumped out of a plane. I kept expecting them to say, 'Who the fuck are you and why are you wasting my time?' Suddenly, getting away from the house – and my inbox – didn't seem so bad. I guess nothing comes more naturally to a coward than running.

Meanwhile, I wanted to change my diet. I wanted to take the edge off those peaks and crashes in blood sugar. I'd read books that mentioned studies had found consuming more fibre was linked with lower anxiety,[1] or that vitamin D supplements could reduce anxiety.[2] I'd also read in several places that excess weight was linked to inflammation, and that chronic inflammation might be both a sign and cause of anxiety.

I contacted Dr Ruihua Hou, an associate professor at the

University of Southampton, who specialises in the field of 'immu-no-psychiatry'. She was researching potential links between anxiety disorders and inflammation.

Inflammation is our body's way of trying to neutralise and clear out pathogens or damaged cells. White blood cells release a variety of chemicals to fight infection and initiate healing. When it happens near the skin's surface you'll have experienced the swelling, redness, heat and pain. In the short term, inflammation is an adaptive – albeit generic – response that combats nasty germs and toxins and helps repair damaged cells. In the long term, it can begin breaking down the very cells it's supposed to defend.

In one study, Ruihua looked at patients with generalised anxiety disorder and their levels of cytokines – little proteins that help modulate the body's immune response. GAD patients had higher levels of pro-inflammatory cytokines and lower levels of anti-inflammatory cytokines than healthy controls.[3] Selye's general adaptation syndrome model suggests chronic stress causes inflammation. But what about the other way round? Does inflammation contribute to anxiety?

Some studies have presented evidence that pro-inflammatory cytokines impair neuroplasticity – in particular the expression of BDNF in the brain.[4] Chronic neuroinflammation might impair our ability to recover from adversity by making it harder to update our thoughts and habits. Other studies suggest inflammation has a stimulant effect on the HPA axis, and alters the metabolism of neurotransmitters like serotonin and dopamine,[5] meaning we might be more easily stressed out and more depressed.

Ruihua told me that while there's good emerging evidence for a bidirectional link between depression and inflammation – including depression symptoms improving in response to anti-inflammatory drugs – at the moment the effect on anxiety is less well-studied. If inflammation contributes to anxiety, she warned me this might only be true for a subset of patients. Still, she was hopeful. 'If I can treat just one subgroup and alleviate their anxiety, I'll be happy.'

Just in case, she recommended some well-evidenced non-pharmaceutical interventions for reducing inflammation: exercise, losing excess weight, eating a Mediterranean diet – lots of fresh fruit and vegetables, nuts, beans, vegetable oils, and less meat – mindfulness meditation, and a final one which caught me by surprise: religion.

One study found that people who regularly attend religious services were 38 per cent less likely to have elevated levels of the inflammation marker C-reactive protein (CRP) after experiencing stressful life events.[6] Another study found that what the authors termed *intrinsic religiosity* – a personal commitment to spirituality, rather than affiliation to a religious organisation – was associated with lower levels of CRP in people who had endured significant stress.[7]

This is probably due to lifestyle factors rather than divine intervention. People with strong religious beliefs are less likely to drink excessive amounts of alcohol or smoke, and participation in a religious community may act as a buffer to stress, offering social support in times of hardship.

Interestingly, the literature doesn't specify which entity you should worship. So if you've ever considered donning a cowl, prostrating towards the nightmare corpse-city of R'lyeh and chanting for the return of the dark lord Cthulhu, you'll be pleased to hear doing so may lower your risk of rheumatoid arthritis.

Undergoing a religious awakening sounded tricky, beneficial as it might be for my neural cytokine profile. By comparison, the other suggestions on her list seemed eminently doable. I had already started an exercise regime. Next up was losing weight. Dave had warned me exercise is 'a really shit way to burn calories – really inefficient'. To lose weight, I'd have to eat better.

I'd read dozens of articles about the gut being our 'second brain'. About how diet and our gut bacteria might influence mood. I'd even read about studies where timid mice were given poop transplants from brave mice, and became brave themselves.

Could changing my diet change a fundamental part of my personality? Could poop be the cure to cowardice?

———

In 2004, Dr Nobuyuki Sudo and colleagues at Kyushu University raised a group of mice from birth in sterile, clear plastic isolators. The mice were given sterile food and water and handled with sterile gloves built into the isolator walls. The aim was to raise the mice in an 'ultraclean', germ-free environment, without any gut bacteria.

At nine weeks, each mouse was pushed by a researcher into the neck of a 50ml conical tube, and trapped there for between thirty minutes and two hours. At the end of this period – known in the literature as an 'acute restraint stress protocol' – the researchers freed the mouse and snapped its neck. Then they punctured the dead mouse's heart to measure levels of ACTH and corticosterone – two hormones released as part of that 'hormone cascade' in the fight, flight or freeze response (corticosterone is the rodent equivalent of cortisol).[8]

Being trapped in a tube is extremely stressful for a mouse, and the researchers found that the germ-free mice produced more than double the amount of stress hormones than regular mice. They also showed reduced BDNF in the cortex and hippocampus. This led some researchers to wonder if gut microbiota – the ecosystem of bacteria in your gut – might have something to do with anxiety.

In 2011, researchers at McMaster University in Canada famously took two types of laboratory mice: the NIH Swiss strain, and the BALB/c strain. BALB/c mice were the type used in Dr Sudo's experiments, a strain that can trace its lineage all the way back to an Ohio mouse dealer in 1913 – the same year Walter Cannon was taking urine samples from the Harvard football squad.* Crucially, BALB/c mice have a reputation for being particularly 'timid and anxious' – in genetic terms they're often described as 'exhibiting an anxiety-like phenotype'. NIH Swiss mice, by contrast, tend to be a bit quicker to explore their environments – behaviour the study's authors characterised as 'adventurous'.

As with the previous experiment, the mice were raised in germ-free environments. Then the 'adventurous' NIH Swiss mice had a tube inserted in their throats and were force-fed the contents of a 'timid' adult BALB/c mouse's cecum – a bacteria-filled fermenting pouch between the small and large intestine that helps break down plant matter (our appendix is the rudiment of that). Conversely, the 'timid' BALB/c mice were force-fed the contents of an adult NIH Swiss mouse's cecum. So the adventurous mice got the timid mice's gut bacteria, and vice versa.

Three weeks later, the researchers got the mice to perform a 'step-down test'. The mouse gets placed on a raised platform, and researchers time how long it takes the mouse to hop down onto the floor below. NIH Swiss mice with normal gut bacteria took an average of about twenty seconds. Normal BALB/c mice took an average of five minutes, peering over the edge, scampering to the other side, peering over, checking and exploring before finally jumping down.

When the researchers swapped the two strains' gut bacteria, they found the 'brave' NIH Swiss mice took an average of around a minute to jump down – almost three times as long as before – whereas the 'timid' BALB/c mice took just over three minutes – about a third faster.[9]

This is a bit less exciting than what I'd understood from popular

---

* 'BALB' is a portmanteau of 'Bagg', from researcher Halsey J. Bagg who first procured the mice, and 'Albino'; the '/c' indicates the substrain. 'NIH Swiss' comes from a laboratory strain bred by the National Institute of Health.

science articles. Most implied that the two mice completely exchanged personalities after snowballing one another's poop. But even after the transplants, the original 'timid' mice still took three times as long as the original 'brave' mice to hop down off a platform.

Still, it should be surprising that there was any change at all. Clearly *something* had taken place. But what? And does it work in humans?

———

To get answers, I went to visit Professor Simon Carding, who researches gut microbiology at the Quadram Institute in Norwich, a striking futuristic building of glass and stippled white cladding that looks like a cross between a Borg cube and a giant QR code.

I asked him whether our gut can influence our mood.

'Yes, is the simple answer.' Your brain and gut, Simon told me, communicate directly via the vagus nerve – a long nerve which starts in the brain stem, goes down your spinal cord and fans out in the middle of your body, spreading across the whole of your gastrointestinal tract. The brain sends signals to the gut to control the speed of digestion. The gut signals to the brain that it's full or that there's a need to eat – hunger. Your gut can also communicate with your brain indirectly, via your bloodstream. It is lined with specialised cells called enteroendocrine cells. There are as many as fifty different subtypes, each one producing a different type of hormone.

About 90 per cent of your serotonin is made in your gut, along with about 50 per cent of your dopamine. But serotonin and dopamine don't cross the blood–brain barrier – 'a big, physical barrier', like a filter, that allows small molecules and nutrients from the bloodstream to reach the brain, but keeps out bigger, more complex structures like microbes and toxins. Thus increasing serotonin production in the gut doesn't increase its availability in the brain (one reason you can't just take a serotonin or dopamine pill).

Serotonin plays many roles. In the gut, it increases motility – a fancy way of saying it stimulates your gut to move faster. High levels of serotonin in the gut give you diarrhoea – extremely useful if your body wants to flush out a toxin before it can do serious harm. Elsewhere, serotonin promotes things like insulin production, or the tightening of blood vessels.[10] Dopamine's role is less well understood, though in the gut it seems to help regulate the absorption of electrolytes and the emptying of the stomach.

The gut has the largest number of neurons in your body outside your brain. They communicate with the enteric nervous system, or ENS, a web of around 500 million neurons that spreads through your gastrointestinal tract, from your oesophagus all the way down to your anus. The ENS regulates all sorts of digestive functions, and can communicate with the central nervous system and the immune system. It's what people usually mean when they call the gut 'the second brain'.

I asked about this incredible research where changing gut bacteria seemed to reduce anxiety.

Simon told me the evidence from animal studies might not be what it seems. 'A lot of the mice studies don't necessarily translate to humans. There's a good reason why they don't. The human [gastrointestinal] tract is not the same as the GI tract of a mouse.' He held his palms about a foot apart. 'A mouse GI tract is about that long – a human one is a couple of metres.' Mice have a special forestomach that stores food. It takes six to seven hours for food to move through a mouse's gut – up to ten times faster than in humans.[11] In common with all rodents, mice can't vomit.[12] Their gastrointestinal musculature is less well-suited to retching than in humans, and researchers believe that they lack critical brain-stem circuitry for generating the emetic reflex. (Gamekeepers and exterminators have long exploited this inability when laying down bait for rats; I read one account where a keeper improvised a 50–50 mix of porridge oats and plaster of Paris, reporting that, when they drink, 'the mixture swells and sets inside the rats', killing them.[13])

Does the length of time a mouse takes to jump down from a raised platform have any relevance to human anxiety? For Simon, the bottom line is: 'Probably not.' Researchers call this behaviour 'anxiety-like' for a reason – we have no idea what mice are feeling. We can't ask them. We can only infer states from how they act.[14] Depending on the paradigm the researcher decides upon, running, staying still,[15] eating a lot, not eating, 'excessive' self-grooming,[16] not self-grooming,[17] startling, hesitating, squealing, urinating, swimming, floating,[18] and a host of other activities count as 'anxiety-like behaviour'.

Not only that, but – clearly – rodent brains aren't simply minia-ture versions of ours. As neuroscientist Alexander Shackman, director of the Affective and Translational Neuroscience Laboratory at the University of Maryland, told me, if you're studying mice and rats which don't have a well-developed prefrontal cortex, and if a big part of anxiety is things like intolerance of uncertainty and worrisome thoughts, how generalisable are your findings likely to be? Have we been choosing these tests not because they're accurate, but because they're easy to do? 'Maybe studying fear conditioning or their reac-tion to an open chamber that's brightly lit – because they prefer the dark – is just the wrong probe, or the wrong species. Maybe we're learning a lot about the wrong things.'

It may seem obvious to point out that a mouse is not a small person, but Simon said he'd found himself having to do just that, repeatedly, when contacted by science journalists. 'A lot of people just don't accept that or don't acknowledge it,' he said – in retrospect a slightly surreal statement. 'Being human is important. We have a human-specific microbiota. You'll never see that in the popular media.' He kept getting press enquiries about the latest discoveries from mouse studies. 'You have to explain why it probably isn't true. Why it's just speculation. Hype. But they don't want to know that.'

I asked if drinking probiotics might help my anxiety. One small double-blind study – funded by Danone, the makers of Activia – found that a group of healthy women, after drinking a 'fermented milk product with probiotic' (I wonder which one) for four weeks, showed significantly decreased activity in brain areas associated with stress and anxiety, such as the amygdala.[19]

In my research, I kept encountering the amygdala. Many articles called it the brain's 'fear centre'. There were headlines like 'Brain's "Fear Center" Skews Emotions in Anxious Kids'[20] and 'Research Reveals How Magic Mushrooms Alter Connectivity in the Brain's Fear Center'.[21] Apparently, the amygdala was responsible for deciding when to trigger the fight, flight or freeze response.

In the probiotics study, the participants didn't report any conscious reduction in anxiety, and they weren't clinically anxious to begin with, but when they were placed in an fMRI scanner, their brains responded less to images of angry or frightened faces than did brains of a control group. 'The European Food Safety Authority has yet to substantiate a health claim for a probiotic,' said Simon. 'The evidence is not there . . . so you'll get some overall vague statement about health and wellbeing.'

He told me the issue with probiotics is that when you drink that little pot of fermented milk, you can't know how much of the bacterial culture is still alive and active. Then the bacteria have got to survive your stomach acid, survive the 'protease enzyme rich environment' of your small intestine, to finally get to the colon, where you've got 100,000,000,000,000 – 100 trillion – microbes filling every niche. 'What are the chances of that little microbe in that pot making it? It's like throwing a pebble into the ocean.'

In the animal studies, the germ-free mice were kept in completely sterile environments before they received their transplants – the bacteria got to colonise relatively untouched real estate in the gut. By contrast, anything we consume – unless we've been very ill or on a heavy course of antibiotics – has to compete with the microbiome that's already established. 'The system is designed to keep equilibrium.

Homeostasis. It resists.' That's how our gut fights off pathogens so efficiently. 'The system is there to push it out, keep what's there, keep it structurally intact.'

A 2018 meta-analysis looking at 12 studies with 1,551 subjects found no significant difference between probiotics and a placebo when treating anxiety.[22] 'I looked at [another] meta-analysis of using probiotics to treat mental health,' Simon told me. 'There were seventeen studies and the conclusion was: there is no compelling evidence here that probiotics can change mood and anxiety.'

Yes, you might get the odd study that finds a positive result. Inevitably, these are the ones that get cherry-picked by the authors of alternative health books. But when you look at the big picture, it's more likely that any improvements to anxiety happened by chance.

It's notoriously hard to get accurate data from human studies – especially ones relating to diet. We can't (ethically) keep humans in sterile bubbles from birth. It's rare that a study can control what they eat. People in dietary trials regularly misremember or misreport what they've been eating. Even in the tiny Danone trial, one participant was excluded after researchers checked her poop and discovered she hadn't been drinking the yoghurt as asked. (Why did she go to the trouble of shitting in a pot and bringing it to the lab? Why was *that* the part she complied with?)

'You can see why it's attractive to use mice, right? They're all the same age, they're all related, they all eat the same diet, they're all living in the same environment.' And, not to put too fine a point on it, we can subject them to ordeals no human participant would ever consent to, and then, when we're done – as in the Kyushu University study – we can kill them. Simon stressed that in the UK we have the strictest regulations worldwide when it comes to using animals in research. 'Breaching the regulations is a criminal offence, with violators facing imprisonment and their host institution major fines and loss of their licence to work with animals.'

There's no common set of international regulations for animal welfare in psychology and neuroscience research, but most countries have an extensive ethical approval process overseen by regulatory bodies.[23] Even so, what a regulator deems an acceptable trade-off between harm and potential benefit may not seem meaningfully distinct from torture, if you're a mouse. In the name of anxiety research, you might be crammed into a tube for two hours then killed,[24] electrocuted 360 times a day for 15 days,[25] burned by a hot plate[26] – what the literature calls a 'noxious thermal stimulus' – or dropped into an inescapable transparent tank full of water and forced to swim or drown – the 'forced swim test'.[27] Even housing rodents in individual cages – a common practice before the actual experimental protocol begins – can constitute a stressful ordeal. Rats and mice are social animals. One recent study found that mice transferred to individual cages displayed 'anhedonia [an inability to experience pleasure], increased anxiety and biological markers of stress' compared to those which were socially housed.[28] Seizures were *sixteen times* more frequent in isolated mice.

To be honest, I started to feel a bit weird about it. After all, these animals were being used in an attempt to understand *my* condition. I spoke to bioethicist and professor of animal sciences Bernard Rollin, who helped write US federal policy on animal welfare and pain control in experiments. He told me the situation has improved, but a lot of cruel and ultimately pointless research still takes place. 'There are good scientists who do good work, but not these idiots in denial. They're technically proficient at implanting electrodes but they don't think about what the hell they're doing.'

The utilitarian philosopher Peter Singer, now at Princeton, formulated a problem with using animals in psychological research that he called the Psychologist's Dilemma. He put it this way: 'Either the animal is not like us, in which case there is no reason for performing the experiment; or else the animal is like us, in which case we ought not to perform an experiment on the animal which would be considered outrageous if performed on one of us.'[29]

In a paper Bernard Rollin co-authored with his son Michael – a double-board-certified psychiatrist – they summarised the dilemma thus: 'One cannot simultaneously defend an animal model as both adequate and ethical.'[30] When we spoke, he put it more bluntly: 'Of course these animals feel pain, you fucking idiots.'

In fairness, most researchers are acutely aware of the shortcomings of animal models. Neuroscientist Dr Alexandra Pike from University College London told me that a common point where drug treatments for anxiety, and neuroscience drugs in general, fail is the translation between animals and humans. 'That's because success in animals is: Can a rat find its way around a maze? Success in humans is: Do you feel less worried?'

Her research suggests that it might not be realistic or useful to attempt to study disordered anxiety in an animal. Instead, what we might reasonably do is attempt to look for a particular process underlying the disorder – say, for example, impairments in working memory in people with PTSD – and then design similar tasks – 'common currency tasks' – to study working memory in, say, mice and humans.[31]

The Psychologist's Dilemma might be putting animal research in an illusory bind. *All* models are inadequate. We develop our knowledge incrementally, testing lots of approximations of the thing we're interested in. Where anxiety research involves a mouse stepping down from a platform or navigating a maze, it's probably no more stressful than being somebody's pet.

Given my monthly intake of battered sausages, pepperoni pizzas and kebabs, it was hard to protest too loudly about animal welfare without – entirely accurate – accusations of hypocrisy. I asked Simon if I should drink probiotics just for the health benefits. His advice was simple: 'Save your money. Eat *pre*biotics.' That is, fresh fruit and vegetables – food rich in plant-based polysaccharides. 'That's the stuff your gut microbes feed on.' He recommended a diet with less processed food. Fewer animal products. More fibre. 'If you have a plate, the more colourful the plate, the better.' This was consistent with Dr Ruihua Hou's advice about eating a Mediterranean diet. Even if it didn't reduce my anxiety, it was likely to improve my health across a range of profiles compared to stuffed-crust pizzas and Irn-Bru.

But, Simon warned, it wasn't enough to just do a short intervention. My microbiota was very resilient. If I didn't stick at it, the old bugs would bounce back with a vengeance. 'If you want to change your gut microbes you've got to stay on the diet,' he said. 'For ever.'

—

Before I left, I had a final query. Remember that thing about the mice and poop transplants? I knew the Quadram Institute researched the equivalent in humans – faecal microbiota transplantation, or FMT. FMT treatments had proven really effective at treating patients with potentially deadly C. difficile infections[32] – taking gut microbiomes from healthy volunteers and transplanting them into the patient to help fight off the dangerous bacteria. They were setting up trials to see if FMT could help with chronic fatigue syndrome or Parkinson's.

In FMT, you whisk up donor poo into a kind of turd milkshake, then the patient ingests it via a tube inserted through the mouth into the stomach or upper small intestine, or via the anus to access the large intestine. Occasionally, they even have it in a pill – what I'd heard Simon refer to as a 'crapsule'. I'd read heartwarming headlines like 'My Dad's Poo Saved My Life'[33] and wondered – as a last resort – if I might be able to find similar salvation, albeit for my mental health. Not from my dad, obviously.

I asked Simon if he thought I might be able to beat my anxiety by swallowing the poo of a very calm stranger.

He took this question remarkably well. Simon told me that currently there's no strong science to justify using FMT for anything other than treating C. difficile. But if I were to try it, the ideal donor would be a relaxed person with a healthy diet. 'Someone who's been screened for infections. Someone whose gut microbiome doesn't contain nasties. Who's had relatively few treatments, insults. So maybe someone between twelve and eighteen is your ideal source.'

I had to find an angst-free teenager and ask if they'd mind pooing into a Tupperware so I could swallow it later. It's for my nerves.

Soliciting random teens for a spot of coprophagy sounded like the sort of activity likely to land me on a register. The evidence wasn't even *that* great in mice.

More practically, both Simon and Ruihua had recommended the so-called Mediterranean diet as a well-evidenced way of reducing inflammation, improving the diversity of my gut microbiome and supporting general health. That meant plenty of fruit and vegetables, whole grains, nuts, seeds, and lean proteins like fish or yoghurt. It meant cutting down on sugar, animal fats and processed meat.

A 2017 meta-analysis found that people who eat a lot of 'fruit, vegetables, whole grain, fish, olive oil, low-fat dairy and antioxidants' and don't eat much meat had a lower risk of depression.[34] A 2019 study found that a high intake of fruit and vegetables was associated with lower odds of anxiety and depression.[35]

Of course, it might just be that fed-up people are more likely to reach for a bacon sandwich than a head of broccoli. Another meta-analysis in the *Journal of Affective Disorders* addressed this by looking at 'prospective studies' – that is, studies which looked at people's diets, then followed them to see who developed depression later. The authors found a mild association between the Mediterranean diet and reduced depression risk, but only in studies that used 'severity of symptoms' scales to measure depression, rather than studies where people had to meet the official diagnostic criteria for clinical depression. They estimated that the number of people who would need to change their diet, on average, to prevent 1 case of depression, was about 47.[36]

That 'number needed to benefit' (or NNB, also called the NNT or 'number needed to treat') might sound high, but the authors point out it's better than, for example, the NNB for statins widely prescribed to prevent cardiovascular disease.[37] Even if the actual number is a bit worse, if there is a causal relationship and everyone in the UK switched to a Mediterranean diet, it might mean many thousands fewer cases of depression and anxiety.

A few months earlier, I'd started toying with becoming vegetarian. I'd felt uneasy about eating meat for years, but I kept doing it because I didn't want to deny myself a pleasure and I didn't believe I could change. I'd taken several 'breaks' from meat but I kept coming back.

After chatting with Ruihua, Simon and Dave, then doing all that angsting about animals in research, I made my mind up: if I was contemplating eating human faeces maybe it was time to consider vegetables. With a rush of intense moral superiority, I quit meat permanently.

As I reflected on all I'd learned, rich vistas opened up in my imagination, full of rainbow plates and tables spread with the bounties of nature. I pictured myself sprinting through fields of golden wheat, shadow-boxing against a blood-red sunset, busting out sets of press-ups then sitting down to write, a haze of hard-earned perspiration misting my brow. I felt strangely optimistic.

Something was changing. Perhaps that religious conversion really might be forthcoming.

———

About a week into my new diet, I was seriously reconsidering eating teenager shit.

I kept track of what I ate with a calorie-counting app. Dave had warned me that starving myself would just make my body break down muscle over fat, as well as increasing stress. I wanted to put myself in a mild calorie deficit. Something healthy and sustainable.

It was horrible. I'd spent years eating fat, sugar and carbs the moment I felt hungry. Or bored. Or anxious. Or happy. Crisps and chocolate bars had been little medals rewarding me for getting through each section of the day. My new diet only put me in a deficit of a couple of hundred calories a day, but for the first week I thought about nothing but food. Sometimes I felt so hungry I wept.

To staunch the pangs, I hunted for foods with the highest volume-to-calorie ratio. Stuff with a lot of mass, but not calorie dense. Porridge became my best friend: it was low calorie, stodgy, but low on the glycaemic index – that is, compared to chocolate or energy drinks, porridge takes longer for the body to break down into sugar, meaning blood-sugar levels rise less, for longer, and you're less likely to trigger those insulin spikes and cortisol-releasing, post-meal crashes.

When I began, I was averaging between one and zero portions of fruit and veg a day – and the one was usually a glass of juice. I don't know if pizzas count as 'Mediterranean'. I was so out of practice with eating vegetables it was embarrassing. I steamed piles of cauliflower and ate it on its own because I couldn't figure out how to use it as part of a meal.

I started to realise I'd been stuck in a routine.

I'd eaten the same breakfast and lunch almost every day since school. Breakfast: four Weetabix with milk. Lunch: a peanut-butter sandwich, a cheese sandwich, a packet of crisps and a chocolate bar for pudding. Dinner was whatever was in the fridge, or a takeaway.

It meant I never had to go through the stress of figuring out what to eat. Choosing meals made me really anxious. I'd start to feel shaky and harassed, like it was a test I could fail.

I know that's not normal. You might think, *Jesus, get a grip*. I don't know what to say, except picking what to eat for lunch felt like defusing a bomb. Especially when I had a limited amount of calories.

Having a routine had let me automate a big part of my life. These changes felt like threats.

For a fortnight, I felt rubbish. Rubbish like when you've got one perpetually wet sock. Rubbish like dropping the ice cream you queued ten minutes for. Rubbish like going on a camping holiday and sharing a tent with people you don't know very well, then on the first night you try to sneak out a fart knowing it'll be muffled by your sleeping bag, only to realise a split second too late that it isn't a fart.

Trying to improve my diet confirmed what I'd always suspected: I was incapable of change, and stupid to try. My weight and health were fixed, just like my anxiety. After all, if I couldn't cope with making myself dinner, how the hell was I going to survive when a real disaster hit me?

———

If you're anxious, a good question to ask yourself is: How good am I at predicting the future?

How good have you been, historically, at calling it? At correctly anticipating what would happen in a week, a month, a year? What's your hit rate like?

It's weird how we can think we're completely useless in every domain of human endeavour except mental time travel. *I'm going to mess this up. They're going to hate me. I'll lose my job. She'll never say yes. I'll have a horrible time. Human beings are doomed.*

Behold the anxiety sufferer: ignoramus in the streets, Nostradamus in the sheets.

Psychologist Aaron Beck – creator of cognitive behavioural therapy – called this the fortune teller error. He pointed out that anxious people often make negative predictions about the future that don't come true. But we don't notice when our predictions are wrong, for two reasons: firstly, we don't test them – we think we'll have a panic attack at the party so we don't go, and we chalk that up as a hit. Secondly, things that go right aren't as memorable as things that go wrong – *especially* when we're anxious, and biased towards noticing danger.

When I make negative predictions about the future, I experience them not as thoughts, not as unsubstantiated gossip or speculation, but as concrete evidence of impending danger. It's like an older, bullet-riddled version of me has staggered out of a time portal and whispered a warning with his dying breath. My mind simulates the catastrophe and a hormone cascade is triggered, readying me for an immediate life-or-death struggle.

Cognitive behavioural therapy (CBT) asks you to critically evaluate these kinds of thoughts. To say, *Hang on, how do I know this is true? Are there other outcomes that are equally as likely? If the feared event does take place, what evidence do I have that it would be as unbearable as I'm predicting?*

The problem is, the brain can supply insults and catastrophes with no effort at all. Deconstructing and debunking them takes a great deal of effort. You start to feel like those people who go round putting little flags in dog shit. Maybe this is why responding with logic often fails. You can launch into a Socratic dialogue with your worry, asking all sorts of questions like: *What evidence do I have that I'm going to mess this up?* But sometimes, the prediction's neither here nor there.

Have you ever gone to a friend with a problem, and they immediately started suggesting solutions, when all you really wanted was a sympathetic ear?

Sometimes, what we need to hear – from others, from ourselves most of all – is: *This is really worrying you, isn't it? I can tell it's getting you down. I'm so sorry you're suffering. Listen. You're allowed to mess this up. You're allowed to mess everything up. I'll be here, whatever happens. Whatever happens, you're enough.*

———

My early predictions of how my diet and exercise would go turned out to be bollocks. It's true I'd never stuck at a diet or exercise regime before. It's true I was trying to change habits of a lifetime. It's true that the first few weeks were grim – full of poor sleep, hunger, discomfort and yo-yoing mood. But I kept going. Maybe because the status quo had got so unbearable. Maybe because Dave had given up his time to help me, and I didn't want to let him down.

This wasn't like me. It didn't fit with my self-image. It didn't match my predictions. Yet on I went. Remembering what Dave had said about NEAT, I got a cheap, mini step machine, balanced my laptop on top of my filing cabinet, and did an hour's writing each day while walking. Instead of two sandwiches, crisps, chocolate and an energy drink, my lunch became soup and half a pitta bread. I started going for walks and runs to clear my head. I bought running shorts that didn't make me look like a sketchy seventies PE teacher.

I started losing weight. My running distances increased.

I went from 5k to 10k to half marathons, to a weekly, long run of at least 18 miles. I lost a stone, then two, then three.

I was still anxious. I was still having panic attacks. I could eat well, go for a big run, and still have a bad evening. I still had those feelings of being a useless, worthless, awful person trapped in a terrifying world, who was going to mess his life up and ruin his marriage and fail his incredible daughter.

One of the most basic theories about why exercise might be good for anxiety is that it's a distraction. It gets you out of the house. At the very least, you can't snap at your partner and make things worse.

But what running also was, was evidence. I was getting up, I was choosing to do something that didn't come easily, and I was achieving it. Every time I ran, it violated some negative prediction I'd made about my own abilities. I felt good for having done it – even as I fretted that I'd been out too long, and maybe Lisa would be annoyed at me by the time I got back. Even as I worried that I was just avoiding my writing.

Every time I ate well instead of bingeing on carbs and fat, I had a similar experience. I felt the exact inverse of those pizza-cheese hangovers – like I'd been kind to myself, looked after myself, and that maybe, just maybe, I deserved that kindness.

Even as I continued to struggle and crash, even as – in many ways – I got worse, my improving physical health planted a powerful seed. *I can't change*, I'd tell myself after a panic attack. *I've always been anxious. It's who I am. I'll never get better.*

Yet even at rock bottom I'd hear this niggling little doubt: *You thought that about your weight. You thought that about running. If you were wrong about them, what else might you be wrong about?*

V.

TERRIFYING ABNORMAL DREAMS
*Antidepressants, tranquillisers, side effects
and withdrawal symptoms*

After chatting to a few researchers, I noticed something odd. As we approached the end of our conversation, their body language would shift. They would lean in, lower their voice, and ask some variation on: 'What are you going to say about antidepressants?'

It felt like being asked to pledge allegiance in a civil war. *Are you with the Empire, or the Rebellion?* Sometimes the real question seemed to be: *Are you one of us?* Off the record, they implied various popular communicators were corporate shills, liars, imbeciles or dangerous quacks. A couple of researchers used phrases like 'complete bollocks' and '[X] is an arsehole.'

I was surprised at the vitriol. I'd thought that science was all about cold data and dispassionate conclusions.

That may well be an accurate summation of the *process* of science. Science isn't a body of knowledge. It's a system for testing theories. It acts as a handbrake on our intuition, our love of stories and coherence. It helps us uncover surprising complexities under the obvious, the stereotypical. It guards against prejudice.

But what we *do* with that data, how we choose to interpret and present it, who gets listened to when we do, the stories we make out of those interpretations, the actions we use those stories to sanction: that's where it gets, well, heated.

With good reason. People live and die because of the stories we spin out of research. Dominant narratives shape national policy and drive individual behaviours. We refuse certain treatments and spend great deals of money on others because of stories we've heard. Since we don't have the time, inclination and know-how to read the estimated 1.3 million academic papers published across all subjects annually (and even if we did, most of that research is behind journal paywalls) we rely on people we trust as authorities to convey the salient points.[1]

This means that a relatively small number of communicators – on YouTube, on Facebook, in the newspapers – have a huge impact on the ideas that reach and are accepted by the public. There's money to be made. Kudos to be harvested. Even well-intentioned 'experts' with no financial ulterior motive make mistakes with serious consequences.

Bad science is why people waste millions every year on expensive supplements with no proven health benefits. It's what drives some people to consume colloidal silver – particles of silver dissolved in water, promoted as a treatment for everything from autoimmune diseases to cancer – until their skin turns blue. It makes people refuse chemotherapy in favour of ineffective 'natural' treatments. It drives vaccine refusal.

It's one thing not to know the answer; it's another to be heading in the wrong direction, and profiting off encouraging others to follow you.

What *was* I going to say? Whichever side I picked, people would be angry with me. Social judgement was one of my biggest anxiety triggers. I just wanted to find something that worked. And there lay my first problem: I was on meds, but they'd stopped working.

———

Sertraline's official list of side effects includes: insomnia, diarrhoea, sweating, 'malaise', nose bleed, haemorrhoids, 'tongue disorder', burping, urinary incontinence, sexual dysfunction, cancer, drug dependence, 'tear problem', hiccups, 'red painful penis and foreskin' and 'terrifying abnormal dreams'. When I started searching for a cure for my anxiety, I'd been on sertraline for almost two years.

Sertraline is an antidepressant of the SSRI class – a selective serotonin reuptake inhibitor. There's almost nothing I can say about it that isn't considered controversial by some people. For example, calling sertraline an 'antidepressant' implies – some argue – that it targets a tangible biological condition called 'depression', in the same way antibiotics target bacterial infections. But – they reason – since we can't see depression or anxiety under a microscope in the same way we can see microbes, we shouldn't call certain medications 'antidepressant' or 'anti-anxiety', because the label is, at best, aspirational.

For some, even calling sertraline 'medication' has ideological overtones. Psychologist Dr Lucy Johnstone is a prominent critic of what she calls 'biomedical model psychiatry'. Lucy emphasises she's not 'anti all psychiatric drugs – nor is anyone I know', but objects to calling them medication because the term 'implies some aspect of the drug that is targeting a known dysfunction and rectifying it'. Similarly, she objects to calling drugs like sertraline a 'treatment' for anxiety. 'If I go to the pub feeling anxious, I can have a glass of wine and feel less anxious, but I don't call that a "treatment" for social phobia. And I don't think that social phobia is caused by a lack of alcohol in the brain.'

Whatever we choose to call them, sertraline (marketed in the US as Zoloft) and other SSRIs like citalopram (Celexa), fluoxetine (Prozac), and paroxetine (Paxil and Seroxat) are 'first line' drugs for anxiety disorders, and are often prescribed by doctors and psychiatrists. (Lucy is one of a number of critics – another is UK psychiatrist Dr Joanna Moncrieff – who also question how useful thinking of severe anxiety as a 'disorder' is, arguing the term implies a medical aberration to be corrected, rather than an understandable emotional response to life experiences.)

SSRIs block the reabsorption of serotonin, so more of it remains available in the brain. Neurons in the brain communicate via long stalks called axons, which send signals to branch-like projections on neighbouring neurons, called dendrites. There's a tiny gap where the end of the axon meets the dendrite, called the synapse. In the case of serotonergic neurons, when the axon emits an action potential – or 'fires' – it releases serotonin. The serotonin molecules cross the synapse to 'dock' with serotonin receptor sites on the neighbouring neuron's dendrite, stimulating them. Afterwards, serotonin molecules disconnect from the receptors. About 10 per cent are lost and the remainder get reabsorbed into the axon. An SSRI inhibits this 'reuptake', meaning more serotonin is left floating around in the synaptic cleft, and may restimulate the receptor sites multiple times.

Critics of SSRIs point out – correctly – that we haven't yet established the precise relationship between serotonin and anxiety, let alone all of serotonin's functions and interactions in the brain. On the other hand, as far as I'm aware, no credible psychiatrist, neuroscientist or psychologist has ever claimed to possess that knowledge.[2]

Here's where we are with serotonin: its chemical name is 5-hydroxytryptamine, or 5-HT. It has a popular image as the 'feelgood' neurotransmitter, but – as I've mentioned – it plays lots of different roles in different parts of the body, not just the brain. In the brain it's been linked to mood, perception, memory, hunger, addiction, depression and anxiety. Outside the brain it can act as a vasoconstrictor, narrowing blood vessels (which is how it first got its name – a substance in blood serum affecting vascular tone). In the gut, it makes the gut walls contract, speeding up the passage of food. It's also been linked to regulation of heart rate, nausea and vomiting, milk release in breastfeeding (in concert with oxytocin), and delay in ejaculation.[3] Phew! What a spunky little workhorse.

In the brain, serotonin seems to play a key role in regulating emotions. Lower levels of serotonergic activity are associated with increased anxiety and depression. But increasing serotonin levels can *also* increase anxiety. A study at Uppsala University in Sweden looked at eighteen individuals with social anxiety disorder. It's hard to measure serotonin synthesis directly, so researchers typically use indirect routes, many of which are invasive or unreliable. In this study, they gave participants 5-hydroxytryptophan, a substance the body turns into serotonin, marked with a special radioactive tracer, and tracked it using a PET scanner. They found that patients with social anxiety disorder synthesised significantly more serotonin than healthy controls, and concluded that the condition is characterised by an overactive serotonin system.[4]

Modern theories distinguish between different types of serotonin receptors in the brain, and different functions serotonin may play. Some researchers have suggested serotonin helps with patience[5] and coping with stress,[6] by helping us passively endure it or take action to address it. Others suggest a model where no serotonin activity results in depression without anxiety, low activity results in anxious depression, and high activity can lead to anxiety without depression.[7]

Every neuroscientist and psychiatrist I spoke to argued that serotonin is unlikely to be the whole story. How could it be? Neurotransmitters interact with one another – partly homeostasis again – so studying serotonin's effect in isolation is tricky and, in a sense, meaningless. Researcher Stefan Brugger at the University of Cardiff told me there's still a lot we don't understand about the underlying neurobiology: 'We know that drugs that act on serotonin seem to work, or do some good. We don't have any direct evidence that there's anything wrong with serotonin in anxiety.'

We can see from a large number of trials that SSRIs seem, on average, to reduce symptoms of generalised anxiety disorder better than a placebo (i.e. a sugar pill). A 2011 meta-analysis found that fluoxetine was, on average, the most effective, while sertraline was the best tolerated, with the fewest people giving it up due to side effects.[8]

Even though we don't have an exhaustive, fundamental model

of the brain and how serotonin interacts with it, people are suffering now, so psychiatrists and doctors try to act based on our best data.

—

The first time I tried sertraline I spent about a week on the toilet, twitching, shitting hot torrents of gravy. I couldn't sleep. When I sat down my legs kept up a jerky, involuntary dance under the table. My face ticked, winking, gurning. My skin prickled with heat and I sweated constantly.

I went back to the doctor and asked for something else.

They switched me to citalopram. I had no side effects at all. Or, indeed, effects. It made no discernible impact on my mood or well-being whatsoever. *You have to wait a few weeks for it to build up in your system*, said the doctor (advice broadly supported by research, which finds overall response rates to SSRIs increase when people stick with the treatment).[9] I waited a few weeks. Nothing. *We might have to up your dose*, said the doctor. We upped my dose. Nothing.

When I said it wasn't doing anything for me, a few family members said, *You never know, you might be much worse without it*, which is true, but happens to be true of literally anything. The same logic could see you wearing a rainbow unicorn-tail butt-plug for the rest of your life because you can't be sure it's not the only thing keeping your pancreas from exploding.

One day I stopped taking my pills. Nothing happened (but it was still a silly thing to do – you should never abruptly discontinue your medication without consulting your doctor first).

This doesn't mean that citalopram is a bogus treatment – as many folks are fond of saying, the plural of anecdote isn't data. But several psychiatrists later told me it was a bit of a weird choice, given my symptoms. There's minor evidence that citalopram might be useful in patients who don't respond well to other SSRIs,[10] but it doesn't even make the top five recommended medications for anxiety disorders.

All the while, I was falling apart.

I thought back to those few days while I'd been on sertraline. Yes, my hands had kept up a constant jittery palsy. Yes, I had soaked the bedsheets in sweat many times over. Yes, my bum had felt like a whoopee cushion full of Bovril. But – when it came to my mental state – as far as I recalled I'd been relatively calm.

Admittedly, leg spasms and infinite diarrhoea are compelling distractions from the customary worry monologue, but I couldn't help but wonder. The doctor had assured me that the worst of the side effects should ease off after a fortnight. What if I gave it another go?

Feeling I had little to lose, I did. This time, I saw a different doctor (not by choice – my GP kept changing as NHS cuts reduced local services), who prescribed me propranolol alongside the sertraline, a beta blocker which reduces the body's production of noradrenaline,[11] slows down your heart rate and helps with things like sweating and shaking. It was originally prescribed for hyperthyroidism – its anxiolytic effects were discovered by accident.

Overnight, my anxiety vanished.

I woke up the next morning, and I just wasn't anxious. In the days that followed, if my wife spoke to me in a way that was a bit brisk or distracted, instead of thinking, *Shit, she hates me*, I'd think, *Ah, she's feeling rushed*, and I wouldn't worry about it. I'd feel able to try to step in and help.

A few times I tried reaching for the old panic reaction, the habitual worry. I sat in bed thinking, *Isn't this the sort of thing I normally get anxious about?* But the feelings wouldn't come. I could imagine their coming, I could call up the relevant thoughts, the usual triggers for a spiral of negative what-ifs, but none of it had any emotional weight. I was just like: *Sure, I could worry about that, but why would I choose to?* The lights had come up in the club, me and anxiety saw each other for the first time, and everyone got sober real quick.

Oh. This is what it feels like to be normal. I didn't need some complicated therapeutic breakthrough or hours of journalling where I challenged my illogical thoughts one after the other. It was obvious not to think frightening things about myself or the future, in the same way it was obvious not to immerse my hand in boiling water or eat a thumbtack. Why would anyone choose to worry? Why would you need years of therapy to figure out that was a bad idea?

Sure, there were side effects. I twitched and sweated. I pooped profusely. But true to what the doctor had said, most of them subsided after a couple of weeks. The main ones that stuck around were anorgasmia and partial impotence. I couldn't get a full erection and when, eventually, I could ejaculate, I didn't feel anything.

In the public mind, impotence is coded somewhere between comic misfortune and character flaw. Men feel more able to talk about stress, despair and suicidal ideation than we did thirty years ago, but side effects like impotence remain rarely discussed. I suppose it's hard to create an ennobling narrative when your case study includes phrases like 'semi-flaccid penis' and 'uncontrollable sharts'. I mentioned the impotence to my doctor, and he said yes, it was a common side effect of sertraline, and after that I shut up about it because there was nothing I could do. It's not great, when you're at your lowest ebb, to discover even wanking has abandoned you. For years, masturbation had been like a faithful rescue dog, sticking with me even as times changed and relationships fell apart. *You still love me, don't you, boy? We'll always have each other. C'mere you!*

In the end, I felt the trade-off was worth it. I got to choose who I wanted to be, instead of acting like a brittle, grumpy arsehole. I didn't lose whole days to sick, shivery dread and exhaustion. I could still laugh. Unlike all the stories I'd heard about medication 'turning you into a zombie', there was no emotional blunting. I still experienced joy, wonder, sadness, delight. Those states were *easier* for me to access because I wasn't drugged with tiredness and fear. I wasn't bracing for the next detonation.

I felt like a whole person.

I'm not saying life was all unicorns and rainbows. But if you've been very anxious or depressed for a long time, normality is a sort of miracle. You sit down to watch TV with your partner and you feel okay. You do your work for the day and you feel okay.

The Vietnamese Buddhist monk Thich Nhat Hanh said: 'When we have a toothache, we know that not having a toothache is happiness.'

I started telling people I was anxiety-free. I began to think of my life in terms of anxiety and post-anxiety.

For a few months, life was normal and it was paradise.

———

Little by little, it wore off. The signs were subtle – flashes of irritation, snapping over something trivial. Afterwards, I'd feel intense guilt. Why had I reacted like that? This wasn't how the New Me behaved. My stand-offish behaviour caused arguments. Afterwards I'd feel stupid, monstrous and abandoned. The downward spiral intensified.

When the first panic attack broke through – that's how it felt in the aftermath, like panic had always been coming for me, clawing at the barbed wire – I felt doubly defeated. Not only were my symptoms back to where they'd been before, but now I knew that even first-line psychiatric drugs couldn't smother them. My true nature was too strong. Sertraline had been like tossing paraffin on a fading campfire – a brief, glorious flare, a blast of light, then nothing, just the memory of warmth.

Worse, now I had all of the side effects with none of the benefits. *Best keep taking it*, said people close to me, *you might be much worse without it.*

I was terrified to come off sertraline in case they were right.

On the other hand – it had clearly done *something*. For a while, sertraline gave me the biggest relief from my symptoms I'd ever experienced. I'd seen that my feelings and me, the human being, were in relationship but distinct. I wasn't anxious: anxiety was an experience I was having.

That glimpse was huge. It might be the only reason I entertained the possibility of recovery.

So what the hell was going on?

———

'I have no doubt that something like sertraline has an effect on people,' Lucy Johnstone told me, 'and some of those effects can be experienced as helpful.' But, she said, some are non-specific effects – like stimulation or sedation – that merely distract you from your distressing thoughts. Any other benefits are probably down to the placebo effect. On the other hand, she said, drugs like sertraline have significant side effects, some of which persist after you stop taking them.

It's true that, if you give someone an inert sugar pill and tell them it might be antidepressant like sertraline, they're likely to show improvement in terms of their anxiety symptoms. Similar effects are found throughout medicine. A famous British study found that branded placebo tablets worked better at relieving headaches than non-branded ones.[12] Another found that stomach ulcers in patients who took placebo pills four times a day were more likely to heal than those in people who took placebo pills only twice a day.[13] Another study found that participants reported that red placebo pills acted as stimulants and blue ones as sedatives[14] – and these effects of branding, number and colour on placebos have been replicated across other studies.

The 'placebo effect' is probably, in reality, a cluster of phenomena. Some are pretty awe-inspiring, to do with our innate capacity for physical and mental healing, and some are dismally boring artefacts of the way we record and measure trial data.

Take clinical trials. People generally sign up when their symptoms are at their worst. That's when they're most motivated to seek help, or when their doctor or psychiatrist is most likely to refer them. Conditions like anxiety disorders and depression tend to be cyclical. There are bad spells, and there are times where, though you're not cured, symptoms ease. You're having a better week.

Even if people are just given a sugar pill, if they sign up to a trial when they're feeling their shittiest, chances are some of them are going to be in a better phase of the anxiety cycle in four or six or eight weeks' time when the study finishes. If they're already reporting near-ceiling levels of anxiety or depression, they can't get worse.

This is known as 'regression to the mean' and it's one of the least exciting contributors to the placebo effect. Lots of conditions have natural histories where they get better by themselves – from rashes to gastric complaints to anxiety – and if you don't factor that in, it can look like almost any intervention is moving the needle.

With studies that involve adhering to some regimen – like remembering to take pills – it may be that taking meds isn't the cause of good outcomes, but a proxy indicator. People who remember to take their medication might be better at sticking to all sorts of healthy routines. If the sample group is elderly, they might be less cognitively impaired. They might have people who visit them regularly to remind them. They might be generally happier and more motivated to look after themselves. Chronic stress and social isolation are major risk factors when it comes to an increased chance of death. So taking pills regularly – whether active or placebo – might *correlate* with better outcomes, not *cause* them.

Anxiety is particularly susceptible to placebo effects. If you've been anxious for a long time, if you've felt like there's no hope, imagine being selected for a trial of a new drug that might cure your condition. That prospect of a reprieve – *even before you've taken the drug* – might lift your mood and reduce your anxiety on its own.

I felt it every time a new researcher agreed to speak with me. *Maybe this is the one. Maybe today I'll figure it out.* Hope is a hell of a tonic.

Drs Howard Brody and David B. Waters argued that the act of diagnosis is a form of therapy. Putting a name to unpleasant symptoms can give the patient an 'understandable, acceptable explanation of his behavior'. We may find it easier to forgive ourselves for struggling, and to experience more positive feelings towards ourselves and others. Our suffering becomes meaningful. When it comes to anxiety, this may be medicine in itself.[15]

Whatever the case, meta-analyses of many hundreds of trials show that SSRIs like sertraline and other psychopharmacological therapies consistently perform better, on average, than placebos when it comes to alleviating distressing symptoms of disordered anxiety[16] and depression.[17] The placebo effect is real – and perhaps growing – but antidepressants beat it.

But by how much? Do these drugs outperform placebos by enough of a margin to justify the cost, the side effects, and the potential after-effects? Big meta-analyses where you average out the scores people get on things like the 'Ham-D' – the Hamilton depression rating scale – hide a lot of individual variation in responses. Some people seem to respond really well. Some people don't, or even get worse. 'There's this thing that's almost like a rule of threes in all psychiatric treatment,' researcher and psychiatrist Stefan Brugger told me. 'A third of people will get better with the treatment, or get better to the extent we say they're "in remission", a third of people will get some benefit, and a third of people won't get any significant benefit.'

When I spoke to Dr Oliver Robinson at University College London's Institute of Cognitive Neuroscience, he told me a similar story – currently, when we treat anxiety disorders with medication alone, 'sixty to seventy per cent don't get better'. On the face of it, that sounds unimpressive. If a GP sees ten people with severe anxiety and prescribes them an SSRI, two months later six or seven of them will still be clinically anxious.

Stefan said that in placebo-controlled studies of antidepressants, if you look at the NNB number – the number needed to benefit

– it can seem quite high. Some studies put it between five and seven – that is, you need to give around six people an antidepressant if you want one to get better who wouldn't have got better if you'd just given them a placebo.

But – as we saw with statins – that's not too different to NNBs across general medicine.

'If psychiatric medications are rubbish,' said Stefan, 'they're no more rubbish than blood pressure tablets.'

In 2012 Professor Stefan Leucht, deputy director of the Department of Psychiatry and Psychotherapy at the Technical University of Munich, published a paper where he compared the effectiveness of psychiatric drugs to a range of common treatments in general medicine. Looking across ninety-four meta-analyses covering both medical diseases and psychiatric disorders, he found the effect size of most psychiatric drugs was 'in the same range as most general medical pharmacotherapeutics' – that is to say, psychiatric drugs work about as well, for about as many people, as a variety of commonly prescribed medications for stroke, arthritis, migraine, heart attacks and cancer.[18]

But – as Professor Leucht points out – you have to view this in the context of the seriousness of the disease. A 4 per cent chance of preventing a fatal heart attack is different to a 4 per cent chance of slightly reducing anxiety, especially when there might be significant costs and side effects.

For Lucy Johnstone, the issue was one of informed consent. She said that people with anxiety are told, '"It's an illness, this is the treatment. It's because you've got a chemical imbalance." Those are lies. And they have profound implications for people's lives and their sense of identity. Any semi-decent psychiatrist who's read anything will know that if they're saying that kind of stuff there's no evidence to support it.'

'Chemical imbalance' is a term that gets brought up a lot by people who have misgivings about psychiatric drugs, as if it represents the mainstream viewpoint. In all my years managing severe anxiety, and throughout all my conversations speaking to researchers, I've never heard a GP, psychiatrist, psychologist or neuroscientist tell me anxiety is caused solely by a 'chemical imbalance'. The NHS's official advice lists 'upbringing and environment' and 'life experiences' as the first two primary contributors to poor mental health, going on to mention discrimination, unemployment and homelessness.[19] Look for 'chemical imbalance' and you won't find it.

Psychiatrists – who, unlike psychologists like Lucy, are licensed to prescribe medication – are often accused of promoting this position, so I asked Dr Adrian James, president of the Royal College of Psychiatrists, what he thought. 'Even the most organic of organic psychiatrists talk about the social determinants of mental illness,' he said. Apart from someone on the total margins, nobody doubts this, 'because all the indicators are going the wrong way. If you take a simplistic view that there is a chemical that causes anxiety and there's not enough of it or too much of it, and we can pour something in which rights that imbalance, there is nothing of the sort. We do know there are some chemicals to do with arousal and we know that some of the medications we use act on things like GABA receptors,* but to talk of it in terms of being a purely organic thing is clearly wrong. It is a clear combination of biological, psychological and social.'

This is usually referred to as the biopsychosocial model of mental illness: some contributing factors are to do with the brain, some are to do with thoughts and beliefs, and some are to do with the environment. It's such a mainstream, utterly commonplace position within mental health research that I'm always surprised when I see authors presenting it as some dangerous, radical assault on orthodoxy – or better yet, as a secret hidden by Big Pharma that they, through diligence and guile, have somehow uncovered. For Adrian, the central

---

* 'GABA' stands for gamma-Aminobutyric acid, the main inhibitory neurotransmitter in the brain.

front he emphasised in the war on anxiety was not medication but systems – supportive workplaces where people are psychologically open to colleagues expressing their concerns, online help that they can access rapidly, and reductions in social stresses like unemployment and pressures on young people around academic performance.

When I spoke to Stefan Brugger, he admitted psychiatry is still a work in progress. 'I don't know many psychiatrists who think we know everything and our drugs are great – cos they're clearly not. A lot of people criticise the biomedical model of psychiatry, which is a bit of a strawman. In terms of my role as a doctor I'm happily promiscuous and ambivalent about methods. I spend half my time telling patients no, I'm not giving you another drug, you need to go and see the psychologists.'

I challenged Lucy over the term 'lies'. I said that I'd never heard anyone blame my anxiety purely on a 'chemical imbalance'. I told her that, at least initially, sertraline had given me a glimpse of what it was like not to be plagued continually by worry. It showed me other ways of living were possible. 'That's fair enough,' she replied, and went on to say that she thinks the chemical imbalance theory has taken root in the popular imagination, and that psychiatrists, when challenged, will claim they were only using it as a metaphor. She thought some professionals who prescribed psychiatric drugs were acting in good faith, because they believed what they'd been told. 'What you need to avoid is the trap of staying on them long-term, where you'll find they'll be decreasingly effective and where it may become hard to come off them. And I'd say there could be other ways of achieving more manageable levels of anxiety.'

That coming off them can be difficult definitely rang true with my experience. A systematic review of twenty-four studies found that more than half of people who attempt to come off antidepressants experience withdrawal symptoms, and that nearly half of those describe the symptoms as 'severe'.[20] The authors found 'a consistently low research interest in antidepressant withdrawal'.

The effects of coming off SSRIs and other antidepressants are more commonly known as 'discontinuation syndrome'. A piece in the *British Journal of Psychiatry* argued that 'the use of the term in the literature grew markedly after pharmaceutical company-sponsored conferences in 1997 and 2006', and claimed that the makers of psychiatric drugs pushed the phrase 'discontinuation syndrome' because they wanted to avoid the stigma associated with 'withdrawal'.[21]

Was this a deliberate misrepresentation by pharmaceutical companies, or – as suggested in the article itself – were physicians just keen to reduce stigma around psychiatric medication and allay the fears of patients worried about becoming 'addicted' to antidepressants? It could be both.

Potential SSRI withdrawal effects include flu-like symptoms, headaches, tiredness, abdominal cramps, diarrhoea, vomiting, insomnia, vertigo, blurred vision, electric shock sensations – sometimes known as 'brain zaps' – tremors, irritability, low mood and anxiety.[22] The longer someone has been taking the drug, the more likely they are to experience some of these symptoms.

By the time I spoke to Lucy and Stefan, I'd been on sertraline for two years.

Whether SSRIs become 'decreasingly effective' at preventing anxiety is hard to say. Obviously, the longer you monitor a group, the higher the chance of relapse – you'll see more relapses over twenty-four months than three. That doesn't mean the SSRIs are wearing off, necessarily. On the other hand, studies claiming that continued SSRI use reduces relapse rates[23] might have found increased symptoms in groups who come off medication partly because of withdrawal effects *caused by* that medication – something the authors acknowledge and attempt to control for, though how effective these controls are is debatable.

Remember how an SSRI increases serotonin levels in the synapse by blocking the axon from reabsorbing serotonin? And remember Walter Cannon's principle of homeostasis – how the body tries to maintain internal balance and stability? It turns out that's true of systems all over the body, including the brain. When postsynaptic receptors are exposed to chronically elevated levels of serotonin floating around in the cleft between the axon and the dendrite, they eventually down-regulate.[24] That is to say, the number of receptors decreases. It's as if the cell has an internal 'set point' of how much stimulation it wants. If you turn up the heat, eventually it cracks a window or takes its shirt off.

Since the exact relationship between serotonin and anxiety isn't clear, it's not obvious that this change is a bad thing. Some researchers have speculated that anxiety may be to do with hypersensitive serotonin receptors, and thus this long-term down-regulation is how SSRIs affect a cure.

One thing that everyone agrees on, however – from psychiatrists who prescribe medication every day, to the subset of psychologists and campaigners who are deeply sceptical of medication's benefits – is that it is unwise to come off these drugs cold turkey. While gently tapering off the dosage over weeks doesn't guarantee a lack of withdrawal symptoms, abruptly stopping your medication is the most risky, potentially harmful choice you can make. No one thinks it's a good idea.

I emphasise this because, in this story, I'm about to do exactly that. That's what happens next. It's a really stupid thing to do. Don't do it.

—

'Hand on heart – I worked it out with my dad – between the ages of four and sixteen I didn't cry at all. Never. I just refused.'

Back when I'd been chatting with gym-owner and trainer Dave Thomas, he told me that if, in the morning, my cortisol and testosterone were high – which is good – there would be, for a man, an obvious way to tell, 'even at our age'.

I had mumbled something about how, since I'd started taking sertraline, that had been a problem for me.

'I was put on SSRIs when I was sixteen,' said Dave, 'looking back, erroneously. I was literally just an angsty teen.' During a rugby match, he got into a fight, threw a punch, 'and I just broke down crying'.

One physiological effect of the fight, flight or freeze response is temporary inhibition of the lacrimal gland – it's harder to cry.[25] Once the initial arousal passes, this inhibition recedes, and two neuro-transmitters released during fight or flight, noradrenaline and acetylcholine, stimulate the gland to secrete tears. Hence the sudden sobbing that can come in the wake of a shock.

'They took me to see the GP,' said Dave. 'He just put me straight on Seroxat.'

Seroxat is a brand name of the SSRI paroxetine. It was the first antidepressant approved for use for panic disorders. A 2015 system-atic review found it has one of the highest rates and intensities of withdrawal symptoms of any medication in its class.[26]

'Those drugs fucked me up. I basically had one episode of being sad as a sixteen-year-old, and I was immediately medicated. I was never offered any chance to talk to anyone.' He stopped getting erections. He couldn't orgasm. 'If that's not going to screw you up as a sixteen-year-old, what will?'

In 2012, GlaxoSmithKline, the makers of Seroxat, agreed to pay the US Department of Justice a $3 billion settlement, including a criminal fine of $1 billion, for a number of charges, including promoting paroxetine for treating depression in under-18s, even though the drug's effectiveness for teenagers had not been proven. The company was found to have withheld data from two studies where paroxetine did not perform better than placebo, and to have hired a PR firm to ghost-write a study which concluded paroxetine was 'generally well tolerated and effective for major depression in adolescents', though the data the study contained showed it performed no better than placebo.

In the UK, the Medicines and Healthcare products Regulatory Agency looked at nine clinical trials conducted by GSK and found they had 'failed to show that Seroxat was effective' at treating social anxiety disorder, depression or obsessive-compulsive disorder, but that there was 'robust evidence' that it was associated with 'an increased rate of events relating to suicidal behaviour among paediatric patients'. GSK was found to have merged data from under-18 trials with adult trials, so the data on teenagers' suicide attempts, self-harm and suicidal thoughts were 'swamped' by the relatively large number of adult trials. A leaked GSK memo said that including a statement that paroxetine's efficacy was unproven would 'undermine the profile' of the drug and therefore would be 'commercially unacceptable'.[27]

'I was asked to take part in a lawsuit,' said Dave, 'and I just didn't want to. It's my past.' He told me his GP was an older guy who didn't seem very comfortable talking about things like anxiety or depression. 'He was just quite . . . northern. He was just, like, "Take these pills, you'll get better."' In the end, Dave's parents saw he was much worse on the drugs and helped wean him off them. 'I look at it as I lost my teenage years to some really bad medical advice.'

I bring up Dave's story because sometimes people who express caution or distrust around antidepressants get pilloried as dangerous cranks. Honestly, I've joined in with that on occasion. We've spent decades fighting stigma surrounding mental illness, rejecting the scaremongering stereotype of psychiatric medication as a 'chemical lobotomy' – that taking meds is a sign of weakness, or turns you into a zombie.

There's good reason to be cautious. Anxiety makes a few companies colossal amounts of money. Many manufacturers of antidepressants have faced multi-million dollar civil suits for mispromoting drugs and offering kickbacks to medical professionals. In 2009, Pfizer, the makers of sertraline, paid a $2.3 billion settlement after criminal and civil allegations that it had illegally marketed four drugs – including pregabalin (brand name Lyrica), which is often used to treat generalised anxiety disorder – for non-approved uses. This was the largest-ever pharmaceutical settlement until GlaxoSmithKline's settlement three years later.[28] Despite its size, the fine accounted for less than three weeks' worth of Pfizer's sales.

On the other hand, financial conflicts of interest are hardly exclusive to antidepressants, or even pharmacology in general. There are huge profits to be made from many far less well-evidenced treatments for anxiety. The mindfulness meditation market in the US alone is estimated to be worth over $1 billion, with the broader 'wellness' industry raking in upwards of $4 trillion.[29] Whereas the pharmaceutical industry has multiple regulatory bodies, claims about mental health made by companies in the alternative health sector undergo very little scrutiny. Antidepressants are almost certainly the most rigorously studied treatment for anxiety in human history.

Though I've heard many emotive stories about people having a crap time on antidepressants – including my own – I've also spoken to loads of people whose experience was broadly positive. In terms of potential side effects, as neuroscientist Dr Oliver Robinson told me: 'Don't let anyone tell you that something has no side effects. Everything has side effects.'

If you run you get aches and pains. You can sprain an ankle or permanently bugger up your knees. Therapy can be costly, time-consuming and can bring up difficult feelings that make you feel worse – even if only temporarily. If your therapist is shit, or uses a modality that isn't backed by rigorous research, they might introduce problems you didn't have before. Meditation and mindfulness practices have been linked to psychotic episodes in vulnerable individuals (though whether these episodes might have happened anyway is difficult to establish). Changing your diet can cause gastric distress, fatigue, cravings, poor concentration, irritability and sleeplessness.

Though antidepressants seem to offer, on average, only a small benefit versus a placebo, they can be part of a suite of interventions attempted simultaneously. A 2014 meta-analysis of fifty-two studies looking at anxiety disorders and depression found that combining antidepressants with talking therapy produced an effect twice as large as taking antidepressants on their own when it came to panic disorder, OCD and depression.[30] Other studies have failed to find a significant difference between antidepressants and therapy when it comes to treating anxiety disorders[31] – that is, on their own, both perform as well as each other.

One clear advantage that medication has over therapy is there's no waiting list. CBT has a solid evidence base when it comes to treating anxiety,[32] but in the UK, the gap between getting a referral and your first session can be anything from weeks to months. Although in recent years wait times for the first session improved, the wait for a *second* session widened, with one in six patients waiting over ninety days, on top of the initial waiting time – suggesting that chronically underfunded mental health services simply shifted their priorities to meet targets.[33] During the pandemic, waiting times across all NHS services in England hit record highs,[34] while referrals to IAPT, the Improving Access to Psychological Therapies service, dropped dramatically,[35] making a situation already criticised as 'unacceptable' by the British Association for Counselling and Psychotherapy substantially worse.

By contrast, if you visit your GP and say you're horribly anxious, you're not coping and you don't know how you're going to get through the next week (as I have), she can write you a prescription for sertraline and you'll be taking your first pill the same day.

Most studies testing treatments for anxiety compare two groups, or 'arms': the group getting the medication or the therapy or whatever treatment, and the 'control' group, who get a placebo – a psychopharmacologically inert pill, or an interview instead of therapy. As we've seen, placebo groups often do surprisingly well. But it's still a form of intervention.

To find the 'true' effect of a treatment, some studies include a third arm. What they want to find out is what happens if you're offered no help at all. It's not ethical to deny people treatment, but what researchers might do is take a comparable population of, say, people with generalised anxiety disorder, who are on a waiting list for treatment, and ask them to fill in a questionnaire about their symptoms at the beginning and end of a six-week period. These third, 'no intervention' arms are often called 'wait list' groups.

Wait lists consistently show far worse outcomes than both placebo and treatment groups. They have worse symptoms. More panic attacks. Lower moods. Greater anxiety.

'Anxiety is all about uncertainty,' Dr Oli Robinson told me. Having a credible authority figure offer a confident diagnosis and prescribe a treatment reduces that uncertainty. Even their explanation of possible side effects and the suggestion it may take two weeks for the effects to be felt give a timeline, a sense of process. These acts are themselves therapeutic.

That doesn't mean that antidepressants aren't doing anything. Just that, faced with the dysphoria of the unknown, almost *any* intervention that isn't actively harmful is better than nothing. As philosopher David A. Jopling puts it, for many non-life-threatening conditions: 'Diagnosis is treatment even if the diagnosis is incorrect.'[36]

For someone with an anxiety disorder, the worst thing you can do is stick them on a waiting list.

———

Of course, this is less of a problem for wealthy middle-class people who can afford to pay for private therapy as soon as they want it, and who get to choose between a variety of practitioners and modalities. They can also pay for private consultations with psychiatrists, who can take more time than NHS doctors to come to a diagnosis, and who, as specialists, have far more experience of prescribing a variety of medications for mental illnesses. (When my GP referred me to a psychiatrist, I was quoted a price of £395 for a single 90-minute consultation – an offer which I could not afford to accept.)[37]

This means those in poverty – who suffer the most stress[38] and are most at risk of anxiety-related disorders (unemployment more than doubles the odds of generalised anxiety disorder, and trebles the odds of phobia)[39] – get the absolute worst care. They get the least choice and the longest delays.

Even the *best* care currently isn't very reliable. Oli Robinson reckoned that for about 25 per cent of people, neither meds nor CBT work – and that's assuming they can get access to either in the first place. Anxiety disorders are the most common form of mental illness on the planet, so there are huge numbers of people for whom the standard solutions do nothing.

Not only that, but 'CBT' means different things to different people. Therapists sometimes exclude the behavioural or cognitive component entirely (which some research suggests, worryingly, has zero impact on outcomes).[40] Two people can conceivably receive two treatments called CBT that share no common elements. The CBT we've studied in clinical trials isn't always what people are receiving.

By contrast, when a physician prescribes you medication there's remarkable consistency. Every molecule of sertraline has 17 hydrogen atoms, 17 carbon atoms, 2 chlorine atoms and 1 nitrogen atom. Each intervention is identical at the atomic level.

Doesn't mean it's better. Doesn't mean it works. But it's cheap, there's no waiting list, and everyone gets the same treatment. Doctors and psychiatrists have limited resources. You can see the attraction.

—

I asked Stefan what my options were, drug-wise.

'Okay,' he said, 'I'll give you what I would do if you were me.'

I was on 50mg of sertraline daily. He reckoned I could go higher – 'up to 200mg' – but if I was already getting side effects those might get worse. As well as SSRIs he suggested two SNRIs – serotonin-noradrenaline reuptake inhibitors – venlafaxine and duloxetine (a meta-analysis ranked them seventh and third respectively for the number of patients that reduced their anxiety score by at least half).[41] He added that they seem to have fewer sexual side effects than sertraline.

Stefan also mentioned a drug called quetiapine that seems to be 'quite good' for treating anxiety at lower doses. It's not approved for use in generalised anxiety disorder – it's more often prescribed for schizophrenia or bipolar disorder – so a doctor giving me this would be prescribing 'off-label', one of the practices big pharmaceutical companies have received fines for promoting. Stefan warned that quetiapine might make me very sleepy and put on weight.

He asked if I felt calmer when I drank booze. 'If you do, it'll be the effects on GABA – basically the major inhibitory neurotransmitter in the brain. It quietens everything down.'

I said I'd been teetotal for just over seven years. My anxiety had got a lot worse when I quit.

'Alcohol is the ultimate dirty drug,' said Stefan. 'It sort of whacks every neurotransmitter in the brain. The anxiolytic effect of alcohol is probably mediated by its action on GABA.'

This points to a fallacy in Lucy's point about anxiety not being caused by 'a lack of alcohol in the brain'. It's debunking a position no one argues for. Alcohol binds to the same receptors as GABA and mimics its effects. There is plenty of evidence for GABA's role in modulating anxiety,[42] and that patients with panic disorder have lower levels of GABA in the brain than healthy controls.[43] Cough syrup can soothe a persistent cough, and so can whisky. That doesn't mean that coughs are caused by a lack of whisky in the throat, but neither does it debunk the effectiveness of cough syrup. Both act on relieving symptoms. Cough syrup doesn't cure the common cold, but that doesn't mean it's useless.

Stefan suggested pregabalin and gabapentin, two drugs that affect GABA and are used to treat things like chronic nerve pain. He thought they had the fewest side effects, though 'if you take a shit load of them you'll probably get high'. He said I could even combine them with sertraline.

As Stefan listed pharmaceuticals and their side effects, I felt a rising nausea. I think of myself as an open-minded, 'better living through science' sort of chap – not anti-meds, not anti-psychiatry. I'd been through my youthful R. D. Laing phase – my dissertation was on the literature of the anti-psychiatry movement – and read classic jeremiads like Erving Goffman's *Asylums* and Thomas Szasz's *The Myth of Mental Illness*. I thought there was much to criticise in psychiatry's history – especially how it had treated women, people of colour and LGBTQ+ folk – and that it still had institutional biases and much room for improvement. But I also believed in rational enquiry, and evidence. I knew sertraline had helped me – albeit temporarily.

Yet I was scared. Remembering to take my meds was itself a source of huge anxiety. Once, when I was due to fly out to Brunei to teach, I realised at the last moment I'd forgotten my medication. Lisa drove all night to the airport to bring it to me, before driving home and heading to work the next morning having had zero sleep. (Fortunately she doesn't operate cranes or perform heart surgery.) It was one of the kindest things anyone has ever done for me. I didn't want to put either of us through that stress ever again.

Sometimes my pharmacy wouldn't fill my prescription on time and I'd have to make frantic phone calls and several trips across town to secure an emergency supply. If I ever went away somewhere, I had to make sure I had enough to last the journey, plus back-ups in a coat pocket in case I lost my bag.

Taking psychiatric meds means you're only ever twenty-four hours and a tiny oversight away from an emergency. You spend your whole life tethered to these little silver blister packs.

———

Maybe I'd internalised a lot of the stigma around meds. That taking them was a sign of failure. Lucy had said there were pros and cons to taking medication, but that most people probably hadn't been introduced to the cons. I told her that wasn't my experience. There's still stigma, shame and moralising. I can't imagine it's a decision anyone takes lightly.

Still, by the time someone finds themselves in their GP's office asking for help, they're desperate. Given how poor the choices available to most of us are, are people really free to decide?

One thing I never had, that no doctor ever discussed, was a long-term plan. How long am I likely to be on this medication? Six months? A year? Two? How will we decide if I'm ready to come off it? Standard consultations with a British GP last minutes. They simply aren't long enough to have that kind of – let's be honest, *essential* – discussion.

Maybe taking medication for anxiety just isn't a very satisfying story. I don't just mean for the purposes of this book (although, admittedly, if the solution to my anxiety had been upping my dosage from 50 to 100mg of sertraline, that would have been a little anti-climactic). You feel worried and hopeless, then you take a pill and you're all right again. To some people that's a wonderful, meaningful idea – a triumph of medicine. We've found a way of giving people back their lives, of empowering them at their lowest.

To others, it's positively dystopian. It short-circuits a cry for help. In their eyes, anxiety, worry, panic attacks are all meaningful responses to pain – cries of hurt and outrage – that medication shuts down. Instead of asking what neurotransmitters dysregulate in anxious mice, they argue, we ought to be asking: 'Why are so many people so anxious?'

Prominent medical sociologist and disability rights campaigner Dr Irving Zola used the analogy of a man who is kept so busy dragging bodies from a river, hauling them onto the bank and resuscitating them, that he has no time to wonder, 'Who is upstream pushing them all in?' Lucy thinks the key driver of what we call anxiety and depression is our modern, industrialised, capitalist society. 'Neo-liberalism takes advantage of people, and takes advantage of their suffering to sell cures which aren't cures. It's self-perpetuating. And they're usually very individualistic cures. Do this mindfulness for ten minutes a day and if you're in an exploitative job you'll feel better. Buy my self-help book. Oh, it hasn't worked? Buy another one. Buy another one. They offer this false solution which is itself a form of exploitation.'

I'd heard this from many people. Prescribing medication to blunt anxiety was missing the point. It was like turning the car radio up to drown out the rattle in the engine.

Was searching for personal solutions folly? What if the problem wasn't in me at all? What if the problem was the world?

—

A couple of weeks later, I glanced at the multicoloured pill spacer my wife had given me and realised that for the past two days I'd forgotten to take my sertraline.

That was odd.

I paused to take stock. Was I more worried than usual? Was my heart racing?

No. I felt completely normal.

Sure, I was still having thundering panic attacks, intrusive worries, and fractious, anxious episodes where I'd get frozen in doorways or words would pour out in a stream of gibbering, repetitive nonsense. But I was no *worse*.

I had been reading about an experimental new treatment for anxiety, one that sounded very powerful. If I wanted to try it I'd have to come off sertraline, because if I did it while on sertraline there was a chance I might die.

Sitting at my desk, it did not seem like such a big step to leave that day's little white pill sitting in its compartment, shut down my laptop and go to bed. I felt okay. Probably, I thought, withdrawal only affected you if you were getting benefits from the drug in the first place.

I told myself, if I wrote about this later, I'd have to tell people not to copy me, because they might not find it so easy.

Because that's how coming off my meds cold turkey was going to be, right?

Easy.

———

I was walking into the city when I got a message from Lisa. Did I know where the car keys were? She had to pick up a birthday present for Suki.

I patted my pockets and realised I'd accidentally taken them with me.

I messaged her back. Oh God, I was so sorry. I must have picked them up by force of habit. I hadn't been thinking. I was so stupid. I knew she'd put this time aside to fetch Suki's present – a specially made mud kitchen for the back garden.

As I texted my apologies, I started crying. I was such a waste of space. I should just kill myself.

Wait a minute, I thought. *That's . . . extreme.*

It was my first clue that coming off my meds wasn't going to be as easy as I'd anticipated.

Over the next few days my mood rollercoastered. I felt as if I had woken up strapped to the nose cone of a rocket during re-entry. Every emotion was magnified to the nth degree.

On Suki's birthday we took her out for pizza. She was three. As we chatted, she mentioned the sunflower she'd been growing in her grandmother's garden.

'It might die,' she said, quietly. She looked me in the eyes. 'I might die.'

She'd never mentioned death before. I had to look away.

Out the window, behind her, a tree's leaves blazed vermillion, impossibly bright. Colours and sounds were surging. Everything was so impossibly fragile and precious. I loved Suki so much, I loved my whole family so, so much and the universe was so vast and uncontrollable. The sunlight through the branches, the people around us eating, everything was suffused with meaning. Why weren't they all crying? How could anyone think or smile or be normal knowing it's all so temporary?

We're all dying! I wanted to scream. *How can you be so bloody calm?*

But I kept quiet, and that's why I'm still welcome in the Norwich Forum branch of Pizza Express.

A day later, I crashed. I slumped in bed and sobbed. Everything felt too much, too strong. I'd glimpsed a maddening, Lovecraftian cosmic truth and I'd never be able to eat a fried egg sandwich or watch TV again because I'd be forever burdened with this Terrible Knowledge.

Over the weeks that followed, the dark heaviness eased off. I started to feel like maybe life wasn't so unbearably intense that I'd rather be dead. I managed to keep going without sertraline.

I was shaken. For the first time in years, I'd experienced genuine, crushing depression. I'd thought my search for a cure and all these changes I was making would make my life better. But right now, they were making it worse.

VI.

MODERN LIFE IS RUBBISH
The anxiety of modern life and the history of stress

One morning, I received a WhatsApp message from my wife: *Shall we buy a nuclear bunker?*

I tried to think if this was something we'd discussed.

When we first met she had been stockpiling food in anticipation of a swine-flu pandemic. My chest tightened. Was she joking? What was she getting us into?

I felt my anxiety rising, and with it a rush of shame. I was always like this when Lisa suggested something new. I hated change. Where was my spontaneity, my sense of adventure? After all, she had been right about painting the living room wall yellow.

I took a couple of deep breaths and considered my response. While I wanted to *seem* supportive, I did not actually want to support her. Maybe if I faked an easy-going indifference she would lose interest.

Woozy with dread, I messaged back: *Where is it? How much does it cost?*

———

Five days later we were levering up a rusted hatch and peering down an unlit shaft. The bunker's entrance sat in the lee of a huge haystack, concealed by blackberry bushes.

We had driven up a dirt track and then walked across a field. Flat, windswept Norfolk countryside spread for miles. Reaching the hatch meant navigating a twisting path of trampled-down brambles.

If anything, Lisa's enthusiasm had grown. My lack of protest had caught her off-guard. Anything less than a gibbering meltdown was so rare she apparently now considered the whole enterprise blessed – fated, almost. 'You could use the plot above as an allotment,' she had suggested – rather optimistically, I felt, given that I had neither gardened nor expressed any interest in gardening for the entirety of our marriage. By the same logic, I could use it to make chainsaw ice sculptures or teach Malay.

When my turn came to climb through the hatch, I felt an ominous loosening in my bowels. I dangled a leg over the void. The drop was at least fifteen feet onto concrete. Imagine slipping. You'd smash a hip, at the very least. What if you came here alone? There'd be no way to call for help – there was no phone signal – no chance of being seen by a passer-by. If no one thought to come looking for you, you might die underground.

When my foot found a rung, I startled. Adrenaline pumped through me. What if the ladder gave way?

A lot of my life has involved shutting down instincts, despite knowing I am definitely going to die. It's a trade-off where I leverage social anxiety – my fear of judgement – to override physical anxiety – my fear of falling from the ladder of a disused fall-out shelter, shattering my pelvis and lying for hours in agony until paramedics hoist my body through the narrow hatch.

The ladder did not collapse beneath me (*this time*, my brain noted helpfully). As I descended, the sound of the wind dropped away and the warmth of the sun faded to a musty, gothic chill. Insulated cables ran down the wall, beside a mechanism that let you shut the hatch via a handle below.

The bunker consisted of a single room with white Formica cabinets along one wall, covered in 'No Smoking' stickers. There was a fold-down bunk, a shower space and a chemical toilet. The desk and floor were caked in brown dust. Next to the sink in the corner was an electric kettle, a bottle of Worcestershire sauce, and several bottles of bleach.

When we'd climbed back to daylight we chatted with the owner, an amiable guy not much older than me with tattoos and faded black t-shirt. He'd bought it so he and his mum could use it at weekends as a holiday home, but he'd been living for years now in Thailand, and she was too old to manage the ladder. This he said with a kind of wistfulness, gazing out across the wheat stubble. Time had passed swiftly, and his dream of spending Saturday nights underground with his elderly mother in a cramped nuclear bunker would remain forever unfulfilled.

It felt weird, standing there by the hatch surrounded by nothing but open countryside, an old grey church in the distance. This was the same landscape the original owner would have seen when the bunker was built. Wind rushed through hedgerows with a soft crash. The little plot of land felt like a raft on a wide, empty ocean.

Imagine thinking such a refuge might be necessary. Imagine living with the belief that one day you might arrive in the midst of a global crisis. That you might pause to take a last look at those oaks and beeches and hawthorns, a last look at England, then retreat underground. That one day you might pull that lever, and watch a little rectangle of sky wink shut.

——

The *Diagnostic and Statistical Manual of Mental Disorders*, or DSM-5, is the current standard for psychiatric diagnosis in the US. It says that to qualify for generalised anxiety disorder, worry must be 'excessive'. The existence of anxiety itself isn't enough to make you mentally ill, even if it's really distressing and making you feel horrible. A key feature is that your feelings have to be out of proportion to what's going on.[1]

Is it 'excessive' to feel anxious in the face of climate breakdown? Is it excessive to feel fear when you're faced with a – terrifyingly plausible – future where our world grows increasingly hostile to life, where my daughter faces floods, food shortages, mass destruction of homes and armed conflict over resources? These are already happening, right? Is it excessive to feel constant worry during a global pandemic? To feel brutalised by the dire, apocalyptic theatre unfolding outside my window while politicians look on with the gormless indifference of an anime body pillow during a hammer murder?

As psychiatrist and concentration camp survivor Viktor E. Frankl put it: 'An abnormal reaction to an abnormal situation is normal behaviour.'[2]

Can anxiety disorders even *exist* at the end of the world?

We live in an anxious age.

I think you would struggle to find anyone who would challenge that statement. It's something anxiety sufferers hear a lot. 'Of course you're anxious – these are anxious times.' 'It's the pace of modern life.' 'There'd be something wrong with you if you *weren't* anxious.'

When I told people I was searching for a cure for my anxiety, lots of them responded with lines like this – I think to try to make me feel better. Anxiety wasn't my fault. What I was experiencing was not a mental disorder. It was a symptom of our sick society.

'Few people today,' says Scott Stossel in his memoir *My Age of Anxiety*, 'would dispute that chronic stress is a hallmark of our times or that anxiety has become a kind of cultural condition of modernity.' Similar assertions appeared in every pop-psych book on anxiety I picked up. They appeared in lectures and research papers. Dr Lucy Johnstone told me young people in schools were suffering 'epidemic levels' of anxiety. She said mental health was better during the Second World War.

I wasn't even ill. Just exquisitely tuned into the zeitgeist.

Do we live in the age of anxiety? This isn't some dry philosoph-ical question. If someone calls 999 in a frenzied panic because they're trapped in the attic of a burning building, you need to send the fire brigade, not sedatives. The problem is not their feelings, but the unbearable circumstances giving rise to those feelings.

If modern life is the cause of our anxiety, there's no point looking for solutions in our genes, or the brain, or medication, or new ther-apies, or new ways of thinking.

We have to change the world.

———

Years ago, when I was passing through the lower intestine of a deep, intractable depression, tearing off the latest of my one-page-a-day Chinese propaganda-poster desk calendar began to feel like an oppressive, bewildering ordeal. Untorn pages lay there like a rebuke.

I'm so shit, I can't keep a calendar up to date, I'd think, having spent the last few days staring at an image exhorting me to 'Angrily denounce the renegade and traitor Lin Biao'. All it would have taken was the simple act of extending my arm, tightening my fingers around the out-of-date pages, and tugging. Yet the gap between reality and the exertion of will seemed like an unbridgeable chasm.

The author M. Molly Backes calls this common symptom of depression 'The Impossible Task': 'The Impossible Task could be anything: going to the bank, refilling a prescription, making your bed, checking your email, paying a bill. From the outside, its sudden impossibility makes ZERO sense.'[3] The Impossible Task is usually something small, simple – something you've done a hundred times. All at once, You. Just. Can't.

You can understand, then, how telling someone who's chronically anxious or depressed that solving their plight requires nothing less than collective mobilisation to deconstruct centuries-old monolithic forces of global oppression feels like a bit of an ask. It's hard to stir the old revolutionary zeal when putting on clean underpants feels like an achievement tantamount to launching Sputnik.

—

So then, to the facts. A recent report from the World Health Organisation claims anxiety disorders and depression rose nearly 50 per cent worldwide between 1990 and 2013.[4] In big, epidemiological studies, anxiety disorders and depression often get lumped together because they share symptoms; they're frequently co-morbid, i.e. people often have both; they seem to respond to similar treatments; and historically, terms for either – neurosis, nervous breakdown – have often been used interchangeably. In fact, many researchers argued and continue to argue that generalised anxiety disorder is better understood as a symptom of major depression than its own disorder.[5] The number of anti-anxiety and antidepressant items dispensed by the NHS has more than doubled over the last decade, rising to 70.9 million prescriptions per annum.[6] Between 1996 and 2013 the number of adults in the US filling a prescription for benzo-diazepines, a class of anti-anxiety medication that includes Valium, rose by 67 per cent from 8.1 million to 13.5 million.[7]

To support her claim that young people are suffering an 'epidemic' of anxiety and depression, Lucy pointed me to a 2017 NHS study which concluded that 1 in 8 children in the UK had at least one mental disorder,[8] anxiety disorders being among the most common. (I noticed that Lucy was willing to use the language and diagnostic criteria of the medical model when it supported her argument. When I mentioned this, she conceded that 'perhaps "epidemic" was a poor choice of words'.)

Some sources suggest 2.5–7 per cent of the world's population may be suffering from a recognised anxiety disorder at any given time, though the number varies by country.[9] Others suggest up to a 33.7 per cent lifetime prevalence rate – that is to say, up to one-third of human beings globally will meet the criteria for an anxiety disorder at some point in their lives.[10] With an estimated 284 million people experiencing an anxiety disorder globally in a single year (more than four times the entire population of the UK),[11] anxiety is the most commonly diagnosed mental health disorder.

After reading these figures, in one sense I felt a little miffed. I had taken anxiety to be evidence of my Rich Inner Life. But it was naff and mainstream, the Michael McIntyre of mental illness. In another sense, seeing anxiety everywhere was paradoxically comforting. My condition was less a personal failing, more a tragic sign of the times. Perhaps one day anxiety would be seen as quaintly synonymous with a bygone era, like whalebone corsets, or syphilis.

Reading all these statistics, the case for our living in a uniquely anxious age seemed like a slam-dunk. The perception that the world has grown increasingly anxious is pervasive. Scott Stossel is probably correct that 'few would argue' if I concluded that anxiety is our uniquely modern curse.

But I was reluctant to move on. If we do live in heart-crushing, uniquely terrifying times, an age so dreadful that anxiety is an inevitable consequence, then yes, perhaps we're off the hook, the blame falling on that nebulous construct 'society'. I suspect that's why anxiety sufferers get told this so often. It's supposed to free us from self-blame.

It also robs us, largely, of control. If anxiety is inevitable – the *proper* response, even – then, in the absence of a global sea-change in attitudes, lifestyles, economic systems and the distribution of resources unprecedented in human history, we're condemned to misery.

Was my anxiety an inevitable crop flowering from civilisation's poisoned soil? Would the Tim Clare of an earlier epoch have been a chilled-out country-dwelling gentleman of leisure, composing verses about peat while gazing wistfully across the Fens? Is our world a more stressful, more anxiety-inducing place than it was, say, half a century ago? Has modernity turned us into nervous wrecks? Do we live in the age of anxiety?

And if so, when exactly did it all go wrong?

—

In 1970, Alvin Toffler published *Future Shock*, which went on to sell over 6 million copies. In it, he argued that rapid technological advances since the end of the war had led to 'information overload' and pervasive cultural trauma, 'the shattering stress and disorientation that we induce in individuals by subjecting them to too much change in too short a time'. For Toffler, everything from too much consumer choice to new buildings replacing old ones created a state of horrible, alienating transience where nothing was stable or certain. Rising rates of heart disease, obesity and anxiety were all down to the unprecedented stress of modern life.

Toffler argued that this new age of anxiety had emerged since 1950, before which western societies enjoyed a slower, more stable existence buttressed by the reassuring predictability of lifelong jobs in farm or factory, and institutions like the church, family and national identity. His thesis pulled the neat trick of flattering both left-wing progressives (we're miserable because capitalism) and conservatives (we're miserable because we've abandoned tradition).

Apocalyptic visions of anxious modernity were on trend. Ethologist John B. Calhoun had spent decades exploring the stressful effects of overcrowding on rats and mice. In the same year Toffler's book came out, Calhoun's most infamous work would reach a grim climax.

Calhoun built something he called 'Universe 25' – an enclosed habitat for mice with ample food and shelter, free from disease and predators. He described it as a 'closed Utopian universe'.[12]

Initially the mouse population grew explosively. Then, as growth began to slow, their behaviour began to change. Mothers started abandoning or attacking their babies. Males who failed to find roles in the social hierarchy 'withdrew physically and psychologically; they became very inactive and aggregated in large pools near the centre of the floor'. Mice stopped breeding. Some males retreated from society entirely, spending all their time alone, obsessively grooming themselves. Unlike their peers, they had no scars from fighting, so Calhoun dubbed them 'the beautiful ones'.

Calhoun believed that once a population passed a certain point, deep, prolonged social interactions became impossible. He thought that rodents and people had evolved to handle maximum group sizes of about twelve. In the city, there were too many stressful interruptions, too many strangers getting in the way. Two mice would be trying to communicate when another would crawl over their heads or squeeze between them. To 'maximise gratification', social behaviours became more numerous, but shorter and less intense. Meanwhile, constant unwanted interactions generated fear, withdrawal and aggression. Think of the difference between encountering one person on a country footpath and fifty people in a busy Tube carriage – or hundreds of digital representations of people on social media.

Rising stress combined with the destruction of close bonds would, Calhoun believed, lead to a permanent breakdown in society – what he termed the 'behavioral sink' – a cultural event horizon from which there was no return. He predicted that 1984 was the point at which humankind would hit this threshold, beyond which life would become so unbearably anxiety-provoking that our chance 'to avoid population catastrophe would be quickly lost'.

Today most psychologists are careful to emphasise the limitations of animal models when it comes to explaining complex human emotions – at least within their papers – using terms like 'anxiety-like behaviour' to describe activities like freezing or withdrawal. If you're used to this kind of cautious language, reading Calhoun is quite a trip.

Calhoun explicitly presents his mice as little humans. He calls their nesting pens 'tower blocks', and refers to withdrawn mice as 'dropouts', and violent ones as 'juvenile delinquents'. He might as well have given half of them tiny longbows and claimed he was restaging the Battle of Crécy. When critics accused him of anthropomorphism, he would retort that the burden of proof was on them to prove that human beings were unique.[13]

To which they might well have replied: 'We drive cars, John. We're using verbal representations of complex abstract concepts right now to have this stupid argument, *you massive pillock*.'

Calhoun's work is astonishingly tendentious, littered with grand references to the Garden of Eden and the Four Horsemen of the Apocalypse. At times it resembles the jottings of a man who is not very well. He lays out Byzantine formulae to show that, in removing war, famine and pestilence from his mouse universe, he has brought about 'the death of death', which he calls 'death squared'. Eventually he had his funding cut.

Yet this barely mattered. As with Toffler, the fears Calhoun raised resonated with a broad coalition of thinkers. They were, as Murray Davis would have it, *interesting*, which liberated them from the dowdy impediments of scientific rigour. Conservatives saw ready analogies for cultural degeneration in his vivid descriptions of females abandoning traditional maternal roles, violent, disaffected youths, and the rise of 'sub-cultures' like homosexuality, all brought about by Calhoun's construction of what they saw as a rodent welfare state. Progressives read off stark warnings about urban consumerist excess and ecological collapse in the wake of the post-war baby boom.

But were Toffler and Calhoun right? Had the world, with its rising population and shifting social mores, grown more intolerably stressful since the halcyon days of . . . *checks notes* . . . the Second World War?

Despite Lucy's contention that mental health was 'better' during the war, civilians had a higher lifetime risk of both anxiety disorder and major depressive disorder if they lived in war zones or areas that were bombed, than if they lived in areas that didn't see combat,[14] to say nothing of the 70 million soldiers who actually fought.

American psychiatrists Roy G. Grinker and John P. Spiegel worked with many traumatised soldiers, and concluded nervous breakdown was not a matter of if but when – they estimated a man could last between a hundred days and one year of active duty before reaching his breaking point: 'It would seem to be a more rational question to ask why the soldier does not succumb to anxiety, rather than why he does.'[15]

The idea that British psyches were in rude health during the Blitz stems from a combination of wartime propaganda and the fact that physicians had expected nothing short of a psychological apocalypse. In 1938, a panel of eighteen leading psychiatrists predicted that, with bombs falling on a civilian population that included the elderly, women and children, 'psychiatric casualties might exceed physical casualties by three to one'. They estimated that, within the first six months of war, Britain would see 3–4 million cases of hysteria, severe panic and other anxiety disorders.[16] When this historically unprecedented wave of neurosis failed to emerge, many concluded that the phlegmatic Brits were doing just fine.

In a 1942 article in the *Lancet*, psychiatrist Aubrey Lewis collected data from psychiatric outpatient clinics all over England, and concluded, 'Air-raids have not been responsible for any striking increase in neurotic illness.'[17] But neither did they result in civilians becoming calmer and happier.

Lewis' report only concerned anxiety cases so severe that people were admitted to clinics. If you're frightened during fifty-seven consecutive days of bombs falling from the sky, you're not mentally ill. But – I think it's uncontroversial to say – you are under a great deal of stress.

What about before the war?

In 1937, we find British cardiologist Thomas Horder lamenting 'the stress of modern life', created by the 'monotony and drabness' of work, an 'increasing sense of international insecurity', and the 'anxiety connected with the competition of living'.[18]

During the Great Depression, a staggering 25 per cent of the US population were without work. As we've seen, poverty and unemployment are huge risk factors for anxiety disorders, doubling or trebling your chances of experiencing them. Franklin D. Roosevelt opened his 1933 inaugural address with the famous words: 'The only thing we have to fear is . . . fear itself,' going on to lament the 'nameless, unreasoning, unjustified terror' gripping his country.

Even before the Crash of '29, writing in the *New York Times* in 1925, physician William S. Sadler proclaimed a new 'group of preventable conditions' which he dubbed 'Americanitis': 'The excitement, the incessant drive of American life, the excited strain of the American temperament, are responsible for a marked mortality increase between the decade of 40 and 50 . . . Adaptation and natural selection have not had time to produce a race suited to the stress of a civilization which counts on the airplane and the wireless as commonplaces.'[19]

Go back even further and we find similar warnings.

'The mechanical facilities for cheap, quick carriage of persons, goods, and news, signify that each average man or woman of to-day is habitually susceptible to the direct influence of a thousand times as many other persons as were their ancestors before the age of steam and electricity,' wrote the English social scientist J. A. Hobson in his 1901 book *The Psychology of Jingoism*. He believed that town life and 'the strain of adaptation' had a deleterious impact on people's 'nervous organisation', arguing that: 'In every nation which has proceeded far in modern industrialism the prevalence of neurotic diseases attests the general nervous strain to which the population is subjected.'

During the same period, a rash of self-help books purported to aid readers with 'weak nerves', 'nervous collapse' and 'neurasthenia', along with an explosion of new treatments for the apparently congenitally anxious middle-classes, such as French psychologist Émile

Coué's 'autosuggestion' – essentially a practice of repeating positive affirmations which followers claimed could, in addition to treating emotional maladies, cure everything from a prolapsed uterus to deafness. Many physicians, preferring the term 'nervous breakdown' to the distinctly Victorian 'hysteria', believed that the human body was like a battery, with a finite store of energy that, in severely anxious or depressed patients, had been drained by the pressures of contemporary living.

In 1897 French sociologist Émile Durkheim argued that modernity and the rapid changes it wrought left people alienated from society, anxious, depressed and without meaning. People in cities killed themselves at a far higher rate than in the countryside, he said, because of the disintegration of traditional communities like family and church. What remained was unbearable anxiety and loneliness.

But this fear of mechanisation, crowded cities and societal change was long-established. The 1881 publication of George M. Beard's *American Nervousness: Its Causes and Consequences*, placed the blame for the 'very rapid increase' of 'nervous exhaustion' or neurasthenia on '*modern civilization*, which is distinguished from the ancient by these five characteristics: steam power, the periodical press, the telegraph, the sciences, and the mental activity of women'. Beard was unequivocal in linking progress with anxiety. 'Civilization', he warned, 'is the one constant factor without which there can be little or no nervousness, and under which in its modern form nervousness in its many varieties must arise inevitably.'

Perhaps his – I want to say 'quaintly bigoted' – dismay at women's thinking gives us our first clue that something else is going on here. For Beard, women's access to education was itself a horror of modernity.

In 1876, almost a century before Toffler's *Future Shock*, Dr Benjamin Ward Richardson wrote *Diseases of Modern Life*, devoting two whole chapters to 'diseases from worry or mental strain', blaming urban living and the pace of change in the Industrial Age.

In his 1860 address to the Royal Medical College of Edinburgh, physician James Crichton-Browne declared, 'We live in an age of electricity, of railways, of gas, and of velocity in thought and action. In the course of one brief month more impressions are conveyed to our brains than reached our ancestors in the course of years . . . [more] than was required of our grandfathers in the course of a lifetime.'

For Crichton-Browne, train travel and 'over-pressure' in schools of a 'superior description' were leading to an epidemic of nervousness, fatigue, sleeplessness and brain disease. Twenty years later, he would warn of a 'morbid nervousness, unknown to the ancients or to the fathers of medicine' afflicting Britain, with a huge increase in nervous conditions and a concomitant rise in the popularity of 'neurotic remedies' like morphia, arsenic and tobacco.[20]

Indeed, this line of argument was so common that in 1895, distinguished physician Thomas Clifford Allbutt – inventor of the medical thermometer – felt the need to write an exasperated piece for the *Contemporary Review*, bemoaning the popular belief that 'affections of the nervous system are on the increase'. In a pungently sarcastic riff, he mocked newspapers' routinely blaming 'the fret-fulness, the melancholy, the unrest due to living at a high pressure, to the whirl of the railway, the pelting of telegrams, the strife of business, the hunger for riches, the lust of vulgar minds for coarse and instant pleasures'. For Allbutt, this talk of modern surges in 'nervous debility', 'neurasthenia' and 'hysteria' was just 'the fashionable fad of the day; what was "liver" fifty years ago has become "nerves" to-day'.

Reading Victorian physicians like Crichton-Browne and Beard with their jarring warnings about 'over-taxing' the female brain, you get the impression their concern may not have been entirely about society's emotional welfare, but troubling shifts in traditional bases of power. Norms were changing, and not in a way many white middle-class men found comfortable.

For many British commentators, the subtext to their laments about the rise of nervous disorders was fears about racial degeneration, shifting gender roles and the fitness of succeeding generations to defend the Empire and its various colonial possessions. Britain needed factory workers and financiers to keep her in the manner to which she had become accustomed. The ruling classes fretted that urban work was producing an enfeebled, sickly underclass managed by pampered cosmopolitan cowards. Where could Britain find virile, robust men to maintain her global supremacy?

In India, after the uprising of 1857, the British began a policy of recruiting soldiers from so-called 'martial races'. The doctrine postulated that Indians from agricultural or mountain areas were strong and brave – albeit backward – whereas better-educated Indians in towns and cities were 'cowards',[21] unused to fighting and apt to run when the going got tough. This nonsense offered a convenient pretext to divide and conquer the population, but it's clear that many British officers were true believers. They had absorbed the warnings laid out in Edward Gibbon's supremely influential *Decline and Fall of the Roman Empire* some eighty years prior: the trappings of civilisation led to easy living and cosmopolitan decadence, the decay of martial virtues, and ultimately a population of weak, anxious cowards, ripe for destruction by the barbarian hordes.

Anyone who suffers from anxiety has heard this a lot – not the stuff about barbarians, but how, in the old days, 'people didn't have time to get anxious; they just had to get on with things'. Anxiety and panic, goes the argument, are luxury problems. Calhoun's rodents only became chronically stressed when he took away predators and disease, and gave them all the food they could ever need. Even Clifford Allbutt, while sceptical that modern life created *more* anxiety, believed that the modern neurotic was invariably 'rich and idle'. He might as well have called them snowflakes.

The logical conclusion of this belief – even if Allbutt failed to join the dots – is precisely the lesson many would take from Calhoun's

'Utopian' mouse universe: as prosperity increases, so too must anxiety. Indeed, no lesser author than Voltaire, in his 1764 *Dictionnaire philosophique*, asked: 'Why do we have fewer suicides in the country than in cities? ... in the fields it is only the body which suffers; in the city it is the mind. The ploughman doesn't have time to be melancholic. It is the idle who kill themselves.'

Voltaire, of course, was not a ploughman, nor had he wasted much time interviewing farm labourers to ascertain their experiences of mental illness. Like so many of these writers, he arrived at his conclusions through an alternative process, called guessing.

Even back in 1733, Scottish physician George Cheyne was arguing that modern life, with its abundance of rich food, sedentary jobs, and densely packed urban living had riddled society with nervous disorders almost unknown to previous generations. His book on 'nervous diseases of all kinds' was titled *The English Malady*.

I could go on, but if I don't stop I might burst into the chorus of 'We Didn't Start the Fire'. Suffice to say that, when the Buddha was delivering his sermons in the sixth century BC, he was speaking to an audience uprooted by an industrial revolution sweeping the Gangetic plains, with a shift from subsistence economies to economies of surplus, the emergence of a cosmopolitan mercantile class, and the rise of great urban centres linked by improved transport. His messages of renunciation and retreat from everyday life spoke directly to an anxious population, overwhelmed by a brave new world of bankers, vast armies and urban bureaucracy.[22]

It is, I suppose, possible that human history describes an unbroken descent from bucolic grace to a perpetually more hectic, miserable shit-storm of stress, anxiety and disenchantment. But if life was less stressful fifty years, or a century, or even three centuries ago, people seem to have felt extreme anxiety, worry and nervous exhaustion just the same. They tell us so, over and over.

We can imagine them deluded. We can imagine ourselves unique in human history, the first people to finally exist in an age where our feelings of dread are justified. Alternatively, we can ask: What else might be going on here?

———

The 'availability heuristic' is a mental rule of thumb proposed by psychologists Amos Tversky and Daniel Kahneman.[23] What it says is: the easier we can bring to mind instances of a thing, the more common we judge it to be. It's easy for us to bring to mind modern worries. They're more available. As a result, we tend to judge that those worries are more frequent than they were in the past.

You've probably heard of confirmation bias – a cognitive distortion that makes us seek information that confirms our existing beliefs, resist information that challenges them, and interpret ambiguous information in a way that supports what we already think. This is a sensible shortcut most of the time. We don't have to waste time assembling a list of evidence for and against every nonsensical proposition someone puts to us. Some claims simply aren't worth considering.

But relying on shortcuts can make us intellectually lazy. Availability and confirmation bias link together, perniciously, to make us *feel* like we know the answers to all sorts of complex questions, when really we've done almost no investigation at all.

———

Alvin Toffler was forty-two when *Future Shock* came out, which would have made him eleven at the outbreak of war – the precise point he located society's lurch into the hectic incomprehensible nightmare of modernity. It's exactly the sort of book you'd predict from someone hitting middle-age just as sixties counterculture reached its zenith.

For Alvin Toffler, the last time things were simpler, better and less stressful was his childhood.

One of our oldest and best-known myths is the story of how the first two humans got evicted from their safe, rural paradise for becoming too sophisticated. It resonates because we've gone through it ourselves. We were all kids once. All of us have experienced the loss of innocence. Some sooner than others.

I half-remember the days before the Fall. Running headlong across Welsh and Cornish beaches towards the ocean. Tumbling into rock pools. Filling book after book with drawings and stories. Strutting around showing off, singing loudly, talking to strangers. Getting my bum out. No concept of war or finances, climate collapse, pandemics, ageing or miscarriages, cruelty, injustice or deep, festering shame. For me, the early eighties were an age before anxiety.

In 1996, when I was fifteen, we came home from a family holiday in Wales to discover our house had been burgled. They had stripped the duvet cover off my bed – a red-patterned one I'd had since I was little – to use as a sack. They stole my CD player. They stole a camcorder with cassettes of little Lego movies me, my dad and brother had made together. They stole my parents' engagement rings. The police came and dusted my room for fingerprints. Months later, my yellow Mr Money moneybox (which the burglars had emptied) was still coated in a silvery layer of fingerprint powder.

My memories from just before our return are especially vivid. I remember sitting on the first floor of the Guildhall Market in Cardigan, flicking through the liner notes of the album I'd just bought – *The It Girl* by Sleeper. Below, my dad was buying a vinyl copy of *Red Octopus* by Jefferson Starship. Back in the static caravan, I popped my new album into a portable CD player, and when the first distorted guitar chord of 'Lie Detector' kicked in – I want to say D# minor – I immediately knew I was going to love it. I remember sitting in the garden after we got back, dazed, still clutching the same album in its plastic jewel case. I'd been so excited to finally play it on my own CD player, the one I'd got as a joint Christmas and birthday present.

A few months later, the bullying started. You never notice it at the time, but when I look back at that younger me, sitting in the garden, reading lyrics to songs I didn't know yet, listening to my parents making an inventory of everything that had been stolen, I see a hard, bright line marking the transition between two worlds. I've come to think of it as the moment my childhood ended.

———

This isn't to make a cult of progress.

Its blessings are decidedly mixed. The problems we face today are many and grave. The modern world inflicts incredible stress on humanity, and it does not distribute that burden equally. But the past we yearn to flee to never existed.

Many studies have found robust associations between poverty, stress hormone levels,[24] and increased rates of mental illness.[25] Globally, the number of people in extreme poverty fell by roughly 1.25 billion between 1990 and 2018.[26] The farther we head back in search of a simpler past, the more we contend with rampant suffering, deprivation and high mortality, even amongst the most privileged. Our ancestors in the seventeenth century were 'exceedingly liable to pain, sickness and premature death' – the average life expectancy of male nobility born in the second half of that century was 29.6 years.[27] Repeated epidemics swept through Europe, the Black Death sometimes killing half a city's population. Outbreaks of smallpox, typhus and dysentery meant that children who beat the 1-in-3 odds of a pregnancy ending in miscarriage or stillbirth still only had a 50–50 chance of reaching twelve. Everyone who survived was grieving lost siblings, friends and parents.[28]

People hankering for 'simpler' times seldom cast themselves as polio survivors confined to iron lungs, indentured servants or women denied suffrage. Nostalgia transforms Victorian chimney sweeps into chipper musical avatars rather than brutalised children as young as four climbing hot cramped flues lined with carcinogenic soot. Subsistence farmers become carefree natural philosophers rather than grizzled survivalists for whom sickness, arson, banditry, crop failure, predation by wolves, diseased cattle or a single season of bad weather could – and often did – spell death.

But hang on. What about those widely quoted statistics from the World Health Organization, reporting that anxiety disorders rose nearly 50 per cent between 1990 and 2013?

The first thing I noticed when I read the WHO's report was that the 49 per cent rise in cases of anxiety and depression represents absolute numbers, not a rise per capita.[29] Between 1990 and 2013, the global population rose from 5.3 billion to 7.2 billion – an increase of nearly 2 billion people, or just over 35 per cent. If the prevalence of anxiety and depression remained completely flat for those 23 years, the number of anxious and depressed people would rise by 35 per cent too. So actually, if we're looking at the *proportion* of humans who are anxious and depressed, the increase is closer to 14 per cent. Much, much smaller. But still an increase, right?

But an increase of what? Well – perhaps surprisingly – not anxiety and depression. The figures don't show how many people were anxious or depressed. Instead, they record how many people were *diagnosed with* an anxiety disorder or depression.

An anxiety disorder only gets recorded if you visit a doctor or a psychiatrist, explain your experience, and they decide to diagnose you with that disorder. What the statistics record isn't anxiety per se, but the frequency of 'diagnostic events'. Mental illness has the same fuzzy status as, say, crime. As far as statistics are concerned, crimes don't exist unless they're reported, and what a crime *is* varies from country to country and within the same country over time.

Between 1990 and 2013, global attitudes to mental illness underwent a major shift. Though it's still hard in many cultures for politicians and public figures to talk openly about personal experiences of anxiety and depression, the conversation around these conditions has evolved. Lots of people are more willing to seek help.

But something strange happens when we create categories for types of human experience. Unlike, say, starfish, humans are aware of these taxa and may change their behaviour to embrace or rebel against them. This can create what the philosopher Ian Hacking called 'looping effects', where labels we create to explain social reality change social reality.[30] Governments base policy decisions on them. Individuals use new terminology in understanding themselves and defining the borders of their identity. Journalists write articles about new theories based on these categories. Support groups grow up around them, connecting people and creating new power bases. Reality shifts.

This isn't a *bad* thing, but it definitely is a thing. As awareness of anxiety disorders grows, so more people may look at their lived experience and think, *Ah, I'm suffering from anxiety/depression*. Certainly, that was what first made me approach my doctor for help – the realisation that maybe I wasn't just sad, but that I 'had depression'. Without that framework to understand my feelings, I doubt I would have thought to approach a medical professional. If I hadn't, I would never have been diagnosed, thus my condition would have remained statistically invisible.

Global anxiety figures are massively sensitive to access to healthcare, stigma around mental illness, medical training, shifting trends in diagnosis and a community's trust in the system. Europe has 50 mental health workers per 100,000 of population, versus Africa's 0.9.[31] An anxiety disorder can't be diagnosed without a professional to record it. As we've seen, during the period in question, extreme global poverty dropped significantly. As incomes and infrastructure grow, so too does the number of professionals qualified to generate those diagnostic events.

And even what an anxiety disorder *is* hasn't remained stable over twenty-odd years. Take generalised anxiety disorder, one of my menagerie of diagnoses. In 1990, physicians in the US were going from DSM-3-R, the revised third edition of the *Diagnostic and Statistical Manual of Mental Disorders*. To meet the criteria for GAD, you needed to have experienced 'unrealistic/excessive anxiety and worry' for at least six months, and meet at least six of eighteen possible symptoms. By 2013, the DSM was in its fifth edition, the symptom list for GAD had been reduced to three out of a possible six, and you only needed to have experienced excessive anxiety and worry for more than half the days over the past six months.[32] The latter is a better, clearer set of criteria. But they're different. It's easier to qualify for generalised anxiety disorder in the twenty-first century than it was in 1990. (In the UK, doctors and psychiatrists now use the criteria from ICD-11, the eleventh revision of the WHO's *International Classification of Diseases*. These are different again, and the criteria have been revised many times.)

In 2006, multinational pharmaceutical company Pfizer released the GAD-7, a seven-question 'screening test' for generalised anxiety disorder that asks 'Over the last two weeks, how often have you been bothered by any of the following problems?' Though it's not supposed to be used as a diagnostic tool, I know from personal experience that it is – especially by doctors who don't have time for an in-depth discussion of symptoms. Critics have argued that the GAD-7 is 'setting the bar for diagnosis too low', dropping the original 1990 requirement that excessive anxiety and worry must have lasted six months, to experiencing the symptoms most days for a mere fortnight.[33]

Since then, a hyper-shortened version, the GAD-2, reduces the test to just two questions.[34] Again, it's only meant to be a screening test, but both the GAD-7 and GAD-2 get used in epidemiology studies gauging the prevalence of anxiety disorders in a population, where participants fill in the answers online.[35] The GAD-2's sensitivity is estimated at between 66 and 89 per cent, depending on the condition you're looking for, meaning that a difference between the populations you're studying of less than – at best – 11 per cent is indistinguishable from noise.

This isn't to imply some conspiracy of overdiagnosis, though Pfizer has certainly profited. In 1990, Pfizer launched sertraline in the UK. It became available in the US the following year under the name Zoloft. Advertising prescription drugs direct to consumers is illegal in most countries, but in the US guidelines were relaxed in 1997. This resulted in a 'higher prescribing volume' and over-prescription of psychiatric medication to patients with temporary anxiety conditions like adjustment disorder.[36] By 2016, Zoloft had become the most-prescribed psychiatric medication in the US.

Psychologist Dr Katherine Button of the University of Bath told me a big impetus behind capturing data with the GAD-7 and its depression equivalent, the Patient Health Questionnaire-9 (PHQ-9), is an economic argument – collecting evidence to justify an expansion in mental health services to policy-makers. The subtitle of the WHO report mentioned above is 'A global return on investment analysis'. Often, mental illness is framed in terms of economic burden, as 'working days lost', rather than a humanitarian crisis, because otherwise governments simply don't see it as a priority. The WHO even puts a net value on scaling up anxiety treatments globally: $50 billion in improved annual productivity.

'As researchers and funders and policy-makers, we have pressures on us to sell certain messages so we can increase funding,' Kate told me.

It's hard, getting governments and voters to care about supporting well-resourced mental-health services. Thanks to the stigma that still surrounds mental illness, most of us don't like to think about it until we, or someone we love, needs help. As a result, researchers and organisations have to fight for their budgets – a state of affairs rarely conducive to nuance. The WHO and the NHS produce amazing research, but it shouldn't be surprising that, when presenting their findings to a general audience, they emphasise interpretations that justify their continued existence.

If anxiety disorders are being more commonly diagnosed, and if pharmacological interventions are being more commonly prescribed, it doesn't follow that a higher percentage of us are pathologically stressed compared to twenty, thirty or fifty years ago.

I can't say with absolute certainty which of many factors account for the headline-grabbing statistics. Given the immense complexity of the problem, caution is the only intellectually honest position. Some of the change may be down to 'concept creep'.[37] Our definition of a disorder has broadened. Some of it may stem from overdiagnosis – from the pathologising of painful but entirely healthy and normal emotional responses.

But there's also less stigma and more access to mental health services. We have better medications.

Maybe we're not more stressed. Maybe what society views as an acceptable level of misery has fallen. Maybe more of us are getting help.

VII.

THIS IS FINE

Social media and our addiction to doomscrolling

In Samuel Johnson's novel *The History of Rasselas*, an Abyssinian prince sets off in search of happiness, the best way to live – what he calls 'The Choice of Life'. Late in the story, he and his party encounter an astronomer in a tower. After years of isolation, the astronomer has become convinced he controls the weather with his mind. 'I have restrained the rage of the dog-star,' he says, 'and mitigated the fervours of the crab.' The astronomer is exhausted, wracked with guilt at his failure to protect people killed in storms. Ultimately, Rasselas and his friends convince the astronomer to join them in exploring the wider world, at which point the astronomer realises he was deluded – he was never really in control.

As an author, I spend a lot of time in a tiny room, alone. For many people who aspire to become professional writers, this may be the chief attraction. As author Chris McCrudden put it to me: 'In a world where everybody is expected to be accountable to other people for what they do with their time, I think it's an incredibly tempting prospect to think: what if I can do something that involves just being left the fuck alone?'

But solitude isn't always great for the old noggin. I have no colleagues. I rarely leave my tower. For a lot of writers, the telescope we use to peer out across the world has become social media. In the aftermath of coming off my meds, I found it almost impossible to write. When I wasn't parenting, I spent a lot of time sitting in bed, scrolling through Facebook and Twitter. What I saw daily *terrified* me.

People I followed shared disaster after crime after outrage, often with little commentary beyond 'oh no', 'ugh' or 'this government'. Day and night, they toiled with the diligence of medieval monks to find and spread bad news, to make sure no terrible event went unshared. They seemed to think they were performing a vital public service.

Why were so many of us obsessed with amplifying bad news? And why was I, an anxious person, so addicted to doomscrolling?

———

In 1968, psychologists John Darley and Bibb Latané had participants complete a questionnaire in a waiting room which gradually began to fill with smoke. Seventy-five per cent reported the smoke when alone, but only 10 per cent did so when in the presence of 'passive others' – stooges who pretended to be indifferent to the clouds rolling in under the door.[1]

By now, most Twitter-users have seen artist KC Green's cartoon of a dog in a bowler hat, sipping tea in the middle of a burning room, smiling while saying: 'This is fine.' For some it's become emblematic of the age – shorthand for that feeling of living in a parallel reality, where others seem pathologically incapable of acknowledging the multiple ongoing crises hurrying on our demise.

You might think an anxious person would crave the company of calm, stoic types. If I'm worried about something in my environment, and the people around me *aren't* worried, isn't that reassuring? After all, plenty of anxiety sufferers are intelligent people with self-insight. We know we have a tendency to fret. We know most of the things we worry about don't come true. So you'd think – hell, *I'd* think – that a useful metric of whether a fear we're experiencing is, to accept the language of the DSM-5, *excessive*, would be the extent to which people around us are experiencing the same fear. Surely if no one else seems bothered, that's a good indicator that what I'm encountering isn't looming danger, but anxiety – right? Phew. Panic over.

Imagine being in the window seat on a plane. You look outside and see the engines are on fire. All around you, your fellow passengers are asleep. You shove the person next to you. 'Hey, hey, wake up, the plane's on fire.' They yawn, shoot you an irritated look. 'Everything's fine. Go back to sleep.' You start to yell, 'We're going to crash! Everyone wake up!' But no one's listening.

When you tell an anxious person, 'There's nothing to worry about,' the message received is, 'You're on your own.' Vigilance is a burden we instinctively distribute through the group. Remember Gloria, the anxious guinea pig? Most gregarious species have an instinctual anxiety response when they see other group members looking worried. One study taught a rat to associate a particular sound with painful electric shocks. Researchers found that when they placed that rat in a cage with another rat and played the sound, the second rat learned to fear the sound from observing the first.[2]

Our brains have an incredible capacity for instantaneous interpretation of people's body language[3] and facial expressions, particularly when it comes to fear. A standard means of eliciting anxiety-like responses in a lab setting is to show someone an image of a frightened human face.[4]

Species which spread panic effectively tend to survive longer. Throughout evolution, signs of fear from your peers – fur standing on end (called 'piloerection'), freezing, screeches, fearful facial expressions – have been reliable proxy indicators of threat. They trigger a state of arousal, the sympathetic nervous system activates, and increased levels of adrenaline and cortisol make us alert so we can quickly scan our environment and locate the danger.

Even people who are cortically blind (where the eye is intact but brain damage results in a total loss of vision) show emotional responses to body language cues they're consciously unaware of.[5] And even deciding how many calories to consume is determined more by social cues rather than hunger or personal choice, an effect called 'norm matching'. The more we perceive those around us to be like us, part of our in-group or 'tribe', the stronger the effect becomes.[6]

This applies across a dizzying range of human behaviours. We rely intimately on each other to know when to eat, speak, laugh, where to stand, what to wear, what to want, when to be afraid. Unconsciously, we choose models we believe are similar to us. We may use obvious markers like age and sex, or indirect ones, like whether we believe they attended the same university as us.[7] Most of us recognise this conformity in others, but refuse to believe our own behaviours come from anything but personal choice – the so-called 'third-person effect'.[8] Oh sure, *other* people buy stuff because they saw it in an advert, but not me.

Some psychologists attribute this to 'affiliation motives' – our 'need to be liked, accepted and to belong'.[9] We copy the behaviours of those we perceive as being part of our tribe because we fear being ostracised. From an evolutionary perspective, social rejection meant loss of protection, and loss of access to food and mates. It was one step away from death.

It feels good to conform, especially when we're feeling uncertain. One study found that a conflict with the group consensus triggers a temporary dip in midbrain dopamine – part of a process that signals that a behaviour resulted in less of a reward than we expected.[10] As well as recruiting part of the brain known as the rostral cingulate zone,* which is implicated in adjusting our behaviour when we don't get what we want, researchers found that conflicting with group opinion led to deactivation in the nucleus accumbens; part of the brain associated with reward and pleasure. The stronger the activation and deactivation of these two areas respectively, the more likely the

---

* 'Rostral' meaning 'front', and 'cingulate' meaning 'girdle-like'; the cingulate cortex, when viewed from the side, curves across the middle of the brain.

participant was to subsequently change their opinion to conform with group norms.

Choice is cognitively taxing. We face thousands of decisions every day, many trivial, some life-changing. We're working from limited data sets. The more we use our peers as models, the more we get to spread that cognitive burden amongst the group. Taking all that work 'in-house' reduces our ability to focus on salient tasks. It's metabolically costly.

Given all this, is it any wonder that anxious people are drawn towards places where they find large groups of similarly terrified, hypervigilant human beings? Frightened, beleaguered people at least appear to be watching for threats. They're shouldering some of our collective burden – cataloguing and distributing every peril, every putative future disaster, every enemy. They're angrily denouncing the renegade and traitor Lin Biao.

This might be why, in times of national crisis, a non-trivial portion of habitual worriers report feeling strangely serene. Finally, they can stop worrying on behalf of humanity. At last, other humans see the danger too. Someone else is taking a turn sounding the alarm.

—

Not everyone who sinks a pint of Guinness ends up pissed in a hedge at 3 a.m. spattered with their own vomit. Not everyone who buys a scratch card ends up tens of thousands of pounds in debt. Lots of people are capable of casual, non-problematic use that offers a little fun.

The issue was, I was starting to get the sense I was not one of those people. Not with alcohol, and definitely not with social media.

Social media, with its tribes and fandoms, accelerates our innate tendency to seek relevant models for our behaviour. But these are not neutral spaces. They're commercial ventures. Algorithms partition us, then advertisers try to flog us an ever-more-thinly julienned platter of micro-identities.

At first I found this comforting. Everywhere were tiny curated communities that tessellated near perfectly with some aspect of my character. *I've found my people*, I'd think.

And then, a moment later: *What if they hate me?*

Maybe the real risk wasn't that social media was making me more anxious. Maybe it was that it had become a bromide that I was using to numb difficult emotions. I don't want one of my deathbed regrets to be: 'Missed my daughter's clarinet recital because I was dunking on a politician for displaying "huge Bean Dad energy". I already regret knowing what that phrase means.

I deleted Facebook and Twitter from my phone. In a concession to self-publicity, I created a bot to post on my behalf on Twitter, which generated nonsensical 'writing tips' out of random nouns and adjectives. Then I left both sites for the year. (Gallingly, I would later discover that my bot alter-ego, posting gibberish, got better engagement than the real me – on Twitter, not being sentient didn't seem to be much of a barrier.)

It took me a week or so to get over the sense that I was missing out – that whole meme cycles were rising and falling without me. I missed reading posts by extended family members and friends living abroad. But a massive source of daily stress vanished.

I stopped reading the news, too. Like social media, the selection pressure that sculpts it is not public wellbeing but consumerism.

It's scary, realising you don't control the weather. That the storms rage on no matter if you write a very clever tweet skewering a moral hypocrite or calling out injustice. Social media is the island of the lotus eaters, except instead of narcotic fruits it's onion-flavoured Monster Munch. We all know at some level it's bad for us. That compulsively monitoring the news is a waste of our precious lives. But it's hard to admit the fistfuls of social capital you spent years grinding for is just joke money.

—

In the aftermath of a natural disaster, or a humanitarian crisis like war, it's not surprising to find that many of the survivors bear profound psychological scars. What is surprising, however, is how many of them don't. Estimates vary, but several studies suggest approximately 1 in 4 survivors of traumatic events go on to develop major depressive disorder[11] and/or PTSD,[12] though others have found a rate of PTSD among trauma survivors as low as 1 in 100.[13] In other words, 75 per cent of survivors process their loss without long-term severe negative psychological consequences. It's horrible, but they recover.

Our world, though perhaps not *more* stressful than it ever was, has ample reasons for us to worry. We're strange, fragile robots, our most vulnerable organ defended by the equivalent of a pudding bowl wrapped in ham, moving through a universe full of speeding cars, pathogens, heights and other people – things that could kill us with ease. Yet not everyone presents with symptoms of severe, uncontrollable anxiety. Not everyone experiences panic attacks.

Why do different people under the same circumstances have such wildly different reactions? How come some people endure, or alchemise their suffering into righteous anger or compassion or gratitude or the motivation to create change, while others – like me – become scared?

VIII.

THE ANXIETY GENE
The genetic roots of anxiety

It's spring 1945, somewhere west of Dresden, and a Russian soldier is pointing a Mosin–Nagant carbine at a girl's head. The girl leans on crutches. She is eighteen years old, and trying to return to her family, who have fled to Rosenthal. Until recently the entire lower half of her body was encased in plaster.

The soldier is guarding a bridge she wishes to cross.

He shouts at her, in broken German, to turn back. Many people – including members of her family – have been killed or raped by the advancing Red Army. Still, she holds her ground.

She begins telling him about her journey. She discharged herself from hospital. She walked along railway tracks. She rode a tram through the bombed-out ruins of Dresden. She has survived on handouts. She is simply trying to get home to her mother.

When she reaches that word – a word that is the same in English, Russian and German, 'mama' – the soldier begins to weep. She sees that he is not much older than her. He says he has not seen his mother in years.

Thinking quickly, the girl says: Pretend that I approached you from the other side of the bridge. The soldier – the boy – agrees. He turns round, and begins to shout out at her to turn back, to go away, thrusting his rifle at her as she continues across the bridge to her family.

—

That girl was my grandmother.

Without her guts, calm and quick thinking, which saw her across Germany and created that moment of empathy between two humans on opposite sides of a global conflict, I would not exist.

She did not have an easy childhood. A congenital deformity in her hips meant that, at seven years old, she spent nearly eighteen months in hospital, in plaster. The nuns at the hospital could be tremendously cruel – once, when she screamed during a nightmare, a nun beat her with fir-tree branches and made her lie on the needles.

She grew up during the rise of fascism, a disabled child mocked by her teachers. Her teenage years were entirely circumscribed by the Second World War. Yet she was not bitter, nor given to panic. As a pensioner, she tackled a burglar who had broken into her house, grabbing his arm to try to stop him getting away.

How did this resilient woman produce such a querulous, weak, maudlin grandson?

I'd read worrying mentions of anxiety having a genetic component. About how people have an internal anxiety 'set point' that we naturally return to. Might I have inherited a genetic predisposition for worry from some other branch of the family tree? Had I already passed on my anxious tendencies to Suki?

On the other end of the scale, lots of pop-psych I'd read said my anxiety was a product of my upbringing and early experiences. Trauma was growing in the public consciousness as an important source of mental health issues later in life.

Did my childhood make me this way? Or was anxiety like an ancestral curse, a doomed bloodline? Were some of us just stuffed from the get-go? Is there such a thing as an anxiety gene?

———

We saw in the mouse-poop transplant study that there are certain strains of rodent, like BALB/c albino mice, which researchers consider more timid than others. In rats, the Wistar-Kyoto strain has a similar reputation. They are more reluctant to explore open spaces, and their HPA-axis triggers more cortisol and adrenaline more often. When dropped into a beaker of water with sheer sides, a rat will swim furiously before eventually giving up and floating. Once the rat is taken out of the water and put back in their cage, they remain motionless for a while before moving. Wistar-Kyoto rats remain motionless after this 'forced swim test' for longer than other strains – they 'exhibit an increased immobility duration' – which many researchers interpret as depression or despair, especially since the effect is reduced if they've been given antidepressants. Wistar-Kyoto rats have duly been used in many thousands of studies on stress and depression, often screening new antidepressants.

To some researchers, these kinds of models are patently ludicrous.[1] Floating is an adaptive behaviour which conserves energy. Antidepressants, they argue, suppress not 'despair' but memory – the rats are less able to learn from the experience and switch to their natural survival behaviour. A forced swim lacks 'construct validity' – it's not remotely like the thing it claims to represent. Depression comes on slowly, in response to sustained hardship – not immediately after falling into a body of water. The idea that the 'floating rodent phenotype' is a good model for human depression is, they conclude, nonsense.[2]

Whether or not these rodents make good test subjects, if things like the strength, duration and sensitivity of a creature's fight, flight or freeze response can be inherited, it makes sense that some of us might be more prone to stress and anxiety than others. On the other hand, BALB/c mice and Wistar-Kyoto rats have been inbred for decades – with the exception of royalty, most humans enjoy far greater diversity in their mating partners.

Big epidemiological studies have found that anxiety disorders have an estimated heritability of 30–40 per cent.[3] Heritability is . . . bloody complicated. At first, I thought it just meant around a third of my anxiety is down to genes. If I were a big smoothie (some say I am already) then about a third of the bottle would be genetic ingredients from my parents, leaving me and my environment to top up the rest.

Except that's not what it means at all. Saying that anxiety disorders are 30–40 per cent heritable doesn't mean that 30–40 per cent of your anxiety is fixed, or 'caused by your genes'. Nor does it tell you that your environment is 60–70 per cent responsible. Heritability doesn't tell you much about how easy something is to change, either. Hair colour, for example, is highly heritable (between 73 and 99 per cent) but trivially easy to alter (albeit temporarily).

But saying what heritability doesn't mean is a lot easier than saying what it does. We know that if you're looking at two very similar people and one of them has a close family member with generalised anxiety disorder or a phobia, statistically speaking they're more likely to have GAD or a phobia than the other person. If you repeated the process over hundreds of people, guessing whether someone had an anxiety disorder based on whether their close family members had one, often you'd get it wrong, but you could do better than chance.

I read a mountain of genetics papers to try to get a handle on it, but they're not really geared towards the casual beginner. I could feel my brain transmuting to blancmange and oozing out through my ears.

So I went to speak to geneticist Adam Rutherford, who has written several popular books on the subject and actually knew what the fuck he was talking about.

—

We met for coffee at the bar of a hotel in Norwich. It's a little unnerving, meeting someone for the first time and saying 'Hi, I'm Tim – the anxious guy.' I worried – of course I did – that people would feel responsible, somehow, for my wellbeing, so I'd overcompensate.

Adam weathered ten minutes of my rattling off every anxiety

factoid in my repertoire (many of them incorrect) with incredible patience, before asking if I had a question.

Oh, right. Yes, I wanted to know if my anxiety might be genetic. He started with the basics.

'In genetics, the first genes we identified were ones associated with well-understood hereditary diseases.' These were cystic fibrosis, Huntingdon's, and muscular dystrophy. 'But the reason they were the first is because those diseases run in families in very well-understood, clear patterns. That's why we learn them at school.' The history of genetics had suggested there was one gene for every disease or trait of interest. 'There's a gene for cystic fibrosis. Same with the next set of diseases we found.'

A lot of us non-geneticists still understand genes through this early 'one gene, one trait' model. When something goes wrong, we imagine there's one gene responsible. This holds true for monogenetic disorders like cystic fibrosis and Huntingdon's. But the reason these scientists picked up on these diseases early was because they were the easiest to spot. They were outliers.

Before the human genome was finally published in 2001 – something Adam considers 'the most ambitious and successful scientific project of the twentieth century' – we had no idea how many genes humans had. In the last meeting where they were assembling the human genome, a young PhD researcher called Ewan Birney opened a sweepstake, and went round asking geneticists, at a dollar a bet, to guess how many genes a human had. 'Every single one of them predicted way too high. The top prediction was something like 150,000. And the lowest prediction was a French guy who went for 29,000, but we're pretty sure he was only doing that to undercut the book.'

The real answer came out at 20,000. 'So basically we had a reset in genetics. Because we have way too few genes for that model of one gene for one characteristic to work . . . What emerges from this is that genes work in networks. Most genes do multiple things. Sometimes they work with other genes at the same time, sometimes they regulate other genes in different tissues. Some genes do some things during [early] development then do completely different things later in development.'

To address these more complicated relationships, a new technique was invented – the genome-wide association study, or GWAS (pronounced 'gwaz'). In order to find genes that are involved in complex disorders or traits, you take a bunch of people who have the same condition, then you get them to give you genomic samples – spit in a tube – and you look across their genome at places of interest, and plot them on a graph. The graph is called the Manhattan plot – so called because, with all the little vertical bars, 'it looks like the skyline of Manhattan'. What you're looking for are places where those skyscrapers are tall. Spikes on the graph mean there are statistically significant genetic markers – bits in the genome – which associate with a particular condition.

'Say you did a genome-wide association study for cystic fibrosis. Take a thousand people with cystic fibrosis, you get them to spit in a tube, you sequence their genomes, then when you plot your graph . . . you have your chromosomes on the bottom, and statistical significance on the y axis. What you'd see is a massive spike – one spike of significance – because there's one gene which is largely responsible for cystic fibrosis: CFTR.'

But with more complex diseases or conditions like anxiety, you may see dozens – even hundreds – of genes that have smaller, but statistically significant, spikes for people with that condition.

Before meeting Adam, I'd taken part in the Genetic Links to Anxiety and Depression (GLAD) study. I'd gobbed in a tube, then filled in questionnaires about my mood, my history of anxiety, and lots of other questions about my age, lifestyle, family, income and so forth. Adam said they'd probably use my answers to put me in a group of people with a similar diagnosis, then they'd sequence our DNA and plot the results on a graph, looking for any significant spikes.

Are there certain genes that show up more often in people with, say, generalised anxiety disorder?

Several genes have been associated with anxiety. 'One of them is of particular interest. It's a classic example of the fetishisation of one gene associated with an interesting trait, which in this case is violence, but actually it's a massive misinterpretation of how genetics works.'

The gene in question is the monoamine oxidase A (MAO-A) gene. In 1993, Professor Han Brunner published a paper on a large Dutch family who had multigenerational criminal activity. All the men in the family had 'a tendency toward aggressive outbursts, often in response to anger, fear, or frustration' and 'impulsive behaviour' including 'arson, attempted rape, and exhibitionism'.[4] Brunner and his colleagues identified a mutation in the MAO-A gene common to all of them. The researchers speculated the mutation might cause dysregulated levels of serotonin, dopamine and noradrenaline, and impair the men's REM sleep, making them chronically sleep-deprived.

'So the press then go fucking nuts for this,' said Adam, 'because they've identified the "gene for violence". Then a bunch of other – often really bad – studies emerged out of this looking at variants in monoamine oxidase for different behaviour types.' One study found a link between the gene and high-risk gambling in City boys. Another found that people with self-reported Maori descent had a higher chance of having this version of the MAO-A gene than those without Maori ancestry. As a result, MAO-A became known as 'the warrior gene'.

'And it was a terrible study. Just because stuff is published in an academic journal, doesn't mean that it's right, or necessarily good. I think a lot of people assume that because you are Professor J. B. Science, you're just right about everything. There are plenty of scientists who are fucking hopeless.'

Adam said MAO-A has been associated with anxiety too. 'Which is completely unsurprising. There aren't that many neurotransmitters and there are a lot of places where neurotransmitters get transmitted. It is but one of not that many messenger molecules which are associated with *all* neural activity.' That's not to dismiss the association out of hand, just to acknowledge that we still have a lot of research ahead. 'A long way down the pipeline, the hope is that because you know this gene is involved, and because we've researched it for twenty years, and we know what the biochemical pathways are, that actually you can target specific drugs to that pathway. Most of our pharmacological interventions are pretty blunderbuss approaches.'

So can we conclude anything from what we currently know?

'That's a brilliant question and it's not going to be a very satisfactory answer, I'm afraid,' said Adam. 'We used to talk about nature versus nurture. That was a phrase coined by Francis Galton in the 1890s. He's kind of like the father of human genetics – massive racist, by the way.'

The half-cousin of Charles Darwin, Galton pioneered concepts used in almost every piece of psychological research today: things like the questionnaire, and testing for correlation – i.e. checking if there's a statistical relationship between two variables, such as frequency of exercise and levels of anxiety. He was also, as Adam pointed out, a massive racist – unapologetically so, openly calling for the cultivation of a ruling white master race.[5]

Adam told me that geneticists worked out a few decades ago that 'nature versus nurture' is not a useful way to frame the interaction between what is innate and our environment. 'The environment doesn't mean whether your parents read to you or cuddled you or beat you as a child, although that is part of it. The environment means: literally everything in the universe that isn't genes. So it includes loads of stochastic and random shit like your orientation as a foetus in your mother's womb. Even the point of entry of the sperm into the egg has an effect on the development of the egg.' In mice, where the sperm enters the cell is important in setting up the head-to-tail axis. We don't know it definitely works this way in humans, but it might well do.

'So everything that is not DNA is environment. That's the baseline statement. In the press, when people say "Is it nature or is it nurture?" the answer is always, always, always: both.'

The real question is then: Is one more significant than the other?

'Go back to a really straightforward, easy case: cystic fibrosis. One gene. If you have the deltaF508 mutation for cystic fibrosis, then you almost certainly will have cystic fibrosis.' Though its impact on life expectancy is being reduced due to better treatments, 'your life will be curtailed as a result of that mutation. However, the thousands of people who have exactly the same genetic mutation have different severity with the disease. That's a concept called penetrance. And the penetrance of cystic fibrosis is hypervariable because it's reliant on a whole set of other genes, which we really only just discovered, that have a small but significant effect, and also the environmental constraints of what's going on while they have this one particular mutation.'

So even a monogenetic disease like cystic fibrosis turns out to be more complicated than we first thought. Basic concepts of genetics get crunchy when you dig deeper. Take eye colour: we're taught that there's a gene responsible for either brown or blue eyes, and since brown is dominant, you only need one copy of the brown-eyed gene to inherit brown eyes, and two blue-eyed genes to inherit blue eyes.

Adam said that's sort of true. 'But it's not really true in any meaningful sense. Any colour combination in parents' eyes can produce any colour combination in their children's eyes. And what this shows really clearly is the key thing about genetics. The central message of genetics. Which is that it is *probabilistic.*'

He told me there could be a version of me in a different universe who had an identical genome, including all the variants which may yet be shown to be associated with anxiety disorders, who did not have any of my symptoms. 'Sorry if that sounds a bit harsh.' True, many genes might be associated with generalised anxiety disorder. None of them are the genes *for* that disorder.

'Here's the next sucker punch: the way we understand the probabilistic nature of particular gene variants as they're associated with any condition or trait or behaviour only works at a population level. Doesn't work in individuals. It's really, really almost impossible to predict these complex disorders.'

Adam discovered he's got apoE4, a gene variant which puts him in a high-risk category for Parkinson's. 'It doubles the lifetime risk from something minuscule like 0.05 per cent to 0.1 per cent. There's literally nothing you can do about it which goes beyond standard health advice. So when companies purport to use genomics to advise on diets and things like that, none of it is more significant than the following pieces of advice: don't smoke, do lots of exercise, eat a balanced diet and as little meat as possible.'

So what does it actually mean when people say anxiety disorders are 30–40 per cent heritable?

Adam described heritability as 'one of the most tricky areas in science', which was a relief, because I'd felt stupid for not understanding it. He said it comes with masses of caveats, and people often get it massively wrong. 'Heritability measures the proportion of differences in a population that can be accounted for by genetics.' So, for example, measures of cognitive ability suggest a heritability of between 40 and 60 per cent. 'That doesn't mean 40 per cent is determined genetically. It means 40 per cent of *the difference within a population* can be determined genetically.'

But again, this only holds at a population level. It accounts for broad averages. It can't tell you anything about an individual.

Adam said he felt like we're drawn to genetics in the hope that it will bestow upon us a sense of belonging, and an explanation for why we are the way we are. But consider the maths of tracing back your family tree. Your parents both had two parents, all four of whom had two parents each, and so on. By the time you reach the eleventh century, you'd need 1 trillion ancestors. Clearly it can't be true that the human population gets exponentially larger the further you go into the past. Instead, our family trees continually spread and collapse, with the same people occupying multiple positions. If you go back far enough, everyone is your ancestor – the so-called genetic isopoint. For Europe, the isopoint is around the tenth century. Everyone who had children then is the ancestor of everyone alive today. The global isopoint for all humans is around the fourteenth century BC – though some estimates put it later.

'Spitting in a tube does literally nothing to explain yourself. People think "I need something to explain why I am the way I am." Genetics is fulfilling that role in the public eye.'

—

Anxiety is, in part, a condition of self-condemnation. Of terrible guilt.

Early on in my search, I made a survey asking people to share their experiences of anxiety. The last question read: 'If you could have one question about anxiety and/or panic definitively answered, what would it be?'

The most common response was two words: 'Why me?'

What if it wasn't our fault? What if we were somehow mis-designed? What if we have this baked-in flaw, this vulnerability, that means all our attempts to cope like our peers are as doomed to failure as a penguin's trying to fly? What if we could finally let go of all that striving?

Part of me had longed to hear Adam say: Look, we've analysed your DNA and you've got the coward gene. No wonder you're anxious.

My longing for genetic proof of my cowardice reminds me of the Christmas episode of *Bottom*, in which they take in an abandoned baby. Richie becomes convinced the baby is the reborn Jesus Christ.

Seeing his three friends wearing paper crowns and bearing gifts, he decides they must be the Three Wise Men, which makes him the Virgin Mary. His eyes widen. '*That's* why I never got a shag!'

Attempts to find a heritable component to anxiety susceptibility have focused on 5-HTTLPR, a polymorphism in the SLC6A4 gene. The polymorphism affects the promoter part of the gene – the bit which decides when and where it will be expressed – and results in either long or short versions of that gene, known as 'alleles'. A short allele seems to lead to lower serotonin transporter 'transcription' (in which information in a gene's DNA sequence is copied onto a molecule of messenger RNA – mRNA – which then gives ribosomes instructions on what kinds of proteins to make). An early study suggested that people with one or two copies of the short allele were more likely to suffer from anxiety.[6] Other studies linked the polymorphism to greater susceptibility to depression[7] or bipolar disorder,[8] or suggested that the long allele variant predicted a faster response to antidepressants.[9]

But as research has continued, these associations have become murkier. Some studies simply failed to find a link,[10] while others emphasised that we need to look at gene-environment interaction. One study found that children with two short alleles of 5-HTTLPR were more sad and anxious than controls if they were raised in unsupportive environments, but happier and more confident than controls if raised in supportive environments.[11] The polymorphism might be associated with greater sensitivity in general, they argue, leading to inconsistent results if a study doesn't take environment into account. On the other hand, a comprehensive 2017 meta-analysis looked at precisely this and failed to find compelling evidence that the 5-HTTLPR short allele increases risk of depression in response to stress.[12]

Some researchers argue that it's wrong to treat 5-HTTLPR as simply having two variations: long or short alleles. Rather than being 'biallelic' (having two allele states), it's functionally triallelic (having three), because of single nucleotide polymorphism within the long allele that results in two further versions. One of these versions is equivalent to the short allele in terms of promoter activity – meaning that it would make more sense to group it with the short allele variations. So confusion around the association between 5-HTTLPR might be down to not differentiating between these two types of long allele.[13]

Then again, a neuroscientist who specialises in molecular genetics told me he thinks the vast majority of studies addressing effects of the triallelic 5-HTLLPR are 'desperately underpowered' – meaning the sample sizes are too small to reliably detect the effect they're looking for.

It's complicated, right? Hard, observable measures like the presence of specific polymorphisms come up against softer, more subjective metrics like: How worried have you been in the past two weeks on a scale of one to seven? How kind were your parents?

And again, we're only talking about *likelihoods*. These tendencies are observable in groups but don't work at the level of the individual.

There's no such thing as an anxiety gene – no single mutation pumping terror juice into your otherwise immaculate brain. Anxiety and depression are complex, polygenic conditions. Even the most significantly associated genomic regions account for a tiny percentage of total risk.[14] But it's possible that in future we will clarify the relationship between certain gene variants and clusters of variants, how those variants might influence how and when our brains and bodies produce neurotransmitters and hormones, and how these neurotransmitters and hormones might modulate our experience of emotions like anxiety.

'It's the old joke,' said Adam. 'Give me a one-armed scientist so he can't say "on the other hand".'

Geneticists, like all scientists, are chipping away at complex problems. Medical researchers have improved outcomes across all sorts of diseases, but they're continually looking for ways to make improvements, noting exceptions, places where our current model breaks down.

Genetics couldn't yet give me absolute answers. But Adam thought there was meaning in my participating in things like the GLAD study. After all, it wasn't just about me. 'You're doing stuff to help people. You're helping knowledge, and that can help future people, future generations. In future, cancer will be a disease of interest only to historians.'

Tackling problems like severe anxiety, panic and PTSD will require research. Years and years of it. Adam's challenge to me – to everyone – was to be part of the process. 'Don't just ask for the answer – come with us.'

I found this oddly consoling. Odd, because it suggested the answers I wanted might be beyond my reach. Consoling, because it meant that, even if I failed, my efforts might not be wasted. Maybe, in taking part in research like GLAD, I could hand something on to help the people who followed. In generations to come, the worried and beleaguered might have an easier time of it. Some baby not yet born might one day be spared the hell of chronic anxiety, in part because of people like me.

Of course, I would rather have been told, 'Here's the anxiety gene, you have it, and we've developed a new treatment that can switch it off.' That would have been really neat, and I suspect all my aspirations for helping the children of the future would have been forgotten. Sorry babies. I'm off skydiving.

But there was comfort in knowing that if I failed in my search for a cure, I could still offer myself as a case study – a kind of scientific cautionary tale. I'd be the Marley's Ghost of anxiety, rattling chains made of a thousand paranoid cognitions.

IX.

AND IT FEELS LIKE HOME

Childhood trauma, brain development
and the power of nostalgia

When I was young, maybe nine or ten, I was walking home when, out of the corner of my eye, I saw a shadow move. From behind a hedge, a boy jumped out and blocked my path.

He was older than me. I glanced down. He was holding a six-inch bowie knife.

He flicked it back and forth, a glimmering fish.

'Want a fight?' he said.

I was hypnotised by the blade.

He stepped forward, aiming it towards my stomach.

He feinted left, then right. My gaze followed the knife. The whetted silver edge.

He tossed it into the grass. While I was distracted he slugged me in the gut. I doubled up.

He stood over me, waiting for me to straighten up. I ran.

I remember getting home and knocking on our front door. When my dad answered, he said: 'Are you all right?'

'No,' I said. I broke down crying.

My dad never went to the police. I didn't know the boy but we knew where he lived, so my dad went round. Later he told me the boy's dad had said: 'Oh, he's always stealing his sister's knife.'

It's easy for me to take that incident, the bullying I went through when I was a teenager, the sudden death of my grandfather, and the time we came home to find we'd been burgled, to imply a childhood filled with anxiety and trauma. In the aftermath of a panic attack, you find yourself wondering how you ended up like this, freaking out over nothing. You think back to times when you felt threatened or powerless. Did they count as 'traumas'? Did they leave permanent scars?

Most of my childhood was blissfully safe. I had plenty of food. I had friends. Structure. Loads of toys. I was cared for by loving parents. (I'm still struck by how brave my dad must have been, going round to a stranger's house, knocking on the door and saying: 'Hi, I think your son just mugged my son at knife point.')

My dad wasn't particularly given to anxiety. My mum was – and is – a bit of a worrier, but not to my pathological extent. Crucially, she combined anxiety with competence. If she felt anxious about something, she took action. She'd check the lock, she'd make a contingency plan, she'd pack an extra pair of socks. She wasn't *paralysed* by it.

We know from landmark studies like the Adverse Childhood Experiences Study (ACES) that stressful, traumatic events during childhood are associated with higher risks of physical and mental health problems later in life, many of which seem to be related to strategies for coping with stress, such as increased risk of smoking, alcoholism and obesity.[1] Similar studies have found that, generally, the greater the exposure to physical and mental abuse in childhood – either witnessed or received – and the worse the intensity of that abuse, the greater the decline in adult mental health.[2]

Though tragic and unsurprising, these findings are subject to some of the same limitations as genome-wide association studies. They're epidemiological. They talk about probabilities of risk at a population level. They're important for hammering home the terrible, ongoing impact of things like domestic abuse, and why every society should be investing heavily to tackle these problems through every means available. They don't, however, tell us much at the individual level. Some people survive horrendous experiences and do not go on to experience significant episodes of mental illness as adults. Some people enjoy wonderful childhoods yet go on to struggle with severe anxiety, depression and addiction. What these studies show are trends, not absolute causes.

Predicting who will be affected by adverse childhood events is difficult, partly because the negative effects seem to stem from how a child *interprets* an event, rather than the event itself. Clearly there are some experiences more likely to lead to negative interpretations – *I'm worthless, I'm unlovable, I'm a bad person* – than others, but none of these interpretations are inevitable. Further, it follows that children can come to these conclusions off the back of events that might seem relatively innocuous.[3]

Some neuroscientists have suggested that our whole conception of stress is backwards – that it's not about too much threat, but too little safety. In this model, our default state is one of vigilance and watching for danger. Safety cues – like the presence of a loving caregiver – engage brain circuits to do with self-control and emotional regulation, including the ventromedial prefrontal cortex, which inhibit our threat response.

We're not looking for danger. We're looking for signs that we're safe.[4]

—

Neuroscientist Nim Tottenham of Columbia University has devoted her career to studying how experiences in our early life may affect our ability to cope with stress later on, and may even reshape the function and anatomy of our brains. Mice usually prefer to nest in silence, but one study found that mice exposed to music when they were between fifteen and twenty-four days old later preferred to nest where the same music was playing. The effect was not found when they were exposed to a simple beep, suggesting something about music itself was affecting them during this crucial early period which they later came to associate with safety.[5]

Nim wanted to explore if there was a similar association in

humans. Participants aged eighteen to twenty-three had to complete a stressful task – answering maths questions while a researcher watched them. But it was a trick. As psychologist Nick Walsh of UEA explained to me: 'Humans are really sensitive to two things: negative social evaluation, and doing things under time pressure.' Nim was using a version of a protocol called the Trier social stress test, developed at the University of Trier by Clemens Kirschbaum. It has people stand and attempt taxing maths problems, like subtracting 17 serially from 344 while a group of researchers – typically wearing white lab coats – sit with clipboards. The researchers are instructed to remain stony-faced, and not to give any encouragement or sign of approval whatsoever. If you make a mistake, they'll say, 'Please continue,' and make little marks on their clipboards.

Nick has administered a variant called the Montreal imaging stress task, or MIST, which allows participants to perform the task inside an fMRI scanner.[6] 'We give people a feedback bar on the top, that shows how you're doing, and how well you should be doing – and you're doing really bad. And we do things like we stand over them and say "You need to do better."' As he told me this, Nick flashed a conflicted smile. 'In that study we do an eye-tracking task, and people were crying into the eye tracker.'

Neuroscientist Alexander Shackman told me the Trier was 'probably the most robust, widely used protocol for eliciting social stress in human beings. Many people perceive it as actually more aversive than things like painful heat or electric shocks or threat of shock or fear conditioning or even scary films.' It reliably produces a physiological response, stimulating the release of adrenaline and cortisol. Alex said he'd been involved in a study where participants went through various stressful trials: looking at horrible photographs, 'things like mutilated bodies and toilets filled with disgusting things', having painfully hot thermodes attached to their arms, and doing the Trier. Which one did they say was worst? The Trier. 'Because it's the most life-like.'

In Nim's study, participants completed maths problems while a researcher watched over their shoulder. The timer was manipulated so it was hard to answer in the time permitted. If they failed to answer before the next question appeared, or they answered wrong, they lost points and a loud buzzer sounded. They were told their scores would be compared with their peers.

After this stressful task, they were given five minutes' rest, during which time they could listen to some music. They could choose between two 'radio stations': one playing clips of pop music from when they were between six and ten years old, the other playing pop music from when they were fifteen to nineteen. Neither station was labelled as belonging to a particular era. After five minutes, they did another round of maths questions.

Nim and her colleagues found that, in adult participants, stress created a preference for the music that had been popular when they were between six and ten. The more they'd been exposed to that music as a child, the larger this preference became. This was despite not explicitly expressing a preference for one period of music over another. Listening to pop music from when they were six to ten significantly reduced their stress levels compared to a control group who had not grown up in the USA and were less familiar with it. They reported feeling calmer, their skin sweatiness dropped, and those studied in an fMRI scanner showed activation in an area of the brain called the anterior cingulate cortex – the front of that belt-like part – and greater connectivity to another part called the amygdala – an area I would soon become very familiar with.

Nim concluded that, like mice, humans have a sensitive period where we develop associations with music, and that, later on, listening to this music can help us cope with acute stress. But she also found that early adversity, like the death of a parent or parental divorce before the age of six, seemed to shift this critical period earlier. Under stress, people who had undergone early adversity showed a greater preference for music from preschool years (ages four to six) and it seemed to work better at helping them feel calm.[7]

You might think 'Well, they just felt calmer because of nostalgia,' but that's precisely the argument being made. 'Nostalgia' is derived from *nost*, 'to return home', and *algia*, 'pain', literally a painful yearning to return home. Music from this critical developmental period, Nim speculates, may act as a powerful safety cue, activating the anterior cingulate and prefrontal cortex, and helping us soothe and shut down our instinctive threat circuits. It's a way of returning home, to a time before anxiety.

———

I had a go at putting together a playlist of popular music from my critical period, which, according to this model, was between 1987 and 1991. Tracks like George Michael's 'Faith', Lisa Lougheed's 'Run With Us' – the end theme to *The Raccoons* – and Bowie's 'Magic Dance' are straight-up bangers and if you disagree I will fight you, no joke. (I was gutted that 'We Don't Have to Take Our Clothes Off', Jermaine Stewart's anti-rawdogging anthem, fell just outside my critical period.) But just because something was popular during a certain era, does that make it comforting?

Take the most successful track from my critical period: Bryan Adams' '(Everything I Do) I Do It for You'. Relistening to it instantly transported me to the hellish sixteen weeks it spent in the number one spot, the longest uninterrupted run in UK chart history. For nearly four months that song hung over Britain like nuclear fallout. Adams' hoarse caterwauling continued as we brushed our teeth, as we slept. We grew so accustomed to his oppressive, grating refrain, it would have felt odd *not* to have our every thought accompanied by a soundtrack of airless heterosexual mediocrity.

'(Everything I Do) I Do It for You' does not engender in me a feeling of safety or home. It makes me rue that our ancestors ever crawled out of the oceans.

Whenever a psychology experiment claims to find that some

intervention has an effect, you have to ask: Compared to what? Listening to tracks that were hits when you were a child might have a slightly better stress-reducing effect than random pop from your teens, but is the effect bigger than, say, choosing music that you *actually like*? Am I likely to feel happier listening to Bros or Bananarama than the Beatles' *White Album* or MF DOOM? Even if the effect exists – and we should apply this question to every piece of research we read – is it so tiny that it might as well not? 'Significant' doesn't mean 'big', remember. It just means 'unlikely to be down to chance'.

Still, it was lovely to realise I could indulge in deeply uncool tracks and not instantly burst into flame. Listening to Madonna's 'Borderline' while running made me deliriously happy. Soon I was jogging down the streets of Norwich lip-syncing and voguing to my little heart's delight.

———

Nim has also found that childhood adversity can affect later structural and functional development of parts of the brain, particularly the amygdala and hippocampus. Childhood trauma has been associated with a smaller hippocampus as an adult, and a smaller, more reactive amygdala. But the picture is not clear – other studies found stressful childhoods led to enlarged amygdalae.[8]

Prolonged and intense stressors can have a profound impact on the developing brain, in ways that don't always become apparent until many years later. But Nim told me that determining the precise timing of this key period 'is an incredibly difficult question to answer in humans, since it's very difficult to control timing effects.' You can't experimentally randomise cruelty amongst children to see what happens to their brains. 'However, early and chronic stresses, especially those that disrupt the parent–child relationship, seem to exert particularly enduring risk.' She said that large individual differences modulate how we respond, and pointed me towards a concept called 'differential susceptibility'. Some researchers have argued that it's evolutionarily adaptive for children born to the same parents to exhibit different temperaments – some being very responsive to their environment, or 'plastic', and some less so.[9] (Indeed, this is precisely the trait that the 5-HTTLPR short allele polymorphism has been implicated in, albeit with mixed evidence.) Paediatrician Tom Boyce of University of California argues that children with heightened sensitivity (who he refers to as 'orchids') feel bad and good experiences more keenly. If they experience a lot of stress growing up, they'll do worse than their less sensitive peers ('dandelions'). In a very stable, safe environment, they may do much better.[10]

Certainly, my brother is a lot more stoic than me – although, given that I exhibit near-ceiling levels of anti-stoicism, he could hardly be less so. His work has centred around supporting autistic children and adults with additional needs, roles that require patience, resourcefulness and calm. He was always less inclined towards academic and creative pursuits, but much better at being a grown-up. He's heir to a similar genetic legacy, but his temperament is quite different.

It was briefly comforting to consider myself in Boyce's flattering terms, a rare bloom who needs special care and attention in order to thrive. But I could also feel the turbine-like energy of thousands of eyes rolling in unison, including my own. It sounded awkwardly close to the old concept of Indigo Children, first promoted by parapsychologist and self-proclaimed psychic Nancy Ann Tappe in the 1970s. She claimed a special new generation of children were being born with indigo auras, all of whom demonstrated strong wills, deep intuition, a sense of entitlement, and behaviour mainstream society would think of as 'strange'. If your child was having angry outbursts or bullying other children, it wasn't because you were a bad parent. It was because they were a future spiritual leader.

I have a lot of sympathy for anything that reduces parents' feelings of shame and encourages them to value their children for who they are. But that doesn't make it scientific.

———

Like any diagnosis, the labels we attach to children aren't neutral. They affect our expectations of that child, and how the child views themselves. Those expectations affect how the child acts, what kinds of challenges they choose to face, and how adults treat them. All of which has a huge impact on how they view the world. A label like 'gifted', 'special needs', 'indigo', 'orchid' or 'dandelion' can seem helpful, exculpatory even, but if we're not very, very careful it can turn into a shackle.

Canadian psychologist Eric Berne, creator of transactional analysis, proposed a series of 'social games' that people play – for the most part unconsciously. One of these he called 'Wooden Leg', in which a person emphasises some personal disadvantage to evade responsibility for their choices – thus the purest form of this plea is: 'What do you expect of a man with a wooden leg?'[11] Berne's thesis is unscientific (not to mention, in this instance, lazily ableist) but it speaks to fears I had about my motives. Much as I hated the idea that my emotional state was forever trapped in the aspic of genetic inheritance or events from my childhood, maybe some part of me longed to be found 'not guilty' by reason of insanity.

Even as I continued my research, I seemed no closer to beating my panic attacks. On one particularly horrible string of days, I found myself collapsing into gibbering fits where I rocked myself, begging God to save me. Part of me yearned for an out. To be told, definitively, that I was a lost cause. 'What do you expect of a man with the intronic rs1067327 polymorphism on chromosome 2p21?'

I was confident many of my friends and family – if they were feeling polite – would endorse a diagnosis of 'highly sensitive'. Perhaps my particular repertoire of genes and childhood experiences had raised my likelihood of experiencing disordered anxiety. That didn't mean I was fated to forever be this tender, soft-bellied creature, collapsing on the chaise-longue, snapping open a fan and sighing: 'Whatever shall become of us?'

I was intrigued by Nim's research into changes in the developing brain – particularly her focus on the area called the amygdala. I'd heard it mentioned before.

Not only that, but one genetic mutation had caught my attention. It did something incredible.

It eliminated fear altogether.

X.

PIECE OF MIND
The neuroscience of anxiety

'S.' had been receiving anonymous letters explaining in detail how – unless she stopped talking to the police – she was going to be murdered.

She was standing alone outside her apartment when the gunman arrived.

He emerged suddenly from a corridor, walked up to her and pressed a pistol to her head.

'BAM!'

He yelled the word. Then he ran away.

Later that day, S. answered her door to a worried police officer. Was she all right? he asked.

Very well, she said. What could she help him with?

The officer hesitated, wondering if he had the wrong address. A very upset neighbour, he said, had reported seeing someone put a gun to her head.

Oh yes, said S., but he ran off afterwards.

The officer was bewildered. She seemed indifferent.

S. was used to threats on her life. After her son found a bag of crack in the backyard, S. had given it to the police and told them which of her neighbours she suspected of dealing drugs. Soon she began receiving written death threats. Even so, when she found a second bag, she went to the police again.

S. did not connect the threats with the gunman. She recalled the encounter as 'strange'. She could not understand his motivation.[1] If he meant to intimidate her, he failed spectacularly. Even with a pistol muzzle pressed to her temple, S. said she had felt no fear at all.

Neither did she feel afraid when an addict held a knife to her throat and threatened to kill her. Nor when a stranger drove her to an abandoned barn and attempted to rape her. Nor when, after confronting her husband over his infidelity, he wrestled her to the ground and strangled her until she blacked out.

In fact, S. – known in the medical literature as 'Patient S.M.' – says she experiences no fear at all. Over decades, researchers have put her through a battery of tests, from questionnaires, analysing her personal diaries, having her carry a handheld computer to record her emotional state daily for three months, and interviewing friends and family, to showing her horror films, exposing her to live tarantulas and snakes, and even taking her to a haunted house. (Not only did the haunted house fail to frighten her, but she managed to startle an actor dressed up as Pinhead from the movie *Hellraiser* – she approached him and prodded one of the nails extending from his mask, because she was 'curious'.)[2]

When I heard about Patient S.M. it was like gazing into a magic mirror that showed my exact opposite. Two psychologists were asked to assess S.M. without being told the specifics of her condition. They concluded she was 'resilient', a 'survivor', and that she had 'exceptional coping skills'. They were impressed with how 'she takes "hard times" in stride and considers them to be just part of the flow of life' and noted her view that most people are 'fine, well intentioned, and positive'.[3]

Patient S.M. has a rare recessive genetic disorder called Urbach-Wiethe disease. There have only been around 400 reported cases since its discovery in 1929. It's caused by mutations of a gene called ECM1 – in S.M.'s case, the deletion of a single nucleotide, the basic building block of DNA. Since Urbach-Wiethe is a recessive disease, people can be carriers without showing any symptoms. When symptoms are present, the most obvious are a hoarse voice and prematurely wrinkled skin. But in a high percentage of cases, the disease causes calcifications in the brain that build up and destroy specific areas. It's not yet understood why, but in the vast majority of cases Urbach-Wiethe disease selectively calcifies the two small almond-shaped regions on either side of the brain called the amygdala.

When the psychologists in the above study were informed of S.M.'s condition, they revised their opinion that she was a 'survivor', instead attributing her reactions to 'an abnormally low level of negative emotional phenomenology' – a response I find *fascinating*. The instant they were told her attitude stemmed from a genetic disease rather than character or learned coping strategies, it became necessarily pathological. After all, brain damage can't possibly lead to better mental health.

Or can it?

———

Although they're commonly referred to in the singular, we have two amygdalae,* one on either side of the brain. These two tiny almond-shaped areas sit below the hypothalamus and on top of the hippocampus, comprising about 0.3 per cent of the brain's volume. Though they represent a relatively tiny proportion of the estimated 100 billion neurons in the human brain, they quickly became the target of intense study as researchers raced to unlock the secrets of human emotion, and in particular fear.

Once, as I understood it, the amygdalae had protected us from snakes and wolves, but the kinds of threats I faced were ecological, existential, emotional or logistical – worries about catching the wrong train, or growing old and regretful. I was hyped up on adrenaline I had no use for.

By contrast, Patient S.M. seemed like a model of resilience,

---

* From the Latin *amygdalon*, meaning 'almond'.

positivity and courage. Surely if I could rewire my amygdalae, or shut them down, or get them removed, I would be free.

I understand the squeamishness around directly manipulating our brains to fix our thoughts and emotions. Three pounds of water and fatty tissue encased in a delicate cockpit of bone, holding memories from a cherished birthday, our love towards a special someone, our child's name, the concept of 'smoke'. Severing connections between areas or – worse still – removing whole sections altogether, feels at some core level like taking a scalpel to the soul.

But modern medicine is brilliant, isn't it? It seemed to me that what those psychologists had classed as 'abnormal' in Patient S.M. might better be described as exceptional. Perhaps a life of happiness, trust and calm *is* abnormal. Perhaps human beings are wired for a world where joy is low on the list of priorities.

If brain surgery sounds drastic, you've probably never had a panic attack. With every bout of stomach-churning anxiety, every panic attack that saw me pinned to the kitchen floor, I felt another piece of myself getting chipped away.

Did my brain really *need* a fear centre? Why not remove this outdated piece of hardware, this neural anachronism? Why not embrace the possibility of a life without fear?

Even given the terrifying permanence of cutting part of my brain out, I chewed on the thought for a long, long time. What would actually happen to me if I found a surgeon willing to do the operation?

———

To understand what the amygdala is and how we started to develop theories about what it does, we need to head back to a laboratory in the University of Chicago on 7 December 1936. It was Monday, it had just gone 5 p.m., and Dr Paul Bucy was performing brain surgery on a monkey.

'Oh God, she was the most vicious animal you ever laid eyes on,' he would recall nearly fifty years later. 'It was dangerous to get near her. If she didn't hurt you she would tear your clothes – just nasty.'[4]

The monkey – who went by the name Aurora – was so violent, the original researcher working with her had palmed her off on a colleague known for his unusual skill with primates, Professor Heinrich Klüver. Klüver had a reputation as a brilliant, if eccentric, researcher. He had served as a private in the German army during the Great War before coming to America to train as a psychologist. 'He was something,' Bucy said. 'One of the most brilliant men and most knowledgeable that I ever knew.'

During Klüver's early research he was fascinated by children with so-called photographic memories, known as *eidetic memory*. In one of the imaginative leaps that characterised his career, he wondered if eating peyote, a spineless cactus with hallucinogenic properties, would help him understand these children's visual experiences better. He began consuming large quantities of dried peyote buttons in the lab, recording his trips in a short book he titled *The Divine Plant*.[5] Ultimately he found its relevance to his work 'minimal'.

'Well, then he gave the drug to his monkeys,' said Bucy. 'He gave everything to his monkeys, even his lunch.'

Klüver remained convinced that mescaline, the psychoactive component of peyote, had potential when it came to understanding how the brain processes visual information. He trained rhesus monkeys to pull strings attached to different coloured or textured objects in return for food rewards. Then he tested how mescaline affected their performance. Could they still recognise the right textures and colours while hallucinating? It was during these experiments that a chance remark by Bucy changed the direction of his research entirely.

While the monkeys were tripping, Bucy noticed they would chew and lick their lips. 'I said to Heinrich: "This business of the lips and mouth is not unlike what you see in cases of temporal lobe epilepsy

– they chew and smack their lips and so forth – so let's take out the uncus."'

The uncus is a small hook-shaped area deep in the brain (*uncus* is Latin for hook). Klüver wanted him to extract a smaller, more specific area, but Bucy wasn't sure he could manage such a delicate operation. Finally, late on a Monday afternoon, Bucy sedated Aurora and removed her entire left temporal lobe – including, deep within it, the amygdala.

'The next morning, my phone was ringing like mad. It was Heinrich on the other end saying "Paul – what did you do to my monkey?"'

Aurora's personality had completely changed. The formerly aggressive monkey had become tame – docile, even.

Subsequent research, in which Bucy performed similar surgeries removing both medial temporal lobes from a variety of rhesus monkeys induced a cluster of behaviours now known as Klüver-Bucy syndrome. The post-operative monkeys became obsessed with putting objects in their mouths and licking things. They became hypersexual, humping almost everything in their environment and masturbating frequently.

But the biggest change was to their emotions.

The monkeys had all been captured from the wild and transferred from their natural habitat to wire cages. Formerly, when humans approached, they screeched and jumped about in fear. Yet after the surgery they seemed indifferent, even when experimenters stroked or picked them up. They didn't react with fear when presented with a snake – one of the most frightening stimuli to a rhesus monkey.[6]

Heinrich Klüver and Paul Bucy's findings triggered a wave of experiments. But though most textbooks credit them with the breakthrough, they weren't the first to perform this experiment nor to make this discovery.

Nearly fifty years previously, at University College London, Professor Edward Albert Sharpey-Schafer – who made no less a contribution to the field of anxiety research than discovering the hormone adrenaline – and his American student Sanger Brown worked to identify the visual cortex in monkeys. In one study, they removed a large male rhesus monkey's left and right temporal lobes. They reported:

> A remarkable change is . . . manifested in the disposition of the Monkey. Prior to the operations he was very wild and even fierce, assaulting any person who teased or tried to handle him. Now he voluntarily approaches all persons indifferently, allows himself to be handled, or even to be teased or slapped, without making any attempt at retaliation or endeavouring to escape . . . Everything he endeavours to feel, taste, and smell, and to carefully examine from every point of view . . . not only with inanimate objects, but also with persons and with his fellow Monkeys . . . a strange Monkey, wild and savage, was put into the common cage. Our Monkey immediately began to investigate the newcomer in the way described, but his attentions were repulsed, and a fight resulted, in which he was being considerably worsted. The animals were, however, separated and tied up away from one another, but our Monkey soon managed to free himself and at once proceeded, without any signs of fear or suspicion, again to investigate the stranger, having apparently already entirely forgotten the result of the former investigation.[7]

I couldn't help but find the hapless curiosity of 'our Monkey' endearing. He reminded me of me when I used to drink (although I'm not sure anyone on the receiving end of my charmless crapulence would pounce on the adjective 'endearing').

After Klüver and Bucy's experiment in the 1930s, other researchers quickly discovered that the emotional changes they had observed in monkeys could be produced with the removal of the amygdala alone.

In the late 1950s, again at University College London, John Downer cut out the amygdala in one hemisphere of a rhesus monkey's brain and severed the connections between the remaining amygdala and the eye on the opposite side of the brain (our brains are wired contralaterally, meaning either side of the body is controlled by the opposite side of the brain). In transecting the monkey's optic chiasm and a few other connections – called 'commissures' – Downer effectively marooned each eye on its half of the brain.

Using eye patches, he found the monkey's behaviour changed depending on whether it viewed the world with or without an amygdala. When looking through the eye connected to the amygdala, the monkey reacted to approaching humans with fear and aggression – screeching, backing away and urinating. When it viewed the world through the eye with no connections to the amygdala, it remained calm and indifferent in the presence of humans – just like Aurora and 'our Monkey'. The monkey could *perceive* the humans just fine – it wasn't blind – but it no longer processed the thing in front of it as a threat. These observations led to the theory that the amygdala is necessary to 'invest sensory experience with emotional significance'.[8]

Imagine closing one eye and opening the other, and something that was *terrifying* for you just moments before – enough to make your heart pound out of your chest, to make you do everything in your power to scramble away, enough to make you literally piss yourself with fear – is suddenly neutral. Empty. Of no more emotional consequence than a tin of beans or a sieve. Oh look. An axe-wielding maniac.

It reminded me of the states reported by Buddhist monks, who, after meditating on impermanence and formlessness, claimed to view the whole world as empty. Maybe it sounds weird to feel jealous of a caged monkey who's just had part of its brain forcibly removed by scientists. I suppose technically it is. But I was.

———

A lack of fear may be a virtue in a monk, but it's probably less helpful for a monkey – certainly not one expected to survive in the wild.

In the late sixties, psychiatrist Arthur Kling tried surgically removing the amygdalae from two groups of rhesus and vervet monkeys – an operation called an amygdalectomy – before releasing them back into the wild. The first group of monkeys were quickly rejected by their peers, beaten up and chased into the sea. In less than a fortnight they were all dead from drowning, bites and scratches, or starvation. The second group, released along the Zambesi river, showed no interest in eating or drinking, and within seven hours became lost in the wild, never to be seen again. Kling wrote that the amygdala-less monkeys 'appear retarded in their ability to foresee and avoid dangerous confrontations . . . they are vulnerable to attack and unable to compete for food'.[9]

Unlike the monkeys, I did not have to engage in physical combat in order to eat, nor was I likely to be mauled and eaten by apex predators prowling the understorey. What was so wrong with cutting out a tiny part of my brain responsible for instinctual fear and mistrust? Why shouldn't we customise our brains the way we modify our bodies? Can't we rebrand it as 'neurohacking' or something similarly buzzy so it doesn't sound too ghoulish?

Why is psychosurgery so taboo?

—

On 14 September 1936, three months before Bucy performed his historic operation on Aurora the monkey, the anaesthetist came for Alice Hammatt. She had agreed to undergo a highly experimental procedure, never before performed in America, at the suggestion of a man who had lost his licence to perform surgery after his last patient died on the operating table.

The new procedure was called a lobotomy.

When the anaesthetist appeared, Alice became agitated. 'Who is that man?' she said. 'What does he want here? What's he going to do to me? Tell him to go away.'[10]

The previous day, sixty-three-year-old Alice had withdrawn her consent to be operated on. She relented when the doctors lied that they would try to spare her curly hair. Besides, they warned her, either she allowed them to operate or she would spend the rest of her life in state institutions.

By the morning of the operation, she had apparently changed her mind. Staff ignored her protests. They pinned Alice to her bed, and as she struggled the anaesthetist administered a rectal dose of the sedative Avertin. When at last she passed out, they shaved her bald.

Alice had come to the hospital suffering from 'insomnia, anxiety and debilitating depression'. For years she had worried about the future, about her appearance, about how others saw her. Tiny things bothered her. She hated herself. Her husband complained her recent behaviour had become unmanageable. She did embarrassing things like undressing at the window and urinating on the floor.

'Anxiety disorder' did not exist as a diagnosis at the time, but the physician who saw her, Dr Walter Freeman, diagnosed her with 'agitated depression', noting she 'showed "uncontrollable apprehension"'. Freeman decided she would be a good candidate for a new type of surgery being trialled in Portugal.

'The state of psychiatric care of the seriously mentally ill was a disaster when he began his career,' Freeman's biographer, Jack El-Hai, told me. There were almost no effective treatments for people with severe, chronic conditions. As Freeman noted, the one event that ended most psychiatric illness at the time was death. Many doctors felt their skills were useless. In many of the huge state institutions, the prevailing mood was despair. 'And Walter Freeman was not somebody who could tolerate despair.'

The inspiration for the procedure – originally known as a 'leucotomy' – came from Portuguese neurologist António Egas Moniz, who had overseen the first lobotomy less than a year earlier. Moniz was not trained in neurosurgery and could not perform the operation himself as his hands were incapacitated with gout, but he formulated a theory that mentally ill patients had, through habit, developed strong neural pathways in which 'predominant, obsessive ideas' had 'become more or less fixed'. His idea was to sever these connections, disrupting unhelpful automatic emotional responses and forcing the brain to adapt and grow new, healthier circuits.

Freeman's colleague, the neurosurgeon James W. Watts, used an auger to drill two holes into Alice Hammatt's skull over the left and right frontal lobes. Watts then inserted an instrument resembling a steel syringe, called a leucotome, into one of the holes. When he pressed the back of the instrument, a loop of wire extended from the tip. He then rotated it, the wire slicing through tracts of fatty white matter in her brain.

When she woke up after the operation, Alice seemed much calmer. When Freeman asked what had caused her anxiety in the past, she replied: 'I seem to have forgotten. It doesn't seem important now.'

She was ultimately able to go home, and sleep without the strong bromide sedatives she had taken for a decade. Her anxiety was all but gone. She said: 'I can go to the theatre now and not think whether my shoes pinch or what my back hair looks like, but can really concentrate on the show and enjoy it.' Her husband called the next five years the happiest of his wife's life. She died aged sixty-eight, from pneumonia.

Encouraged by the apparent success of the procedure, Freeman went on to oversee nearly 3,500 lobotomies. Later, he would 'refine' the technique so it did not require drilling holes in the patient's skull, meaning it could be performed without operating rooms, surgeons – or anaesthesia. It also meant that, despite losing his licence, he could perform the operations himself.

Looking at Alice Hammatt's personal history, it's not hard to understand why she suffered with worry. Her first child died at the age of two. Just three years prior to her lobotomy, her brother-in-law murdered her sister-in-law then killed himself. More recently, Alice had 'developed a crush on another man', told her husband about it, and become miserable with guilt.

To me, at least, Alice Hammatt doesn't sound like someone with intractable brain problems. She sounds like someone in understandable pain. She had experienced a series of horrible traumas and apparently had no one with whom she could talk about them openly. Even her more extreme behaviours feel intelligible as a kind of protest against her domestic prison.

In the throes of anxiety I've screamed, paced, wept, babbled to myself. The feelings Alice described felt uncomfortably familiar – the self-hatred, the agitation, the inability to relax in public places. If the outcome Freeman described is accurate, I'm glad for her.

But even if she did get some relief, I wonder if it was a happy accident of the procedure. I'm not sure her anxiety was the true target, so much as the disruption her behaviour caused men. In his own notes, Freeman dubbed her 'shrewish and demanding'. As in the notorious case of Rosemary Kennedy, sister of future president John F. Kennedy, where Freeman left her incontinent and unable to walk or talk, Alice Hammatt wasn't lobotomised with the knowledge that it was the best treatment available, nor even – ultimately – with her consent. Staff pinned her down and cut her open because a man in her life thought she was 'difficult'. Her husband may have loved her, just as Rosemary Kennedy's father, Joe, no doubt loved his daughter. But, like Freeman, both men seemed to view these women's behaviours as problems to be solved rather than messages to be listened to.

When you believe you have to save someone from themselves, their self becomes acceptable collateral damage.

———

In 1992, a new Batman villain was introduced – a rage-filled, muscle-bound psychiatric inmate called Amygdala.[11] Born Aaron Helzinger, he had his amygdala removed to control his fits of anger. 'Usually,' a caption explains, 'when it's surgically removed the patient becomes exceptionally calm and placid . . . However, in Helzinger's case, something went badly wrong.'

Compared to lobotomies, surgical removal of both amygdalae for the treatment of mental illness has been relatively rare. Approximately 40,000 lobotomies were performed in the US, and a further 17,000 in the UK. For amygdalotomies – where both amygdala were removed – the number globally may be under 1,000.

Around 10 per cent of these were performed in the 1960s by Japanese neurosurgeon Professor Hirotaro Narabayashi and his colleagues. He destroyed the amygdala by injecting a mixture of wax and poppy-seed oil. His subjects were as young as five.[12]

It's hard to say with confidence how successful these procedures were, because we only have Narabayashi's word to go on. Though his official reason for performing amygdalotomies was to relieve the symptoms of temporal lobe epilepsy, he stated frankly: 'It has been our intention to improve the emotional state of the patient with behavior disorders and not primarily to utilize this technique in order to achieve control of epileptic seizures.' It's telling that the most common positive adjective he uses to describe his patients, post-op, is 'cooperative'.

Many more amygdalotomies were performed in India between the sixties and eighties under Dr Balasubramaniam Ramamurthi, a man often regarded as the father of Indian neurosurgery. He claimed to have performed 481 amygdalotomies for the 'control of aggressive behaviour'.[13] The majority of his patients were children under the age of fifteen.

These days, removal of the amygdala is generally reserved for severe epilepsy that has resisted other treatments. But its use for altering behaviour has not entirely disappeared. In 2017, a nineteen-year-old woman in China with what the case report described as 'mild mental retardation' had an amygdalotomy for 'psychiatric symptoms and

COWARD

aggression'. The authors claimed the procedure led to 'significant alleviation' of her symptoms.[14]

———

These cases – mostly – happened long in the past, when neuroimaging technology was crude or non-existent. Surely now, in an era when I could apparently *watch my daughter think* live on screen, there were alternatives?

Alexander Shackman told me that, at least in animal studies, our methods for knocking out specific brain regions have massively advanced since the time of Klüver and Bucy. 'For years, what were the techniques that were available? You could use a scalpel, you could cauterise different parts of the brain tissue, burn it away, vacuum it away – these are very traditional neuroanatomical techniques, "gross perturbation", for turning off a brain area. We just destroy it.'

One alternative researchers developed is 'excitotoxic lesions'. 'This is a process where you inject an excitatory transmitter into . . . a small region of the brain, like one nucleus of the amygdala, and essentially cause the neurons in that region to fire themselves to death.' The advantage of this technique over dropping a scalpel in is that any axions coursing through that region that have nothing to do with it are preserved. If you have two other brain regions communicating with each other and those fibres are passing through the amygdala, with traditional lesions you'd destroy not only the amygdala but the superhighway running through it. With excito-toxic lesions you can knock down the houses but keep the roads open.

Another approach that became popular in the 1990s was injecting muscimol, an inhibitory neurotransmitter, into a brain region. 'You could transiently or acutely suppress the cells,' Alex said. 'You can turn them off.' Muscimol is the main psychoactive compound in fly agaric toadstools, which cause delirium and hallucinations if ingested.

It strongly stimulates the production of GABA, that neurotransmitter Stefan Brugger told me about which dampens brain activity.

A rarer technique involves suppressing activity in a region like the dorsolateral prefrontal cortex by cooling it. 'You can cool it down so much that the neurons are healthy and alive but they're quiescent, they're in hibernation.' Then researchers can observe a creature's behaviour before, during and after turning off a specific area of its brain.

These methods are less of a blunderbuss than scalpels or poppy-seed oil, and crucially – in the case of muscimol injections and cooling – temporary. But they're not practical for humans. You'd need to remove part of the skull and administer an injection in exactly the right place every time you wanted anxiety relief. Worse, despite what pop-science would have us think, the brain isn't divided up into discrete, convenient departments. You're still potentially knocking out lots of different cellular populations or little ensembles that live in the same region.

Two breakthrough techniques offer answers: chemogenetics and optogenetics.

In chemogenetics, you use a virus to mutate target cells, creating special receptors known by the thrillingly cyberpunk name DREADDs ('designer receptors exclusively activated by designer drugs').[15] These receptors are selectively responsive to a biologically inert drug, clozapine N-oxide (CNO). After waiting a fortnight or so for receptors to form in the cells, you can introduce CNO via an injection, and, depending on whether your DREADDs are coupled to excitatory or inhibitory signalling pathways, they either silence the chosen neurons or trigger burst firing.[16]

In other words, you can use a harmless drug to temporarily make brain cells of your choosing either shut down or activate.

This technique, Alex told me, allows researchers to transiently target subpopulations of cells sitting right on top of each other. 'Interdigitated,' he said, threading his fingers together to demonstrate, 'or a term that's sometimes used is a "salt and pepper" pattern.' With a lesion or muscimol or excitotoxins, you'd be knocking out all those cells. With chemogenetics you can differentiate with incredible precision, so you hit only the salt or only the pepper. Preliminary studies have used DREADDs to inhibit amygdala activation in rhesus monkeys, with the aim of one day developing similar treatments for anxious humans.[17]

Optogenetics offers similar accuracy, and in some ways is even more impressive. The field began in the mid-nineties, when scientists discovered they could transfer a gene from a bioluminescent jellyfish to a worm, making the worm's neurons glow green.[18] A search followed for more and brighter colours. Scientists explored coral reefs armed with fluorescence spectrometers, hunting for fluorescent corals and sea anemones, and cloning their genes. One result was the breathtaking, nightmarish 'brainbow mouse', where each neuron in a mouse's brain glows a different colour, making it easier for scientists to monitor the axons and dendrites of individual cells.[19]

Mice and rats can be genetically engineered so their brain cells are photosensitive. Researchers then use a laser to directly stimulate individual cells. In chemogenetics, CNO – the harmless chemical – has a relatively slow wash-out, meaning it takes a while for the effects to wear off.[20] In optogenetics, you're working at the speed of light. 'It affords a millisecond-resolution lever for turning cells on and off,' said Alex. 'You can do things like record cellular activity, then – in principle at least – play that back. Imagine it as a keyboard or piano – you could actually play the song of anxiety at the same speed as it actually happens. And that's completely unlike what we had before.'

One limitation with optogenetics is that you have to drop a fibre-optic cable directly into the brain. Mice have tiny brains, so relative to the width of the cable you can target a reasonably large surface area. But once you get to non-human primates with fist-sized brains, you need many more cables to cover a comparable area. Alex said it was 'proving very difficult to get working . . . Monkeys have hands. They can grab things that are implanted in their skull and try to rip it out of their heads.' He later clarified that he didn't think this was a major stumbling block compared to brain size, but it would require implanting an ambulatory battery system under the creature's skin.

I felt a bit queasy. I'd got so caught up in the possibilities, I'd forgotten these are living creatures – creatures which presumably don't enjoy being repeatedly stressed or bionically modified while researchers record and analyse their brain activity.

Still. Neurons you can play like a piano. Anxiety as the 'Minute Waltz'. One day, might we learn enough to 'play' the song of peace right into someone's brain?

Sadly, human brains don't come with a sunroof. You'd have to remove most of the skull and replace it with a docking station for fibre-optic cables. Even then, the amygdala is nowhere near the surface. You wouldn't be able to get at it without additional invasive surgery.

The future applications of psychosurgery were almost literally mindblowing. But for now, directly triggering neurons to stimulate specific parts of my brain was a far-off dream.

Or so I thought.

XI.

BRAIN STORM

Stimulating parts of the brain with electricity and magnets, and taming our 'threat circuit'

When I was five, I went to see *Return to Oz* at our local cinema. It's set six months after the events of *The Wizard of Oz*, when a tornado carried Dorothy away from Kansas to the magical land of Oz. Since then, she has been unable to sleep. Her Aunt Em and Uncle Henry think her stories of talking animals and slain witches are the product of emotional trauma, and borrow money to take her to the city to see Dr J. B. Worley, a psychiatrist who offers 'electric healing'.

'The brain itself is an electrical machine,' he explains in his lavish office. 'It's nothing but a machine. When it malfunctions, a blow to the head, for example, then the brain produces useless excess currents, and these excess currents are our dreams and delusions . . . Now we have the means to control these excess currents.'

A few scenes later, Dorothy lies strapped to a gurney as a hatchet-faced nurse in black bombazine slips the metal contacts of an electroshock device over the young girl's temples. Dr Worley tinkers with dials and switches as the orchestra rises to a crescendo.

As a child, I was terrified.

So it was with understandable trepidation that I adjusted the damp electrical pads over my left and right prefrontal cortex, and tapped the button marked 'Start'. Brine trickled from the sponges into my eyes. I felt a tingling, prickling sensation on my upper scalp. A few seconds later, the prickling became burning.

———

Transcranial direct-current stimulation (tDCS) – also known as exogenous neurostimulation or, as neuroscientist and tDCS researcher Adam Green cheerfully described it to me, 'brain zapping' – uses electrodes to pass a weak electric current through the scalp into the brain. Unlike electroconvulsive therapy (ECT), which intentionally induces seizures and nowadays is performed under general anaesthetic, tDCS is relatively gentle. The electrical current depolarises targeted neurons' resting membrane potential – that is, it lowers the threshold at which those neurons generate an action potential, or 'fire'. It's like blowing on the embers of a fire, making them more likely to reach a heat where they burst into flame.

It can also be used to make neurons *less* likely to fire, effectively inhibiting activity in the area beneath the electrode. By increasing or decreasing the excitability of specific parts of the brain – or connections between regions – tDCS aims to jumpstart the formation of new, stronger neural pathways. This is known as Hebb's postulate: What fires together, wires together.[1]

In this sense, neurostimulation is a milder, noninvasive alternative to the procedures Alex was describing. It's far less precise, but it can transiently quieten or excite particular regions of the brain without the necessity of removing portions of the skull or genetically engineering new receptors.

I spoke to Dr Camilla Nord, a neuroscientist at Cambridge University's MRC Cognition and Brain Sciences Unit, who has looked at using brain stimulation techniques like tDCS in treating psychiatric disorders.

When I asked Camilla how tDCS worked, she was quick to temper my expectations. 'If you'd asked me ten years ago I would have said what it's doing is roughly increasing the global activity in one region known to be disrupted in depression and other disorders – the dorsolateral prefrontal cortex. In reality, it's more like the prefrontal cortex because it's pretty diffuse stimulation, but we thought it might be able to cause patients to be better able to dampen down emotional reactions to things: maybe they're better able to pay attention, maybe they have better working memory.' PTSD survivors consistently show impaired working memory, although attempts to treat PTSD by boosting working memory have had, at best, mixed results. I'd read some research on generalised anxiety disorder – albeit with small sample sizes – that suggested stimulating the left dorsolateral prefrontal cortex allowed it to exert greater control over the amygdala.[2] 'But over the past ten years it seems not to work in every patient with depression – in fact there are many for whom it doesn't work at all.'

She told me that there had been a number of robust tDCS trials. To control for the placebo effect, these often include a 'sham stimulation' condition, where experimenters attach electrodes to the participant but don't pass the full current through the target areas.

In the beginning, Camilla said, the results were impressive. 'It looked like it was a very large effect size even in a very small number of patients. The majority of people were showing some kind of response or remission, even after five or eight sessions.' But – as so often happens with treatments in development – as the samples got bigger and different researchers tried to replicate the results, the picture grew muddier. 'In more recent papers, and this includes mine, it is not something you see in every patient, or even overall. And there have been even bigger clinical trials where there was truly no difference compared to sham stimulation – some patients even seemed better off on the sham stimulation. That makes it very unclear if it's actually better than placebo.' She said she thought it still might be, but, like Dr Ruihua Hou's hunch about how anxiety might be connected to inflammation, she suspected it might only work for a subgroup of depression sufferers.

There was another type of exogenous neurostimulation where the evidence was stronger – transcranial magnetic stimulation, or TMS. 'It's a kind of figure-of-eight coil about the size of a large mango, but a lot heavier.' A long, thick cable connects it to the stimulator.

You hold it over the region you want to stimulate. 'If you do this over one region of the motor cortex, it will make you twitch your finger, and then if you move it along you'll twitch your ring finger then your little finger – so it's anatomically very specific.' She said the sensations were stronger than with tDCS – a tapping sensation which can be very uncomfortable (some people have even likened it to having their skull drilled into).

So far, results for depression had been promising. But when I asked about why we target the dorsolateral prefrontal cortex, she admitted that part of the reason was 'convenience'. The prefrontal regions are not the only regions implicated in anxiety and depression, but they're the only ones we can reach from the outside. Direct stimulation of other regions – like the amygdala – is currently only possible with invasive surgery. But Camilla said new technologies were on the horizon that she was 'keeping an eye on. Things like ultrasound stimulation.'

In the not-too-distant future we might be able to target deep brain regions and activate or inhibit them as we please. For now, treatment with TMS was way beyond my budget – thousands of pounds for six half-hour sessions.

But there's a new wave of consumer tDCS devices that you can use at home. The marketing makes all sorts of claims about boosting creativity and learning speed, and relieving anxiety symptoms. Are they equivalent to tDCS administered by trained professionals in a clinic? Probably not.

Was I going to try one anyway? You bet.

—

My device was a grey plastic headset with three rubber pads into which I had to put white sponges soaked in saline solution. I set the device to boost activity in my left prefrontal cortex, put it on, and, using the app on my phone, cranked the ampage slider up to 2mA.

I felt a prickling, burning sensation beneath the contacts, as if someone were jabbing pins into my scalp. Saltwater dripped down my face onto my t-shirt and the crotch of my jeans (resolving into suspicious-looking stains – somehow the truth was more embarrassing). After a few minutes my vision seemed to be narrowing. Was that a good sign? I tried to get on with work but it was hard to forget I was wearing a cumbersome electrical hat that was burning me.

I didn't feel less anxious – it's difficult to completely relax when there's a non-zero percent chance you're irreversibly frying prime acres of neural real estate with a crowdfunded plastic hair-slide – and the only thing my first session stimulated was a sore red patch on my forehead the size of a Garibaldi.

In fairness, the purpose of tDCS isn't to reduce anxiety or depression in the moment. (It would be pretty useless if the effects stopped the second you took it off.) Like exercise, what you're really after are the long-term gains from repeated sessions. There's not yet good evidence that tDCS – especially a consumer kit – is an effective treatment for anxiety. I added it to my ever-expanding suite of anti-anxiety habits, alongside the new, healthier diet, running, and the news and social media embargo. After all, I'd bought the fucking thing now. No harm (well, potentially *some* harm) in tossing it into the mix.[3]

Until now, my approaches had been piecemeal. I was picking away at my anxiety like a scab, when I wanted a decisive duel to the death.

Looking through some of the research on tDCS and anxiety, I thought about what Camilla had said about her original hypothesis – that neurostimulation helped the prefrontal cortex 'dampen down' emotional reactions. Some studies suggested the prefrontal cortex did this by suppressing the amygdala – it was like a trip switch, modulating instinctual fear.

From what I'd learned, it sounded like the bit of me that was going wrong was the amygdala.

In all the neuroscience textbooks about the amygdala, one name kept cropping up again and again. His work with rodents seemed to complete the story that Paul Bucy and Heinrich Klüver's monkeys began. Decades of work had made him arguably the best-known anxiety researcher in the world.

If I was going to crack the amygdala, I had to speak to Joseph LeDoux.

—

Joe was very accommodating when I emailed him, but he was also very busy, so it was months before he finally had a gap in his schedule. Unfortunately, that week we were going on holiday (me and my family, not me and Joe LeDoux.)

Rather than miss perhaps my only chance to talk to him, I decided I'd just call him from our cabin at Center Parcs. I sprinted back after watching Suki on her first ever pony ride. I'd been so worried she was going to miss the slot we'd booked, I nearly ruined the whole experience for her and Lisa.

As our video call started, I saw myself on my phone screen – poorly lit, out of breath and very obviously in bed. The bedroom had been the only place I could think of where we wouldn't be disturbed.

'Hi,' I panted, red-faced and sweaty. 'Can you see me?'

Joe suggested we switch off video.

I asked him about the amygdala.

'Fear is not what the amygdala's doing.'

He had an electric guitar propped against the wall beside his desk. When he isn't working as a neuroscientist, he's lead singer for his band: the Amygdaloids.

'I think it's been totally misconceived and scientists like me are partly at fault.' He paused. 'Other scientists are even more at fault.'

Joe particularly blames the late Estonian neuroscientist Jaak Panksepp – don't we all – for popularising the idea of the amygdala as the brain's fear centre.[4] 'It gave people an excuse not to deal with the subtleties because the thing they had thought all along, that the amygdala is a fear centre – okay, here's a scientist, Panksepp, who's saying yes, it's a fear centre.'

Now in his seventies, Joe LeDoux is as close as the fields of neuroscience and anxiety get to a rock star. Nearly everyone I talked to brought him up. In the mid-nineties, his work took up an entire chapter of Daniel Goleman's bestselling book *Emotional Intelligence*, in which Goleman coined the term 'amygdala hijack' to explain moments where we – apparently – lose our self-control as the primitive amygdala takes over. Whereas previous researchers had formulated theories of what the amygdala did, Joe and his team at New York University built on previous discoveries to try to nail down the *how*.

The basic model he proposed goes like this: say you're walking through the woods and your eye catches something long and coiled lying in the path.[5] The visual stimulus – a long, coiled thing – hits your retinas and travels backwards through the brain; first to the thalamus, which acts as a kind of relay station. The thalamus makes a quick determination – what *type* of thing is this? A threat? Food? Another human? It passes this 'rough, almost archetypal' assessment directly to the amygdala, which has outputs to circuits governing motor control and heart rate via the hypothalamus, and can rapidly prompt us to take evasive action before we even realise what we're looking at.

Meanwhile, the thalamus also passes the information back through the brain to the visual cortex, which sits at the rear. The visual cortex can process and interpret visual stimuli with much more sophistication than the thalamus, making higher-order assessments like, 'Oh no, a venomous snake.' The visual cortex's assessment then *also* passes to the amygdala directly, which may prompt our blood pressure to increase, the release of adrenaline, etc. On the other hand, if, when the visual stimulus reaches the visual cortex from the thalamus, the visual cortex decides, 'Wait, that's just an old hose pipe,' then this new interpretation travels to the amygdala instead, conveying a message to stand down and quell the sympathetic nervous system's response.[6]

These cortical and sub-cortical pathways are what Joe called the 'top-down' and the 'quick and dirty' routes to the amygdala respectively. A key feature of this model is that a visual or auditory stimulus can be interpreted as a threat by the thalamus and conveyed to the amygdala – which starts marshalling a threat response – before you realise what you're looking at.

If this model is accurate, the system it describes may have saved your life several times. It certainly saved the lives of our distant ancestors.

The direct link between the thalamus (the part of the brain lobotomist Walter Freeman believed was the 'seat of emotion' that he was trying to disconnect from the prefrontal cortex) and amygdala means you can react to something that might be a threat at the earliest possible moment. You don't have to wait while the more sophisticated, slower part of your brain performs the complex taxonomical calculus of figuring out what this thing in front of you is, what it might do, and what your response ought to be. The thalamus just says to the amygdala: 'FUCK! SNAKE!' And you jump back. As Joe said in a 1989 interview with the *New York Times*: 'Those extra milliseconds may be lifesaving, which is a powerful advantage in evolution. But it's a quick and dirty process; the cells are fast, but not very precise.'

From a survival perspective, the costs of false positives are relatively low. Think of Gloria, our anxious guinea pig. If she startles at a strange noise and it turns out to have been harmless old me sneezing, it's no great loss. Speed is more important than accuracy. Better safe than sorry.

Once – if – other, slower areas of the brain decide the threat-like stimulus is not a threat, they signal the amygdala, which – theoretically – signals our aroused sympathetic nervous system to stand down. (I say 'if' and 'theoretically' because, of course, these systems can go wrong.) There's a metabolic cost from all that cortisol and adrenaline, where our heart's beating faster than it needs to. But even if that happens fifty or a hundred times in a single day, those are better outcomes than getting bitten – or, in Gloria's case, eaten – by a snake.

Whereas some fears like snakes, heights and sudden loud noises may be instinctual, we learn others over time. Joe and his team developed and tested this theory through years of working with rats, using a process called fear conditioning.

You've probably heard of the Russian physiologist Ivan Pavlov, who trained dogs to associate a buzzer or metronome – amongst other things – with the appearance of food. Seeing the food, the dogs would salivate (a response Pavlov measured by collecting drool via tubes inserted through cuts in the dogs' cheeks). He and his researchers repeatedly paired the food's arrival with a particular sound. Eventually, just the sound of the buzzer or tick of the metronome on their own made the dogs salivate.

Pavlov found that, over time, the dogs' responses became more refined, so that, for example, they could be trained to salivate in response to a metronome ticking at sixty beats per minute, while ignoring one ticking at forty. But he only had general hypotheses about how this might take place in the brain. (His methods for analysis were crude and his dogs rarely lived long – many had their oesophagus removed and a hole cut in their throat so any food they ate simply dropped out.)

In the 1980s and '90s, Joe used things like flashing lights or buzzers to test rats' visual and auditory cortices. In one set of experiments, he trained rats to associate hearing a particular tone with getting a painful electric shock to the foot. His team gauged the rats' threat response by their blood pressure and how long they spent frozen to the spot. Eventually, the rats only had to hear the tone for them to freeze and their blood pressure to rise.

Unlike Pavlov, Joe was able to explore the mechanisms behind the conditioned response with great precision. Each rat was anaesthetised and placed in a stereotaxic frame – a rigid clamp-like apparatus that held its head in place. Joe's team would consult a 'rat brain atlas' to find the precise coordinates of the brain area they wanted to destroy. (*John Peel voice*: 'That was "Rat Brain Atlas", the new track from Ilford synth-punk duo Stereotaxic Frame, from their debut EP, *Pavlov's Fistula*.') Next, they would bore a hole in the rat's skull with a dental drill and insert a steel electrode. By passing a current through the electrode for ten to fifteen seconds, they could destroy – or 'lesion' – the target brain area before closing the wound and returning the rat to its cage.

In this way, over years, Joe and his team painstakingly destroyed specific sections of thousands of rats' brains, then tested to see if the rats could still learn to freeze in response to – for example – a specific tone, if it was repeatedly paired with a painful shock. They discovered that if either the 'top-down' cortical pathway (ear–thalamus–auditory cortex–amygdala) or the subcortical 'quick and dirty' pathway (ear–thalamus–amygdala) were intact, freezing in response to the tone still occurred. But when *both* routes were lesioned, freezing drastically reduced.[7] Most of the literature at the time talks of this discovery in terms of 'fear conditioning'. In 1998, Joe wrote: 'The key to the fear pathways in the brain is a small region called the amygdala.'

When I had been to visit Dr Oliver Robinson at University College London, he'd told me Joe would 'be an interesting one for you to talk to because he's going through a bit of a mea culpa right now'.

'What happens,' Joe explained a little ruefully, 'is you start doing research, and you find something, you give it a name, because that's just what the field is calling it. So we called what the amygdala does "fear" because we were using a task called Pavlovian fear conditioning – so it must be conditioning fear.' But he says he was always uncomfortable with the term. Back in the 1990s, based on his work in rats, he claimed that 'Some emotional reactions and emotional memories can be formed without any conscious, cognitive participation at all.'[8] Now he believes that explanation is misleading. In his view, an emotion is a conscious experience – an act of interpretation. 'Anxiety is the awareness that you are in harm's way. That requires that your brain have a representation of you, and that is a very complicated thing and something that may be unique to the human brain: the ability to know that it's you that's having a certain experience.'

He thinks that when we talk about the amygdala's role in detecting and responding to danger, what we should be talking about is the activity of a *survival circuit* – something that has arisen through evolution to help the organism stay alive. Such a circuit does not need any kind of conscious awareness. That function is present in every organism that lives today or has ever lived. Every organism, whether it's a single cell or a complex human being or anything in between, has to be able to detect and respond to danger to stay alive. 'This is about keeping the organism alive; it's not about making psychological states. Bacterial cells detect and respond to danger.'

Just because the amygdala detects a threat and prompts a physiological response, that doesn't mean the organism experiences what we would recognise as an emotion. I asked Joe what was happening, then, in the hundreds of anxiety studies which use fMRI scans that show the amygdala's activating.

'Let's say we're talking about the amygdala being activated by a threat. Now, we can present that threat to a person subliminally [for example flashing up an image of a spider so quickly they aren't consciously aware of it], the threat will go to the amygdala and activate it, the person's heart will race, their palms will sweat, but the person has no idea what the stimulus is, doesn't know it's there, and doesn't report fear.' So, in Joe's view, fear isn't what's causing the amygdala to respond.

'The amygdala is detecting danger and responding to danger. That is a kind of behavioural, physiologically non-conscious process from start to finish. If you're conscious of what the stimulus is – you know that what you're looking at is a snake – in addition to the amygdala non-consciously responding, you begin to cognitively interpret what that means. You know that snakes are dangerous, you notice that your heart is beating faster, so you notice a picture of a snake and those two things come together to equal fear. We cognitively put together what's happening in the outside world with what's happening in our brain and body to assemble what I call a "fear schema".'

In other words, behavioural responses are not the same as emotions. Things like anxiety, dread and love necessarily involve a concept of self, and the conscious interpretations of experiences both in our body – interoception – and outside, in our environment. 'Our feelings are higher-established processes that require a lot of cognitive processing.'

I brought up a 1974 study by the psychologists Donald Dutton and Arthur Aron called 'Some Evidence for Heightened Sexual Attraction Under Conditions of High Anxiety' (which would also work as a caption for my wedding photos). It's more commonly known as the 'Love on a suspension bridge study'.

The study took place across a 5-foot-wide, 450-foot-long bridge made of wooden boards attached to wire cables, spanning the Capilano Canyon in North Vancouver. The bridge was chosen for its 'many arousal-inducing features', including very low wire handrails, a tendency to wobble and sway, and 'a 230-foot drop to rocks and shallow rapids below'. The researchers placed an 'attractive' female interviewer in the middle of the bridge and had her approach men between eighteen and thirty-five as they crossed, explaining she was doing a project about 'the effects of exposure to scenic attractions on creative expression'. The men were asked to fill in a short questionnaire then write a short story on the following page.

The stories were later rated for sexual content and compared with the stories of a control group, who had been approached on a bridge of 'heavy cedar', just 10 feet high, some miles away. There were also two more groups who were approached on either bridge by a male interviewer. Men on the high, anxiety-inducing suspension bridge wrote stories containing the most sexual content. One explanation the authors suggested was that the men were misinterpreting their physiological symptoms of anxiety – racing heart, trembling hands, sweaty palms – as sexual attraction, the so-called 'misattribution of arousal' model.[9] (The researchers apparently assumed that every participant was either heterosexual or bisexual and shared their opinion of what constitutes 'attractive'.) They found similar results when men were given painful electric shocks in the presence of an 'attractive' woman. The more painful the shocks, the more attraction the men reported. (How the authors decided who met the criteria for 'attractive' is not mentioned in the paper.)

This seems to hold true even when the physiological response is bogus. Psychologist Stuart Valins had participants view erotic slides while listening to a soundtrack, supposedly of their own heartbeat, but actually faked. When they heard their alleged 'heartbeat' markedly increase for half the slides, they rated those slides as significantly more attractive.[10]

'Right,' said Joe, 'that's a good example. What all of these states are, are cognitive interpretations, based on a kind of best guess by your brain about what it is that's happening. So the physiology and all of that is not so much a determining factor but a supporting factor. It's really all about the attribution of mental states to situations.'

In this model, these cognitive interpretations are a mix of contextual clues and beliefs about ourselves and the world. If your heart's pounding, your knees feel weak and you've gone lightheaded, you might have just received devastating news of the suicide of a friend over the phone, you might be standing on the edge of a 10-metre-high diving board, or the love of your life might be kissing you moments after you complete your wedding vows.

I've been through each of these scenarios, and the bodily symptoms are very similar. In what's known as the two-factor theory of emotion, we decide what emotion we're feeling by linking those symptoms to context – our immediate environment, our beliefs about ourselves and the world, and our memories.[11] According to this model, it's possible that certain people – like the men in Dutton and Aron's study – don't like to see themselves as anxious, and so, given ambiguous circumstances, choose an option that fits better with their self-image – like 'horny'. Other people – perhaps those who see themselves as timid, or who've been brought up to believe that feeling lust or anger is wrong – might experience emotional arousal in the presence of an attractive person, or in response to a co-worker's rudeness, and interpret their racing heart and sweaty palms as fear.

Weirdly – perhaps worryingly – this model doesn't imply that there's a 'correct' emotion sitting there waiting to be discovered. Emotional experience is *always* an interpretative act.

'We often hear that fear is universal,' said Joe, 'because people round the world have words for fear.' But that doesn't mean that different cultures have identical understandings of what 'fear' is. Each term – *die Angst, la peur, huoli* – exists amongst a constellation of options within each language, each with distinct connotations representing subtly different conscious experiences. 'Fear is a culturally defined state, cognitively assembled in the presence of danger.'

But there's an amygdaloid baby bobbing in neuroscience's increasingly murky bathwater. Though the amygdala's response to a threat may not in itself be fear, according to Joe it's still an essential part of the process. It has the power to trigger the fight, flight or freeze response, releasing stress hormones and raising your heart rate. We don't need to learn how to freeze or flee, or how to produce cortisol and adrenaline – those responses are hardwired – but what we can learn are new cues which trigger those responses.

Just as the rats' amygdalae learned to associate a tone with a painful shock – meaning the tone on its own could trigger raised blood pressure and freezing – so too can we learn nonconscious associations between a sound, a visual cue, even a smell, and that hardwired threat response.

When I spoke to Oli Robinson at UCL, he told me about how panic attacks are sometimes triggered by sensory reminders of trauma: 'A lot of the early work with PTSD was done with Vietnam vets in the US, and there are all these references to chop suey. They'd be in Vietnam and they'd smell chop suey, and then back in the US they'd smell chop suey and they'd have a panic attack.'

Being able to distinguish between a theatre of war and a quiet peacetime neighbourhood – and thus respond appropriately – is partly a conscious, cognitive process. But it also involves apparently nonconscious associations, not all of them residing in the amygdala. I thought of all the situations I got anxious in. Some made sense – like just before I was about to go on stage at a gig – but some were really weird, like if I was in the kitchen by the fridge and my wife came up behind me. All at once I'd feel boxed-in, trapped, as if something dreadful were about to happen.

'The brain is learning lots of different things in any given situation,' said Joe. 'We can't just mush them all together. That's what we've done in the case of fear. We've put all of the workload into the amygdala when in fact the workload is distributed across a lot of different systems.'

As well as the amygdala, he said, we need to look at how it interacts with the hippocampus.

—

The hippocampus is popularly known for its role in memory. It seems to play an important part in how we form autobiographical memories – memories of things we've experienced – and spatial memories – memories of where things are in relation to one another. Like the amygdala, we have two hippocampi, one on either side of the brain.

The hippocampus and the amygdala have many direct and indirect connections via other brain areas.[12]

Much research has explored how the hippocampus may use context to help guide our behaviour when we're learning – or unlearning – threat responses.[13]

When I spoke to Alexander Shackman at the University of Maryland, he told me about animal studies that have attempted to explore the hippocampus' role in this process. 'The hippocampus is a system in our brain for encoding information about the environment and associating that information in the environment with safety.' So as well as learning to freeze in response to a tone paired with a shock, a rat can learn to freeze when it's placed in the particular cage where the shocks happened. The context *itself* becomes threatening – a bit like how returning to your old school, or the house you lived in when you went through your divorce, might bring up anxiety in the absence of specific cues.

So, Alex told me, imagine you're a rat, and you've learned to associate a cage with painful electric shocks. Then you're placed in another cage. Perhaps it has a different kind of bedding – the last one had wood chips, this one has stone. Maybe it smells different. Maybe the walls are painted a different colour. 'If you couldn't distinguish between those two environments after being exposed to shock in one, you would probably treat both environments as equally dangerous.' Researchers are trying to figure out how the hippocampus gives us spatial information about our environment and how it associates that information with safety. 'So you can be like "I'm in the box with wood chips, I know I'm safe," [or] "I know I'm back in the United States, I'm not in Afghanistan."'

Other studies have suggested that the hippocampus plays a primary role in acquiring contextual fears and extinguishing them later.[14] Some research suggests it may not be *essential* for an animal to learn to associate context with threat,[15] but when the hippocampus is damaged – either through physical injury ('gross perturbation'), chronic stress or severe trauma – learning is impaired, particularly when it comes to learning that an environment is safe.[16]

Nonconscious and conscious associations can, of course, exist in parallel.[17] A human can be trained to associate a particular tone with an electric shock, but – unlike a rat – we can also have the conscious thought, *Oh, it's that noise again – a shock must be coming.* Or – more perniciously – we can consciously appraise our inner physiological experience, our racing heart, our clenched fists, our trembling knees, and think, *Oh, it's those feelings again – a panic attack must be coming.*

———

I asked Joe if he had any suggestions for me.

'What I think we need to do first is somehow tame the amygdala.' Joe gave the example of someone who is terrified of spiders: they can't stand looking at spiders, they avoid places spiders might be, and their fight, flight or freeze response is triggered by spiders. 'What you have to do is bypass the conscious awareness that the spider is present, in order to do the initial exposure therapy nonconsciously.'

He suggested presenting a spider picture subliminally – a very brief flash followed by a 'visual mask' which hides the picture. 'What you'll find is you can weaken the amygdala's response, without the person experiencing what's called flooding.' It's a bit like vaccination: giving the amygdala a tiny dose of the learned threat – the 'conditioned stimulus' – without the usual conscious, cognitive components that help construct the conscious experience of fear. Usually, for a phobic person, prolonged exposure to a spider picture results in an overwhelming increase in anxiety as the amygdala prompts a threat response, releasing adrenaline and cortisol, along with chains of unpleasant conscious thoughts like, *Oh no, a spider – I've got to get out of here!* Done subliminally, Joe believes the amygdala can gradually be desensitised through repeated exposures.

'The second step would be to go to the more cognitive memories involving the hippocampus.' In other words, now we get to do tradi-tional exposure therapy. In this instance, that means showing our arachnophobe a picture of a spider long enough that they consciously perceive it, and letting them gradually build up their tolerance. 'If you do that before you've tamed the amygdala, then the amygdala's going to be activated simultaneously and when you present the spider, the arousal and other consequences of hippocampal activation are going to store that memory stronger and stronger each time. So rather than weakening the hippocampal memory you get recondi-tioning or reconsolidation of the memory through exposure.'

Step three is the brain. Once you've conditioned the amygdala and the hippocampus to no longer respond to the thing you were scared of as a threat, Joe thinks your brain is 'ready for psychotherapy, in the sense of talking about your problems, and taking positive steps to move your life forward, with the understanding you've regulated two systems in your brain that were causing you some difficulties and making it hard for you to think through the situation. You can now more effectively go through things like belief change and cogni-tive restructuring.'

Spider phobia works fine as a test case, but Joe acknowledged that most anxiety disorders don't have a single, specific cue. Generalised anxiety disorder involves excessive worry about 'a number of events and activities'. By its very nature, it can't be reduced to one trigger.

Joe has suggested that, in the case of GAD, it's *the anxious thoughts themselves* – not the events to which they pertain – to which we can apply the principles of exposure therapy. So an anxiety sufferer like me might try – with the help of a therapist – bringing anxious thoughts to mind and rehearsing muscle relaxation or slow breathing. Other strategies might include challenging automatic thoughts and misbeliefs that arise in our conscious mind – classic CBT, basically.[18]

He had warned me right at the beginning of our chat that he was not a therapist. The majority of his work has been about formulating and testing theories, rather than developing treatments.

Still, I admit I was a bit disappointed. Here was the world's best-known expert on the neuroscience of anxiety. He had even written a book called *Anxious*. I'd thought he might have access to some super-advanced secret technique – a spot I could press just so that would kill the fear. But as we chatted, he denied that anxiety had ever been his real area of study.

Researchers talked, he said, 'as if working on the amygdala's going to solve the problem of how people experience fear and anxiety. And I don't think that is the case. If you look at the effort to develop drugs to treat people with anxiety by studying these behavioural tasks in animals, you don't necessarily end up with a medication that helps people.' He claimed that big pharmaceutical companies 'are all getting out of the business' of developing anti-anxiety drugs because they can't find ones that help fear and anxiety.

I'm not sure that's the whole story – SSRIs like Zoloft and benzo-diazepines like Valium account for hundreds of millions of prescriptions annually. Their efficacy may be debatable but the demand is not. It's more likely that, since their patents have expired and they're available in off-brand forms, it's more of a risk to invest in developing new ones which may, at best, only result in marginal improvements relative to cheap generics.

The number of new drugs approved per $1 billion spent on research and development has roughly halved every nine years since 1950, after adjusting for inflation. Any sustainable health-care system would only agree to pay for a new, more expensive drug if a patient failed to respond to the existing cheaper generic. This massively limits drug companies' potential market. The issue isn't that they can't find drugs that help fear and anxiety – it's that they already have.[19] To make the risky, protracted R&D process financially viable, they would have to hit upon a medication which so massively improved upon existing generics that health-care providers' denying it to patients would be unethical.

Joe told me the failure of animal studies like his to produce results for anxiety sufferers was 'a misperception of what was being asked of the animal studies in the first place'. We confused mice that were more willing to hop down off a platform, like the BALB/c mice in the McMaster microbiome study, with mice that were less fearful. But those are two different things. He said he thinks drugs that make mice less timid might make a person less timid too, but they do nothing for that person's conscious experience of *fear*. 'So a person with social anxiety might find it easier to go to the party, but still feel anxious while she's there.'

I was confused by this analogy. I've taken benzos, SSRIs, SNRIs, MAOIs, quetiapine and the beta blocker propranolol, and I've self-medicated with booze and other substances. Never once have I had the experience of feeling more able to do something – like go to a party, perform on stage, etc. – while still feeling an identical amount of problematic anxiety. For me, the anxiety *is* the inhibition. They're one and the same. The DSM-5's criteria for phobias, social anxiety and generalised anxiety disorder state that your anxiety must make you habitually *avoid* the events or objects you're afraid of. If you can do the thing, by definition you no longer have an anxiety disorder.

If someone does public speaking and they experience worried thoughts or a raised heartbeat as they walk on stage, we don't say they have an anxiety disorder. We say that's natural. And, as we've seen, it's someone's *interpretation* of their somatic experiences – the sweat, the rapid breaths, etc. – that makes an emotion. I didn't understand what Joe thought anti-anxiety drugs did. I asked if it was possible to feel those things – braver, disinhibited – and still feel anxious.

Joe said he wouldn't talk about someone *feeling* those things; instead he sees bravery and avoidance as behavioural responses. In his view, the systems in our brains that control our behaviour are separate to those that give rise to our feelings.

'It's not simply your desire to avoid a party, which is a behavioural phenomenon.' You might give yourself a drug that weakens the amygdala's response, and be less inhibited about going to the party, yet consciously worry on your way there. 'And then when you're there you'll feel anxious because the drug has not necessarily changed these higher cognitive systems that make your feeling of fear.'

This still felt weird and counterintuitive. When I took sertraline I felt like it explicitly changed my conscious experience of anxiety. I felt less anxious, I worried less, and I behaved accordingly. I had fewer anxious cognitions. Most measures of the effectiveness of anti-depressants on anxiety are based on self-reports – people reporting their subjective, internal experience via a numerical scale – not on behaviour or amygdala response.[20]

That his explanation felt counterintuitive is not, necessarily, a strike against it. Much of psychology – nay, science in general – is a reminder that our instinctive, intuitive explanations for things are not always reliable. Patients suffering from Alzheimer's disease, for example, often spontaneously invent autobiographical details to explain gaps in their memory, or to make sense of the situation they find themselves in, a phenomenon called confabulation. They don't realise they're doing it – they have complete confidence in their story, even if it contains outlandish or illogical details.

Joe's early career was as a student of neuroscientist Michael Gazzaniga, researching so-called split-brain patients – epileptics who had undergone surgery to separate the left and right sides of their brains, like John Downer's monkeys in the 1950s. There he saw for himself that the explanations we give for our behaviours – even to ourselves – are not always correct.

He and Michael worked with a split-brain teenager from Vermont known as 'Case P.S.' They would flash words and commands to either brain hemisphere via its contralaterally wired eye. Many brain functions are typically – though not always – lateralised, with one side dominating. Language is a well-known example, where the left hemisphere tends to do the bulk of the work relating to things like vocabulary and grammar, at least in a sample of right-handed participants (left-handed people are less likely to demonstrate prototypical patterns of brain lateralisation – this is why many neuroscience studies specify that their sample is comprised entirely of right-handed participants).[21] Though P.S.'s right hemisphere was unable to speak, when they flashed questions to it his left hand could grab Scrabble tiles and spell out answers. Through this process, Joe found that the left and right sides of P.S.'s brain both had a sense of self, but different goals for the future.

'We were giving the right hemisphere written commands ('stand', 'wave', 'laugh'), and P.S. responded appropriately in each case. Had Mike not been there that's probably as far as it would have gone.' Michael Gazzaniga suggested they ask P.S. *why* he was doing what he was doing. Only the left hemisphere had the power of speech, yet the right hemisphere was perceiving and initiating the actions. 'When the command to the right hemisphere was "stand", P.S. would explain his behaviour by saying he needed to stretch. When it was "wave" he said he thought he saw a friend. When it was "laugh" he said we were funny.'[22]

This is neither intuitive nor comforting. Michael and Joe would come to view human consciousness as a kind of interpreter that came up with justifications for our behaviours. Even if those interpretations were nonsense.

———

It's funny how, in psychology, you can spend ages learning complex theoretical models, jargon about neuroanatomy, read dozens of systematic reviews, absorb decades of research, and at the end of it all you burrow up somewhere very familiar. When I started learning about the amygdala, I was ready for psychosurgery – a little snip inside my head, a sort of mental vasectomy that would cut off my anxiety for good. In the end, Joe's final advice for remoulding my anxious brain was . . . having a chat.

'What we have to do to change a conscious experience is to have an interaction with another conscious being.' In therapy, he said, the conscious mind of the therapist and the conscious mind of the client talk to each other. But underneath that, the unconscious schemas are also interacting, normalising brain function. 'And that's where I think the hard work gets done. Underneath the talking.'

Okay, so the amygdala wasn't the brain's 'fear centre'. Fear and anxiety, in Joe's view, are stories we tell ourselves to explain our behavioural and physiological responses in certain situations.

Geneticist Adam Rutherford had warned me that today we think of the brain less in terms of modularity – certain parts being responsible for certain things – and more in terms of *connections*. Alex Shackman believed that two decades of neuroimaging research show that anxiety disorders are associated with heightened reactivity to emotional challenges in an extended 'threat circuit', comprising parts of the amygdala, the bed nucleus of the stria terminalis, the periaqueductal grey, midcingulate cortex and anterior insula. Studying how these areas speak to each other in disordered anxiety might give us some clues as to what's going on.

But wasn't the amygdala still the big boss of the brain's 'threat circuit'? Wouldn't – as Joe put it – 'taming' my amygdala help relieve my anxiety?

Several researchers warned me that the amygdala doesn't only handle our threat response. 'Bring in an addict and show them photographs of their preferred drug,' said Alex. 'Bring in someone who's been food-deprived for twelve hours and show them photographs of delicious food. That lights the amygdala up like mad.'

He told me that the 'vast majority' of neuroimaging studies related to anxiety use the so-called 'emotional faces protocol', where participants are shown pictures of unfamiliar adults making prototypical expressions of fear and anger. 'With neuroimaging – and this is a dirty secret, a widely known skeleton in the closet – we tend to study things that are well-aligned with the methods that are available. Conventional fMRI is very good at studying transient, short, phasic responses, and it's essentially unusable for anything lasting greater than, perhaps, two minutes.' He said researchers gravitate towards fearful faces 'because they know they're going to get a very strong, pretty consistent amygdala response. They know it's relatively easy to do.'

But participants don't report feeling fear during the process. They don't show a raised heart rate. In fact, a big problem researchers deal with when using the fearful faces probe is people falling asleep in the scanner, 'cos it's kinda boring'.

Oli Robinson at UCL told me that in his post-doc years he'd tried showing non-clinical individuals fearful faces and happy faces to get this amygdala activation. To his surprise, they couldn't find it.

'It turns out that the amygdala is just activating like crazy for *any* face.'

In as much as we can associate any area of the brain with a single purpose, the amygdala may be better characterised as investing salient stimuli with emotional significance to help orient our attention towards them.

Still, smaller amygdalae = less emotional reactivity, right?

'Neuroplasticity' – the brain's ability to grow new pathways – had become a pop-science buzzword. One study found eight weeks of mindfulness training – meditation, awareness of the body and so forth – significantly reduced the density of grey matter in the right amygdala,[23] and another that conducted MRI scans of 155 adults found that 'dispositionally mindful' individuals – that is, people with a natural tendency to pay attention to their thoughts and experiences in a non-judgemental way, moment-by-moment – had a significantly smaller volume of grey matter in the right amygdala.[24]

But most of the mindfulness studies had small sample sizes and the researchers involved were often enthusiastic meditators – not exactly impartial. Smaller amygdalae in calmer people might be a classic example of correlation versus causation in brain-scanning research – or, as German neuroscientist Martin Lotze of Greifswald University once put it to me: 'Here again we have the problem of the hen and egg.'

A 2009 study found that 'amygdala volumes in both hemispheres were significantly smaller in patients with panic disorder compared with control subjects'.[25] Another, conducted in 'healthy' adults who had not been diagnosed with anxiety disorders, found that higher anxiety was associated with decreased volume in the left amygdala.[26] A study of nearly a hundred military veterans with PTSD found it was associated with significant reductions in both left *and* right amygdala volume compared to a control group. The authors concluded their study provided 'robust evidence' that 'a smaller amygdala represents a vulnerability to developing PTSD'.[27]

And remember Patient S.M., the woman without an amygdala? The woman unafraid when a stranger held a gun to her head?

Researchers arranged for her to undergo a '35% CO_2 challenge', a reliable way to induce panic attacks in the lab in those vulnerable to them. She wore a breathing mask and inhaled an air mixture containing 35 per cent carbon dioxide – 875 times more than in the air we usually breathe. After one breath, she began gasping for air. She waved her hand near the mask and cried: 'Help me!'

Experimenters had successfully given Patient S.M. her first panic attack.

Not only that, but it was a *smasher*. Her body went rigid, she grabbed the researcher's hand, clutched at her throat and gasped: 'I can't breathe.' It went on more than twice as long as most CO_2-induced panic attacks.[28]

This finding was replicated in a study involving twins with the same genetic disorder as Patient S.M. Researchers found the CO_2 challenge triggered a panic attack in both.[29] Despite having no amygdala, both participants described sensations of 'fear' and 'panic'.

Not only that, but it turns out that some people who've had their amygdala removed later in life are still capable of experiencing fear. One, known as 'Patient S.P.', had always lived with a damaged left amygdala. Her right amygdala was removed when she was forty-eight because of severe epilepsy. In contrast to Patient S.M., she seemed able to experience anxiety, worry and fear.[30]

Studies in rhesus monkeys that had their amygdalae lesioned at birth found that, by adulthood, their behaviour was only subtly different from unlesioned monkeys, the authors speculating that neural plasticity resulted in the brain creating new pathways to make up for the damaged areas: 'It is clear that the injured brain attempts to establish a compensatory pattern of connectivity and improvises a modified nervous system that interacts as effectively as possible with the environment in which it finds itself.'[31]

Just when I thought I'd cracked it, I felt more baffled than ever.

I contacted more researchers from universities all round the world, asking for their advice. *Help me understand*, I said. To my surprise, almost all of them agreed.

With my neurostimulation device directly zapping my prefrontal cortex, I was already part cyborg. I felt so close to figuring out how to remould my outmoded mammalian brain. After all, robots don't get anxious.

Only, it turns out, they do.

XII.

PARANOID ANDROID
What robots and AI are teaching us about anxiety

In the ending scene of the 1983 movie *WarGames*, a military super-computer, 'Joshua', has the launch codes to America's nuclear arsenal and is about to trigger Armageddon. Seconds before it does, a plucky hacker (played by a young Matthew Broderick) convinces Joshua to take both sides in a simulated global thermonuclear war, and try to win.

Joshua runs some basic tactics – a first strike by the US, a first strike by the USSR – and both superpowers get annihilated. It moves on to increasingly elaborate gambits, with names that sound like obscure fonts – Hong Kong Variant, Arabian Clandestine, Cambodian Heavy – but the result is the same. Joshua's processors overload, coughing sparks.

'He's learning,' breathes Joshua's creator.

The simulations speed up, explosions blooming over the world map, faster and faster, while names of doomed strategies – Arctic Minimal, SEATO Decapitating, Thai Variation, English Thrust – fill the screens in a strange apocalyptic mantra. Every gambit ends in failure. Every choice leads to destruction.

Finally, the war room goes dark. Then Joshua delivers one of the most-quoted lines of the 1980s: 'A strange game. The only winning move is not to play.'

Matthew Broderick saves the world by teaching a computer to be anxious.

—

Consider the problem of the self-driving car.

We want self-driving cars to be accurate – to take us to our intended destination. We want them to be efficient – to get us there in the shortest possible time. But most of all, we want them to be safe.

If we're travelling from London to Edinburgh we don't want to go via Paris. But we also don't want to take shortcuts through school playgrounds, to mount the pavement or drive the wrong way up the M1.

Some hazards, like the position of buildings and rivers, remain fairly static over time. Others, like the behaviour of pedestrians, are less predictable, and so require more complex calculations of risk. For a car, increased ambiguity requires increased caution. Caution means slowing down, stopping or avoiding.

A self-driving car with zero caution would be a disaster. A friend who works as a researcher in the field told me, with palpable excitement, 'The holy grail of self-driving cars is a car that sees a child on one side of the street, an ice-cream van on the other, *recognises that the former might move towards the latter*, and slows down.'

We're trying to teach our AIs to be anxious.

But as we've worked on this, something weird has happened. The more we've taught robots to learn and respond to danger, the more they've started behaving in ways that look . . . oddly human. Self-piloting drones that won't leave the warehouse. Cars that hate crowds.

These discoveries have, in turn, led to the rise of a whole new science of the mind: computational psychology.

Computational psychology attempts to take our thoughts, feelings and behaviours and express them as programs our brains might be running. By creating mathematical models of decisions we're faced with, and expected punishments or rewards, psychologists hope to understand how we make choices, and how, in anxious people, that process might go wrong.

Oli Robinson at UCL's Institute of Cognitive Neuroscience told me: 'I sometimes joke about it as Marvin the Paranoid Android. Why would you make a paranoid android? Well, if you make an anxious robot, you might understand what made the robot anxious in the first place.'

Reducing the squishy complexities of the human heart to a series of equations sounded comforting. I'm shit at maths but I like systems with tables and numbers. I like games with rules and clearly defined win conditions. All of these things suggest predictability, control, the possibility of mastery.

When I started learning about computational psychology, I couldn't see what a neurotic parcel drone had to teach me about worry.

After all, we were nothing alike.

Or so I thought.

—

When I first encountered Nathaniel Daw, professor in computational and theoretical neuroscience at Princeton University, he was slightly out of breath from rushing across a field to get back to his office in time for our meeting. Something about his mild air of furtive urgency, combined with his spectacles and short dark hair, made me think of a healthier, more likeable Dennis Nedry, the computer programmer from *Jurassic Park*. In a sense, his work had shut down the electric fence separating human psychology from computer science. But it was not raptors that had come scrabbling over that once-impermeable barrier. It was robots.

Nathaniel warned me he knew more about anxiety as a sufferer than a researcher, but that he would do his best. As it turned out, he was being modest (he's published many influential papers on anxiety, including one co-authored with Joe LeDoux).

Computational psychology grew out of the science of information processing, with its fundamental questions like: *How do I solve problems?*

What does it mean to solve a problem? What are the quantities that I have to push around? What do those operations cost?

Nathaniel explained that one of the core problems AI systems face is figuring out when to take an action where the reward for it is delayed and dependent on a lot of later choices. Take, for example, a robot learning to navigate a maze in the fastest possible time. Each part of the journey can be broken down into individual actions: rotate ninety degrees to the left. Walk forward five steps. 'The problem is you don't get immediate feedback. You get the goal when you get to the goal.' Only with the final step in the sequence do we actually achieve the reward. 'It relies on the construction of intermediate quantities to predict future rewards.'

In anxiety, the sequential nature of choice makes optimising behaviour particularly hard.

'It's not just that I take an action and I get rewarded for it later, like I find the goal or score the points or whatever, it's that whether or not that happens doesn't just depend on the action I take now, it depends on all the stuff I do in between. And so reasoning about what happens now necessarily is intertwined with consideration of what happens later.

'If we go with the robot in the maze, the shortest path to the goal might be for me to go left now, but to deliver on that, I'm going to have to make a whole bunch of turns properly after that. So the way these algorithms work is, "If I go to the left I'll get to the goal in ten steps, if I go right I'll get to the goal in twenty steps" or whatever. But it's not that simple, because if I go left I'll only get to the goal in ten steps if I make all the correct moves later. There's a dependence – a complicated relationship between what I do now and what I do later.'

As humans, we hold a staggering number of hypothetical futures in our head at any one moment. Each fate diverges from decisions large and small: Shall I cross the road, shall I go to the party, shall

I apply for the job? We predict results, we construct mental models, and we decide how much we like or dislike the probable outcomes. Unlike a robot designed for a single task – such as navigating a maze – we can even determine our own goals, so the choices and possibilities are almost endless.

In researcher Quentin Huys' 2012 paper, 'Bonsai Trees in Your Head', he proposed a model where all these futures spread out before us in the form of a 'decision tree'. Picture each future as a branch, and each choice – do I go out for a run or stay in and eat take-out – as a point where the branch splits.

We have so many options, Huys argued, 'it is usually infeasible to consider all potential future sequences', so we have to 'prune' some branches. Except for all but the smallest problems, getting this exactly right would be – and I love this phrase – 'computationally ruinous'. So we use a bunch of tricks, shortcuts and mental hacks to cut the tree down to size.[1]

Huys proposed that most humans use a simple strategy when making these types of sequential evaluations. When we're weighing up a series of choices, we discard ones that contain large losses – or major costs – early on. In this way, we're able to use our limited cognitive resources deciding 'which of the good options will prove the best, not which of the bad ones are the worst'.

Like many rules of thumb, this 'aversive pruning' works well in many situations. When I come home, I don't have to devote lots of thinking time to deciding whether I ought to unlock the front door or fling myself bodily through the window. Smashing the glass or trying to burrow under the foundations have obvious high upfront costs, so they aren't factored into my decision-making.

But Huys found that 'humans use this strategy even when it is disadvantageous', and even that its use is associated with 'mild depressive symptoms'.

'If you think about a chess computer,' said Nathaniel, 'it's searching through different paths in the game and working out what best moves to do, literally examining millions of positions.' Imagine, to use a simplified example, you have approximately 30 moves available to you, and your opponent chooses from an equal number. Looking just 5 moves ahead asks you to consider 24,300,000 unique sequences. 'Our brain does some of that but it can't go through all of them, so it's using tricks to consider the most promising ones. And what you don't think about is going to mess up your choices in some circumstances. This process in any moderately complex task, let alone the real world, can go badly wrong.'

Nathaniel's explanation differs from Huys' in that he sees anxious pessimists discard potential gains that appear deeper in a decision tree, not because they haven't considered them, but because they doubt their ability to choose well later on. They'd rather pick the least-costly action for right now, even if it means discarding large potential gains further down the line. They don't trust themselves not to screw up.

Look again at our example of the robot in the maze, said Nathaniel: 'If I say, "If I go left I'm going to get to the goal in ten steps", that's assuming I make the right choices later. What if I don't assume I'm going to make the right choices later? What if I have some belief that I'm going to mess it up, or the world's out to get me? That is, in terms of these algorithms, a tweak in this parameter. Which leads you, in terms of this system, to be systematically pessimistic about a particular thing, which in this case is, "How likely am I to deliver on the best possible thing I could do later?" If you do all the math and push that through the model, if I'm too pessimistic about future choices it's going to lead me to be too pessimistic about an action I'm going to take now and it's going to lead me to take the wrong choices.'

One way this manifests is through avoidance.

'Crossing the street can get me killed, right? But I know if I follow the lights and don't run out into the street when I'm not supposed to, I'm pretty much all right. I don't have to protect myself by not leaving my house, because I know that later on I'm not going to run out into the street. I don't trust my kids not to run out into the street so I don't let them leave the house without me.

'So my evaluation of whether it's safe to leave my house is based on my evaluation of what I'm likely to do when I'm near cars. If I expect I'm going to behave reasonably when I get near cars, I'm protected from cars and the danger of cars doesn't infect my whole world. If I think I'm going to make mistakes, I don't get to take advantage of the protectiveness of the assumption that I'm going to behave rationally later. And that will affect my evaluations everywhere. Back in my house, I shouldn't leave my house because I believe I'm going to run out in the street and get run over. So a little change in a restricted belief about a parameter on these algorithms has a monumental effect through my world.'

At this point I sat back and made weird goldfish faces as my mind imploded. All of a sudden I had explanations for all sorts of self-destructive, apparently irrational behaviours. Why bother exercising today if you doubt your ability to stick at it tomorrow? Why ask the cute person out on a date if you expect that, even if they say yes, you'll either chicken out or make an idiot of yourself? Why sit down to write a bit more of your novel tonight when you're convinced you'll never be able to finish it?

If you believe these things and act accordingly, then – by some metrics – the strategy appears to have worked, right? You flinch, you avoid . . . and you feel a tiny surge of relief.

'And then it can get worse and worse, right? Because not leaving your bedroom can save you from potentially leaving your house.'

Okay, so this theory has attractive explanatory power. That doesn't prove it's accurate. How do we test it in humans?

'That's a fair question for a toy model,' said Nathaniel. 'One thing that's good about this idea is that it builds on rough models of the function of brain hardware, like the dopamine system. Back in the nineties there was a set of observations about a particular class of neurons in monkey brains. These neurons carry a neurotransmitter called dopamine which is . . . famously the target of all addictive drugs . . . and clearly involved in reward and addiction. What people knew back then was that it was the pleasure neurotransmitter.'

I knew dopamine was to do with motivation and maybe addictive behaviours like gambling. When I'd chatted to researcher and psychiatrist Stefan Brugger, as soon as these words left my mouth he'd cut me off: 'I would chuck a massive bowl of caution over folk understanding of neurotransmitters. Take dopamine – probably the most researched neurotransmitter going. It seems to gate movement – we know with Parkinson's, low dopamine people have trouble initiating and continuing movement.'

Stefan had warned me that dopamine was 'really really really really complicated', and that new studies were coming out all the time that refined our understanding. Like serotonin, what dopamine does depends on *where* it is. It has various functions in the body as a hormone and various functions in the brain as a neurotransmitter. 'One very well-replicated finding is that one of the things dopamine signals is prediction errors. It was originally shown in reward tasks where you've got mice learning about getting sweets or sugar or whatever. And they showed that unexpected sugar meant dopamine would fire off. But if they were expecting a bit of sugar and they didn't get it, you'd see a drop in dopamine release' – what the literature calls a 'phasic dip'.

Dr Wolfram Schultz, professor of neuroscience at Cambridge University, has a nice analogy where he describes trying to get a blackcurrant juice from a Japanese vending machine. There are six drinks on offer, and he can't read the language, so he just presses the second button from the right. He has a low expectation of getting his preferred blackcurrant juice – 'then a blue can appears with a familiar logo that happens to be exactly the drink I want'. Hooray! A better result than expected. His surprise helps him remember which button to press next time.[2]

This is what we mean by a 'positive reward prediction error'. He predicted he wouldn't get a blackcurrant juice. He was wrong, and the gap between expectation and the better-than-expected outcome activates dopaminergic (i.e. dopamine-releasing) neurons in the mesolimbic pathway – in the jargon, they 'generate action potentials', or as we usually say, they 'fire'. This helps reinforce the lesson: *Ooh, I got something unexpectedly good here. I should remember this and do it again.*

Future presses of the second button from the right that result in a can of blackcurrant juice no longer prompt a prediction error, because the reward is expected. But Schultz recounts pressing the button a few weeks later, only to get a different drink. Someone must have refilled the machine differently. Oh no!

This time, he experiences a 'negative reward prediction error'. He thought he was going to get a blackcurrant juice and he got something that he values less. Firing of dopamine neurons temporarily drops, creating an association between the behaviour and the worse-than-expected outcome.

Now this is the simplified analogy, and as Stefan warned, dopamine is much more complicated than that. 'It's also been shown to look at – let me get this right – motivation prediction errors, so you're doing some task to get something and it takes less effort than you think, you get a bit of dopamine release.' And it's not just to do with rewards. 'It's broader than just pleasure or nice stuff or motivation. You get the same thing in sensory prediction errors.' So if you learn a pattern of lights, then you're shown a red dot where you expected to see a green one, this creates a prediction error that releases dopamine. Red dots aren't a better reward than green ones, as far as we know – but dopamine neurons seem to fire nonetheless. 'You've got an expectation about something that's going to happen, it doesn't happen, and something's got to signal you need to change either your beliefs or your behaviour.'

To summarise: if you think you know what dopamine does, you

don't. Its functions are complex and we're still teasing out how it works in different locations with different receptors and subfamilies of receptors.[3] But in terms of Nathaniel's model it's important for two reasons.

Firstly, we don't only experience an increase in dopamine when we get the unexpected reward. Nathaniel gave the example of a $100 bill. You can exchange it for food and similar. It's not a reward in itself, merely the signal of a reward. But if you find one on the pavement – I suppose in this analogy a more likely place would be the 'sidewalk' – you still get that dopamine 'zing'.[4]

'Predictors of reward act as actual rewards,' he explained. 'If I squirt juice in a thirsty monkey's mouth unexpectedly, he gets the zing. But if I signal to a monkey that he's going to get juice, he gets the same zing.' These little shots of dopamine might solve the problem of how the brain reinforces all the little steps on the way to a pay-off.

The second reason the prediction-error function of dopamine is important, is it gives researchers a way – in a very loose sense – to measure a person's optimism: 'With dopamine, we can measure how surprised you were. We can't directly measure dopamine but we can measure some of its effects, or we can in rodents. How surprised you are by a reward or punishment also tells the experimenter indirectly what the organism was expecting.'

One way of testing this is the balloon analogue risk task, or BART. Participants are shown a picture of a balloon on a computer screen. They inflate the balloon by clicking a button. For each 'pump' of the balloon, they earn a small amount of money – say 5¢ – and by clicking another button they can bank the money earned and move onto the next balloon. Or they can keep going. But with every pump, there's a small risk that the balloon will pop and they will lose all the money earned on this balloon.

It's a classic push-your-luck game only – unlike, say, blackjack – there's no data on the mathematics of the risk you're taking – no cards to count, no obvious threshold of how many pumps the balloon can take.

Nathaniel was cautious about the BART's value as an experimental tool. Individual tests are very 'noisy' – that is, lots of minor factors can affect a player's behaviour. Not everyone gives the prototypical performance: an anxious person might pump the balloon lots and lots of times, and a non-anxious person might play very conservatively. This makes it a poor test for diagnosing anxiety in an individual.

However, when we look at the average performance across the two types of players, there's a significant difference. Anxious players as a group pump the balloon fewer times before banking their money.

For Nathaniel, the big question is: 'When the balloon explodes, what happens in your brain?'

Each time you pump the balloon, you presumably expect it to inflate and your earnings to go up by 5¢. Thus, if it pops, you're a little like Dr Schultz pressing the second button from the right and getting the wrong drink. You expected a reward – you got less than you hoped. This is a negative prediction error.

But here it's the *size* of the error that matters. You might have pressed 'pump' confidently expecting to receive another 5¢. You might – as I did when I tried the BART – have clicked that button with gritted teeth, bracing for the inevitable bang. The size of the dip in dopamine neuron activity suggests the size of the prediction error – i.e. how surprised you were. Were you expecting a bad outcome, or a good one?

Are you always waiting for the balloon to pop?

Nathaniel suggested this model might help distinguish between subgroups in anxious populations. 'One of the problems of psychiatry is that some treatments work on some people and not others.' Which is a bit like saying that one of the problems with space travel is some planets are very far away.

His point was that diagnostic categories are fuzzy. He likened anxiety to a stomach ache – a symptom, not a distinct syndrome.

Stomach aches can have all sorts of causes, and we treat them differently based on those causes. If we didn't, only some sufferers would get better – and some might get worse. In the same way, your anxiety might look like mine, it might have a similar impact on your life, but it might arise from a different source. Take unhelpful thoughts – what the literature calls 'maladaptive cognitions'. One such thought would be about trusting your future self to make good choices, and trusting in your ability to carry those choices out. If you don't trust yourself not to walk out in front of a car later on, it's rational to stay indoors now.

But there's another type of maladaptive cognition where it's not that you don't trust yourself. It's that you don't trust the world. *I could do everything right, but if cars drive up on the sidewalk, it doesn't matter – I'm still going to get run over.* Why go on that first date if you believe people are basically fickle and exploitative? Why stop smoking if you think society might collapse in the next five years?

These beliefs don't arise out of nowhere. When I spoke to Dr Katherine Button, psychologist at the University of Bath, she reminded me that a lot of these 'negative schemas' are formed by real experiences: 'Sometimes people are having genuine adverse reactions to properly shit stuff that's happened.'

We build models of the world – sometimes over years – with rules that become deeply ingrained.

'If you grew up in an environment where you're told the world is your oyster,' she said, '[and] you have nothing but supportive love, you'd expect the world to be this wonderful place where as long as you put your mind to something, you can achieve. If your experiences very early on have been very different – you've learned the world is a hostile place, no one really cares, you have no control over events, you have no idea how your parents are going to act because it doesn't seem contingent on your behaviour – then your schema that you're working with throughout your life is going to be one of hostility.'

The assumptions underlying our schema affect how we process

information moment by moment. It becomes a lens through which we interpret both our environment and our internal experience – physiological symptoms like raised heart rate, sweating, etc. – and it also affects *what* we pay attention to. When you arrive at a party, for example, are you casting round for opportunities, or threats? (The way we talk about anxiety, you could be forgiven for thinking sufferers live thrilling lives of turning down endless party invitations while fleeing packs of sabre-toothed tigers.)

I told Kate that often, in shops, I find it very stressful if I notice another customer making a complaint. My attention gets completely absorbed by the interaction to the exclusion of all else and my heart begins to race – even though it has nothing to do with me.

'Is it that you desperately want social situations to run well?'

'Yes,' I said, already breathless just thinking about it.

Kate suggested I might have developed a schema where I'm hyper-vigilant for signs that social situations are about to fall apart. She said if someone is bullied at school, it can have a big impact on their sense of social competence and anxiety in social situations. 'So that then becomes a sensory prism through which all information is processed.'

We're better at noticing things we decide are important. For anxious people, those things are cues linked to threats, either external ones like angry or worried faces, raised voices or dogs, or internal sensations like sweaty palms or tightened lungs, which might signal the onset of a panic attack. Cues can be explicit (a sign that says 'WARNING: WILD BEARS IN THIS AREA') or implicit (dense woods, poop of indeterminate provenance), and these can help us narrow our perception to filter for particular stimuli.[5] This biases our whole view of the world, so fear-inducing stimuli become more salient. They 'pop'.

Since anxious people notice threats more readily, we tend to over-estimate their frequency. Our sense that the world is a threatening place is reinforced.

Like Nathaniel, Kate is interested in fundamental models we

develop about ourselves and the world. Much of her research focuses on how we learn, and how we update our beliefs.

'As I'm talking to you, or talking to anyone, I have this sort of ongoing working hypothesis or model about how this conversation is going.' If someone's smiling, we might conclude it's going well. If they look bored, we might think, *Shit, it's going south.* We continually update that evaluation based on facial cues, and how the other person responds to our questions.

'My research has been interested in whether or not there might be differences given the same objective information on how I update that inference.' Do anxious people interpret the same information differently to calmer people? Might an anxious person take a neutral expression as a sign the other person is bored, where someone else would completely ignore it or see it as a minor blip in the flow?

To test this, Kate and her colleagues developed something called the social evaluation learning task. It's a very stripped down, bare-bones model of a social situation entirely mediated through text on a computer. Kate admitted it might sound 'a bit artificial' but asked that I bear with her as she explained how it worked.

Word pairs appear on the screen. One has a positive connotation and the other a negative. So perhaps you see the words 'Nice Horrible'. The instructions are: Work out what this imaginary persona thinks about you by selecting the word out of the pair which fits how they view you. Obviously in the first instance, with no information to go from, this is a pure guess.

Next, you get told whether you were correct or not. Then you're presented with another pair of adjectives, say 'Charming Tactless', and you guess again. You have to work out, over repeated trials, whether that person likes you or not. 'You might choose a positive word the first time, get told that's correct. Maybe the second time you choose a positive one and you're told that's not correct, so now you're not so sure. If the positive words are scored correctly 80 per cent of the time, you can guess the computer likes you. If the negative attributes score correctly say 70 per cent of the time, you can guess the computer doesn't like you.'

There's no human behind these word pairs, no body language to interpret, no history of interactions or social context to take into account. Like the BART, it's not a terrific diagnostic tool at the individual level (and was never designed to be). But at a group level, the results are fascinating.

'People with low anxiety and depression make hardly any errors learning that the computer likes them,' said Kate. 'It's almost like they just assume people will like them, and then that's never discon-firmed because they don't get feedback. But they're terrible – and I mean *absolutely terrible* – at learning when the computer dislikes them. It's like they can't quite learn or admit that the evidence shows the computer just doesn't like them.'

This information has been tricky for Kate to reconcile with the traditional model of cognitive behavioural therapy which posits that anxious and depressed people are negatively biased and hypersensi-tive to threat.

'CBT's all about being realistic, right? But what's coming out in my research and some others' is that sometimes people who are low in symptoms seem to be overly optimistic. In our study, as social anxiety levels increased people became more balanced in learning negative and positive evaluations.'

Normal and socially anxious people were equally good at figuring out that a computer persona liked them, but socially anxious people were better at recognising when the persona *dis*liked them. This is terrifying news for the socially anxious – apparent confirmation that relaxing makes you oblivious to the many ways in which you're pissing others off.

Kate said she's used this task over ten years in about eight studies,[6] and it's a really robust effect. She spent a while wondering why being less aware of negative cues might be indicative of better mental health – why a bit of positive bias might be adaptive.

To answer this, consider what the task leaves out. Real social interactions are a feedback loop. We're constantly making evaluations, *while simultaneously being evaluated.* Our judgements on how well the chat is going inform how we act. Those actions – our speech, our tone, our body language – are in turn being evaluated by the person we're talking to, whose subsequent actions are informed by their interpretation.

As in Nathaniel's computational models, tiny biases lead to altered conclusions lead to altered behaviour which changes the material reality.

'When you get sensitive,' said Kate, 'or when someone gets defensive – I've seen this in interviews – things can get awkward and go into a downward spiral.' Your assumption that you're boring the other person – or that they're hostile – changes how you act. If you feel worse, you're less likely to be open, authentic. They may interpret your anxiety as evidence that *you* don't like *them*.

Traditional CBT might seek to challenge thoughts like, *This conversation isn't going well* or, *This person doesn't like me* by asking: What evidence do I have for that? and dismantling the logic of negative interpretations point by point. By contrast, a third-wave therapy like metacognitive therapy might ask: What am I hoping to accomplish by monitoring whether this person likes me?

Kate thought that it wasn't always useful to be hypersensitive to signs of mild irritation. 'If you ignore it for a bit, you'll probably win them round.'

Even if someone does seem annoyed or bored, it's a leap to attribute those cues to permanent negative evaluations they've made of me, rather than temporary states they're feeling. Maybe they've had a tricky day. Maybe they're feeling tired or grumpy.

Some environments teach us to watch closely for clues that someone is annoyed: 'If your father was an alcoholic and there was some volatility in the way he might respond to you, you might be much more sensitive to those early warning signs.' Noticing when you're trying the old man's patience might mean the difference between an uneventful evening and a beating. A glare, or even a conspicuous silence, might have been your equivalent of a sign that says 'WARNING: WILD BEARS'.

These habits are tough to unlearn because – as we've seen – they bias how we perceive the world. Our brain may restructure itself to accommodate them. The incredible human capacity to adapt to our environment becomes a curse when we spend too long in an environment that is pathological.

If you grow up in bear country, learning to watch out for bears is smart. But it's a hard habit to break.

———

One of the most famous experiments on delayed gratification is the so-called 'marshmallow test'. You put a marshmallow in front of a child and tell them: Wait fifteen minutes before eating it and you can have a second one. Then you leave them alone, and observe.

Stanford psychologist Walter Mischel began a series of these tests in the 1970s. In 1990, Mischel, along with fellow psychologists Yuichi Shoda and Philip Peake, published a follow-up study claiming that the length of time young children were able to hold off from eating the marshmallow was a significant predictor of their intelligence, academic performance and ability to cope with stress and frustration as a teenager.[7] A later study even claimed that a child's performance correlated with their weight thirty years later, concluding: 'Each additional minute a preschooler delayed gratification predicted a 0.2 point reduction in BMI [Body Mass Index] in adulthood.'[8]

The study seemed to have a simple message: children able to sacrifice short-term pleasure for long-term gain do better in life. It was immediately seized upon as proof that what really matters is that old-fashioned notion of 'character'. Self-discipline and obedience today were rewarded by success, good health and financial prosperity tomorrow. Children who did well had, by implication, earned their place at the top.

The findings seemed so neat that most commentators ignored the authors' own warnings that the small sample of fewer than ninety children – all from a single preschool on the Stanford University campus – 'could very well exaggerate the magnitude of the true association' between the time delay and how children did later in life.

In 2018, psychologist Tyler Watts from New York University, along with Greg Duncan and Haonan Quan, attempted to replicate the original studies, focusing this time on a much larger and more diverse sample of children.[9] They found that – just as the original researchers had warned – the effect was much smaller than originally claimed, and when they controlled for things like a child's household income and social background, many of the correlations disappeared completely.

It turns out the marshmallow test may not be a test of self-control or character at all, but of a child's beliefs about the world. If you grow up in a household where money is scarce, where the food budget changes week to week, maybe where adults work long hours and can't always make good on promises, a treat left on the table today might not be there tomorrow. How reliable, in this child's experience, are unfamiliar adults like the researcher promising a second marsh-mallow? Taking a guaranteed marshmallow now rather than gambling it for a second one can be a perfectly rational choice – one that doesn't represent a mistrust in your own ability to act well later on, but in the reliability of future rewards. Walter Mischel himself acknowledged this – if the child doubts the stranger's promise, it's no longer a test of self-control, but one of trust.[10]

Guess what? Children who grow up in poverty or care or with absent parents or who are otherwise betrayed by a caregiver might have good reason to trust their own intuition over the assurances of an unfamiliar authority figure. Given the experiments we've seen so far, it's wise to be sceptical. Researchers use deception *all the fucking time*. As psychologist Nicholas Walsh warned me (his tongue firmly in his cheek): 'Don't trust psychologists.'

And now, because of dozens of bell-ends summarising the marshmallow experiment in their TED Talks or articles or bestselling books aimed at competitive middle-class parents, we blame disadvantaged kids for their struggles as adults, their worse-paid jobs, their increased risk of diabetes and incarceration, while lauding the privileged for wealth and status that must, perforce, have arisen from character. Structural inequality, chronically underfunded support services and systemic racism are all off the hook. It's Lerner's 'Just-World' hypothesis again.

Choosing one marshmallow now instead of gambling for two is like pumping the balloon a couple of times before cashing in. Those kids aren't greedy. They are anxious.

———

If you grow up learning the world is unpredictable or dangerous, you might act identically to someone who believes they are useless or unreliable. You might shy away from trying new things. You might give up easily. You might see threats in uncertain situations. But the core beliefs you and the person with low self-efficacy need to challenge are different. (Of course, it is perfectly possible to believe both propositions at once. I certainly have. They come down to the same conviction: I lack the skills to meet the challenges of my environment.)

We become like Joshua the supercomputer, gaming out infinite doomed futures. Every decision ends in apocalypse. We decide the only winning move is not to play.

'One of the things that's wrong with psychiatry,' Nathaniel told me, 'and one of the reasons drugs are less efficacious than they could be, one of the reasons we haven't been able to figure out biological or genetic bases, is that if you just gather up a bunch of people who are labelled with generalised anxiety disorder or major depressive disorder, that's a heterogeneous group. There are subtypes there that can't be appreciated on the basis of asking you a bunch of questions.'

In the DSM, you can get a diagnosis of a condition like generalised anxiety disorder or major depressive disorder by having a certain number of symptoms from a larger list (three of six in GAD, five of nine in depression). This means many different versions of these conditions exist, and – in the case of GAD – two people could share a diagnosis but share no symptoms. (Not to mention that the DSM-5 and ICD-11 criteria for GAD are subtly distinct, so you could have GAD on one side of the Atlantic and not on the other – on top of which, US psychiatrists diagnose using the DSM but *bill* using the ICD.)

'We're trying to understand diseases that aren't defined properly. It's not just that anxiety is several different things – GAD may have several different subtypes – but it's also that generalised anxiety disorder and depression have a huge overlap. The same patients might show up and get diagnosed with one or the other. I've heard over the lifetime, there's something like a ninety per cent comorbidity.'

It's not just the boundary between anxiety and depression that's blurred. One study found that, for people who meet the criteria for one mental health disorder in their lifetime, 66 per cent meet criteria for a second; of those, 53 per cent meet criteria for a third, and of those, 41 per cent meet criteria for a fourth.[11] I'm not suggesting that – as the iconoclastic psychiatrist Thomas Szasz put it – mental illness is a myth. Just that our definitions undergo constant refinement.

———

When Nathaniel was explaining the challenges of creating AI that can learn and adapt, one observation struck me with particular force. 'The problem is,' he said, 'you're trying to design a robot to act reasonably while in the act of learning. Because while it's acting, it's also gathering data.'

This is, of course, true of us.

Whenever we do something, we're actually doing two things: we're performing the behaviour, and we're surreptitiously gathering data on the results of that behaviour. Our predictions about the world are based on the results of our previous choices.

'Not leaving your house is a rational choice if you believe you're going to die in traffic,' said Nathaniel. 'The whole story is a rational story conditioned on one localised misbelief. That's part of what's cool about the mathematics of sequential decision problems. Everything is tied to everything else. So localised changes can have vast effects.'

In Nathaniel's model, the disadvantages of an anxious or pessimistic style are twofold: firstly, we're less likely to work towards long-term rewards because we're not confident we'll make good choices later on (or we think the world is so horrible that our efforts are likely to be negated). But secondly – *and this is the killer* – because we're no longer attempting those longer chains of complex behaviours, we're not gathering data on what happens when we do. Our dataset is increasingly limited. We're not updating our information on the probability of certain results because we're not making those choices and testing those assumptions. Our model of reality becomes a caricature, restricted to the confines of our routine.

If you stay indoors because you're scared of being run over, you don't get to go outside and have the disconfirmatory experience of not getting run over. But you *do* experience being indoors and being safe. Gradually, your whole model of the world skews around a lopsided set of behaviours. This involves a familiar cognitive bias – the availability heuristic. You can bring to mind a hundred times when you stayed indoors and nothing terrible happened. Examples when you went out and had a good experience don't come so readily because you rarely do it.

Since doing a behaviour is also how we gather data, if you stop doing a behaviour, you stop updating your model. You bias the dataset. When it comes to putting your hand on a hot stove, this is appropriate. You don't need to keep testing every day to check it still hurts.

But for more complex risks, or evaluations about maximising rewards, it's disastrous. If the sequential evaluation model is accurate, it's easy to see how a few tiny misbeliefs, a little distortion here or there, can quickly mess up your whole perception of the world.

We're in a constant conversation with reality.

All of this felt really exciting to me. Like Nathaniel, I'm the sort of nerd who can describe 'the mathematics of sequential decision problems' as 'cool' with a straight face. I'm far more comfortable handling my anguish with the oven gloves of progamming jargon. All the algebra and diagrams of bifurcating decision trees reminded me of tapping BASIC commands into my rubber-keyed ZX Spectrum in the early nineties. Models like this made anxiety and panic feel knowable. Things you could assign numerical values to, plot and predict.

But a theory is not a solution. It's all very well creating a three-hour PowerPoint presentation on precisely when and how seagulls keep breaking into your bedroom and shitting all over the duvet, but it's not much use unless it helps you come up with a plan for stopping them. When I asked Nathaniel how all of this might help me beat my anxiety, he faltered.

'You would want to experience getting close to the thing that you're wanting to avoid. And hopefully that would help you learn – help your brain learn.' He paused. 'But that's not good enough. Even if I find out I can cross the street, if the consequences of that thinking have infected my models of the world everywhere, I've got to live my life in the world to relearn all of it. Another thing your brain does to solve these long sequential decision problems is it stores the answer to that question everywhere – and so even if you correct the misbelief, all of its consequences might still be there.'

In other words, having a feared situation go better than predicted doesn't magically erase the anxiety in one swipe. Some of the reasons for this may be, as Nathaniel hypothesises, neurobiological in nature – parts of our brain storing expectancies, as we saw with fear conditioning in the amygdala and hippocampus. But some might also stem from higher order, 'top-down' thinking.

So you do the presentation at work and it goes okay. You aren't horribly humiliated. Surely that constitutes a substantial positive reward prediction error? If a key purpose of this dopaminergic response is to drive learning, shouldn't our encounters with reality cure anxiety naturally?

'It seems like it should be almost a self-correcting problem,' said Nathaniel. 'A recurring puzzle in trying to understand depression and anxiety is, if you think they correspond to some mistaken or pessimistic belief of some sort, why don't people just unlearn it from experience and get better?'

Why not indeed.

One study – co-authored by Camilla Nord – suggests that the degree to which we learn from experience changes depending on our environment. In a stable environment, we're more likely to rely on past experience, but in a volatile environment, we're quicker to update our beliefs. The authors propose a modulatory role for the hormone and neurotransmitter noradrenaline. By studying participants' pupil size and blood pressure while they completed a learning task, researchers found that blocking noradrenaline with the beta blocker propranolol reduced the effect of prediction errors on pupil size – particularly in people who were feeling anxious. They speculated that, in stable environments, we may produce less noradrenaline and thus update our beliefs about the world more slowly. In more volatile, arousing environments, producing more noradrenaline helps us learn new rules and associations faster.[12] Other research has suggested noradrenaline plays an important role in memory – the amount of noradrenaline released in the amygdala predicts how well a rat will learn to avoid a nasty stimulus, like getting its tail pinched.[13] Noradrenaline appears to increase synaptic plasticity, boosting learning. Trials suggest that SNRIs like venlafaxine – which increase the availability of noradrenaline in the brain alongside serotonin – often help ease symptoms of generalised anxiety disorder.[14]

Part of the answer to Nathaniel's conundrum is aversive pruning. When we're anxious, we avoid situations we think will go poorly, so we don't have the disconfirming experience to learn from. Another answer, suggested by Camilla's work, is that when life feels routine, predictable, safe – when we're in a 'stable environment' – we're less neurobiologically primed to update our beliefs. New connections are less likely to form. Taking propranolol might reduce your anxiety in the moment, but if, for example, you took it before giving a speech, it might also reduce your ability to learn that public speaking isn't that bad.

This felt like the inkling of an important truth. Safety – the feeling I craved – might be the very thing keeping me trapped. 'Step out of your comfort zone' had always come off like trite, hackneyed advice, but now it seemed like it might be based in sound science.

But what would stepping out of my comfort zone look like? Had I been playing it too safe? Did I need to take more risks?

A chance comment by Camilla gave me my answer. One that would take me on a journey involving ancient mushroom gods, freezing water and people locked in cupboards.

XIII.

SAFETY

*How we perpetuate our fear, and the
extreme-exposure therapies that conquer it*

'Lisa.'

My wife glanced up from her laptop. I was standing in the doorway, tugging at my hair.

'Sorry,' I said, 'I was just, uh, wondering if you could reassure me because I'm feeling really panicky.'

'You'll be fine.'

I clutched a fistful of my hair and took a deep breath. 'I feel really panicky.' My chest felt tight.

'Go and have a meditate,' she said. She seemed irritated. I'd been short with her earlier – I had been feeling stressed about my writing – and I was worried she was still upset.

'Can you just tell me some reassuring things, please? I'm feeling really worried.'

'I'm just in the middle of something.'

Oh God. She was definitely irritated.

'Please,' I said, stepping from foot to foot, 'I just need some help.' I wrung my hands. 'I can't . . . I feel weird. I feel dizzy. My head's spinning.' As I spoke, I really was beginning to feel lightheaded. My words felt as if they were running away from me. I didn't feel in control of myself.

'Just go and have a meditate.'

'I just . . . I'm not feeling okay. I need some help. I'm really in trouble now and I need your help just for a minute, just to help me calm down.'

'I can't help you,' she said. 'Anything I say just makes you worse.'

'Please! I can tell you're annoyed. It's m-making me w-w-worse.' My stammer had kicked in. I really was getting anxious. 'Just say something nice. Something kind.'

'Everything's all right.'

'You sound annoyed!'

She sighed. 'I *am* annoyed. Just go away and calm yourself down. I can't help you.'

'Please!' I was clutching my head. I felt frozen in the doorway. 'I just . . . I just . . .' I had begun gabbling, repeating the same short phrases over and over. The words didn't feel like they were coming from me any more. I knew I was only making things worse. I couldn't imagine that begging her to try to placate me was going to de-escalate the situation but I didn't feel like I was in control. I couldn't breathe. I clutched at my windpipe. I couldn't hear what she was saying.

I knew, of course, that the healthy thing would be to do as she requested. To back away, to give us both space. To take myself off to a quiet room to calm down, normalise my breathing, and listen to the thoughts caroming round my skull without acting on them. To offer *myself* compassion rather than demanding it from others.

But something in me craved reassurance. If she'd only swaddle me in cooing maternal indulgence, if she would only hug me and tell me 'It's all right, I could never be annoyed with you, I love you, nothing's gone wrong, shh, shh,' finally I'd be able to power down the klaxons wailing in my head and heart. I'd be able to exhale.

I'd be safe.

———

Imagine an experiment where participants sit in front of a screen on which different coloured squares appear in turn: blue, yellow and green. Every time a blue square appears, after an interval of ten seconds they receive an electric shock.

After a while, just the sight of the blue square is enough to give them a little jolt of anxiety – their heart rate goes up, their skin becomes sweatier.

Next they're split into two groups. One group sees the blue square again and again, this time with no shock. The next group are given a button and told if they press it when they see the blue square, they won't get a shock. Guess what happens?

At the end of the experiment, the second group – the ones who could press a button – still feel that 'zap' of anxiety when they see the blue square. They haven't unlearned the association between the event and the bad thing happening because they believe their behaviour is stopping it.

And here's the kicker: the button isn't wired to anything. If they'd just sat there, they wouldn't have got a shock either.

On the other hand, the first group – who weren't given a button, who simply had to face the anxiety without reacting – no longer feel anxious when the blue square appears.

This is an only slightly simplified version of an experiment conducted in the late 2000s by psychologist Peter Lovibond at the University of New South Wales,[1] demonstrating one of the trickiest confounders when it comes to beating anxiety – safety behaviours.

Safety behaviours are little things we do to try to control our physical symptoms of anxiety, or to keep imagined dangers at bay. They range from the apparently rational, or at least logical – like texting a friend for reassurance, sitting near the exit in case you feel the need to escape, or taking a beta blocker or benzodiazepine – to the deeply superstitious – carrying a lucky talisman or holding your breath while climbing a flight of stairs so something 'bad' doesn't happen to you.

The problem is, while safety behaviours reduce anxiety in the moment, in the long-term they maintain and even strengthen it.

One study looked at people who had refused MRI scans due to claustrophobia. (Having an MRI scan feels like being inserted into a massive noisy futuristic doughnut.) Participants were given exposure therapy that involved lying down inside a black foam-padded box (a coffin in all but name) with the lid shut. Before they went in, they were given a pill and told it was a new medication called adomoxin.

After the exposure therapy, one group watched a video explaining that adomoxin's side effects included 'anxiety, tremors, shakiness, breathlessness, and sweating', so it would have made the exposure therapy much more difficult. A second group was told side effects included 'sedation, relaxation, and sleepiness' and that it would have made their exposure in the box 'much easier'. A third group were told the truth – the pill was not the fictitious medication adomoxin, but a placebo (250mg of vitamin C).

All three groups showed significant reductions in claustrophobic fear immediately after the exposure therapy. But a week later, participants who believed they had taken a sedating pill that made the exposure easier showed a 'markedly higher return of fear' than the other two groups. In fact, they were indistinguishable from a control group who had received no therapy at all.[2]

Many anxious people take the physical and emotional experience of anxiety as evidence they're in danger.[3] When they resort to a safety behaviour, their anxiety drops a little, and it *feels* like they just warded off a threat. You expected punishment or harm, you took action, and the expected harm did not come to pass. Instead of learning that your prediction was faulty and updating your model of the world accordingly, you conclude at a conscious and unconscious level that danger was averted thanks to your vigilance.

In debate this is known as the 'post hoc fallacy', from the phrase *Post hoc ergo propter hoc*, 'After this, therefore because of this'. You put in your special noise-cancelling earphones before you got on the bus and played soothing affirmations for the whole journey. You didn't have a panic attack. Therefore your headphones and affirmations prevented your panic attack.

The literature calls this a 'misattribution of safety'. We credit the behaviour for keeping us safe instead of updating our mental schema of the world, or our beliefs about our own resilience.

A follow-up to Peter Lovibond's study found that safety behaviours may do more than just maintain existing anxieties – they may have the potential to create new ones. Researchers at Utrecht University conditioned participants to expect a shock a few seconds after a particular-coloured shape appeared on the screen, then let them press a button to prevent that shock. Then they were given the opportunity to press the button in response to a different shape. If they did so, after a few rounds they became anxious when they saw that shape too, even though it had *never* been followed by a shock. They believed – erroneously – that their button-press was preventing a shock, and generalised their learned fear from one context to another.[4]

From an evolutionary perspective, this kind of fear generalisation is useful. It allows us to build a model of the world and make predictions. We are wired to make the most of negative experiences – to minimise the damage necessary for learning. With each aversive experience, we formulate a new rule. The world becomes a little less uncertain.

In some contexts, safety behaviours may serve a secondary purpose of sparing us the discomfort of disconfirmation. In the 1950s, psychologist Leon Festinger theorised that when we receive information that contradicts something we believe in, we experience psychological discomfort – what he called 'cognitive dissonance'.[5] We're motivated to resolve that conflict, and often the easiest way is to dismiss the disconfirming evidence as a one-off, a fluke, an aberration, or otherwise unrepresentative of how the world works. Accepting that our predictions of danger are wrong means accepting that our model of the world is flawed, which means accepting increased uncertainty. Bizarre as it sounds, sometimes we'd rather believe our predictions of doom than relinquish the comforting illusion that we can see the future.

If anxiety is about intolerance of uncertainty, you can see why it's so hard to shift. The more we cling to certainty, the less amenable we are to the benign doubt that leads to change.

———

When I was seven or eight, I would hear a whisper in my head saying I had to do certain things or I would go to hell. The voice mostly sounded like mine, whispering yet somehow very loud. It said things like, 'May I be damned unless . . .' and then it would tell me I had to get to the stone pillar at the end of my grandparents' drive and touch it without taking a breath, or climb the stairs two at a time without slipping.

I knew it was me thinking these things to myself, even though they frightened me, even though I didn't want to think them. Eternal damnation was forever one reckless thought away. My only defence was to obey.

May I be damned unless I touch the skirting board with my forehead. I wasn't sure I'd go to hell if I didn't, but why take that risk? (I went to a Christian school but I wasn't brought up in an especially religious household, nor do I recall anyone bombarding me with dire, brimstone-tinged warnings of fiery judgement if I didn't perform weird rituals in penance; it was a theology I spontaneously invented.)

Until recently, obsessive-compulsive disorder was classified as an anxiety disorder. The DSM-5 created a distinct category, but OCD and things like generalised anxiety disorder and panic disorder often come in pairs – if you have one during your life it's not uncommon to have the other.[6] In childhood-onset OCD, children often hear an inner voice ordering them to perform certain rituals – like touching particular objects, moving in a specific way – and are more likely than adults to have obsessions around religion or death.[7]

I doubt I ever met the criteria for full-blown OCD. I suspect a lot of anxious children experience relatively mild, subclinical symptoms that never get picked up. I never told anyone. The religious terror faded as I grew older, and the rituals became such a part of life I hardly noticed.

People often talk about OCD colloquially as if it just means fussiness or a preference for symmetry: *Oh, I have to fold all the napkins into swans when we have guests round, I'm a bit OCD.* OCD sufferers and clinicians have – rightly – protested the condition's reduction to a jokey personality quirk.

But an important truth has been lost in the pushback. Diagnostic categories have tricked us into thinking mental illness is a light switch that's either flicked on or off.

None of the rituals I did – or still do – were self-conscious bits of whimsy or funny quirks. They were dead serious to me, so obvious as 'rules' that I was rarely conscious of why I was doing them. If someone or something stopped my following them, I'd often feel very distressed, without being able to articulate why. Those moments were the closest I'd get to realising: *This is crazy.* These behaviours were more than a preference. They felt like a *need*.

OCD, PTSD, GAD, social anxiety disorder and even panic disorder might be better thought of as spectrum disorders. Rather than being a binary 'you either have it or you don't' condition – or even a 'you either are it or you aren't' identity – they're more like sliders on a mixing deck. Not only that, but symptoms can be high one day and low the next. They can rise in different combinations. What we think of as static traits might also be transient states. Human consciousness is far more varied, far more personal, far more gorgeously *weird*, than these diagnostic labels suggest.

Even something that seems unambiguously associated with mental illness, like hearing voices, is pretty common. Estimates vary, but different sources suggest between 5 and 15 per cent of people experience auditory hallucinations at some point in their lives. One survey found that 7.3 per cent of respondents had heard voices, but of those only 16 per cent had sought professional help.[8]

My late grandfather heard a voice just before he underwent a life-threatening operation for throat cancer – an operation that, ironically, would claim his own voice. The voice quoted Ruth's reassurance to her mother-in-law Naomi in the Bible: 'Whither thou goest, I will go.' In that moment, he felt a profound feeling of peace, and the experience remained a comfort to him for the rest of his life. Hearing voices isn't intrinsically pathological.

Nor is performing some comforting ritual to assuage anxiety. Sometimes it's adaptive. Maybe you're stressed about a big exam, so before you step into the hall you give yourself a squirt of Rescue Remedy to calm your nerves. No matter that Rescue Remedy is about as well-evidenced an anxiolytic as a cheese toastie. Even open-label placebos – that is, inert sugar pills, given to people who know they're just sugar pills – seem to significantly reduce test anxiety and improve self-management skills.[9] That little dose of comforting nonsense prior to starting calms you down, and so you perform better.

Some psychologists even argue that safety behaviours – used wisely – can help in the early stages of exposure therapy, by getting patients to begin the process of confronting their fears.[10]

Still, each time you delay that confrontation, it's like you're taking out a loan. Debt accrues.

Sooner or later, you're going to have to pay.

———

'There's something that took me a long time to understand about exposing yourself to something you're afraid of,' Dr Dawn Huebner told me. She's an author and parent coach, specialising in childhood anxiety.

I'd been thinking a lot about my childhood, and my early attempts at coping with fear. I'd come to her for advice on how anxiety begins and takes root in kids.

She said she used to think of exposure and desensitisation as being about getting used to the thing you're afraid of. So if you're afraid of dogs, you need to repeatedly experience being near dogs. If you're afraid of mistakes, you need to repeatedly experience making mistakes.

'But there's a second thing you're exposing yourself to when you're doing those challenges. You're exposing yourself to your fear. You're exposing yourself to your discomfort.'

Anxiety is all about avoiding harm, and discomfort is its early warning system. From anxiety's perspective, the less tolerant we are of discomfort – and the earlier we feel it – the more sensitive we are to potential danger, and the better that early warning system is working. When we try to beat anxiety by taking action to reduce discomfort, we're playing anxiety's game.

Dawn said the successful treatment of anxiety is about learning to tolerate it.

How afraid we are of the symptoms of anxiety – the physical sensations, the associated thoughts, and possibly having others notice we're anxious – is called 'anxiety sensitivity'. Plenty of research suggests this 'fear of fear' creates a brutal feedback loop. Across a range of anxiety disorders, anxiety sensitivity correlates with severity of symptoms.[11]

'Long ago, obsessive-compulsive disorder used to be called "the Doubting Disease"', said Dawn, 'because it's really all about the inability to tolerate doubt or uncertainty. The more people seek certainty, the more caught they are.' As you learn to tolerate uncertainty, anxiety goes down. 'But the going down happens second.'

She gave the example of a child who has separation issues and worries their parent isn't going to be there at the end of the school day to pick them up. The child wants repeated reassurance, but the more the parent provides it, the more the anxiety gets locked into place.

'The thing that anxiety feeds on is doubt. The worrisome situation is the *possibility* of the parent being late. I think what you need to be exposed to is that uncertainty. The possibility of the parent being late. The possibility of a bad thing. Not the actual bad thing.'

Once, Lisa and I hit traffic on our way to a wedding. We felt really stressed up to the point when it became clear we weren't going to make it. Suddenly, we relaxed. Actually *being* late wasn't that unpleasant. It was the uncertainty that we *might be* that caused our anxiety.

Dawn told me parents often unintentionally collude in safety behaviours, accommodating their children's worries and making them grow in the long run. 'It always comes from a well-meaning place. Part of our hardwiring as mammals is that children, when they're distressed, are going to signal distress. And we as parents are wired to respond.'

Yale psychologist Eli Lebowitz has created a model for a programme for anxious children that's focused exclusively on treating the parents. The child never sets foot in the therapist's office, the whole thing is done with the parents, yet research suggests it's as effective as treating the child directly.[12]

When I was growing up my parents were always quick to comfort and protect me. They still are. If they saw me getting frustrated or upset they'd step in to relieve my distress. It would be churlish to complain that I was cursed with parents who were too caring – imagine! But from what Dawn was saying, I wondered if my parents and I had, together, developed some habits that no longer served me. Sometimes, she said, as parents, we feel like we're protecting our child from danger, when actually we're just protecting them from their experience of fear.

Dawn experienced this first-hand when her son Eli developed anxieties around things like splinters, haircuts and bees. At first she helped him avoid places that made him feel uncomfortable. But his anxieties grew worse, until he was afraid to touch wood or even go outside. Eventually she and her husband staged an intervention – a bribe. Go outside, they said, and you can have $30 for Lego if you get stung by a bee.

He ended up getting stung within five minutes. Dawn has said she would do things differently if she tried it again, but ultimately Eli got over his fear of sharp objects enough to take up fencing.

It might be a cliché to say our fear of something is often worse than the thing itself, but it points to a powerful truth. We're often so hypnotised by our physical experience of anxiety, and the messages we're telling ourselves in the moment, that we can't see the object of our fear – the dog, the spider, the disapproval of others – for what it actually is. When we can't tolerate fear, *fear itself* becomes a form of Pavlovian conditioning – the equivalent of a nasty electric shock every time the stimulus appears.

Dawn told me children need to learn how to cope with their anxiety, rather than be protected from it. 'It's an uncomfortable feeling but it's not dangerous in any way. Being afraid is not the same as being in danger.'

She admitted that sometimes, when a kid comes to see her and says, 'I did such-and-such a challenge and I didn't even feel afraid,' part of her thinks *darn it*, 'because it wasn't a big enough challenge and I want them to be afraid'. The aim isn't not to feel fear, it's to change your relationship to fear. 'With anxiety, the more you get caught up in the content, the more you're in the weeds,' she said. 'It's the process of anxiety that's the important piece. Learning to change that is what frees people.'

———

No one is saying this is easy.

Threat circuits have been conserved over millions of years of evolution because they keep creatures alive. It's adaptive that fear feels unpleasant – its aversiveness is what compels a creature to act. To sit with fear, to feel it without reacting, is to go against a fundamental impulse that governs all living creatures. Protect yourself. Be safe.

When I tried to override my desire for reassurance, I didn't feel like I was wisely increasing my tolerance of anxiety. I felt like I was risking divorce. Abandonment. The collapse of my life.

My head said, *Cool it, wait, this is an opportunity to get comfortable with your feelings.*

My heart said, *Jesus Christ, Tim, we have to fix this now!*

And then my head would be like, *What if your heart's right? I mean, she did seem annoyed, and you are quite a lot to handle. Why wouldn't she be getting sick of your shit? Maybe this is a make-or-break moment. You never know.*

Like Joe LeDoux had told me in so many words, it's pretty easy to build a scaffold of rationalisations to gloss whatever horseshit your emotions are trying to sell you as fact.

The more I learned about safety behaviours, the more I felt like I was on the trail of something big. Camilla Nord at Cambridge University mentioned something which turned my interest to obsession.

She said one of the big success stories in psychology is treating panic. As a teenager, she had experienced panic attacks. She said if she were still having them she would seek out an expert in exposure therapy. 'I know a researcher in Oxford who has invented a one-day intervention for people with claustrophobia. It sounds terrible. You're locked in a closet and you cannot be let out. But it works.'

I had to speak to her. Camilla gave me her name – Dr Andrea Reinecke at Oxford University. A week later, she agreed to talk.

———

'What I've spent the last few years doing is trying to get to the bottom of what's different in the brain of someone with an anxiety disorder,' Andrea told me. She spoke with a soft German accent, complimented my questions and laughed a lot – not at all the type of person you'd associate with horrifying imprisonment in tiny spaces.

Her early studies in neuroscience taught her that anxiety biases us towards stimuli relevant to our fears, which changes how we experience the world. For example, if you're spider-phobic and 'a spider comes into the room, unluckily you're the one who detects the spider – but that's not coincidental.'

Psychologists sometimes test anxious people's unconscious biases by presenting them with words and pictures related to their fear and measuring their reaction times.[13] For example, a 'faces dot-probe task' briefly shows two faces side by side expressing different emotions – say one neutral, one fearful – then replaces them with a dot. The participant has to press a key indicating whether the dot is on either the left or right of the screen. If they consistently react faster when the dot is on the same side as a face showing fear, this suggests their eyes were already looking that way.[14] Psychologists interpret this as evidence that the person's attention is biased towards fear-related stimuli. They're vigilant for threats, which might be external – like a spider, or an argument kicking off nearby – or internal – like elevated heart rate, or worrisome thoughts.

In Andrea's studies of people with panic disorders and intense phobias, fMRI scans showed a change in activity in 'one brain area that you have probably come across many, many times. It's the amygdala.'

I laughed. *Ah, we meet again, old friend.*

Andrea and her team took two groups – patients with panic disorder and non-clinical volunteers who had never had a panic attack – and showed them images indirectly related to panic and catastrophic expectations that patients with panic disorder experience. 'So for instance often they are afraid of driving because they might have a heart attack and cause an accident, so some of the images we present are of a crushed-up car. There's nothing gory, nothing terrible.' Other images might include intensive-care scenes or funerals.

Participants rated each image out of ten in terms of how scary it was. Andrea's team found no difference between how the two groups rated the images. But when they compared amygdala activation, they found it was 'extremely exaggerated' in patients with panic disorder compared to healthy volunteers. 'In their case the amygdala is telling a story saying this is really dangerous, something's really wrong here, we have to do something.'

Andrea thinks that the amygdala is probably driving behaviour in very anxious people. 'But what often happens in these patients is that they do certain things that make the amygdala more and more sensitive.'

Imagine someone who is afraid of having a heart attack – especially in places where escape is difficult, like on a crowded bus. Maybe next time they're on the bus, they keep checking their heartbeat to make sure it's all right. Since they're anxious, their heart speeds up a bit. They think: *Oh God, is this the heart attack coming?*

'The amygdala signals "do something about this", said Andrea. Maybe they get off at the next stop, even though they're fifteen minutes from their destination. If that's not possible, they may try safety behaviours. 'They might call someone, they might take a tablet, they might open a window, they might take off their jumper or drink a sip of water to feel more hydrated. And all these things help in the moment – and unfortunately it is what is often recommended by doctors: breathe into a bag, have a tablet – but they mean that the brain learns: if I wouldn't have done these things, I would have definitely had that heart attack.'

In the moment, the safety behaviour brings relief. From the threat circuit's perspective, our anxiety has been vindicated – we detected a threat, took action, and had a lucky escape. That feels like a successful behaviour, and the pathways that facilitate it get strengthened. 'So it will trigger even earlier.' It's Hebb's postulate: what fires together, wires together.

'The key to treating anxiety,' Andrea said, 'is to give the person the chance to learn if they wouldn't have done any of those things, it still wouldn't have happened. But that's not what we do. That's not what our brain tells us to do.'

When she came to Oxford, she started out in a pharmacology group. Everyone was looking at how SSRIs treat depression and how they affect the brain. Andrea's background was as a cognitive behavioural psychologist. Her colleagues were sceptical. 'I think my job was to show cognitive behavioural therapy will take much longer than drugs, the changes in the brain will be very minimal and delayed and only after fifteen, twenty sessions will we see something.'

She took part in a study where they gave patients with agoraphobia a small dose of CBT – one session – to show it had no effect on the brain and no effect on cognitive processing. To everyone's surprise, they found that how the brain processes threat information had changed in just twenty-four hours. 'In the treated group there were already people who showed a processing pattern very similar to that of a healthy volunteer.'

Andrea's research has gone on to challenge the assumption that psychological treatments work on a purely 'top-down' basis – changing conscious thought processes before more automatic responses – suggesting that certain therapies may be closer to the effects of medication than previously thought.[15]

Here's what she thinks is happening: 'After one session of CBT, the hypersensitivity in the amygdala has normalised, and then they go into situations like the crowded bus and nothing's happening, so they gain more and more confidence that they can actually do this without safety behaviours, and so their anxiety will drop over time.'

This is in contrast to Joe LeDoux's belief that CBT should come last, after subliminal techniques have been used to 'take out' the amygdala. For Joe, doing CBT first is, at best, suboptimal. Conscious and unconscious processes might use the same circuits and thus compete with each other, making the therapy less effective.

But for Andrea and her fellow researchers, making a therapy faster and making it more effective can be the same thing. Treatments can be costly, hard to access, and many patients drop out before they're complete – especially with exposure therapies, which are very challenging. If a therapy takes one session instead of six, patients who would have waited two months instead get seen in a fortnight. Creating an elaborate structure for optimal fear extinction is all very well when you're dealing with rats, who have no choice but to participate. Humans have limited time, money and hope.

Andrea is not talking about the kind of CBT I've experienced – sitting in a doctor's office while someone talks you through a photocopied worksheet on 'the anxiety cycle'. 'We can't just draw up a pro-and-con list. It has to be a very physical experience to translate into an amygdala change.' You can read about safety behaviours and why they're bad all you want, but the brain responds to lived experience. It's the difference between reading about the physics of electrostatic discharge, and getting struck by lightning.

'This is going to sound really drastic, but it has to be drastic to work.' It's not enough to simply *tell* the anxious person they're not going to die. They have to put themselves in the situation, drop all the safety behaviours, and *experience* not dying for themselves. Anything else – as far as the amygdala is concerned – is hearsay.

Most of Andrea's patients are agoraphobic, which she told me is basically one aspect of claustrophobia. 'They don't like to be in situations where they have to give up control, because if something happens to them, someone has to be able to get to them. They have to be able to get out.'

Andrea asks them to enter a tiny cleaning cupboard. She doesn't tell them how long they'll have to stay in there. It might be minutes. It might be hours. Then she turns off the light and locks the door.

Beforehand, they're warned to resist relying on any sort of safety behaviour – crossing their fingers, whispering rosaries, even reassuring themselves that, 'Oh she's going to come back, she's a nice person, it's probably just another minute.' The idea is to expose themselves to their fear – the thoughts, the physical sensations – in its fullest, purest form. To relinquish control. To willingly face uncertainty.

Unbeknownst to them, their exposure will be relatively short –

fifteen minutes. Andrea chose this time because it's just long enough to experience the fight, flight or freeze response from beginning to end – the initial rise, a peak, then a gradual tailing off as hormone levels normalise. 'So if you don't try to regulate your anxiety, if you just give in, if you let the wave roll over you, after about fifteen minutes your body can't really do it any more and you will just feel relaxed and depleted.' It's not enough to have the intellectual knowledge that staying in the cupboard won't kill you – the amygdala needs to *learn* this through experience, so it no longer signals the hypothalamus to trigger that hormonal cascade.

There are slower forms of exposure therapy, where patients make a list of anxiety-provoking situations – a 'fear hierarchy' – then work through each one in turn. So, if you were afraid of Roy Orbison, you might start by looking at the cover of his 1965 LP *Orbisongs*. In the next session, you might handle a pair of sunglasses. Next, you might listen to the first sixty seconds of *Pretty Woman*, and so on, slowly learning to normalise your response before moving up to the next level of fear.

Andrea's research suggests patients can get relief from their symptoms much faster – in minutes, rather than months. One study treating patients with panic disorder over four sessions of this 'protocol-driven CBT', where patients confront these extreme fear-inducing situations, had a 71 per cent recovery rate (although the authors concede it's not known how long the effects last).[16] Andrea and her colleagues found that, after the sessions, amygdala activation in the former panic patients 'was comparable to that of healthy controls'.

They also found reduced activation in parts of the prefrontal cortex – often explained to non-neuroscientists like me as the bit of the brain responsible for self-control. That's an oversimplification, but as we've learned from tDCS, specific parts of the prefrontal cortex seem to be associated with planning, decision-making, emotional regulation and choosing not to act on our impulses.

Let me repeat that: post-exposure, Andrea and her colleagues found *reduced* activation in the prefrontal cortex. The traditional assumption is that anxiety is a result of under-regulation from the prefrontal cortex. We're unable to slam the brakes on our primal impulses of fear. We fail to override 'lower order' instinctual responses with 'higher order' conscious thought. You might expect that CBT would boost emotional regulation and thus lead to greater prefrontal cortex activation.

There are a few possible explanations: as the authors suggest in a later paper,[17] these specific parts of the prefrontal cortex associated with fear inhibition – the dorsal-medial prefrontal cortex and the left dorsolateral prefrontal cortex (the bit I'd been zapping with tDCS) – might activate less because of 'a diminished need for inhibitory strategies'. If you're not experiencing that surge of adrenaline and cortisol, you don't need self-control to suppress it.

A second possibility made me think of a conversation I had with psychologist Dr Tim Pychyl, head of the Procrastination Research Group at Carleton University, Canada. Tim has devoted over twenty years to studying the 'breakdown in volitional action' we call procrastination. He sees it as highly linked with anxiety. (A recent German study found that procrastinators have, on average, larger amygdalae and different connections to the prefrontal cortex.)[18]

We often think of procrastination as stemming from a lack of self-regulation. But actually, procrastinators are *continually* taking action to regulate their emotions. That's what procrastination is. A strategy for emotional regulation.

We use avoidance to escape uncomfortable feelings, like fear. We step away from the laptop and grab a biscuit. We check social media. We're actually very sensitive to our emotional state and constantly acting to control it. Procrastination isn't about *under*-regulation – it's about *mis*regulation.

Similarly, high activity in the prefrontal cortex doesn't necessarily imply *effective* emotional regulation – as with procrastinators, it may reflect a great deal of inefficient, poorly executed misregulation. Worrying, for example, may be a prefrontally modulated, maladaptive effort to seek emotional relief by finding solutions. Effort doesn't always translate into results, especially if we persist with bad strategies.

Andrea's super-quick anxiety treatments have one more component I haven't mentioned yet. When the patient goes into the cupboard, they're given drugs. It's usually an antibiotic called D-cycloserine. 'On its own it would probably not do anything,' said Andrea. 'It's not even a good antibiotic.' D-cycloserine is primarily used to treat tuberculosis in people who are allergic to more effective medications. 'What happens during the exposure therapy in the cupboard is the patient learns something new. So there are new connections being made between the amygdala and, let's say, the prefrontal cortex, and all those lower-level areas that deliver the stimulus information. And we think that this tablet primes the brain to learn these things better.'

The theory is that D-cycloserine temporarily increases neuroplasticity – the brain's ability to learn new things. By binding with a type of glutamate receptor called NMDA (N-methyl-D-aspartate) receptors, it seems to improve memory and learning. Glutamate is an excitatory neurotransmitter, often thought of as the opposite of the inhibitory, calming GABA. Between them, glutamate and GABA account for more than 90 per cent of all neurotransmission. Glutamate–GABA disharmony is a key part of the neurobiology of anxiety disorders, but it's proven hard to find medications that address this without considerable adverse side-effects – unsurprising given how much work the pair do across the brain.[19] The idea is, when someone goes in the cupboard, a dose of D-cycloserine helps make the lesson really stick.

You may have spotted a potential drawback.

'What happens if someone uses safety behaviours while they're on D-cycloserine?' I asked.

Andrea was impressed I'd thought of that. 'It's a question that took researchers ten years or something.'

I doubt it took a decade to wonder if locking a claustrophobic in a small cupboard while they're on psychoactive medication might carry risks, but I appreciated the compliment.

'That is the big, major issue with D-cycloserine. If the exposure doesn't go well, then it will improve that kind of learning as well.' This is called 'fear reconsolidation'. A 2014 paper about this 'kill or cure' effect is titled 'D-cycloserine for Treating Anxiety Disorders: Making Good Exposures Better and Bad Exposures Worse'.[20]

Some researchers remain unconvinced that D-cycloserine improves learning or fear extinction, pointing to inconsistent results.[21] Andrea thinks this is partially down to the split between good and bad experiences. 'There was a proportion of people in the cupboard who had a good experience, they got better, and there was another proportion of people who didn't have a good experience in the cupboard and they got worse.' When you take an average, it looks like D-cycloserine isn't performing very well, but actually some people got a lot better – it's just that the risks are greater than placebo too.

D-cycloserine has a narrow therapeutic window – i.e. the time when it works best. It reaches peak levels in the blood four to six hours after ingestion, and key learning processes seem to happen – a little counterintuitively – one to two hours *after* the fear exposure, as the brain rewires itself in response to the experience. Timing is crucial. Give the dose too early, and you might reinforce the experience of intense fear. Too late, and you might miss that critical extinction period.

'We're getting more and more away from D-cycloserine after being extremely enthusiastic about it,' Andrea told me. 'Currently we're looking for drugs that might only augment learning in the cupboard if it actually went well.' She said that studies in rodents suggested that losartan, a blood-pressure medication, might augment fear extinction without the risk of enhanced reconsolidation if things go wrong.

I asked whether they had considered transcranial direct current stimulation – tDCS.

'You would be a very good researcher,' she said. 'That is exactly what we're looking into at the moment.'

(One key reason I wouldn't be a very good researcher – aside from my antipathy towards maths, teamwork, intellectual rigour and having to leave my house for work – is that when Andrea said this, my faith in her conclusions went up by about 200 per cent. I like to think of myself as even-handed and hard to fool, but later I would notice that the researchers whose work felt most convincing to me just happened to be the ones who had been friendly and occasionally flattered my ego.)

'We think that people are very different, and for some people D-cycloserine might work really well, for others it's the losartan, for others it's the tDCS. It depends a lot on how their brain works at baseline.' She thought that certain 'settings' of the brain – observable via fMRI – predicted how well people might respond to CBT, drugs or tDCS. Like Ruihua and Camilla, Andrea thought the criteria for each anxiety disorder may disguise many subgroups, with subtly different needs.

I asked Andrea about my own experiences with anxiety – my worry, my avoidance, and my intense panic attacks. I told her how I could get extremely worried that my wife was annoyed at me, and how in the kitchen, if she came up behind me, I sometimes felt an intense, choking fear that froze me in place.

She said if she were me she would try to figure out where my worry that someone was annoyed at me came from. What was so terrible about it? 'And being trapped in that corner of the kitchen, it almost sounds like . . . From what you described, I have the feeling there probably was a real threat at some point in the past. I would probably go into that and try to make your amygdala learn.' She said she wasn't suggesting I had PTSD, but there might have been some instigating trauma where I learned I wasn't safe.

'It's a traumatic experience to be attacked,' she added, which at the time seemed strange. I'd never mentioned an attack.

—

Speaking to Andrea and Joe LeDoux, I got the frustrating sense that psychologists have got very good at treating specific, single-stimulus phobias. The treatment was brutal – a baptism of fire where you confront actual terror – but compared to most psychiatric disorders the recovery rates were exceptional. It was quick, and more often than not it worked. Changes in brain activity led to changes in thoughts, which led to changes in behaviour in everyday life, re-inforcing the lesson that the feared situation is, in fact, safe.

But what if you're not just scared of spiders? What if the outside world is spiders? What if intimacy is spiders? What if tomorrow, and every day after that, is all spiders?

If your worries shapeshift to suit the occasion, what's the tiny closet you need to lock yourself inside?

XIV.

PSYCHEDELICS

*LSD, magic mushrooms, MDMA,
and the growth of psychedelic therapy*

L ying on the living-room floor in darkness after yet another panic attack, I admitted it to myself.

I wasn't getting better.

If anything, I was getting worse. Since I'd quit my meds, despite exercising hard, losing weight, zapping my brain, learning all about the amygdala and decision trees and exposure therapy, anxiety was still winding up haymakers and knocking me flat.

The more I learned, the less I believed that the cure I sought was out there.

It was like I'd finally yanked the cord that said 'Pull In Case of Emergency' and it had come off in my hand.

If Brody and Waters were right that diagnosis is treatment, what was I doing to myself by introducing all this doubt? Maybe I'd never wanted the messy truth at all. Maybe I'd just wanted a credible authority figure to say, 'Do this.' Maybe all I'd ever wanted was certainty.

If I kept reading research papers I'd go mad. Without social media, it was all I did with my spare time. Each one took me ages because I'd have to keep stopping to find out what a 'voxel' was, or a 'non-ordinal scale', or the difference between diastolic and systolic blood pressure. My online ads were all selling subscriptions to neuroscience journals and therapist training courses.

I needed a showdown. A reckoning. Not a little nudge but a great stack of dynamite. Something you call on when the usual tricks aren't working.

I'd been off sertraline for two months. It was time.

———

You have advanced-stage colon cancer.

The doctors are doing everything they can to manage your physical condition, but your mental health is in bad shape. You are, understandably, distressed. You wake in the night with panic attacks. You worry constantly. You feel trapped, on edge, broken with bitterness and despair.

When we talk about anxiety, a lot of the popular advice boils down to, 'Cheer up, it might never happen.' But for many anxiety sufferers, it *has* happened. It *is* happening, right now.

It's not enough to discuss anxiety is if it were always about 'excessive' worry. As if the fears aren't real. Some of us are grieving lost children. Some of us are caring for elderly parents who are gradually losing their independence, their memories, their capacity for speech. Some us can measure our remaining life in weeks, or days. It doesn't get more real than that.

Severe anxiety under these circumstances heaps suffering upon suffering. It turns those last precious days into a kind of hell. For me, and for the many researchers who study this, it's clear that even when anxiety is completely proportionate to what a person faces, we want to find ways to relieve that suffering.

Imagine now you're taken into a room in the hospital that looks different to the others. The walls are covered in fabric hangings depicting colourful Indian mandalas. Fresh pink chrysanthemums sit in a vase. After a good sleep and a light breakfast, a therapist talks you through what to expect for the rest of the day.

At 10 a.m., you're given a large dose of psilocybin – the active, hallucinogenic component of magic mushrooms. The therapist encourages you to put on an eye mask, and gives you earphones that play gentle, ambient music. They sit with you the whole time, checking in hourly to make sure you're all right, and giving you water or juice if you like.

You lie back and relax. Gradually, as the music rises in intensity, a path of lights opens up in front of you. For the next six hours, you follow it.[1]

———

Psychedelic therapy is not new – in fact, many argue it predates psychology as a discipline and the concept of 'therapy' altogether. Consciousness-altering substances have been drunk, ingested or inhaled in religious ceremonies across a range of cultures throughout human history. Many of these ceremonies had the explicit purpose of bestowing insight, a sense of purpose or community, or prompting personal growth.

But it wasn't until 1943, when Swiss chemist Albert Hofmann accidentally dosed himself with the new drug he'd synthesised five years previously – in the process discovering the psychoactive properties of lysergic acid diethylamide, or LSD – that psychedelic therapy research really took off. After his first, accidental trip – absorbed, he guessed, through his ungloved fingertips – Hofmann attempted a more controlled experience a few days later, taking what he judged to be the minimum effective dose. He wildly underestimated the drug's potency (the actual threshold dose of LSD is less than a tenth of what he took) and ended up cycling home through picturesque Basel, floridly hallucinating, wracked with anxiety and convinced his next-door neighbour was a witch. Afterwards, Hofmann recognised LSD had powerful psychoactive effects and imagined it would become a potent tool for psychiatrists.

The 1950s and '60s saw an explosion in efforts to use psychedelics therapeutically. They were used in attempts to treat alcoholics, prison inmates, to comfort the terminally ill, and to augment conventional psychotherapy. Ultimately, LSD's growing popularity as a recreational drug led to a backlash, possession was made illegal in the United States in 1968, and increased regulations meant much research ceased.

It's easy to read the conventional timeline and conclude that psychedelic therapy's decline in popularity was entirely political. But as Hofmann's infamous bike ride demonstrated, many effects aren't intrinsically therapeutic. Oh, you're depressed, madam? Would it help if you were having sex with a hyperdimensional alligator composed entirely of question marks? Also, psychedelics pose major problems when it comes to designing high-quality studies.

In medicine, the gold standard of evidence is the double-blind placebo-controlled randomised trial. This is a trial where you take a group of patients and randomly assign them into one of two (or more) groups. One group gets the drug you're testing. The other group gets a placebo – a sugar pill, a vitamin C tablet or similar. Crucially, neither the patients *nor the physicians administering the treatment* know which group they're in. That's the 'double-blind' part. In this way, you control for all sorts of expectation effects and the weird ways we've seen in which people's belief that they're receiving – or providing – a fantastic new treatment can change how they act and feel.

Throughout the twentieth century, the standards to which we held clinical trials rose. We understood that it was no longer enough to show a medicine performed better than no intervention at all – you had to show that it did better than pretending to give someone a cure.

You can immediately guess one problem LSD, psilocybin and MDMA studies have complying with this model. If you dutifully drink your glass of water or receive your injection and an hour later the therapist splits down the middle, morphing into a vast cosmic womb swirling with countless unborn universes, you can be reasonably sure you're not in the control group. In psychology-speak this is known by the mildly titillating term 'penetrating the blind'.

This means that a lot of psychedelic research is considered, by its very nature, to be of lower quality – to carry less evidentiary weight – than studies where the effects of treatment are more subtle – like, say, taking a tablet once a day for lowering your blood pressure.

But one can raise similar objections about research into mindfulness training, various forms of therapy, and even antidepressants. You *know* if you're meditating. You know if you're having a conversation with a therapist. You probably have preconceived notions of how effective certain types of intervention are likely to be. Some researchers suggest – convincingly, to my mind – that, given the potent side effects of many antidepressants – and given that participants in both the active and placebo arms of trials are informed of those side effects – many supposedly 'double-blind' trials of antidepressants are nothing of the sort.[2]

Some of the most prominent earlier work in psychedelic therapy was done by a mild-mannered psychiatrist called Albert Kurland. He started with schizophrenic patients, but it was his work in the late sixties with over a hundred alcoholic patients which set the standard for many modern psychedelic trials. He used a model established at Vancouver's Hollywood Hospital, which carefully manipulated patients' expectations and environment – their 'set' and 'setting' – to 'foster a mystical experience'.

Patients in Kurland's programme were given two weeks of intensive psychotherapy, followed by a 'single, overwhelmingly high' dose of LSD in a 'modest cottage' on the grounds of Baltimore's Spring Grove State Hospital, one of the oldest psychiatric hospitals in the United States. They were taken to a 'comfortable living room' fitted with a sound system, and given an eye mask. A therapist and nurse sat with them for the full 10–12 hour trip.[3] A key element of the therapy was that patients received 'a heavy dose of tender loving care'.[4]

———

His transition from working with alcoholics to terminally ill patients arose out of tragedy. In 1966, a forty-three-year-old woman, a member of Kurland's research staff, was diagnosed with metastatic cancer. She had seen how LSD psychotherapy had helped alcoholic patients, and requested it for herself.

Kurland's paper from 1985 describes four case studies of patients with inoperable cancer who were given therapy along with 100–600mcg of LSD – between half and more than double the 250mcg dose Albert Hofmann took before his cycle-delic journey. Kurland describes a 'preparatory period' of two to three weeks, where the therapist and patient outline unresolved issues in the patient's life, with an emphasis on 'making life as meaningful as possible'. Rather than attempting to resolve deep-seated problems, Kurland tried to direct the patient to focus on the 'here and now', with the aim of 'obtaining satisfaction from ordinary situations in life'.

In the drug session itself, the patient was encouraged 'to feel everything that emerged, to experience it fully, and to give full expression of the experiences'. They listened through headphones to a specially designed playlist; it began with soothing Vivaldi to ease them through any initial anxiety, before building, as the psychedelic experience intensified, to pieces like Brahms' *Symphony No. 3*, music with a 'pressing quality, with long phrases leading toward climaxes' – i.e. sick drops.

Here's part of the account of Kurland's terminally ill co-worker, who had undergone a double mastectomy for breast cancer which had, by now, spread to her liver. She had been experiencing severe anxiety and deep despair.

I was alone in a timeless world with no boundaries. There was no atmosphere. There was no color, no imagery, but there may have been light. Suddenly, I recognized that I was a moment in time, created by those before me and in turn the creator of others. This was my moment, and my major function had been completed. By being born, I had given meaning to my parents' existence . . . That night . . . all noticed a change in me. I was radiant, and I seemed at peace, they said. I felt that way too. What has changed for me? I am living now, and being. I can take it as it comes.[5]

She claimed no miraculous transformation in the days that followed: 'I still get irritated occasionally and yell. I am still me, but more at peace. My family senses this and we are closer.'

Five weeks after the session, she died.

Not all of Kurland's case studies fared so well. One patient, described as a '56-year-old, White, Protestant, married female' suffered 'an attack of uncontrollable diarrhea' just as the LSD kicked in. She repeatedly soiled the bed throughout the day-long trip, which, understandably, 'compromised her ability to enter into the LSD experience'. It's not a great advert for psychedelic therapy, but it speaks to Kurland's transparency that he includes it in the paper as a warning of how the process can go wrong.

Ultimately, Kurland concluded that 'approximately one third' of patients responded very well to LSD therapy, overcoming their fear of death, another third 'felt that they had been helped and moved by the experience', though their fears remained, and the remaining third did not respond. It made me think of Stefan Brugger's comment about the 'rule of threes' in psychiatry, and how responses to antidepressants tend to see the same split.

LSD, psilocybin and MDMA are all serotonin agonists – that is, all three stimulate the release of 5-hydroxytryptamine (aka serotonin). Conversely, SSRIs like sertraline increase serotonin levels by blocking its post-release reabsorption back into the axon terminal. This is why you can't combine it with conventional antidepressants.

SSRIs and SNRIs stop serotonin left floating around in the synaptic cleft from being reabsorbed. Most psychedelics increase its release. If you take both at the same time – especially in large doses – the high levels of serotonin can cause a condition called serotonin syndrome. Symptoms range from high blood pressure and racing heart, to tremors, diarrhoea and – in rare cases – death.

Psychedelic therapy's mission – to relieve people's anguish at the end of their lives, to increase their joy – shows how much those WHO reports on 'the global economic burden of mental illness' miss. There are no 'lost working days' when a terminal cancer patient spends their last few weeks wracked with sleepless terror. You can't go to the World Bank with a presentation about net returns to GDP. Few stand to profit from giving a dying woman five weeks of closeness with her family. Yet such a gift is priceless.

Whether psychedelic therapy can deliver it is another matter. On the face of it, the results sound incredible.

One study at New York University looking at twenty-nine patients with advanced cancer reported a single dose of psilocybin resulted in 'immediate, substantial, and sustained improvements in anxiety and depression' and led to reduced 'demoralization and hopelessness, improved spiritual wellbeing, and increased quality of life'.[6] Patients were given 0.3mg of psilocybin per kg of body weight – about 25mg for someone who's 82kg/13 stone. The effective dose for psilocybin – the amount you have to take to feel effects – is around 6mg, so this is a decent amount – most of the literature calls anything in the 20–30mg range a 'high dose'. (Veteran psychonauts in search of a truly mind-bending trip might do double that, but remember, for many of these patients, this was their first time.)

Another study of fifty-one cancer patients at Johns Hopkins University, using a similar set up – a 'living-room-like environment', two trip-sitters, headphones, eye mask – found that high doses of psilocybin led to 'large and significant' decreases in anxiety and depression, and increased 'quality of life, life meaning, death acceptance, and optimism' – effects still evident six months later.[7] Eighty-three per cent were less anxious, according to both their own reports and assessments by a clinician. Participants completed a thirty-item 'mystical experience questionnaire' (the MEQ30), which asks a person to rate on a 0–5 scale the degree to which they experienced things like 'reverence' and 'timelessness' – 0 being 'not at all', and 5 being very strongly, 'more than at any other time in my life'. One question even asks how much they agree that: 'You are convinced now, as you look back on your experience, that in it you encountered ultimate reality.'[8]

The Johns Hopkins study calls itself 'a randomized double-blind trial'. This is, charitably, a stretch. The study used a 'crossover' design, where all the participants did two sessions, one with a high dose of psilocybin and one with a low dose. They weren't told in either session how much they'd be receiving, and neither were the researchers administering the capsule. All they knew was the doses might range 'anywhere from very low to very high', and that the doses might be the same in both sessions or different.

So clearly this wasn't a double-blind trial in the conventional sense. There was no placebo group. They were told they were taking psilocybin, and they were. The only variable was whether they were taking 'some' or 'a metric fucktonne'.

The authors acknowledge that psilocybin produces 'highly discriminable effects' that might lead to both participants and sitters 'penetrating the blind'. At the end of each trip, the staff members acting as primary sitters filled in a questionnaire where they had to guess the intensity of the dose out of 10. There were a few inaccuracies (over 13 per cent of the high-dose sessions were rated at 4 or less, and more than 12 per cent of the low-dose sessions were rated at 4 or more) but overall their estimates were remarkably accurate – especially as they weren't the ones having the trip, which was mostly conducted in silence by someone lying on a bed wearing an eye mask and headphones. Yet the authors conclude: 'The blinding procedures provided some protection against a priori monitor expectancy,' which is a bit like waking up on the beach, sunburnt except for a pale rectangle where you left your paperback, and concluding: 'The book procedure provided some protection against UV light.'

As for the patients actually undergoing the procedure . . . Well, the difference between 3mg and 30mg of psilocybin might not be immediately apparent to the more sheltered reader, but it's the difference between having a glass of wine with dinner and downing an entire wellington bootful of tequila. At 3mg you're a bit giggly. At 30mg the walls are melting. That's a blunt truth the authors disguise with academic euphemisms like 'highly discriminable effects'.

Researchers involved in these kinds of trials told me patients usually realise when they've been given a control dose. They often experience deep disappointment which the monitor then has to manage. They've been struggling daily with severe anxiety, depression, resentment, guilt, and they're psyching themselves up for a profound spiritual journey. Part of the monitor's role, in these cases, is to help them through the resultant dip in mood.

One widely reported finding from the Johns Hopkins study is that over two-thirds of participants (67.4 per cent) rated it as one of the top five most meaningful experiences in their lives, and a similar number (69.6 per cent) rated it as in the top five most spiritually significant. Aside from anything else, I'm not sure that how an intervention rates in a participant's personal 'meaningful events' league table is a relevant endpoint. That's not the problem the treatment is supposed to be tackling.

The language of the MEQ30, with all its talk of 'infinity' and 'ultimate reality', primes people for these sorts of responses, as does the way participants are briefed for the trial. There's also the phenomenon of 'effort justification' – after participating in a somewhat burdensome study, you don't want to feel like your time was wasted, especially if you get the sense some of your fellow patients may have been fusing with gelatinous seraphim or whatever. The psychologist

Leon Festinger theorised that sometimes the easiest way to resolve this unpleasant feeling is to convince ourselves, post hoc, that we actually enjoyed the task or value the outcome more than we really did.[9]

A connected phenomenon is 'the Good-Subject Effect'.[10] In taking part in these trials, patients built up a considerable bond of trust with their session monitors, spending about eight hours with them before the first psychedelic experience developing 'the therapeutic alliance' – considered by many psychologists to be a 'reliable predictor' of successful therapy.[11] Given all this, many participants, who are vulnerable, anxious and desperate for reassurance, may be highly motivated to figure out what the researchers want to hear and give it to them. They don't want to 'ruin' the experiment by saying the wrong thing. They don't want to let down the people in whom they've placed so much trust.

The Johns Hopkins study is one of the more rigorous psychedelics studies, with one of the larger samples, and it still has major methodological weaknesses. Other studies found that psilocybin-based interventions led to large, significant reductions in anxiety, but suffered from small sample sizes, doubtful blinding measures and the risk of bias.[12]

I'm not bashing the researchers. Psychedelic therapy is really, really hard to study well. It takes a lot of money and time, and – as you pass the treatment through increasingly fine meshes, testing a wider range of patients in larger numbers, letting other teams attempt to replicate your findings, relaxing screening criteria – you may find that once-impressive effect sizes shrink, become inconsistent, or vanish altogether, just as Camilla Nord and her colleagues did with tDCS.

———

Psychedelic therapy has pursued other routes.

Back in 1943, when Hofmann was discovering LSD, psychiatrists

Roy G. Grinker and John P. Spiegel were injecting traumatised members of the US Air Force with the barbiturate sodium thiopental. Sodium thiopental seems to dampen higher brain functions, and was sometimes used as a 'truth serum'. It reduced the airmen to a 'dream state' in which they were encouraged to recall their traumatic experiences, hopefully loosening trauma's grip in the process. Grinker and Spiegel claimed of the therapy, in messianic tones: 'The stuporous become alert, the mute can talk, the deaf can hear, the paralyzed can move, and the terror-stricken psychotics become well-organized individuals.'[13]

Dutch psychiatrist Jan Bastiaans used sodium thiopental in his work with Holocaust survivors who were unable to speak about their experiences. Like Grinker and Spiegel, he used the drug to reduce patients to a semi-conscious stupor before exploring their memories, calling the process 'narcoanalysis'. He would later move on to using LSD and psilocybin. It's not clear how effective Bastiaans' methods were; his work remained controversial throughout his life, and he admitted sodium thiopental often meant patients could not remember what they had said.

I spoke off the record to a researcher who has worked with PTSD survivors in therapeutic trials using psilocybin and MDMA. They told me MDMA, not unlike sodium thiopental, seems to allow people to touch and explore very traumatic memories that they otherwise habitually avoid. Trauma often comes with a sense of stuckness, of being trapped and defined by the past. MDMA-based therapy focuses on revisiting and releasing those stuck, frightening memories and feelings in the hope that this will allow them to be reprocessed, with a correspondingly lower emotional intensity, rather than experienced as immediate, present threats.

Alongside formal research into psychedelics there have, of course, been plenty of nonclinical practitioners continuing the tradition for decades, either illegally or in countries where some of the substances are permitted.

The most popular – perhaps notorious – of these psychedelic retreats are ayahuasca ceremonies. Based on indigenous Peruvian traditions, participants consume a bitter brew of mashed bark and leaves that contains the psychoactive compound N,N-dimethyltryptamine, or DMT. Drinking ayahuasca typically induces a long period of altered mood and florid hallucinations, but not before – and I apologise for returning to this theme so soon – vomiting and diarrhoea. Such 'purges' are often glossed as an important part of the emotional catharsis – a very visceral display of ridding oneself of one's emotional poisons.

As word of ayahuasca ceremonies has spread, they've become popular with tourists, and what was once a sacrament preserved by religious elders has become, increasingly, an industry, catering to the demands of white western middle-class backpackers. I don't mean to sound too cranky – or worse, hypocritical – but aside from a dearth of quality research on its therapeutic benefits – which, if they exist, are likely due to its serotonergic effects[14] – I was put off by the drug's reputation as a kind of culturally appropriated cinnamon challenge for wide-eyed yoga Chads.

Psychedelic therapies like the ones researchers were studying for PTSD were already available privately in places like the Netherlands. Though the Netherlands made magic mushrooms illegal in 2008, psilocybin truffles – a sort of scrunched, compacted, bad-weather offshoot of magic mushrooms called 'sclerotia' – were omitted from the ban and quickly became the sacrament of choice for most Dutch psychedelic retreats.

The thought of unmooring myself from the shores of reality while surrounded by a bunch of munted strangers did not fill me with enthusiasm. But I kept coming back to those testimonies. Those reports from people who felt they had touched some deeper reality, some inner truth that brought peace. I spoke to a friend who had tried ayahuasca years before it became popular with gap-year kiddies. He told me how, deep in the Peruvian jungle, along with a nearby town's mayor and the chief of police, he had experienced himself as a tiny speck in a universe made entirely from love. He said the experience had changed him.

I'd never had anything close to a spiritual experience, a sense of oneness, connection. We're not supposed to admit we want those things, for fear of looking like glib and credulous ninnies.

Still, as a writer, who was I to snub the allure of Cool Stories?

—

I contacted a chap who co-runs retreats specialising in 'truffle therapy'. His name is – improbably – Chi Amsterdam. I wanted to get a sense of who I'd be entrusting my safety to if I decided to go ahead.

Chi is a handsome, shaven-headed guy with a wide smile and a gentle demeanour. He told me – as Andrea Reinecke had – that understanding anxiety intellectually isn't enough. 'It's really about going through some kind of experience.' That could be as simple as taking a cold shower – he thought cold showers were 'really amazing for anxiety' – or it could involve a psychedelic experience. 'We witness quite miraculous changes in people, and transformations,' he told me. 'Words can't describe it. You have to go through it.'

I asked him how he had got into running truffle retreats.

He smiled. 'The truffles just . . . they know how to grow. They know how to change people's lives and get people talking about them. Yeah, it's really the power of the truffles, the psilocybin, the mushrooms. There's a reason why people just talk about it a lot after they go through the experience.'

Unsurprisingly, he was a big advocate for the therapeutic power of psilocybin therapy. 'It's unlike anything else. It really reduces depression, reduces anxiety. People's anxiety just . . . it basically disappears completely. For at least a short time there's no anxious thoughts.' But he was quick to warn me that deeper grooves of anxiety in the mind might take longer to shift. 'It's a practice like anything else. There's no magic silver bullet.'

Many people I'd spoken to about anxiety treatments had used variants of, 'There's no magic bullet' or 'it's not a silver bullet'. In medicine, the concept of a 'magic bullet' – in the original German, a *Zauberkugel* – was invented by the Nobel Prize-winning physician Paul Ehrlich in 1900, to describe a hypothetical agent that could selectively destroy specific microbes without harming the body. In folklore, a silver bullet is one of the only ways to kill a werewolf. Either phrase implies the quick, miraculously effective destruction of a problem.

Sometimes, hearing people use it made me feel a bit defensive – like they suspected me of hunting for shortcuts, for easy answers. Mainly I felt defensive because that was true. I wanted a cure and I wanted it now, because I was hanging on by my fingernails.

I asked Chi what he thought was going on when people took psilocybin therapeutically.

'The scientists . . . the way they describe it is it turns off the default mode network.'

The default mode network, or DMN, is a network of several brain areas that is associated with a state of unfocused awareness, like mind-wandering and daydreaming. Many researchers conceptualise it as our brain on standby, usually when we're paying attention to nothing in particular. But the DMN has also been found to be activated when we're thinking about ourselves, or performing a task that involves 'self-referencing' – which has led some researchers to speculate that it may be linked to our concept of a 'self' or 'ego'.

One study found that blood flow in part of the DMN, the posterior cingulate cortex – i.e. the rear of that 'belt' curling across the middle of the brain – decreased by up to 20 per cent under the influence of psilocybin. The authors speculate that perhaps the DMN acts as an agent of 'cognitive integration and constraint' under normal circumstances.[15] By this logic, a consequence of its temporary 'down-regulation' could be freedom from our usual ways of thinking.

Other studies have found altered DMN activity in patients with anxiety disorders[16] and those with comorbid anxiety and depression.[17] One hypothesised role of the DMN is 'retrieval and manipulation of information and past events in an effort to solve problems and develop future plans' – thus, rather than daydreaming about pleasant things, anxiety sufferers' wandering minds may default to imagining future threats or ruminating on dangerous or unhappy situations from the past.

It's not just psilocybin that dampens parts of the DMN. Studies have also found reduced activity in the main nodes of the DMN – the medial prefrontal cortex and posterior cingulate cortex – in experienced meditators 'consistent with decreased mind-wandering'.[18] Quite what these studies prove is still an open question, but if – as Joe LeDoux argued – an essential part of anxiety is a concept of self, then it seems the DMN must be implicated somewhere in the whole dysfunction.

'The ordinary, usual way we think about things is past and future,' Chi told me. 'So we always get anxious about the future. Somehow we're not good enough or we're not going to do enough or it's going to be painful. The truffles just bring us into the moment and help us feel our body. They really shake up all these deep emotions like fear. Usually it's a lot of crying. Most people need to cry a lot.'

On those rare occasions where crying comes from the heart – perhaps when you're in the presence of some compassionate other – it has a cleansing, healing quality. It's what my mum would call a 'good cry'.

I asked Chi what a typical retreat looked like. I imagined they had what psychologists call strong 'demand characteristics' – subtle or even explicit rules for how a 'good' attendee acts and feels. In the febrile atmosphere of a shared trip there was plenty of scope for emotional contagion – what used to be called 'mass hysteria' – like charismatics speaking in tongues. But maybe I was being too cynical.

He told me on the first night, everyone arrives, eats together, then they sit in a circle to share their intentions and feelings. 'A lot of it's about expressing emotion, expressing fear, being vulnerable with other people, then trusting other people.' The next day, everyone does a microdose of psilocybin, just to alleviate any pre-trip jitters. 'It's just like the cold. We think, *Oh, maybe I didn't die. Maybe it's all good.*' Sometimes the group goes on nature walks. They do some meditation, some yin yoga – 'very gentle, restorative yoga that helps people just prepare to surrender for the journey' – and group members spend some time sitting with and getting to know one another.

At last everyone gathers at the ceremony space. There's a mat and an eye mask for everyone.

'Each person comes up to the facilitator and they weigh out their truffles,' Chi explained. 'So they really feel which truffles are calling them. With the guidance of the facilitator they decide how much to take. Then we put on music, people lie down.'

For most people, the journey lasts between five and seven hours. I asked him what the sitters did during that time.

'We help people get tissues, hold people's hands, help them go to the bathroom, refill water bottles – it's really like nursing, actually . . .' He smiled. 'We just do our best to be there for people when they need us, and help people feel safe and stay safe.'

It sounded like running retreats had been a journey for Chi as well.

'Oh yeah,' he said, 'it's been a massive initiation. It's like a shamanic initiation by the mushroom. It only gives us what we're ready for. It just gives us little challenges. We have faith and we make it through.'

He went on: 'Oh God, it's . . . a lot of times I still want to cry every day. Still, every time I'm on a journey I cry. It's the biggest blessing. It's definitely not easy, continually going and dedicating my life to the mushroom. I finally found my guru, and it takes the form of a mushroom. It's like guru-surrender. Really surrendering to the will and the vision of the mushroom. Because there is a species far beyond human intelligence in many ways. We're still in awe and shock, hearing the stories on every retreat about how mushrooms have changed people's lives. We're just so happy to be a part of it, basically.'

My ears pricked up at 'far beyond human intelligence'. When he talked about being 'called to' by the truffles, or the mushroom having a 'will', was that . . . an analogy?

'It's an intelligent species,' said Chi, deadpan. 'It's a kingdom. The fungal kingdom. They look for ways to grow and their mycelial network can break through concrete. Human beings are sort of like concrete blocks. They clean us out and they heal us. They get us talking and other people try it. We spend money to grow it. To share it with people. It's not metaphorical at all. It's a reality. And I think this can only be understood if someone goes through some journeys.'

I wasn't sure what to say.

'I represent the mushroom kingdom,' he said. 'All my clothes are mushrooms.' He stood to reveal he was wearing a mushroom hoodie. 'I have a tattoo here – it's the mushroom vision on a cross.' He rolled up his sleeve to reveal a tattoo of a foot-long rainbow cross bearing what, at first glance, looked like a crucified heart-shaped mushroom with a single eye. 'It's the willingness to die for the vision.'

I nodded. Chi was telling me truffles were a sentient, highly intelligent species using humans to propagate them through a form of semi-benign mind control, and that we should be willing to surrender and die for them.

I think of myself as a pretty broadminded guy, respectful of other people's beliefs. But I worried that, if I went on one of Chi's retreats, my tiny granule of uncertainty around whether I was offering myself up as a vessel for our cosmic fungal overlords would be enough to give me a heinously bad trip.

I admired his willingness to be vulnerable and his lack of cynicism, but I was not ready to pledge fealty to the mushroom kingdom.

I just wanted to be less terrified.

——

I had a couple of false starts with other psychedelic retreat providers.

On impulse, I booked myself onto an ayahuasca retreat at an undisclosed location outside Amsterdam. Through an exchange of emails, I was told we would spend three days drinking the stinking, wax-like brew and undergoing spiritual transformation, all under the direction of a striking blonde woman whose wardrobe appeared to consist exclusively of white linen suit jackets. Shortly before the retreat, I received an email telling me the location and instructing me to wear only white, 'to keep the energies balanced'.

I am not a man with a diverse wardrobe, far less someone who has enough white outfits to survive three days of profuse puking and DMT sharts. Given the high probability of 'purging', white seemed like a poor choice. Who were these people who believed in 'energies' and not diarrhoea? Suddenly I was overcome with a deep, almost mystical, intuition that attending was a terrible idea.

I cancelled. The morning after the retreat finished, the guru posted a video announcing that, effective immediately, she was quitting ayahuasca ceremonies for ever, and that all future bookings were cancelled. I have no idea what happened that weekend – she made only vague reference to ending a 'wonderful and meaningful journey' – but I came away with the sense that this was one *Zauberkugel* I had been lucky to dodge.

My squeamishness came partly from the thought of being spannered amongst strangers. What if someone was really annoying? Sobbing really loudly or baying like a wolf while they listened to Vashti Bunyan on their smartphone? I'd be irritated, then I'd feel guilty for being such a crabby, judgemental penis. What if *I* was really annoying?

I got in touch with two women who ran one-day solo experiences, Amanda and Nikolitsa. I was bracing myself for talk of 'energies' or supplication to the mushroom Christ, but they turned out to be two of the friendliest, most down-to-earth people I've chatted with. Talking over Skype from California, laughing often, and passing the conversation between them with the easy familiarity of veteran podcast hosts – 'We love, love, love talking about this – this is our jam' – they spoke frankly about their pasts, their personal struggles, and how psychedelics had allowed them to go to a place that they weren't able to go to through talk therapy or art.

'I often describe it as meeting this other person,' Nikolitsa told me, 'like my most authentic self, who's like: "I'm sorry – what are you doing here? Why are you so sad?" I meet this person and I get closer and closer and closer to her.'

They told me that, for a psychedelic experience to be transformative, it has to be intentional. They offered a space with a balcony, a private bath, and music piped into the rooms, the tracks selected live throughout the day.

I felt immediately comfortable talking with them. They were open, smart, insightful and humorous.

But when, half an hour later, we finally got to the matter of price, it turned out to be expensive. As in, more than a month's wages. They said they tried to operate a sliding scale to accommodate what people could afford – but look, when you're anxious it can be hard to be assertive. I didn't want to admit it was too much, because I didn't want them to be disappointed in me. Nor did I want to discover that they'd just been nice because I might make them money. I thought if I tried to negotiate down they might think I didn't value their work. Then I might carry that anxiety into my session and have a terrible trip. We'd just been sharing some of our deepest personal struggles. I felt vulnerable. Rather than directly address the issue, and test if my fears were true, I just said 'sure'.

The longer I ruminated and stewed, the more I worried that if I couldn't express my needs about something as simple as the price, how on earth was I going to have an authentic, transformative experience when I got there? Wouldn't I feel pressure just to 'perform' my recovery – especially as I'd paid so much for it?

I've spoken to a lot of anxiety sufferers who've gone through counselling and have ended up trying to please their therapist rather than get their needs met. When you open up to someone, you're in a very vulnerable position. You start wanting to be a 'good' client. You want to show progress, maybe make your therapist laugh with a self-deprecating joke, articulate some insight or share some difficult moment from your past to suggest you're on the verge of a 'breakthrough'.

The therapist takes your behaviour as evidence the therapy is going well. The two of you can end up in a *folie à deux* where you perform your assigned roles with the aim of pleasing one another – the client wanting the therapist to feel competent, the therapist wanting the client to demonstrate progress – rather than with the intent of genuinely grappling with the problem at hand, even if it means risking the other party's disapproval.

For all the talk about the value of the 'therapeutic alliance', from an end-user's perspective I worry that too often it ends up prioritising rapport over authenticity. The therapist asks, 'How have you been feeling?' and you drop your gaze and reply, 'Yeah . . . better', because you don't want to disappoint them, or else you cook up some new problem or insight so the two of you have something to therapute about.

One psychedelic researcher told: me how patients, during their trip, sometimes regressed back to being toddlers, even babies. They said the patients would recall primal moments of infant neglect – for example, crying out for their parents and being ignored. In re-experiencing these formative traumas, the patient could finally break free and begin their journey towards acceptance.

I felt uneasy. When someone had these visions under the influence of psychedelics, how could you be sure they were real memories?

The researcher thought for a moment, then replied that they weren't sure that it mattered. The question was: Was it real for the patient? The 'truth' could be a symbolic one. As long as it acted as a catalyst for healing, its historical accuracy was unimportant.

I'm sure they were coming from a place of compassionate pragmatism. But it sets a dangerous precedent when a therapist is unconcerned about the possibility of inducing false memories of childhood abuse in a vulnerable patient rendered highly suggestible by big doses of psychoactive drugs.

During a psilocybin trial run by Imperial College London on patients with treatment-resistant depression, one participant, Andy, had a vivid hallucination in which he was a child, and someone was trying to smother him with a pillow as he slept. Afterwards, he was understandably disturbed. He remembered his childhood as very happy. Was it a real memory? Had his father tried to kill him in his sleep? In a documentary about the trial, the therapist working with Andy on 'integration' after the experience plays down the necessity of deciding whether the hallucination was a real memory or 'something his mind just made up'. (It's clear that, actually, this was *very* important to Andy. He spends a long time weighing up the evidence, ultimately deciding that it wasn't a real event; he expresses relief that the therapist offered him 'a rationale' – that it was a metaphor for his 'suffocating' childhood.)

Explanations for our mental anguish can be therapeutic, even when those explanations are incorrect. But it's important – essential, even – that before undertaking a psychedelic experience, both patient and therapist understand the unreliability of memory. That the scenes that arise *may* be biographically factual, or they may be a form of psychodrama.

Abuse survivors often get told: 'You're making it up', 'You imagined it', 'You're mentally ill.' Some memories – often from when survivors were very young – get suppressed, or the horrors were so habitual that multiple encounters meld together. Survivors are scorned and threatened and gaslit until they doubt their own experiences.

In the late 1980s and early 1990s there was a spate of litigation arising from the infamous 'repressed memory therapy', where therapists used a mixture of leading questions, hypnosis, and even interrogation under the influence of sedatives to 'uncover' lurid abuse memories. Adults would come in complaining of anxiety and insomnia, only for these to be taken as evidence of repressed trauma. The therapist would then look for apparent lapses in childhood memories, areas where their recall grew hazy, before 'regressing' the person back to that age and gradually, through repeated questions delivered in a role-play format, tease out accounts of elaborate satanic rituals involving incest and child murder.

Given that some people who underwent repressed memory therapies reported having been abducted by UFOs, it's reasonable to conclude that at least some of these supposed memories were 'iatrogenic' – that is, harmful artefacts introduced by therapeutic process. Thousands of close family members found themselves at the centre of abuse allegations derived entirely from ostensibly 'repressed' memories. Overzealous therapists implanted trauma into vulnerable people, who subsequently saw their families torn apart by bogus memories, and amongst whom – according to data from recovered-memory legal claims in Washington State – 'suicidal ideation increased nearly seven-fold and . . . psychiatric hospitalizations increased over five-fold over the course of therapy'.[19] Worse still, the scandal was used to discredit genuine experiences of abuse.

These are extreme examples. But they serve as vivid reminders that therapy can harm as well as heal. There is a power imbalance, which terms like 'the therapeutic alliance' obscure. One party is getting paid, usually by the other. Money and the disclosure of sensitive personal information flows in one direction. Even if we didn't live under the sucky, exploitative system that is capitalism, the fact that one person is coming to another, an expert, for help, necessarily sets up a status gap. If the therapist is a qualified psychiatrist or involved in one of these psychedelic trials, they also control access to psychopharmacological treatments.

This isn't to imply anything sinister – but it's a dynamic that exists. To pretend otherwise doesn't magically create parity between client and therapist; instead, it obscures the ways in which this dynamic colours and biases the therapeutic process (and makes it harder to assign accountability when that process breaks down, as Jo Freeman argued in her essay 'The Tyranny of Structurelessness').[20] You're not mates. It's a transaction.

Maybe, in the end, this was the thing that made me a little queasy about going through with Amanda and Nikolitsa's retreat. Everyone has to make a living, I get that. But these events are unregulated. Travelling to a foreign country and placing your safety and wellbeing in the hands of strangers who stand to profit – regardless of the outcome – just feels . . . I don't know. Compromised?

Maybe it was a weird place to draw the line. I don't have the same issues around, say, hiring someone to fix the guttering. But then, during that process I'm not – usually – blindfolded, spannered and crying. So I bottled it. I made up a vague excuse about having to postpone, and never got back to them.

I felt crappy. Galled at my own gutlessness, my inability to be honest with people who'd been nothing but nice to me, at my chronic indecision.

I thought about what Andrea Reinecke had told me, about how it wasn't enough to just tell people not to be anxious. She had used D-cycloserine to improve learning after a patient faced their fear, locked in that cleaning cupboard. Some research suggests psilocybin might have a similar, albeit more potent, effect on neuroplasticity.

Subjects – and their brains – have to learn through experience. I'd read studies that suggested serotonergic psychedelics like psilo-cybin promote neuroplasticity in the prefrontal cortex,[21] increasing the density of dendritic spines on cortical neurons – and that a single dose of psilocybin reduces the amygdala's response to fearful faces one week later, as well as improving mood.[22]

When patients entered the cupboard in Reinecke's research, they were completely alone. Lights out. Door locked. No safety behaviours. Increased neuroplasticity made good exposures better and bad ones worse. Half-measures were death.

Maybe trying to find the perfect, choreographed experience was itself a safety behaviour. Maybe wanting a sitter 'in case something went wrong' was no different to needing to carry that blister pack of propranolol everywhere, or refusing to get on the bus unless there was a seat near the exit. If, like Dawn Huebner had intimated, my triggers were my own thoughts and uncertainty, then those were the things I had to face.

Maybe I had to be alone.

———

It's not easy, as a working dad, to find time to sneak off for a day-long, solo, drug-fuelled descent into the echoing chasm of your own boundless neuroses – still harder when you haven't admitted to your wife that that's your plan.

I'd told Lisa I was looking into psychedelic retreats. She was not enthusiastic. She worried they might be dangerous, or that they might make me worse. Her concerns were far from stupid – the DSM-5 lists a condition called 'hallucinogen persisting perception disorder', where drug-induced hallucinations continue for 'weeks, months or years'. Estimated prevalence amongst people who use hallucinogens is 4.2 per cent – around 1 in 25. LSD and psilocybin can also trigger psychotic breaks, one reason most studies screen potential participants for a history of psychosis.

More prosaically, Lisa had warned it was unhealthy for me to pin all my hopes on one dramatic cure. She was worried I would crash when I emerged on the other side and wasn't miraculously anxiety-free.

But, like a gambling addict, I had fantasies of betting everything and winning big. I would return home a new man, and shower my family with affection and calm. *You seem happy today*, Lisa would say, and I'd reply – as if noticing it for the first time – *Yeah, I am.*

I'd still be me, but more at peace.

I decided not to tell her I was doing it. I think I felt ashamed. She had solid objections. I didn't have good answers. But I didn't know what else was left.

It was a little like planning an affair. I spotted a gap in the diary. I waited. I lied.

—

For various reasons, I'll remain vague about the location I chose. It was a house less than an hour from Amsterdam, with Wi-Fi, woods within walking distance, and a ground-floor room with a sofa-bed beneath a skylight.

The night before, I still wasn't sure I would go through with it. I hadn't told anyone. I had the lonely sense of standing on a precipice. Possibly a precipice that oversaw a three-foot drop into a puddle.

Because of course it might all be a massive anticlimax. My truffles might be duds.

I had my eye mask. I had my headphones and music. I had set my intention to get well. Most importantly of all, I had a shitload of truffles.

Several people had advised me not to eat a heavy breakfast, as high doses of psilocybin can cause 'gastric distress' as serotonin stimulates the enterochromaffin cells that line the digestive tract to undergo 'peristaltic contraction', like the rippling of a worm's body. On the other hand, psilocybin truffles taste like crap, so you need something to mask the flavour. Just before 9 a.m., I fixed myself a peanut-butter sandwich loaded with 15g of the strongest psychedelic truffles the shop had offered.

Unlike the controlled conditions of an official study – Albert Kurland injected participants with an exact dose of LSD, and psilocybin trials usually administer it in capsules – I had to guesstimate. Gram for gram, truffles are generally reckoned to be milder than mushrooms, but actual psilocybin content varies wildly depending on species and freshness. Since changing my diet and taking up running, I had lost three stone. Based on data from one study I had read,[23] if the truffles I was taking genuinely were as strong as claimed, and still reasonably fresh, I might expect 15g to contain around 25mg of psilocybin – bang on the 'high dose' from the Johns Hopkins study.

I stared at the peanut-butter sandwich for several minutes, my head swimming. After all the trouble I'd gone to, it seemed inconceivable that I'd chicken out now. Yet I couldn't take that final step.

What's the worst it can do? I thought. *Give me a panic attack?*

I began giggling manically. I gobbled the sandwich.

In the room I had designated as my obligatory 'living-room-like environment', I lay down on a woollen rug, my head supported by a pillow and began some deep-breathing exercises, hoping to stave off my rising jitters. I pulled my eye mask on, popped in my ear buds and pressed play on a soundtrack of steady, hypnotic drumming. I had no idea what was going to happen – whether I would start hallucinating, whether I would lose control of my thoughts, or whether the whole thing would be a crushing flop.

Whatever happened, the advice was to accept it. To embrace it as part of the experience. To lean into it. Thank you. More please.

Once you'd taken your dose, there was no way to terminate the experience early. All you could do was surrender.

The absolute worst thing you could do during a trip was resist.

I breathed, my closed eyes scintillating with static. I felt nervous, but okay. The breathing was giving me something to focus on, to stop my thoughts whirling off into paranoid scenarios. *What if someone suddenly hammers on the window? What if the house gets invaded by burglars?* I had no sitter. I was alone and drugged.

Bronze phosphenes rose from the visual noise, resolving into chequerboard patterns of rings, spheres. Slowly, the patterns became glowing, elaborate mosaics, symmetrical shifting mandalas that repeated like a tile texture to form a tunnel bounded by fizzing white rings of light. The image grew brighter and brighter until I felt I was floating in it.

Ooh, I thought, *something's happening.*

———

The word 'anxiety' shares its origin with 'anger', from the Old English *enge*, meaning 'narrow', and the Latin *angere*, meaning 'choke' or 'strangle'. Anxiety, angst and anguish carry a sense of a drawstring bag pulled tight, a shutting off, a restriction.

Contrast them with 'inspire', from the Latin *inspirare*, meaning 'to breathe', 'to blow into', 'to fill with air/breath/*spiritus*'. Inspiration is all about that intake of breath, the bestowing and acceptance of life. Openness. Receiving.

From an etymological perspective, it's hard to be inspired and anxious at the same time. How can you experience that shut down, small, constricted sense of choking, when you're drawing in a deep breath, when you're inhaling that vivifying spiritus, when you're opening yourself up and accepting life in its fullness?

That these two states – anxiety and inspiration – are so antithetical suggests increasing our sense of inspiration should reduce our anxiety.

Rarely, however, anxiety and inspiration co-exist.

It's how you might feel standing at the edge of the Grand Canyon, or looking up from the bottom of the ocean and seeing all those metres of dark blue water heaped on top of you, or holding the hand of a loved one in hospital as they die.

It's what I felt when I first looked down into Suki's eyes, and saw life.

A single moment can be both terrifying and astonishing. You can be afraid and filled with wonder. Even something as prosaic as zip-wiring on a corporate away-day can evoke tiny doses of *argh* and *wow*.

This is the state we call awe. It's what some philosophers might call 'an encounter with the sublime'.

As I lay on the floor beneath a widening fractal lightshow, I was starting to feel that weird, tingling feeling you get when you see a murmuration of starlings over the corn stubble, or an evening cloud-bank underlit in carmine and peach-gold.

I began to rise.

———

Dreams are the world's most perishable commodity. Few survive the journey from brain to mouth. Even the most enthusiastic listener can often do no more than nod and smile politely as you lay out narrative fragments like holiday photos chewed up and regurgitated by a dog.

I'm not saying we should be ashamed of our visions. I've had intimate and deeply therapeutic conversations with friends as they recall a recent, powerful dream, but they don't usually make for great, relatable stories. Trips exist in a category distinct from dreams, but they suffer from the same narrative frailties. Heinrich Klüver recorded his mescaline visions in elaborate, mathematical detail, estimating the dimensions of impossible objects. For a man who did drugs with monkeys, the result is astonishingly dull.

So – in my great mercy – I'm not going to relate a blow-by-blow account of what I experienced over the next six hours. I've omitted some deeply personal moments, too. It related to stuff I've never shared with *anyone*. In a way, the specifics are irrelevant. But just so you know.

———

Right at the beginning I met an angel, and communicated telepathically. Sounds incredibly goofy, but at the time I was euphoric. Eventually I felt myself being pulled upwards towards another vertical tunnel. I didn't want to leave, then I remembered what I'd been told. Don't resist. Go with it. Accept. They waved goodbye to me as I left.

Later I was a jellyfish – something boneless and transparent – and for a time I floated amongst brightly coloured marine creatures. Later still I was a gigantic female statue, lying on an impossibly high mountain top in the attitude of the Buddha in repose. Far below was an entire world, with continents and great plains and people, observed through clouds. Later still I was disintegrating, dissolving into nothing. I made myself think, *Thank you, yes, more,* before blasting to particles.

Sometimes I was aware of laughing or crying – often both, tears streaming down my cheeks. Occasionally I was brought back to my body by stomach or leg cramps.

Occasionally I came round, took my eye mask off, changed the music. The room would appear briefly normal, then everything would begin running like tallow. Textures oozed with a putrid abundance. At one stage, water poured from the ceiling, flooding the room, and the air filled with tropical fish.

I clung to a ship crushed by a glacier, dangling over a bottomless icy crevasse. I could sense the dead. I saw their faces in the clouds. I felt them all around me. They had always been watching over us. I had been foolish to doubt their presence.

When I needed to pee I was – thankfully – able to stagger through the kitchen to the bathroom. I chanced a look in the mirror. I was a zombie, with sunken, discoloured flesh rotting away in chunks. It struck me as a rather childish, obvious illusion. I rolled my eyes and tutted. *Oh honestly*, I thought, *is that the best you can do?* I don't think I've ever felt more English.

Eventually, by around 3 p.m. – six hours into my trip – I felt able to leave the house. I walked through the woods with my headphones

COWARD

in. My depth perception was doing odd things – tiny flowers seemed very far away and massive, a tree might seem like it was an inch from my eyes but only thumb-sized – and occasionally I'd glimpse something bizarre and distorted, but the world was no longer a mass of intense, multicoloured, plopping wax.

It was a sunny day. I sat on a log and gazed across the grass. I had the strangest feeling in my chest. A deep, weary grief.

Wasn't I supposed to feel elated? Reborn?

In retrospect, it's not terribly surprising that, after necking a big dose of a drug that stimulates the release of serotonin, I had a massive comedown. But I didn't remember reading about this in the research, nor had any of the therapists I'd spoken to mentioned it. In fact, many accounts implied the opposite: an extended 'afterglow', a feeling of wellbeing, security and renewed inspiration. I had been advised to bring my notepad and prepare for several days where the ideas would just flow out.

Instead, I just felt really, really sad.

Sad that it had come to this. Sad that I had spent so many years running from fear, hating myself for not having the right feelings. Sad that I'd lied to my wife. Sad that I was out here, walking off a terrific, psychedelic katzenjammer, rather than playing with my daughter.

For months, I'd thought about nothing but anxiety. What is it? Where does it start? How can we nail it down and wipe it out and never have to feel it again? I was exercising to beat anxiety. Eating to beat anxiety. Meditating to beat anxiety. Journalling to beat anxiety. Every spare moment I was reading studies on my phone, the better to understand anxiety.

My entire life had become a monument to anxiety.

What a mess.

—

When I next saw Lisa, I waited until we'd put Suki to bed, then confessed.

I broke down sobbing.

Aside from the small risk of flashbacks, in the right setting psilocybin is comparatively safe – non-addictive, and not, as far as I'm aware, associated with any deaths due to overdose. But something about the way I'd done it – making a plan, lying to people close to me, the belief it would solve all my problems, that final moment of doubt before compulsively swallowing – felt really dark. In my head, it rhymed with a suicide attempt.

I'd felt several times over the past few months that I was worthless and stupid and broken. That my life was not worth living. I love my wife and my daughter more than anything – not to mention my family and my amazing friends – but I felt like I was more of a burden than a net positive. I'd tried everything I could think of, spoken to the world's most knowledgeable experts on the subject, and here I was, worse than ever.

Before I set out, I still had all this ahead of me. I didn't know what I'd find, and how it might change me. I still had hope.

In Schrödinger's famous thought experiment, the cat is both alive and dead till you open the box. The two states co-exist in quantum superposition. It's the act of observing that collapses the waveform down into one of two possibilities. Has the cat been slain by the radioactive isotope, or is it sitting in there, licking its paws? Well, until you check, the answer's both. You've got a living kitty, as long as you promise not to peek.

Until now, there had always been the possibility that I was just feckless or ill-informed. That my wellbeing was waiting inside the box. That box had been a comfort. More than I'd realised. An uneaten Crunchie in a coat pocket.

Think of those parables where characters are warned not to look. Orpheus, Lot's wife, Pandora. Sometimes the truth is shitty, and – since you can't change it – you're better off living in blissful ignorance.

Lisa reminded me that I'd felt this way when I cold-turkeyed off my meds. Admittedly, all this comparing of myself to tragic figures from the Bible and classical myth did seem a bit, well, comedown-y.

I told her I felt like we'd survived some real sadnesses in the past few years, but what with our becoming parents – something that was supposed to offer unvarnished joy – we hadn't found time to grieve. I told her she was my best friend, and with all my fear, I'd shut down and stopped trying to connect with her. I'd become terrified of intimacy. I told her I missed her. I told her I'd known she was probably right about not putting all my hopes into psyche-delics, but I'd gone ahead anyway because I was so, so tired.

She listened so kindly and patiently. Then we held each other, and we both cried.

It was a good cry.

XV.

THE WATER CURE
Cold-water immersion and wild swimming

It's the nineteenth century and you've gone mad.

You don't have generalised anxiety disorder or panic disorder because they don't yet exist, but you find yourself *liverish*, in a state of *nervous collapse*, *melancholic*, or perhaps *hysteric*, and you are conveyed to an asylum.

A doctor escorts you around the grounds. Presently you find yourself beside a pond. A charming wooden bridge spans the water. An orderly stands on the far bank beside a large spoked wheel. The doctor invites you to take in the view from the Tang dynasty-style pagoda at the bridge's centre. Perhaps the tranquil surroundings will ease your troubled mind.

All right then, you think, and you stroll onto the bridge. It's a pleasant, late autumn day. Horsetail clouds drift across a silver sky. As you gaze from the pagoda you reflect that perhaps the nightmarish tales you have heard about asylums were exaggerated.

You hear the rattle of gears. A trapdoor gives way beneath your feet. You drop into freezing water.

You have just experienced the *bain de surprise*.

———

In the weeks that followed my mushroom trip, I felt low and deeply shaken. There were days where I was so on edge I could barely speak for stammering. I paced, wrung my hands, tugged at my hair. Several panic attacks confirmed that no magical neurogenic transformation had occurred in my brain. (A couple of people who had been enthusiastic about psilocybin suggested that my low mood was, in fact, a positive sign – maybe I was purging 'toxic feelings'.)

Read enough research, and a kind of nihilism sets in. For every supposedly robust finding, you can find ten very smart papers pointing out flaws that complicate an apparent slam-dunk with extraneous variables you hadn't considered, or criticising the study design, or failing to replicate the effect, or conceding that yes, the results were credible but the conclusions the researchers drew from them weren't. The phrase 'further research is needed' has become such a cliché, such an in-joke, that several journals have banned it.

This is what good science is. If the price of peace is eternal vigilance, the price of science is eternal scepticism. It's forever accepting that current knowledge is a constellation of best guesses based on our best information at this time. As the mathematician George Box put it, 'All models are wrong.' Science is a continual iteration of theory and practice – assembling an explanatory framework, testing it against reality, going back to the theory to try to improve it, testing it again, and so on.[1] Hopefully, over time, the scale of these refinements – the distance between theory and practice – becomes smaller and smaller.

Clearly progress does happen. The germ theory of disease is a better model than the miasma theory of disease. Fewer people die from infections during surgery. I would rather see a contemporary therapist or neurosurgeon than one from a hundred years ago. But I understand the weariness that drives people to alternative medicine. Sooner or later, you catch yourself gazing towards the *bain de surprise*, thinking: *What have I got to lose?*

Throughout the history of psychiatry, cold-water immersion appears both as a homely folk cure for the well-to-do and a horrible punishment for the incurably insane. Asylum residents were restrained and immersed in water upside-down, nearly (and sometimes actually) drowning in the name of quenching the inner flames of madness. Orderlies doused patients in large quantities of freezing water from on high as a means of 'cooling' manias, or, as with the *bain de surprise*, might suddenly and forcibly submerge their charges in very cold water as a form of sedative.[2] Well into the twentieth century, residents of asylums were given forced cold showers, strapped into stalls and hosed down with jets of freezing water, or else 'mummi-fied' in wet towels and made to lie in cold baths. Some physicians believed that cold-water exposure was an effective treatment for agitation and anxiety. In the military, 'the water cure' became an ironic name for tortures like dunking, drowning ordeals and water-boarding.

At the same time, the great and good of society were being told by their doctors to 'take the waters': to visit spa towns, alpine lakes and seaside resorts and immerse themselves in cold water for the sake of their body and mind. Various – often doubtful – explanations were put forward to explain the benefits of cold-water immersion. In 1715 Lichfield physician John Floyer published his book *Psychrolousia: Or, the History of Cold Bathing* in which he argued that '*Cold Baths* act much on the *Spirits*, and preserve them from *Evaporation*, and render them *Strong* and *Vigorous*.' Floyer claimed that cold bathing was a storied tradition stretching back to the Romans. He blamed its disappearance on the Puritans, who saw baptisms as superstition – rather than full immersion in a baptismal font, they contented themselves with mere 'Sprinkling'. 'Tis certain *Cold Water* contracts and strengthens all *Nervous Parts*,' said Floyer, citing the case of a Yorkshireman who, as a result of regular cold baths, lived to 169.

In Nordic countries, ice swimming – combined with retreats to hot saunas – has long been commonplace. Yet in Britain and America, voluntary immersion in cold water has until recently been more niche, the province of masochistic oddballs who revelled in their status as cultural outliers.

And so, perhaps, it would have remained, were it not for the emergence of an unlikely modern superhero.

———

In 1995 Wim Hof's wife killed herself. He did not see it coming. 'I lived with her for fifteen years and we had four children. She was so alive and so sensitive. She became touched by . . . I don't know. Society, stress . . . She became psychotic. Different personalities . . . She jumped from the eighth storey, down.'[3]

He was left to raise four children alone – 'hopeless, powerless'. As he tells it, one day he was walking in the park when his attention was drawn to the pond, covered in a thin layer of ice. He felt an urge to plunge into the freezing water, and as soon as he gave into it he felt the constant, churning thoughts – what psychologists call 'rumination' – vanish, replaced by a feeling of focus and calm.

This is Wim Hof's origin story – how he claims he was transformed from a tormented, grieving widower to the figure known as the Iceman.

Some call him a visionary, vindicated by multiple scientific studies. Others see him as a dangerous quack whose 'method' makes overblown, unproven health claims and encourages – if only implicitly – vulnerable people to take potentially fatal risks. He has amassed a cult following, many celebrity admirers, and twenty-six world records.

What sets his feats of endurance apart, however, is his claim that anyone can learn to do them. 'Hard nature is merciless, but righteous,' he has said. 'He taught me to do things with my immune system, nervous system, my cardiovascular system and my mind, beyond my thinking.'

A garrulous, Rasputin-like figure with a wild grey beard and the grizzled, dishevelled intensity of a nineteenth-century whaling captain, Wim lent cold-water immersion a wild glamour that it had previously lacked. In the UK, at least, swimming in freezing ponds or the sea was largely associated with amiable, dorky eccentrics clutching thermos flasks – an activity on a par with medieval re-enactments or bell-ringing.

Wim's claims are not without evidence. Researchers at Wayne State University studied his ability to regulate his body temperature by using a specially designed suit into which they pumped cold (15–17°C) or neutral (31–34°C) water while recording his brain activity and physiology with fMRI and PET scanners.[4] They found he was able to maintain his skin temperature regardless of fluctuations in water temperature when compared to both controls and himself when he was not attempting the method. The authors concluded their findings 'suggest the compelling possibility that the WHM (Wim Hof Method) might allow practitioners to develop higher levels of control over key components of the autonomous system, with implications for lifestyle interventions that might ameliorate multiple clinical syndromes.'

Many – including Wim himself – have made grand claims for the method, saying it has the potential to cure autoimmune disorders and fight off various diseases without medication (on Russell Brand's *Under The Skin* podcast, Wim claimed it could help people protect themselves against Covid-19: 'I am able to tackle the problem of what the coronavirus is causing – and that is the deregulation of the innate immune system'). My interest, however, was purely in the psychological side.

A 2014 study suggested that volunteers trained for ten days in the WHM were able to assert some control over their immune system after being injected with a bacterial endotoxin, through conscious control of their sympathetic nervous system. The study reported that the breathing techniques seemed to help volunteers release more adrenaline, and that their cortisol levels normalised more quickly than controls after injection with the endotoxin.[5] Imagine training yourself to take control of previously automatic processes – of being able to consciously control the release of stress hormones, or even modulate your immune response to fight off disease.

My enthusiasm was only slightly muted when I dug deeper. A follow-up study, co-authored by one of the original researchers, Matthijs Kox, suggests that the volunteers' enthusiasm for the WHM and their belief in its efficacy may partially explain why they did better than controls; higher optimism when it comes to treatment outcomes appears to result in higher blood adrenaline levels and lower self-ratings of flu-like symptoms when reporting back.[6] Maybe they had more adrenaline because they were just more excited, and maybe they reported fewer symptoms because they expected to feel better.

Still, might not breathing techniques and cold-water exposure be the perfect remedy for my anxiety and panic? To my layman's mind they sounded like they might retrain a key component of my malfunction, my autonomic nervous system. Suffocation and freezing might be two of our most primal fears – threats that predate our humanity, threats that almost every species on Earth has evolved to sense and avoid.

I imagined myself sinking into an icy clear lake, my whole body alive with freezing fire. The silence. The ecstatic rebirth.

Perhaps this was what I had been craving all along. Not to run from my body's ancient systems of survival, but to embrace them. To return to nature. To come home.

Years ago, I was sat round a campfire singing songs with an ex-convict turned cook – a big, stolid, shaven-headed Mancunian – when he told us about the time he and his band decided to play 'Piggies' by the Beatles at a police gala.

'We knew it would be bad,' he said, 'but it was *really* bad.'

His words came back to me the first time I tried a cold shower.

I screamed. Fully shrieked as if I were being murdered. Thank God no one else was in the house – or the street outside – because you don't hear a noise like that without calling the emergency services.

I lasted all of twenty seconds before jumping out angry and shivering, feeling deeply betrayed. Where was this ecstatic bliss I had been promised?

It's hard to exaggerate how little I enjoyed my first cold shower. I'd forgotten we've all had brief, involuntary cold showers in those moments where someone else in the house turns a hot tap on. Those are never profound spiritual experiences. Something about the gap between the paltriness of the experience – a brief splash of cold water – and my melodramatic response rankled. So many things in my life made me overreact, scream when there was no need to scream.

But unlike fears about work, or my wife hating me, or the world ending, this was obviously just a cold shower. I could *see* it wasn't going to kill me.

Maybe what I really hated wasn't the cold itself. It was the reminder that I was a wimp.

A few days later, I tried again.

I spent two minutes dancing from foot to foot on the bathmat, delaying the inevitable. In the end I stepped in. Cold water hit my scalp. The sensation was like needles. I turned and it struck me between the shoulder blades, taking my breath away. It was *so* much worse than I had imagined. It actually hurt. My knuckles ached when the water hit them. Still, I counted to sixty, twisting and rotating to make sure no part of me escaped.

My skin was glowing, my whole body buzzing with energy. I couldn't stop laughing. YouTube entrepreneur douche-bros talk about cold showers like some supremely masculine rite of passage, on a par with scarification rituals or wrestling a polar bear while trekking through Arctic tundra.

It was just a bit silly. I'd gone really giggly. I felt like my whole body had tensed as hard as it would go, then just relaxed.

The process let me watch my anxiety play out from beginning to end – the growing anticipation, the avoidance, the pain of procrastination, then the encounter itself, somehow both worse than I'd feared and completely survivable. Then the aftermath, the relief, the weird sense of accomplishment.

Like Andrea's cupboard exposure therapy, taking a cold shower was – in itself – pointless. I didn't need to do it. Nothing bad would happen if I 'failed'.

The comedian Marc Maron has talked about people who were bullied as children going into stand-up because it allows them to control *why* people laugh at them. Cold showers, I quickly realised, allowed me to control why I was anxious. They allowed me complete control over one very specific source of anxiety. They let me rehearse facing anxiety in a ridiculous situation where the stakes were zero.

———

It's hard to keep up cold showers every day, but with my war on anxiety going badly, I had the motivation to get back on the gross, freezing horse. Soon I was doing three minutes from a cold start.

I experimented with turning the shower on, then immediately stepping in without blinking, like a psychopath. It worked pretty well. No matter how long I dithered, the water didn't get even a fraction of a degree warmer. If I delayed, all I did was prolong the least enjoyable part – the anticipation.

Within a week, my body was adapting. When the water hit me, I didn't feel the same jolt, the same involuntary gasp. In as little as thirty seconds, the water didn't feel cold at all. I saved time, too. Showering in freezing water is great motivation to wash quickly.

It wasn't a miracle cure. On days when I was anxious, I could rarely muster the courage to get in the shower in the first place, even though I knew it would probably help (it never made me feel worse, except during that first minute).

Maybe this was the exposure therapy I'd been looking for. I wanted more.

Could I go colder?

—

For anaesthetist Mark Harper, cold was originally the enemy. If a patient gets cold during an operation, it's generally bad for them. But after swimming in the cold sea, he noticed he felt great. 'Essentially, getting into cold water creates a stress response,' he told me. 'When you first do it, it's a really big stress response. The more you do it, the less that stress response becomes. It doesn't go away, but it comes right down.'

Mark started reading up on how cold water affects you physiologically, and how adapting to it reduces inflammation. When he read new research suggesting – as Dr Ruihua Hou had told me – that inflammation is linked to depression, he wondered if you could use cold-water adaptation and swimming to treat it.

The theory he's exploring is cross-adaptation. Immersing yourself in cold water triggers that same fight, flight or freeze response as daily psychological stressors – in this case, the 'cold-shock response'. The body thinks, *Fuck, I'm in danger,* and works to give you enough energy to escape a potentially lethal environment.

With repeated exposures, your body starts to adapt. As your cold-shock response decreases – so the theory goes – so does your physiological response to stress right across the board. 'That stress becomes less because you're adapted to stress.'

In toxicology, this principle is called hormesis – 'a process in which exposure to a low dose of a chemical agent or environmental factor that is damaging at higher doses induces an adaptive beneficial effect on the cell or organism'.[7] Sometimes brief, controlled exposure to a small amount of something bad like a toxin or a stressor gives us practice at fighting it. It's the principle behind vaccines.

The dose makes the poison.

Cold-water swimming – so the theory goes – induces a specific hormetic response known as the 'adaptive stress response'. Sudden skin cooling – as in cold-water immersion – triggers the cold-shock response: constriction of blood vessels close to the surface of the skin as your body tries to conserve heat round your core, a gasp reflex, increased heart rate and hyperventilation.

In untrained, unhabituated individuals, this can be a fatal combination. People who fall into very cold water can rapidly become panicked and disoriented, and the gasp reflex often means they inhale water. However, repeated exposure diminishes the intensity of the cold-shock response. According to Mark, this can be achieved with as little as six immersions at 10–14°C, three minutes a time, over a week. In the UK, that's the rough sea temperature in April and May, or from October to December.

'Sixty per cent of your stress response as measured by blood pressure and heart rate changes,' said Mark, 'and fifty per cent of that's still there fourteen months later.'[8]

In 2018, Mark co-authored a case study where a twenty-four-year-old woman who had suffered from major depressive disorder since she was seventeen took up a programme of weekly swimming in cold open water. Her depression had resisted treatment with the SSRIs citalopram and fluoxetine, but according to the study, swimming in cold water 'led to an immediate improvement in mood following each swim and a sustained and gradual reduction in symptoms of depression'.[9]

A case study isn't convincing evidence on its own – at best, it's proof of concept, a hint that an area deserves further investigation. Another 2018 study found that elements of the cold-shock response are mediated by anxiety – specifically, the more anxious you are when you enter very cold water, the faster and deeper you tend to breathe and the higher your heart rate. This effect can delay or even prevent the adaptation Mark talks about through repeated immersions.[10]

Like Mark, I'd already experienced a lift in mood from cold water. I thought it was worth a try.

Autumn was sliding towards winter. Mark had said that, although you can adapt at any temperature below 20°C – i.e. the British sea in summer – the 'optimal temperature' was 10–14°C. If I wanted to enact the protocol he suggested – six cold-water immersions of three minutes each on consecutive days, outdoors, I would have to act soon.

Looking on Google Maps, I found a spot twenty minutes' walk from my house, in the River Wensum. I stuffed a towel in a plastic bag by way of committing myself. The experiment would start on Monday.

—

A brief warning: I swam alone. This was not ideal.

Yes, I was in a public park with people in sight. Yes, I was never more than a couple of metres from the bank. Most people go through their entire outdoor swimming career without ever finding themselves in a situation where they need assistance. But swimming with a partner is an important safety net for the rare occasions where something goes wrong.

Drowning is the most obvious danger (and is one of the UK's leading causes of accidental death, though 44 per cent of the people who drown each year never intended to enter the water),[11] but there are others. Transient global amnesia affects roughly 1 in every 20,000 people per year, especially those over 40. It involves severe confusion that lasts 1–8 hours, where the person temporarily loses the ability to make new memories. Transient global amnesia is often triggered by intense physical stress such as immersion in cold water. It usually passes with no lasting neurological effects, but it can be very traumatic.[12] In the highly unlikely event you were to suffer such an attack – even if you were at home, in an ice bath – you'd want a friend present to look after you.

I went alone because most of my friends have got jobs, and because I was desperate. I realise you might be desperate too, but *please don't be a dickhead*. If you want to do a cold outdoor swim, do it somewhere safe and legal, and take a friend.

The air temperature was 10°C. As I made my way through the park, a wet mulch of leaves squelched beneath my trainers. I passed a guy in duffel coat, gloves and woolly hat walking his Doberman. Under my trousers I was wearing bright orange swimming trunks.

It was a typical dreary, grey, late-autumn English day. Not extreme conditions by any stretch of the imagination, but odd ones for taking a dip. I followed a slope down to the water's edge. Between bramble bushes, a grooved ramp eased into the river.

I stood there for a while, staring at the water, wondering if I'd lost my mind. It didn't look like a swimming spot, nor did today feel like a swimming day. Lorries rumbled over the nearby bridge. The wet grass was salted with fag ends. I wasn't worried about the cold so much as appearing mentally ill. I toyed with the zip on my jeans (in retrospect not a great look for someone trying to seem normal in a public park). I felt like I was about to strip off and climb into a shopping mall fountain.

Was I deluded for trying to swim myself sane? Or would the real delusion be to come this far, only to back away? I had so little trust left in my own judgement.

In the end, I thought back to all those cold showers, and how stringing it out just made it worse. I thought how bad I'd feel about myself if I backed down now. How it would bug me, like a hangnail or a misattributed quote on a pub blackboard.

I sat down and started taking off my shoes. By the time my first sock came off, I knew that, one way or the other, I was committed.

Mud squelched beneath my toes. I balanced my clothes on top of the plastic bag, then walked down to the submerged end of the ramp. The water came to just below my knees. It was very cold. On the opposite bank was a canoe club, closed for the winter.

I glanced back into the park, half-hoping I had drawn a small, astonished crowd goggling at this liberated maverick. The man I'd passed earlier was standing about fifty metres away with his back to me, smoking a roll-up while the Doberman took a shit.

I turned to the river. I'd been looking forward to this – glorious union with the elements, escape from my worry and anxious thoughts. But now I was here, in a damp park, it seemed a bit crap.

I sat down on the lip of the ramp, lowering my body into the water up to my navel. Okay, it was definitely cold. I had to do it now. If I just sat here gazing morosely at the water people would definitely think I was having some sort of breakdown. I mean, I probably *was* – I just didn't want anyone to notice.

It doesn't begin until your heart goes under. That's when you get the shock of being submerged – the sense of being on a timer. A crushing pain enveloped my hands and feet. I started counting: *One, Mississippi, two, Mississippi.*

Mark had told me to stay in until I had brought my breath down to a normal speed and volume. When you immerse yourself in cold water, your body narrows all the capillaries near the surface of your skin, reducing blood flow to preserve warmth round your vital organs. After all, it's better to lose a finger than to damage your heart. But after a certain point – much of the literature I'd read on cold-water immersion suggested fifteen minutes as a rough average – that cold reaches your core. At that point, you're becoming hypothermic – as Mark put it, 'thermically injuring yourself' – and the survival rate plunges vertiginously.

I didn't want to come anywhere near that danger zone, and I was aware that once I got out I'd still be losing heat, so I had committed to sticking it out for three minutes max.

Away from the bank, the current was stronger than I had expected. It began pulling me downriver and I had to swim against it just to stay in place. A minute in, my skin had gone numb and my fingers and toes felt like I'd crushed them in a door. I dunked my head under to get the full hit, coming up with a throbbing ice-cream headache.

I swam breaststroke against the current, concentrating on slowing my breathing. For the last thirty seconds I held onto the submerged ramp and kicked the way we used to back in swimming classes.

When I hauled myself out I was shuddering. I staggered to the plastic bag and fumbled with numb fingers for my towel. It felt like wire wool across my reddening flesh. I did my best to dry my hair and drag my clothes on. Sensation was returning to my extremities, and with it, pain. My feet felt broken. I stuffed my dripping shorts into the bag and hobbled back across the park to where I'd left the car.

Mark had advised me that warming up from the inside out is best, through thermogenesis – for example, by going for a run. Inside the car, I did something I knew was unwise: I turned on the heater full blast. Air scorched my face and hands, painfully hot. The danger with heating yourself up quickly after a cold swim – especially from the outside in – is that all those little capillaries around the periphery dilate and cold blood flows back into your core. Sure enough, thirty seconds later I felt a chill run through my heart and belly. That's not a metaphor – I could actually feel the icy blood worming its way into my vital organs. I started shivering and sweating at the same time. My toes and fingers throbbed. I felt nauseous.

It was a challenging start, and I still had five days left.

What I had failed to do when I committed to the six-day experiment was to check the weather forecast the rest of the week. Turned out it was due to get colder.

Much colder.

The temperature dropped from 9°C the next day, to 8, to 6, to 4.

On Tuesday I knew what I was in for. I hesitated on the riverbank.

What was I afraid of? *Come on, Tim, you're briefly entering water of slightly suboptimal temperature, not going over the top at Passchendaele.*

I thought of my Finnish in-laws who swam in holes cut in frozen lakes. Again, I had that feeling of ridiculousness.

As humans we can tolerate much more than we realise. Anxiety is a very conservative impulse that keeps us safe. It takes discomfort as an early warning signal for loss and injury. This is a useful heuristic if you're about to trap your winky in a zip. But if you follow it too rigidly, you're going to miss a lot of life's juice. In the words of the great Finnish scholar and explorer Moominpappa: 'If you want an adventure, you've got to be prepared to rough it a little.'[13]

I climbed in. It was bad for about a minute, then it was fine.

On Wednesday, I marched down to the river with clenched fists, amped up, ready to assert myself and be a warrior. I had learned my lesson. Time to be brave.

Two swans were in my usual swimming spot.

They spotted me and started swimming towards me, presumably hoping for bread. If I got in the water my head would be at optimal pecking height. I spent the next ten minutes hiding behind a bramble bush. At last they glided away. The swim that followed was coloured with terror. I kept expecting them to reappear, to hear the thump of those infamous, arm-breaking wings.

If it weren't for the experiment I would have given up. Six days, Mark had said. That was the protocol. If I missed one, I'd have to start all over again from scratch. Each day I got up, dreading it. Each day I thought how shit I'd feel if I backed down now. Each day, it got colder.

On Saturday, the final day, I woke to frost on the ground. The air temperature was −2°C. Leaving the house, I felt strangely elated. I could see my breath.

When I reached the park, buttery sunlight was breaking over the slanted white roof of the canoe club. Grass crunched under my trainers. Where sun struck the bramble bushes, vapour rose in a glistening mist. I walked down to the water's edge and stripped to my swim shorts.

A running club were staging a 10k race that passed through the park, and as I lowered myself into the river, dozens of people in gloves and woolly hats were jogging past. I heard a woman exclaim: 'Oh my God!' Finally, the sheeple had noticed the liberated radical in their midst. Nice middle-class sense of propriety you've got there, madam. Be a shame if someone were to . . . disregard it.

When I sank into the water, my breath didn't catch. I breathed steadily and deeply, swimming away from the bank.

Sunlight thrilled the river with hundreds of silver flakes. Steam rose from the bramble bushes. Everything shone. I swam against the current, counting in my head: *One, Mississippi, two, Mississippi.*

Over the last decade, there's been a resurgence in middle-class writers treating 'wild swimming' as some sort of mystic communion with nature. Something special and exalted. Ooh, look at me, I'm in a body of open water and I have a degree. If we're not careful, it becomes a bit of a performance, even if only to ourselves. We can't do it without thinking about what it *means*, what it says about us, without mentally preparing a commentary so we can Instagram it later.

The truth is, in Britain, swimming outdoors is like sex. It's not always great, but doing it is less important than establishing a reputation as someone who does it.

What the cold did, at least for me, was strip away the continual worried, self-conscious chatter in my head. I was very aware that I was a guest in an environment that could not support me for more than a few minutes. My mind wasn't wandering to that email I hadn't replied to, or fretting about someone I suspected didn't like me. I wasn't asking myself if I was okay this morning. I wasn't checking for signs of an impending panic attack.

I was swimming, and I was counting, and everything was beautiful.

When I got out, I towelled myself down, then laced up my trainers and ran along the river for four miles, warming myself through thermogenesis in a way I hoped Mark and Dave would have approved of. As sensation came back my feet stung and ached. Parts of the track were slick with ice, and I skidded. I kept going. Eventually the pain faded and I was warm, running beside the river in the morning sun, my skin and belly tingling. Calm.

———

At the moment we don't have much data on whether cold-water immersion is an effective treatment for anxiety and panic. That might be because no one's funded large, high-quality studies to find out. We only develop an evidence base for treatments that researchers investigate. But then you could say the same about watching episodes of *M*A*S*H* while lying in a bathtub of mayonnaise. Large, high-quality studies might well find out that cold-water immersion, compared to placebo, does nothing.

On a wide scale, even if it proved effective, I imagine compliance would be a problem. Cold exposure is painful, it *induces* anxiety in the short-term, and it's a hassle to arrange. More saliently, done unsupervised, it can be dangerous – even fatal. But, assuming you could arrange professionally supervised sessions, are the other downsides significantly worse than the side effects of anti-anxiety medications, or the time and cost involved in seeing a therapist?

Mark's theories about cross-adaptation are biologically plausible, but just because something *can* happen doesn't mean that it *does*. As he rightly observed, simply being in nature and doing exercise can have an impact in themselves. We have data on those interventions already. Why add an arctic endurance component? Is the effect really that much larger?

I wonder if, for some of us, there's an element of *overcoming* – what psychologist Albert Bandura calls 'self-efficacy'.[14] Taking those cold showers, and eventually turning up for that cold dip six days in a row, challenged my self-image. I've often thought of myself as a lazy, fearful person who can't accomplish very much, who likes to stay in his comfort zone, who retreats if he feels anxiety. For six consecutive days I felt anxiety, discomfort and actual physical pain . . . and I went and did the thing anyway. Not only that, but knowing what I was facing, I kept doing it. I was surprised. That final Saturday swim was one of my most memorable, pleasurable moments of the year.

By doing something I wouldn't ordinarily do, by behaving in a way I wouldn't ordinarily behave, I discovered that some of my predictions about myself and the world were wrong. My mental schema's validity was thrown into question. I became more uncertain.

I'm not sure cold exposure helped my immune system – that final Saturday night I was woken at 2 a.m. by stomach pains and explosive diarrhoea that kept me up till sunrise. (Possibly something I picked up from my swim, which was a hundred metres downriver from the city tip.) Aside from that ignominious footnote, I enjoyed the experience. It felt meaningful to me.

What I didn't know when I emerged from the river on that freezing Saturday was if the experience would stick; if I was somehow better prepared, more resilient. Of course, we can never know the future. Given what was on its way, I'm glad I didn't.

XVI.

BREATHING
Pulmonary biology and the science of panic attacks

Reading about panic-attack symptoms is like licking a photograph of an ice cream. The DSM-5's entry for panic disorder describes a panic attack as 'an abrupt surge of intense fear or intense discomfort that reaches a peak within minutes' – which is technically accurate, but a bit like describing getting kicked in the nuts as 'an intense external pressure applied abruptly to the testicles'.

Even I forgot how bad they were between episodes.

The DSM-5 says a panic attack must have four or more of thirteen symptoms, including a pounding heart, trembling, feelings of choking, stomach cramps, dizziness, numbness, a feeling that nothing is real, fears of going insane and fears of dying. Crunching the combinatorics – what neuroscientist Nathaniel Daw described to me as 'the Taco Bell combination of ingredients' – I make that a total of 7,814 flavours of diagnostically acceptable panic attack.

In addition, the DSM-5 lists culturally specific symptoms, like ringing in the ears and a sore neck during what Cambodians call *khyâl cap* or 'wind attacks', or 'uncontrollable screaming and crying' in an *ataque de nervios* as reported by people of Latinx descent. I find the exclusion from the standard list of these particular panic-attack symptoms slightly weird – I've certainly experienced them – but the point is that some people might experience a sore neck as a warning sign that a panic attack is about to erupt and feel so afraid that they trigger a panic attack, whereas others without those cultural associations would not.

When we say 'panic attack', we're not always talking about the same thing. Some people go completely still and silent. Some people run, scrambling for the nearest exit. Some people freak out, scream, wail. There's no such thing as the definitive panic attack á la mode.

Going into this it's important you know what a panic attack feels like. Why don't I walk you through the one I just had?

—

It was late. I was sitting at the kitchen table. Lisa came in and asked if I'd put any of the cauliflower cheese she'd just made into Suki's packed lunch for when she went to the childminder the next day.

Now, intellectually I knew I was unlikely to need to:

a) fight hand-to-hand for my life,
b) flee at high speed,
c) remain absolutely motionless so as to go undetected by a predator.

I just needed to have a simple, open discussion. You know, like a person. My brain and body, however, had other plans.

I felt tightness in my chest. I hadn't used the cauliflower cheese – I'd used some pasta I made yesterday instead – and I had a presentiment that this would be Wrong. That Lisa wouldn't think I'd chosen well, and she would want to change it or at least express disapproval.

These are what a cognitive behavioural therapist would call automatic thoughts.[1] They are habitual reactions to a stimulus, interpretative choices so familiar, made so quickly, that they feel identical with reality.

I must have recognised I was being irrational because, instead of getting outwardly defensive, I braced myself against feelings of vulnerability and resentment and said no, I hadn't realised that it was okay to use the cauliflower cheese. My wife said, smiling, that she'd told me. I said, smiling, that I must not have heard but it sounded like a really good idea and the dinner I'd prepared was in the fridge if she wanted to change it.

As she opened the fridge and took out our daughter Suki's red Postman Pat lunchbox, all sorts of emotions were rising in me. I often felt scared to even try to prepare Suki's meals for the next day – even though I did it several nights a week – for fear of Lisa taking it out and examining it later, telling me that I'd done some aspect of it wrong, or that she would have chosen a different food. I'd stand in front of the fridge imagining scenes of judgement and criticism, my heart would start to race and my vision would get blurry and it'd be hard to concentrate on what I was supposed to be doing. Which would make me less confident in choosing well. Which would increase my anxiety. Which would increase the symptoms. Which would make it harder to think. And so on. Sometimes I would end up grabbing the first thing I saw, just to get the ordeal over with.

In this instance, as Lisa took the lid off the bowl, she tried to get my attention, saying that I'd cut the cherry tomatoes into halves instead of quarters, and that was dangerous because it was a potential choking hazard. She began spooning out the pasta I'd prepared and replacing it with her cauliflower cheese. I felt heartbroken. I'd failed again. Nothing I did was ever good enough. I was constantly being judged and it wasn't fair. I wasn't respected or valued as a parent. I was just shoved aside.

If I sound, in this moment, brittle, melodramatic, self-centred, illogical, petty and unfair; if, dear confidante, I sound like a nightmare to live with, that may well be because, at times, I am. Peering inside a mentally ill person's head during periods of dysfunction rarely flatters them. That's why it's called 'mental illness' and not 'cool, reasonable thoughts syndrome'. Well-meaning people often tell anxiety sufferers: *Don't be so hard on yourself*. This can lead to very black-and-white thinking where we're either horrible monsters or passive victims. Sometimes it feels like our only choices are self-blame or self-pity.

Having anxiety or depression doesn't grant you diplomatic immunity from acting like a bell-end. And that's okay, because humans are allowed to make mistakes. We can behave like twats sometimes, and that doesn't make us beasts, broken, or failures. We can give ourselves permission to forgive ourselves, but only if we also take responsibility for our behaviour – those aspects which were under our control – and acknowledge the possibility for change.

The thoughts I was having in that moment and the ways I was acting on them were both a product and a process of mental illness. But they were also me. My habits, arising from my decisions. They happened so fast, so *effortlessly*, it would be easy to believe I had no choice.

We always have a choice. And thank goodness for that.

Back in the kitchen, I chose to share my feelings. I told Lisa how miserable I felt, how gutted I was that I could never do anything right, how constantly scared I was of her analysing and criticising my dinner choices for our daughter. She told me she was tired of my not listening to simple safety instructions. Suki could choke on half a cherry tomato.

Oh great. Now she was saying I didn't care if our daughter lived or died. Now she was looking at my efforts and not only saying she could do better, but she was more or less calling me a child murderer.

I started crying. Lisa tried to ignore me. I started sobbing that I couldn't do anything right, that I was scared to even try because she always criticised me. It's worth noting that, at this point, there was still a commentary going on in my head observing: *Tim, this is unlikely to result in either of you feeling happier*, and, *Tim, this is not strictly true*.

I ignored those thoughts, because I felt *wounded*. I had this pain that I wanted acknowledged and tended to and healed. Like a toddler pushing a cereal bowl off the table, I was saying, *Listen to me listen to me listen*.

BREATHING

This was neither of our first times at the sad-panic rodeo and so my wife mostly tried to ignore me. I repeated my grievances, helpfully clarifying that I could never do anything right and I was never good enough for her. She said she was sick of not being listened to and she didn't want the stress of this.

By this point the physiological changes brought on by my thoughts were intensifying. My heart rate was increasing. I was breathing faster. My vision had started narrowing. I had the thought that I'd let things slip out of control and if I didn't act fast they would get a lot worse.

I felt a stabbing pain in my heart, like I was worthless. I wanted to hit myself in the head over and over, to punish myself for being so stupid and useless and selfish, for letting my emotions get out of control and starting an argument, and just to distract myself from the whirling cycle of thoughts and self-loathing.

I tried to leave the kitchen. The room seemed to tilt like the deck of a ship. The lights were too bright and everything looked unreal. I felt like I was going to pass out – despite the fact that I have never once lost consciousness during a panic attack – and took a few deep, sucking breaths. The muscles in my neck were tightening. My throat felt like it was closing.

I cried out to Lisa for help. I said I couldn't breathe, couldn't think straight. I was going mad.

She said I should go out of the room and calm down.

I stared at an empty plug socket. In the sickly light, it seemed to be vibrating. I clutched at my throat. I shouted that I couldn't breathe, I couldn't move. I was frozen to the spot. I was sure that anything I said now would make things worse.

She said I was having a panic attack and it would be okay.

But I could tell she was still – understandably – annoyed at me. It would not be okay because now she was upset, I'd screwed things up – over the most trivial of issues – and failed again and now my panic was back after it had seemed like I was getting better, and I'd never be free of this and now my wife hated me. And who could blame her? She'd never want to spend any time with me again. She was thinking I was a failure, my anxiety disorder was permanent and she was already making plans to leave me.

I said I was so sorry and please could she help me, I was sorry that my panic had ruined her evening.

In retrospect, this was a semi-conscious rhetorical ploy to bait her into saying that the evening wasn't ruined, and everything was all right. Some part of me calculated that by overstating the case, I would force her to make a verbal correction in my favour. I imagined hearing that bit of reassurance would give me some relief and my symptoms would calm down a little. I craved that reassurance. I felt it was my only hope.

She said: 'It's not your panic that's ruined my evening.'

It took me a moment to understand the distinction. Like when the samurai looks down and realises he's impaled on his opponent's katana.

I was filled with a rush of adrenalised terror. We weren't just having an argument – I had *ruined the evening*. I'd failed and screwed up and it was happening all over again, the powerless paralysed terror, the anxiety that seemed to control every moment of my life, that told me where I could and couldn't go, that stopped my being able to think straight, that let me believe I was free only to yank on the leash and drag me shrieking back, this useless pathetic fucked-up man-child approaching forty who couldn't even have the world's safest, most middle-class parent conversation with his wife about the merits of wholewheat pasta versus cauliflower cheese without losing his mind. How was I going to deal with the rest of my life if I couldn't deal with this? What hope did I have?

The literature calls this 'ruminative flooding' – the point where the cycle of negative thoughts becomes so rapid and intense you start to feel confused and out of control. It's as if you took the low, bleak, repeated thoughts of depression and began accelerating them in a salad spinner. Life seems dreadful, unliveable, and anxiety turns these dark thoughts to threats which require an answer *now*. Depression becomes a state of emergency. Ruminative flooding can combine with 'frantic hopelessness' – an *urgent* sense that life cannot improve, of being trapped – to push someone over the edge to a suicide attempt.[2]

I dropped to the floor and started screaming.

I shrieked and contorted and shoved a towel in my mouth to muffle the sound. For some reason I kept saying over and over, 'Please don't hit me, please don't hit me.' Lisa has never hit me, but in that moment I was cowering on the cold tiles, my arms over my head, terrified I was about to be beaten up. I know it sounds bizarre – because it is, that's why what I'm describing is a symptom of mental illness – but in the moment begging for mercy felt like a compulsion. I wasn't even especially addressing her. I just felt this intense conviction that punches and kicks would rain down any second. That retribution was imminent.

I couldn't breathe yet somehow I hadn't passed out. My muscles were tensed, my arms folded, my hands twisted into claws. The floor tiles looked unreal, like cell-shaded animation. I felt like a character in a TV show.

Eventually I crawled into the adjacent room and lay shuddering on the carpet, the towel over my head, alternately screaming and catching my breath. Aware that I had failed, that panic and anxiety had got the better of me again, that I had stressed out and alienated the one I love most in the world, that the consequences of this lapse – the shameful, humiliating memory – would last days, weeks, months even. After about ten minutes I felt able to stand, and I came up to my office, where I wrote down a version of the account I'm telling you now.

———

I know none of this reflects on me well. I would rather be sharing a gently self-deprecating story about how I was too shy to accept some award for my amazing humanitarian work. But it's important you understand what a panic attack can look like *in vivo*, as the literature puts it. And, to be clear, I had been through *hundreds* of these fuckers. Maybe more than a thousand, often three or four a day, for nearly fifteen years. I lived in terror of them. Of that choking sensation. The brain fog and cascading thoughts. The air hunger. The emotional fallout.

So yeah, when I heard there might be a way to silence my mind and regain control of my breathing? That got my attention.

As well as swimming in cold open water, I decided to try some Wim Hof-style breathing exercises too. There was, after all, some research supporting both practices, and trying it was free. Sure, it was a little on the woo-woo end of scientific, but if I got nothing out of it I'd have lost nothing except a few minutes of my time.

Hof's breathing techniques draw upon – some would say 'plunder wholesale and secularise' – Tibetan *tummo*: a tradition of yogic breathing where adherents breathe heavily while visualising inner heat. There are amazing tales of ceremonies where monks sit in the freezing Himalayan cold with wet sheets wrapped around their bodies, trying to generate enough heat to dry the sheets. Experienced meditators – so eyewitnesses claim – can dry multiple sheets in a session, steam rising from their bodies as they breathe.

Tummo itself has been the subject of research – a 2013 study by psychologist Maria Kozhevnikov and colleagues looked at meditators in remote monasteries of eastern Tibet, monitoring their external temperature and brainwaves via electroencephalography.[3] They also looked at western participants who were taught aspects of the *tummo* practice. Kozhevnikov concluded that *tummo*'s ability to raise and maintain core body temperature was likely down to two things: the physical exertion of the breathing techniques, which leads to thermogenesis, and meditators' visualisation of inner heat. The latter correlated with increased alpha waves in the brain, which seemed to extend the length of time core body temperature increased, leading to higher core body temperature overall.

Which is interesting, but doesn't imply anything mystical – you can increase thermogenesis in your body by walking upstairs or straining during a bowel movement. Go for a run on a cold day, and you'll soon find yourself sweating. Even the visualisation aspect – what Kozhevnikov calls the 'neurocognitive component' – while on the face of it a bit more surprising, reflects what every anxiety sufferer knows only too well: thoughts can stimulate physiological reactions in the body.

Imagine having to give a presentation at work. The light from the projector is in your eyes. Everyone is staring at you, blank-faced. You can't remember what your next slide was supposed to be about. You're pretty sure everyone is pissed off and bored.

Picture this with enough vividness – the dust motes caught in the projector beam, the dryness of your tongue against the roof of your mouth, the disapproving expressions – and your sympathetic nervous system will stimulate the production of adrenaline, noradrenaline and cortisol. Your pulse will quicken, your skin conductance will increase, more antibodies will enter your bloodstream. Our thoughts affect our physiology all the time. It's not weird or unusual and you certainly don't need to learn a special 'method' to be able to do it.

In the *tummo* style of breathing, you perform controlled hyperventilation. After 30 to 40 deep breaths, you partially empty your lungs and refrain from breathing for between 60 seconds and 4 minutes – *hypo*ventilation. When eventually you feel the urge to breathe, you inhale, holding the breath for 10 to 15 seconds.

Wim and adherents of his system claim it lets us 'change the physiology', and 'get into' our nervous system, gaining conscious control. He has claimed the breathing technique is 'oxygenising the blood and all the cells', allowing people to hold their breath for much longer than normally possible.

This explanation is inaccurate. The truth is quite complicated and technical, and it took several days of research – and eventually a chat with one of the world's leading experts on panic attacks – for me to properly understand it. But in getting to grips with the physiology of hyperventilation, in understanding how counterintuitive it is, I learned something valuable about panic attacks themselves – why they're so harrowing, why so much of what I'd been doing to avoid them hadn't worked, and why it might be easy for a non-scientist like Wim Hof to misunderstand his own technique.

———

Take a breath. Hold it.

When you inhale, you draw oxygen down into your lungs. Oxygen binds to haemoglobin,* a protein that carries it through the blood and delivers it to the cells.

Breathe out.

When you exhale, you expel carbon dioxide. CO_2 is like the exhaust fumes of our mitochondria – the little engines that power each cell.

As Walter Cannon discovered, when an animal thinks it's under threat, its body prepares to run away or fight for its life. Both require more energy. Thus the instinct is to breathe more – to draw more oxygen down into the blood (which flows faster thanks to a raised heart rate), to help muscles work harder, which produces more CO_2, which gets carried away by the blood and exhaled. In this way, balance – homeostasis – is maintained. But, crucially, *only* if the predicted flurry of activity happens. If you're not vaulting dried riverbeds or wrestling an aardwolf, oxygen supply is going to vastly outstrip demand. Homeostasis gets disrupted. Weird things start to happen.

When you hyperventilate – as I've done literally hundreds of times in the build up to and during a panic attack – you increase the frequency and volume of your breathing.

Though you take in more oxygen, oddly that doesn't mean

---

* 'Haemo' meaning blood, and 'globin', ball-shaped.

more oxygen reaches your cells. When you're breathing normally, blood oxygen saturation levels are usually around 98 per cent. Most of this oxygen is bound to haemoglobin, with a tiny bit dissolved in your blood. Haemoglobin molecules can carry a maximum of four oxygen molecules each. You can't 'load them up' with oxygen any further.

Each time you exhale, you breathe out CO_2. Since when you hyperventilate you're breathing out more frequently, you eliminate much more CO_2 than usual. Of course, if you were engaged in high-effort, high-intensity activity, your cells would be *producing* much more CO_2, so the proportions in your bloodstream would stay about the same. But if you're just standing or sitting, this rapidly creates an imbalance.

As the level of CO_2 dissolved in your blood drops, you enter a state called hypocapnia. Since CO_2 is acidic, your blood pH rises, becoming more alkaline.

Transports like haemoglobin use the presence of CO_2 and increased blood acidity as a signal to release oxygen into the blood for absorption into the surrounding tissues. Under normal circumstances, CO_2 concentrations in the blood naturally increase as a waste product of metabolism. High levels of acidic CO_2 suggest those mitochondrial engines in each cell have been working hard, so a dip in local blood pH is a handy indicator to haemoglobin that here's a good place to drop their cargo of oxygen.

The reverse is also true. If haemoglobin passes through an area with low amounts of CO_2, that suggests demand in this region is relatively low – the engines haven't been pumping out fumes. So the haemoglobin clings tighter to its four oxygen molecules, saving them for where they're needed.

As you eliminate CO_2 through hyperventilation, your blood becomes more alkaline. As a result, oxygen binds more tightly to haemoglobin. Your blood undergoes what's known as 'a leftward shift on the oxygen–haemoglobin dissociation curve': haemoglobin has an increased affinity for oxygen, leaving less available for absorption into the cells.

A similar thing happens with calcium ions. When CO_2 levels drop, they bond more tightly to transport proteins in the blood, starving your extremities of calcium and quickly leading to symptoms like tingling in your fingers and toes, and numbness (sensations that panic-attack sufferers often take as signs of an impending heart attack). Remember how, during my panic attack, I described my hands twisting into claws? The technical name for that is 'tetany' – involuntary muscle contractions caused by localised calcium deficiency.

Increased blood alkalinity triggers another reaction, called bronchoconstriction, which makes the airways in your lungs tighten. It's your body's way of trying to regain balance, but when you're having a panic attack it creates the sensation that you're choking. Unless you know why it's happening, the natural response is to breathe faster and deeper, which increases CO_2 washout, which intensifies symptoms of choking, tingling and numbness.

Worst of all, raised blood pH stimulates cerebral vasoconstriction – a narrowing of blood vessels in the brain. Being your most important and delicate organ, the brain is particularly sensitive to changes in blood acidity and reacts quickly to restore homeostasis. Lowered CO_2 levels result in reduced blood flow to the brain – up to 50 per cent during acute hyperventilation.

So not only are you cutting blood flow to your brain by up to half, but – since oxygen clings to haemoglobin more tightly in the absence of CO_2 – there's less oxygen available in the blood that *does* get there. This means when you hyperventilate – either deliberately or out of panic – instead of 'oxygenising the cells' you rapidly starve your brain of oxygen, a state called 'cerebral hypoxia'. Hence the frighteningly quick onset of dizziness, confusion, a sense of unreality, and in acute cases fainting or even seizures. It's hard to think rationally, because you're starving your brain.

When these symptoms arise seemingly out of nowhere – rather

than being deliberately induced by a breathing exercise – it's easy to misinterpret the physical sensations of pounding heart, shortness of breath, numb, tingling extremities, faintness and confusion as a cardiac arrest, a brain haemorrhage, or insanity. This extra layer of – not unreasonable – misinterpretation (*I'm dying/going mad*) adds fear and stress, which triggers the HPA axis, stimulating the urge to breathe faster and deeper.

In the WHM technique, after hyperventilation comes a long breath-hold. Most people think what triggers the breath reflex is low oxygen. In fact, the urge to breathe is prompted by the build-up of carbon dioxide. As CO_2 rises, so does blood acidity. If you don't consciously inhale, chemoreceptors in the brain detect falling blood pH and stimulate breathing. Normally it's a good system, signalling your cells have used up the available oxygen and need some more. But like all rules of thumb, there are edge cases where it doesn't work. If you hold your breath after hyperventilating, although the concentration of oxygen in your blood begins dropping, the low levels of CO_2 mean your blood pH doesn't dip enough to alert those acid-sensitive chemoreceptors.

As a result, your blood oxygen levels can drop to abnormally low levels – low enough for you to pass out – without your feeling the urge to breathe. It's not because, as Wim has claimed, you've 'charged up the cells with oxygen' but because the waste product your body usually relies on to trigger that urge is missing. Eventually, if you lose consciousness, the reflex will once again take over.

Given the wonky science, the weird side effects and some apparent dangers, why would any sane person subject themselves to such an ordeal?

I can't speak for sane people, but many researchers I spoke to – in psychology, neuroscience and physiology – wondered aloud if breathing exercises such as this might work as a form of exposure therapy or 'challenge'. I had learned to watch for symptoms of an approaching panic attack – the rapid breathing, the brain fog – to fear them, to instinctively try to distract or soothe myself if I felt them arising. Doing a practice like this, some researchers speculated, might help me unlearn negative associations between rapid breathing and the horror of a panic attack. The drop in blood CO_2, the dizziness, the tightening airways – these were all just physical symptoms. Even the confusion and sense of unreality had a relatively benign explanation. Maybe if I could make some new associations – voluntarily expose myself to these sensations, over and over – I'd stop fearing them, and the self-fulfilling prophecy of panic attacks, the spiral of terror, would finally be broken.

While this specific technique hasn't yet been widely studied – and a lot of breathwork is shot through with New Agey beliefs that have nothing to do with evidence – there's been plenty of interesting research into the physiology of breath-holding, including studies that looked at experienced freedivers who have trained themselves to hold their breath for up to ten minutes while swimming deep underwater. Some research found the body seems to adapt through practice, becoming more efficient at maintaining the flow of oxygen to the brain.[4] The parasympathetic nervous system gets better at slowing the heart rate, blood vessels throughout the body's periphery constrict – raising blood pressure – and blood flow elevates in the brain. Freedivers have reported that dives consist of an easy initial stage, followed by a 'struggling' stage and a final, very uncomfortable, 'fighting' stage. Holding the breath as air hunger increases therefore requires considerable emotional regulation, which may lead to the development of stronger 'top-down' executive control of stress responses from the prefrontal cortex.[5]

Was it faddish, pseudoscientific claptrap? Or was there something in it? Could the answer be: both?

———

Before starting, I tested my blood oxygen level with a pulse oximeter clipped to my index finger. Red digits showed a steady 97–98 per cent. Holding my breath, my oxygen levels only had to drop to about

95 per cent for me to feel that ache in my lungs that signalled I wanted to breathe.

I lay down in bed and began.

You're supposed to breathe with your diaphragm then expand your chest as fully as you can before exhaling. This quickly became arduous and unpleasant. Nasty memories started surfacing of lying in this same spot, gasping for air, feeling like my life was over. My head swum. My fingertips started to tingle.

After thirty breaths, I exhaled gently – not all the way – and stopped breathing. I gazed at the ceiling. My pulse beat against my temple. I raised my index finger and glanced at the pulse oximeter. My blood oxygen held at 98 per cent for the first minute, then began ticking down: 94, 90, 87. When it hit 70 per cent – at around the 90 second mark – my lungs started clenching, like a gag reflex.

I took a long deep breath and held it.

To return to that question: why would anyone practise a breathing technique that starves your brain of oxygen and occasionally induces seizures?

The same reason we do any drug. It feels fucking *great*.

Bear in mind I haven't had a beer in almost a decade, so my hedonism bar may be set low enough to function as a draft-excluder, but in the seconds following that deep breath, I experienced a rush of calm, followed by a strange clarity and euphoria. My whole body tingled. I felt like my vision was sharpening. Tensions and worries melted away.

The closest thing I can liken it to is nitrous oxide, popularly known as laughing gas. If you've ever inhaled an $N_2O–O_2$ mix in hospital, or huffed a balloon of N_2O at a festival, you'll remember the loose, pillowy feeling that spreads through your body, the strange stretching of time, the Dopplered sounds and the afterglow as you return to the world. It wasn't as potent, but it felt really good. And with each round of breathing, that relaxed, almost ecstatic feeling at the end of the breath-hold grew.

The WHM's dirty little secret – the reason, I suspect, it has gained such popularity – is that it's basically autoerotic asphyxiation without the wanking.

The high wasn't always so intense. As the days went on, my body seemed to acclimatise. I felt less lightheaded and I could hold my breath for longer. I always felt better for having done it. Calmer.

A couple of times I passed out. Once I came round to find myself shuddering in what might have been the tail end of a seizure. Which I suspect will be enough to make most people conclude: 'This sounds like a profoundly stupid and dangerous idea.' I can't say I blame you.

A few years ago at a family gathering, I saw an eight-year-old knock himself out by holding his breath. He fell backwards, smacked his head on the parquet floor and began jerking spasmodically. He was fine afterwards, but it looked *terrifying*. We'd all agree that was a dumb thing to do – albeit forgivable for an eight-year-old – but add a few celebrity endorsements and a steel drum backing track and suddenly it's a lifestyle.

We don't know what the long-term health consequences of doing a practice like this are. We don't know if it's dangerous. It's not unreasonable to have concerns that it might be.

Yes, sometimes the breathing made my fingers tingle or cramp up. Yes, sometimes I briefly lost consciousness. But it also helped a bit. It shut up my anxious, despondent thoughts. Even if it was a placebo, it made me feel like I was doing *something*.

———

A week later I was chatting to Dr John Wemmie, professor of psychiatry, neuroscience, molecular physiology and biophysics at the University of Iowa. His specialist area of research is panic attacks. If anyone had the answers, it was him.

I asked him to explain panic to me.

'Anything you can encounter that has danger associated with it represents a threat,' he said. 'There's a whole range of threats in terms of their likelihood, their risk, their severity. And then consequently there's a spectrum of potential responses to all of these threats.' Some threats are internal, like an illness. Some are external, like a predator. 'Somehow the brain has to figure out: What's the severity of the threat? And how do I match the appropriate defensive response to the severity of this threat? And as you can imagine, that's an extremely complicated process.'

For John, what we call 'anxiety' is on the lower end of that spectrum of responses. The threat may not be imminent, it may not be certain. Stress hormones make us alert, and top-down cognitive processes bias our attention towards danger.

Panic is at the extreme end. 'If you're caught by a predator, you either just give yourself up and be eaten, or you fight like hell and hope the predator will give up or decide it's not worth the effort.' The threat is here. Now. Eating your heart out of your chest. Panic is your all-or-nothing, last-ditch attempt to survive.

In low or indeterminate threat situations, we can consciously reflect on the danger – to, as John put it, engage in 'some cognitive, frontal contemplation', asking ourselves whether our response is appropriate. But conscious processes are slow. 'When it's life or death, that stuff has to happen very fast.'

I asked about one of the ways he induces panic attacks in the lab: the CO_2 challenge, the same as Patient S.M., the fearless, amygdala-less woman, undertook that induced her first ever panic attack. It involves donning a mask and inhaling a mix of 35 per cent CO_2 and 21 per cent oxygen. It usually triggers a panic attack in people vulnerable to them, but it's unpleasant for anyone. John said he had done it himself 'many, many times'.

He told me about a student in his lab who volunteered to try. 'She had a panic attack that lasted minutes. She hyperventilated. She wasn't expecting to have it, we weren't expecting her to have it, but this panic attack lasted like five minutes. Just from one breath of CO_2. And it was sort of terrifying, because we thought: well, crap. We just did something really bad.' He laughed sheepishly.

From his own experience, he said it triggers a strong feeling of air hunger: 'There's this sense that you just cannot get enough air.'

A study published in 2000 found that healthy first-degree relatives of patients with panic disorder are more reactive to CO_2 challenges than matched controls, implying that vulnerability to panic attacks may have a genetic component.[6]

One thing I didn't understand – the main thing I'd wanted to ask John about – was: why carbon dioxide? I'd thought it was a *lack* of carbon dioxide, caused by hyperventilation, that triggered a panic attack. All that business with reduced oxygen levels in the brain even though you're breathing in more oxygen had been counterintuitive enough, but now he was saying a panic attack came from *too much* CO_2? What about the old folk remedy of calming someone down by getting them to breathe into a paper bag? Wasn't the whole idea that they would breathe waste CO_2 back in, thus raising their CO_2 levels? What was going on?

As well as the CO_2 challenge, John told me he's deliberately hyperventilated to manipulate his brain pH in an fMRI scanner, and the two states feel quite different. With hyperventilation there can be feelings of lightheadedness, detachment, derealisation. With CO_2, it's that horrible feeling of choking and suffocating.

John mentioned studies where researchers fitted panic-disorder patients with portable devices that monitored their breathing. One study led by psychologist Alicia Meuret measured patients' 'end tidal' CO_2 levels – the amount of CO_2 released at the end of each breath – and their breathing patterns in the periods of time around the panic attack. In the lead up to an attack, their breathing patterns become abnormal. Tidal volume decreases (they breathe more shallowly). They sigh more (perhaps unconsciously trying to expel CO_2).[7]

Psychiatrist Donald F. Klein theorised that panic attacks were a form of 'suffocation false alarm',[8] noting that patients with a history of respiratory disease are more likely to suffer from panic disorder. Chemoreceptors in the brainstem monitor CO_2 and pH levels, stimulating the desire to breathe, and, in emergencies, triggering the fight, flight or freeze response to help us reach air quickly. Since starving brain cells of oxygen for frighteningly short periods of time can cause irreparable brain damage, this reaction needs to be rapid and powerful. Klein thought that, in patients with panic disorder, this chemical alarm system might be oversensitive.

Meuret agrees – she believes that panic sufferers habitually over-breathe, resulting in abnormally low levels of CO_2. This chronic hypocapnia makes them increasingly sensitive to even small amounts of carbon dioxide, meaning those chemoreceptors respond to the slightest rise, triggering that suffocation alarm.[9]

Recent research suggests that breathing in the range of six to ten breaths per minute – taking six to ten seconds to inhale and exhale, breathing in through the nose and using the diaphragm to pull air down towards the belly – constitutes 'autonomically optimised respiration'.[10] Our lungs exchange oxygen for carbon dioxide in little sacs called alveoli. When we breathe rapidly, less air reaches fewer of these sacs, increasing 'dead space' where our lungs aren't working, and our breathing becomes less efficient. Breathing slower, with increased tidal volume, decreases dead space, filling more alveoli with more oxygen. We recruit the whole of our lungs, and breathing becomes easier and more sustainable.

When we're calm, parasympathetic activation stimulates the release of acetylcholine, which results in reduced heart rate and inhibits the release of noradrenaline. A slower heart rate results in lower oxygen consumption and thus lower blood acidosis, meaning a panic attack is less likely to be triggered. In addition, a study in the *Journal of Hypertension* found that slow breathing reduces the sensitivity to CO_2 of the chemoreflex response that makes us want to take an in-breath.[11] Those chemoreceptors tolerate a wider range of pH levels before they ping.

'One can argue about the theory,' said John, 'but for me it's really attractive. It can resolve some of these issues.' John's hunch is that, before a panic attack, our breathing dysregulates a bit. CO_2 rises. (This would explain why many people with panic disorder are woken from sleep by panic attacks.) These people may be more sensitive to changes in their brain's pH, and so small increases in acidosis caused by rising CO_2 may trigger powerful feelings of dread and terror. We feel like we're drowning – and we may have conscious thoughts that we're dying or choking or having a stroke or a heart attack – so we breathe faster and deeper. But we're *not* drowning, so, although this hyperventilation is initially adaptive, lowering CO_2, it then causes all those problems associated with hypocapnia: dizziness, confusion, and constriction of the airways. But for John, these effects are 'after-effects' of the panic attack. Rising CO_2 is the trigger. 'It's a continuous experience, but I suspect the CO_2 is changing – it's high, you trigger a panic attack, then it's low and you've got all this other stuff going on.'

Some researchers have found that serotonin neurons act as CO_2 chemoreceptors, which might explain why SSRIs sometimes help people with panic disorder.[12] In his own research, John has found evidence that the amygdala itself acts as a chemosensor, detecting changes in pH and eliciting fear in response.[13] 'We've got a couple of papers out now where in humans we've electrically stimulated the amygdala.' These are young patients with epilepsy, who were having their seizures monitored and mapped with intracranial electrodes – that is, electrodes inserted through holes drilled in the skull. 'And they don't know they've stopped breathing. Their CO_2 is rising, and they're fine.'

Electrically stimulating the amygdala simulates the effects of a seizure reaching that part of the brain. In a recent paper, John and his colleagues noted: 'Strikingly, the pediatric patients were completely unaware that they had stopped breathing and did not report any shortness of breath, air hunger, desire to breathe, or display any visible signs of respiratory distress during or after the periods of stimulation-induced apnea.'*14

'I'm sort of imagining there are some people where stimulating this particular location in the amygdala may suppress panic attacks,' John said.

Many people – particularly children – with epilepsy, die suddenly and unexpectedly during the night.[15] One explanation – still somewhat speculative – is that a seizure may prevent the amygdala from responding as it should. 'It may actually suppress their drive to breathe, and all the alarms that go off that say, "Hey! I'm not breathing," and they just die.'

In some ways, these epilepsy patients may be the exact opposite of panic-disorder sufferers. Whereas someone with panic disorder may be too sensitive to rising CO_2, someone having a seizure may be completely oblivious. It was a sobering reminder that I could have it a lot, lot worse.

Even if temporary electrical stimulation of this particular subregion in the amygdala was effective at shutting down panic attacks, because of how deep the amygdala is within the brain, the site can't be reached with something like tDCS. John and his colleagues were only able to get at it because these children were already having their seizures monitored.

'You know it's pretty interesting,' he said, 'these patients who don't have an amygdala. They don't have an anxiety disorder. They don't have panic disorder.'

I said I'd heard that the famous Patient S.M. had had an extreme and extended panic attack.

'Yeah, and we were sort of dumbstruck when we first observed that. We know the amygdala's sensitive to CO_2.'

---

* 'Apnea' ('apnoea'), a temporary suspension of breathing, from the Greek *ápnoia*: *á*, 'absence of', and *pnoia*, 'breathing'.

Until that moment I hadn't connected John with the account I'd read of S.M. doing the CO_2 challenge. Suddenly I realised – that was his name on the paper, along with neurologist Daniel Tranel and neuropsychologist Justin Feinstein.[16] I was talking to the guy who gave Patient S.M. her first panic attack.

He said they know the amygdala plays a pivotal role. 'And we're beginning to understand ... it looks like the amygdala's actually *suppressing*, to some degree, these panic attacks.'

Wait. What? Suddenly it was making people *less* frightened?

'If an animal freezes, it can't fight. And if it fights, it can't freeze. It has to make a choice. You can't do both things at the same time.' This is what most accounts of the fight, flight or freeze response leave out. How do we choose which one to do? John emphasised he was speculating, but he thought the amygdala might be a crucial part of that decision-making circuit. 'I think it's influencing that decision.' There may be areas involved in more conscious, cognitive choices, but they're slower – like the cortical and subcortical pathways to the amygdala in Joe LeDoux's 'quick and dirty' threat-circuit model.

'So,' I said, 'you're thinking that, without the amygdala, there's no way really to make that decision and the default response is panic?'

'I think it's biased towards the more extreme response. Which again from a survival perspective makes sense. If you can do nothing or do something extreme, the default that would be more protective would be the extreme response.' When systems that modulate reflexive responses malfunction, the default – panic – is more likely to be triggered. Remember, as well as taking cues directly from the thalamus, the amygdala maintains a 'dialogue' with the prefrontal cortex,[17] which is implicated in decision-making, judgement, self-perception and assessing feedback.[18]

The amygdala might be responsible for triggering physiological reactions to fear, but it also throttles them. Trying to stop panic attacks by removing the amygdala is like trying to fix a leaky tap by hacking it off with an axe.

John said patients without an amygdala describe the CO_2 challenge as 'the most fearful, most terrifying experience they've ever had. Yet you say: "Do you want to do it again?" "Okay."' In the moment, they find the panic attack terrifying, but it doesn't stick. There's no lasting fear. 'There's tons of research to say the amygdala's important for learning in the memory of these traumas, and I think that's true. And they don't have that system.'

I said – and I meant it – that I could see ways in which the inability to be traumatised could be adaptive.

John wasn't so sure. 'I'm not telling you anything that hasn't been published,' he said, but S.M. 'has gotten into situations in her life that have been very maladaptive.' Psychologists have speculated that it's because of her inability both to feel fear in the moment, and to learn about these dangerous situations for the future.

Terms like 'very maladaptive' might sound clinical and distant, but his tone was anything but. He sounded genuinely concerned.

As our chat came to a close, I asked the big question: How do we beat panic attacks?

Like so many researchers I'd spoken to, John's suspicion is that panic-attack sufferers fall into subgroups. As we've seen, the range of symptoms is vast. Some patients may be having panic attacks because the amygdala isn't controlling their response normally. 'But there may be other people who are just terrified by the panic attack and the uncertainty of what it means.' Having a panic attack is traumatic in itself, especially if you think you're having a stroke or going mad. Some anxious people may be chronically over-breathing or under-breathing in the lead-up to an attack. 'There may be other people where they freeze too much. They're frozen with fear to the point they can't move. It's not that they're having a panic attack, they're just frozen with fear.' That might involve a different brain mechanism altogether.

Alicia Meuret trialled an intervention for panic-disorder patients who were taught about hypocapnia's potential role in panic sensitivity, then spent four weeks doing a twice-daily, seventeen-minute breathing exercise where they gradually learned to slow their breathing down while monitoring their CO_2 levels on a portable capnometer. She called this an 'interoceptive exposure therapy'. That is, participants practised experiencing the symptoms they most feared – the rise in CO_2 associated with an incipient panic attack. The study found the intervention was successful in 'substantially reducing panicogenic cognitions' by the end of the four weeks.[19]

There was no control group for the above study and no placebo condition (where patients, say, did relaxing visualisation for two sessions a day), so we can't draw too many conclusions, but it's interesting to consider that the traditional advice to anxious panic-attack sufferers – take some deep breaths – may actually increase their CO_2 sensitivity and make their risk of panic attacks worse.

John thought that different interventions might work best for different individuals. CO_2 exposure therapies were more popular in the past than they are now. We discussed the Wim Hof breathing technique, which is more an accidental hyperventilation exposure therapy – alternating between hyperoxia and hypoxia – which he found 'awfully interesting', particularly the feeling of euphoria that comes on at the end. He wondered if the euphoria might reflect the release of 'endogenous opioids', something suggested by the authors of a 2018 paper using fMRI and PET scans of Wim Hof, who hypothesised that hyperventilation triggers the sympathetic nervous system's stress response, releasing these naturally occurring pain suppressors which produce 'a feeling of euphoria, anxiolysis [reduced anxiety] and a sense of wellbeing'.[20] Still, they're quick to emphasise that, at this point, it's just a theory.

—

Panic attacks happen fast. Or they seem to. But maybe, I'd learned, the build-up takes weeks. All that heavy breathing. All that training the canary in the mineshaft of your brain till it's exquisitely sensitive, till the merest whiff of CO_2 sees it keeling over with a case of the vapours.

Klein's suffocation alarm theory is attractive, but it doesn't cover all situations. Some of us have specific, obvious triggers for our panic attacks. I suspect some of us experience a souped-up fight, flight or freeze response, hyperventilate, and spin out into that confused state of choking, breathless, surreal depersonalisation – terror's sour ecstasy. Some of us freeze like an electrocuted rat. These varied experiences that we smoosh into one bin labelled 'panic attacks' might have varied causes and respond best to varied solutions.

Panic attacks come in over 7,000 flavours, but they all share some things in common. Your brain shuts down, so it's hard to make smart decisions. Every instinct you have – escape, cower, breathe harder – is the wrong one. Every action you take to try to break free is actually digging you deeper, making it worse. Some primal part of your brain, a legacy from when we were tiny, burrowing creatures whose underground homes might cave in on us while we slept, is screaming: *Emergency, emergency, find air or die.* But the more we breathe, the more we feel like we're choking.

We're not so different from that E. coli bacterium, forever checking its internal pH and adjusting to keep its cytoplasm in that 7.2–7.8 sweet spot. It's just our cover stories are more elaborate. We have future-vision. Actions we take to keep oxygen flowing to the brain might lead to social disgrace, which might jeopardise our access to food or shelter. Multiple, overlaid systems of escalating sophistication watch and monitor and warn – a bizarre, paranoid alliance of mathematicians, sniffer dogs and feverish clairvoyants.

COWARD

—

Let us now recite the Coward's Prayer: 'Lord, grant me the foresight to predict threats, the strength not to let my guard down, and the wisdom to know that things can always, *always*, get worse.'

XVII.

HYPNOSIS
Hypnotherapy and placebos

O n a winter evening in 1917, Dr Lewis Yealland led a young, shell-shocked private into the 'electrical room' of London's National Hospital, drew the blinds and locked the doors. The only light came from the resistance bulbs of a large battery. Dr Yealland attached one electrode to the base of the young man's spine and a second long electrode to the back of his throat. Matter-of-factly, Dr Yealland informed the private that he would not leave the room until he was fully cured.[1]

Then he turned on the current.

The twenty-four-year-old soldier was suffering from one of a growing number of 'hysterical' conditions found in veterans of the Great War. He had been fighting since the opening weeks of the conflict, a veteran of some of its most famous engagements: the Mons retreat, the so-called 'Miracle of the Marne' (where the German advance was halted just miles from Paris), the disastrous crossing of the River Aisne on pontoon boats only days later, and the first and second battles of Ypres. By the most conservative estimates they had a combined toll of over 620,000 dead and injured.

Machine-guns and artillery pieces would scythe through regiments in minutes, leaving heaps of rotting bodies that later regiments sometimes used as makeshift sandbags. At the second battle of Ypres, the Germans made their first foray into chemical warfare with Operation Disinfectant, unleashing nearly 6,000 barrels of greenish-yellow chlorine gas that left Allied troops drowning in their own fluid-filled lungs. Shelling persisted for hours, days – a continuous bombardment that wore down the most even-tempered of soldiers.

German lieutenant Ernst Jünger described the psychological impact of heavy shelling thus: 'You must imagine you are securely tied to a post, being threatened by a man swinging a heavy hammer. Now the hammer has been taken back over his head, ready to be swung, now it's cleaving the air towards you, on the point of touching your skull, then it's struck the post, and splinters are flying . . .'[2]

In July 1916, while stationed in Salonica, Greece, the private had collapsed while tending to the horses, 'on account of the intense heat'. He remained unconscious for five hours. On waking, he 'shook all over' and could no longer speak.

Before his session with Dr Yealland, the soldier had been strapped to a chair for twenty minutes at a time and electrocuted. Lit cigarette ends had been stubbed out on his tongue. Hot plates had been applied to the back of his throat. None of these methods, the doctor would later lament, had proven successful in restoring his voice.

In the electrical room, the resistance bulbs flared. When the current reached the man's pharynx, it was so strong that he jerked backwards, detaching the wires from the battery. At this, Dr Yealland grew impatient: 'You must behave as becomes the hero I expect you to be,' he snapped. 'A man who has gone through so many battles should have better control of himself.'

Yealland went on to electrocute the soldier repeatedly over a period of four hours, ordering him to march back and forth mouthing 'Ah, bah, cah'. Eventually the private broke down, whispering that he wanted a drink of water. The doctor refused. 'It has been my experience with these cases,' he told the man, 'to find two types of patients; those who want to recover, and those who do not want to recover. Though you appear to be indifferent, I recognise the fact that you belong to the latter group. I understand your condition thoroughly and it makes no difference to me which group you belong to. You must recover your speech at once.'

Dr Yealland believed that nervous disorders such as mutism, hysterical blindness and paralysed limbs with no obvious physical cause were the product of 'negativism' – a form of internal resistance, a subconscious bloody-mindedness that had to be overcome through hypnotic suggestion, subterfuge, and – if necessary – punishment. In his view, open displays of sympathy – even shaking the patient's hand – reinforced the reality of their condition and made it harder to cure.

Yealland's accounts of the various treatments he presided over come off less like medical procedures and more like exorcisms. He seems to be speaking past the patient, addressing his remarks to the condition itself, the hysterical tendency. But whereas a priest invokes the authority of Christ, Yealland instead calls upon the irresistible power of modern medicine. Sometimes he accuses patients of 'shamming' or 'malingering' and threatens to report them to the military authorities if they leave before the treatment has been successful. Sometimes he announces the electrical current will increase every five minutes until they are cured.

If Yealland seems cruel by modern standards, remember that physicians were still struggling to understand the condition that would come to be known as 'shell-shock'. One issue was the sheer range of symptoms: blindness, deafness, limbs that hung limp or lost all feeling, men who shook uncontrollably or walked in a tremulous, creeping shuffle as if crossing a tightrope. Doctors proposed all sorts of explanations: the absorption of toxic gases from shells, concussion from the impact of nearby explosions, a rash of fakery by cowards.

As the war continued, the consensus would eventually shift. A report by Dr Harold Wiltshire in a 1916 edition of the *Lancet* found that, of 52 cases of shell-shock where the soldier had been exposed to the physical effects of an explosion, only 5 per cent favoured 'physical concussion as the cause of the subsequent neurosis'.[3] Instead, he proposed psychological causes, grouped into categories such as 'Gradual psychic exhaustion from continued psychic strain', 'Sudden psychic shock' and 'Horrible sights'. One nineteen-year-old private had assisted with clearing up body parts after twenty soldiers were blown up by shrapnel. After tending to the wounded, he became unable to recognise his friends and began screaming. The patient had no memory of the incident, only of hearing an explosion. He reported waking on a train two days later, feeling 'swimmy in the head, as if expecting something, something seems to be coming, as if something is going to happen, something nasty, when I hear anything like the whistle of a shell coming towards me'.

Yealland, at least, seemed to regard the origin of the ailments he saw as mental rather than physical. In this, he was influenced by the work of two rival schools of hypnosis that arose in late nineteenth-century France. Neurologist Jean-Martin Charcot's Paris School believed that susceptibility to hypnosis was a sign of hysteria – a catch-all diagnosis with symptoms ranging from mutism, deafness and convulsions to severe anxiety. (Later in the twentieth century, hysteria's decline in popularity as a diagnosis was almost directly proportional to anxiety's rise.) Physician Ambroise-Auguste Liébeault's Nancy School, by contrast, believed that hypnosis was merely a state of enhanced suggestibility, usable on healthy subjects.

Thus, in the lead-up to the First World War, Polish neurologist Joseph Babinski used his infamous *traitement brusqué*, where patients were stripped naked and subjected to 'the painful application of Faradic electricity' while Babinski, a striking moustachioed figure reminiscent of a circus strongman, barked 'suggestions' that their ailments were, in fact, imaginary.[4] Babinski believed many anxious patients convinced themselves they had a condition and thus began acting out its symptoms. All he had to do was show them that their leg or arm or tongue worked just fine, and they would be cured.

The French psychologist Pierre Janet – whose ideas were a major influence on Freud – had theorised that, under trauma, the mind of the hysteric split into a 'conscious' and 'subconscious' component.

He called this process 'dissociation', and used it to account for why patients frequently could not remember the traumatic incidents that had triggered their hysteria. For Janet, unexplained physical symptoms were the work of this suffering, dissociated subconscious, and many psychotherapists who followed him concluded that effective treatment required addressing this subconscious mind directly.

I get the impression that Yealland, for all his faults – of which excessive modesty was not one – was trying to do the best by his patients based on what he believed. In the case of the mute private, Yealland reported that when his speech returned the private exclaimed: 'Doctor, doctor, I am a champion.' Yealland replied: 'You are a hero.'

Yealland – and many of his contemporaries – saw the nervous mind as an antagonistic little brother who had to be tricked or disciplined into compliance. Many nervous disorders – so the reasoning went – were the result of spontaneously accepted erroneous beliefs, a kind of self-hypnosis or 'autosuggestion', and thus ought to respond to counter-suggestions, providing they were delivered with sufficient determination and authority.

It was all about the exertion of will. As popular author Annie Payson Call wrote at the time in her book *Nerves and the War*, the anxious soldier 'must take his muscles and nerves in hand, as he would guide a refractory horse – quiet them down and insist upon dropping their resistances.'

—

On 10 March 1994, Christopher Gates went to the Swan Theatre, High Wycombe, to watch a show by popular stage hypnotist Paul McKenna. When the show started, he began to feel very strange. The music sounded 'spooky' and the lights seemed to be flickering. When the hypnotist instructed anyone who wanted to volunteer to be hypnotised to come on stage 'now', Christopher felt suddenly compelled to obey.

Over the next two hours he took part in various sketches which, he claimed, caused him emotional distress. At various points he was told he was Mick Jagger, a ballet dancer, and a contestant on *Blind Date*. Early on, McKenna told participants that he had become invisible. He then walked across the stage, sweeping it with a broom. Christopher claimed to have seen the broom moving by itself, which he found 'extremely disturbing'. During the interval, he was told that, whatever questions were put to him, he had to answer 'Yes'. Someone asked him if he was gay, and – though he was not – he later said he found himself 'compelled' to answer yes, which he found 'distressing'.

That night, Christopher was unable to sleep. The next day, he was called into a redundancy meeting at his work at a furniture polisher's, and found himself giggling and crying. Over the next few days his mental state deteriorated. He was afraid of falling asleep in case he died. He heard muttering voices which he believed belonged to Jesus or Moses. He became convinced his staircase led to Heaven. He thought he could stop cars with his eyes. Ultimately he was admitted to the psychiatric unit at Amersham General Hospital and diagnosed with schizophrenia.

In a subsequent court case, Christopher Gates contended that being hypnotised had caused him to become schizophrenic. He attempted to sue Paul McKenna for £200,000 in damages. At the time, McKenna had released many self-help books and cassettes offering hypnotic solutions to common problems. He's continued to publish similar books – many of them bestsellers – with titles like *I Can Make You Happy*, *I Can Make You Sleep*, *Hypnotic Gastric Band: The New Surgery-Free Weight-Loss System* and *Change Your Life In 7 Days*. During the case, when cross-examined about his 'extravagant claims for the powers of hypnosis', the judge reported that McKenna 'recanted or qualified those views to a considerable extent', describing some of what he'd written as, in the judge's words, 'advertising hype'.

A good portion of the defence's case was to argue that McKenna couldn't possibly be responsible because hypnosis is mostly placebo.

They brought in witnesses who argued against the idea of a special 'trance state' and instead said that 'hypnosis' could be explained by mundane social pressures. Dr Graham Wagstaff, a researcher of hypnosis from the University of Liverpool, said: 'Stage hypnosis, like a game-show, or many domestic situations, can be a powerful social situation in which people feel a strong social obligation to do what they are told (which increases the more things they actually consent to do). It has what psychologists term powerful "demand character-istics". When people are asked to do something embarrassing on stage, 'they may feel socially obliged to do it, but also apprehensive about what they may be asked to do next, and annoyed to find themselves in this situation. Occasionally, therefore, some hypnotic subjects report feeling "embarrassed", "out of control" and "annoyed", and, because they underestimate the influence of social or situational pressures, they may even express some surprise at their compliance, and attribute it to some feature of "hypnosis".'[5]

A hypnotist can't really cause hallucinatory blindness – and the defence presented studies supporting this – nor can they make someone do anything they don't want to do, so (the defence's case went) all 'hypnotised' people are really doing is a form of play-acting, either because the social context allows it – i.e. for fun – or out of embarrassment. Afterwards, they may rationalise it by convincing themselves they had no choice.

In the end, the judge concluded it was 'highly improbable' that Christopher Gates' schizophrenia had been caused by hypnosis and cleared Paul McKenna of the allegations.

———

In contemporary psychology, hypnosis and hypnotherapy exist in a no-man's land between legitimate treatments and alternative medi-cine. Certainly, there's little evidence of some special, altered state called 'trance'. But when it comes to *suggestibility* – the idea that people, or a subset of especially receptive people, might alter their behaviour or emotional state in response to commands, instructions or verbal nudges, hidden or explicit – the jury is still deliberating. After all, it's an incredibly broad claim. If, while I'm walking down the street, a car drives by and someone yells out the window, 'You're a big twat!', in the moments that follow I probably feel a bit more of a big twat. Does that make it a hypnotic suggestion?

Psychologist Irving Kirsch – whose work on antidepressants has excited much controversy – defines a suggestion as a communication indicating that someone will respond in a particular way 'nonvolitionally' – that is, without trying. '"Raise your hand,"' he argues, 'is an instruction, whereas "Your hand is getting lighter and beginning to rise" is a suggestion.' Which seems like a clear enough distinction – only he immediately abandons it, claiming instead that whether something is a suggestion or instruction is reliant on context. Take the word 'Sleep!' for example: 'When given to a child who is still awake at 11 p.m., it is clearly a command; when given to a volunteer at a stage hypnosis performance, it is a suggestion.'[6]

Kirsch claims that 'Sleep' is a suggestion rather than a command because – unlike raising an arm – we can't ordinarily *choose* to sleep. His distinction would make sense if the subject actually fell asleep when a hypnotist said 'Sleep', but of course they don't. 'Sleep' is understood not as a command to become instantly unconscious, but to lower your head, close your eyes, and listen to the hypnotist's instructions.

Kirsch goes on to argue that suggestions don't even need to be verbal. A suggestion might come from 'the size, shape, and color of a pill' or how someone else in the room behaves. Suggestions, then, are just a form of 'expectancy modifications' – that is, little cues or hints that help us decide what to expect in the current situation. Our behaviour and mood may then change to account for those expectations.

If you're getting flashbacks to research on the placebo effect, that's no accident. Kirsch views hypnosis as a type of 'nondeceptive placebo' that triggers the same responses, resulting in people, for example, reporting less pain during surgery.

You'd think, then, that there would be a wealth of clinical evidence backing up the effectiveness of hypnosis and suggestion in treating anxiety disorders. On the face of it, anxiety would seem to be hugely amenable to expectancy effects, since it feeds on expectations, particularly negative ones. However, proof that hypnosis works any better than placebo interventions in the treatment of anxiety disorders is scant. One systematic review lamented the 'lack of high quality trials', and found that current evidence 'is insufficient to support the use of hypnosis for treating anxiety'[7]. But there are two caveats here: one, absence of evidence is not evidence of absence. Large randomised controlled trials are expensive, so we only get data on interventions that attract funding.

Two, placebos work pretty well. As we've seen, people receiving a placebo treatment for anxiety do considerably better than people stuck on a wait list. Is there any functional difference between getting less anxious through a 'real' method, and simply *believing* you're less anxious in response to a placebo? What if we gave people a well-evidenced intervention like CBT, *and* hypnosis? As I and my nerd friends are forever asking when trying to mix magical items in *Dungeons & Dragons*: Do the effects stack?

Irving Kirsch certainly thinks so. He published a meta-analysis looking at eighteen studies of weight-loss where CBT was supplemented with hypnosis. He and his co-authors concluded: 'The addition of hypnosis substantially enhanced treatment outcome, so that the average client receiving cognitive–behavioral hypnotherapy showed greater improvement than at least 70% of clients receiving nonhypnotic treatment.'[8]

However, these were studies looking at obesity rather than clinical anxiety. More concerningly, a study published the following year by the same journal found 'several transcription and computational inaccuracies in the original meta-analysis'. The authors had been sceptical of the 'surprisingly large' effect size Kirsch had found, especially as it was inconsistent with previous research. Adjusting for the mistakes in Kirsch's original analysis, the authors found that when hypnosis was added to CBT the effect was small. When they removed one study with 'questionable' design, the effect became statistically insignificant.[9]

It seems like hypnotherapy exists in a liminal space between legitimacy and outright quackery. To suggest it *might* work in certain circumstances as an adjunct to better-evidenced treatments is a reasonable position – one that most psychologists I spoke to were fairly comfortable with. To assert it *does* work, however, is quite another thing – a claim we don't have the studies to support.

But look. Slap me across the face with a rolled-up copy of *Medical Hypotheses* and call me a credulous hypno-simp, but the best-evidenced stuff had done jack shit for me. What if there are subgroups of anxiety sufferers who respond best to less conventional treatments? Some of the literature around hypnosis talked about people who were particularly 'suggestible', even 'hypersuggestible'. What if that was me?

My mum had been suggesting I try hypnotherapy for years. I kept chickening out. I'd told myself it was because there wasn't much science backing it up, but now I wondered if I'd been resisting because it was an idea from my mum. I'd already tried doing the absolute opposite of what she'd approve of – coming cold turkey off my meds, jumping in a freezing river and high-dosing magic mushrooms. Maybe it was time I started listening to her?

What if it didn't matter whether hypnosis was real? What if, like a sugar pill, it worked anyway?

One morning, a few hours after a panic attack, I went online and searched for hypnotherapists. I found a number for a guy called Graham, and before I could change my mind, I rang it.

When he answered, I ended up blurting out my whole story: I'd been anxious for years, I had panic attacks, nothing had worked, and it had got so bad I was writing a book about it. In a weird way, I think I was a bit proud. I also felt bad. Was I setting Graham up? Most people who rang him didn't do so with the belief that what he practised – the discipline he had built his entire career around – was pseudo-scientific rubbish. He seemed nice, friendly and understanding. I emphasised how hopeless my case was so we both had an out when the treatment didn't work. 'I'm not expecting miracles,' I said, 'I'd just like to feel a little less anxious.'

'Wouldn't you like to do better than that?' he said. 'Why don't we get you cured?'

I stammered, not knowing what to say. What I was thinking was: *Because it's impossible.* I wanted to protect us both from inevitable disappointment, but I worried that would come off as defeatist – as 'negativism'. So, although I was full of doubts, I said: 'That would be great.'

It would take four appointments, Graham said. I could come to the first, see how I liked it, and if I wanted to we'd do the following three on subsequent weeks. Then, he said, I'd be free of panic attacks. For ever.

'Okay,' I said.

———

When I arrived at Graham's house, he made me a cup of tea, then led me out to a cabin in his back garden. Inside there were padded benches covered in plush cushions, an aromatherapy diffuser and a big leather chair. A cherry-red sunburst electric guitar was bracketed to the wall and there were shelves full of therapy books.

We sat down, and he got out a clipboard and had me fill in a sheet with all sorts of details about the names of family members and what I wanted hypnotherapy for.

'My success rate is one hundred per cent,' he said.

I felt huge pressure. I felt mean-spirited for turning up, and a bit resentful towards him for not saying that it was all right to fail – that we would just do our best.

I wondered how he knew. How many people, if their panic attacks started up again, were likely to ring him to complain? Anxious people, by our nature, hate confrontation.

I talked a bit about my anxiety and panic attacks – how long I had had them, what seemed to trigger them – but mostly I listened to Graham as he explained his understanding of how the conscious and unconscious mind worked, and how we acquired beliefs about ourselves.

A lot of our beliefs, he said, we acquire when we're very young. Someone may have told us something like 'You're so lazy', or we may have figured them out based on how others treat us, maybe thinking, *People always ignore me, I must be boring*. Later on, whenever the world tries to give us a new belief, we check it against our existing beliefs before we accept it.

He likened the conscious mind to a bouncer. Every suggestion the world gives us has to get past this bouncer. The suggestion approaches the door, and the bouncer turns to 'a little guy called Luigi' ('I don't know why he's called Luigi,' said Graham) and tells him to check in the back. The little guy goes into the back room – our unconscious – and looks through all these filing cabinets for something similar. If the suggestion matches a file we've already got in the back, he returns and nods and the bouncer lets it in. If it doesn't match the stuff we've already got stored away, he comes back, shakes his head, and the bouncer rejects it.

But a lot of those beliefs weren't put there by us, or they made it in while we were still small and didn't have many beliefs in the filing cabinets to compare them with. Hypnosis, Graham said, was like sending the bouncer off for a break. With the conscious mind out of the way, you could slip some helpful suggestions into the filing cabinets – and then, once the bouncer was back, positive beliefs were more likely to get in because they matched the ones stored in the unconscious.

He tried a couple of hypnotic inductions with me, asking me to imagine I had an electromagnet on one palm and an electromagnet on the other palm, and then asking me to imagine their switching on. I moved my palms together. 'Very good,' said Graham. Then he asked me to imagine a helium balloon tied to one hand and a lead weight tied to the other. I moved one hand down and the other hand up. 'Very good,' said Graham.

He told me I was very suggestible and should be easy to hypnotise. He said I was going into a light hypnotic trance and he hadn't even done anything yet. I liked hearing I was doing a good job. I felt relieved I wasn't mucking it up.

We talked for about an hour and a half, then he led me over to the big leather chair and sat beside me with his head just above my right ear. The diffuser, which was the shape of a big pink salt crystal, was blowing out vapour with a faint floral aroma. He started counting down from ten, saying with every number he wanted me to 'double that feeling of relaxation'.

I worried I was doing it wrong – I couldn't see how I was supposed to keep my relaxation doubling exponentially. By the time he reached '1' I would have to be 512 times as relaxed as when he started counting. He had given me impossible instructions.

Each time he said a number I tried to let my body go floppy and pretend I was feeling more relaxed. I didn't want to seem like I was being obstructive. I kept thinking about that business of 'negativism' and Lewis Yealland saying some people don't want to get better. Probably normal people didn't overthink things like exponential growth. Probably they just doubled their relaxation and got well.

Graham took me through some visualisations where I imagined a safe, relaxing place, and also a big portrait gallery full of paintings that represented parts of my past. I had to take out all the paintings I didn't want any more and toss them into a big furnace. I find picturing things really hard – often I couldn't see anything consistent at all – but I didn't want to seem like I was being difficult, so every time Graham asked if I was ready or if I had collected up all the paintings, I'd lift my index finger to indicate 'yes'.

Eventually he counted back up to ten and told me to wake up. I felt woozy after lying in a chair for half an hour, but okay.

The following week, he warned me that I shouldn't make any big life decisions after the session, as it sometimes took a while for people's emotions to settle. We talked for about an hour about holding on to the past and learning to let things go, and then we went to the chair for more hypnosis. This time, he asked me to imagine a hall lined with doors. I had to go into a room, and there would be someone in there from my past, waiting to talk with me. He said it would be someone who had hurt me. Someone I still held unresolved anger towards.

He told me not to decide on someone, just to look and trust my subconscious. But how could I know it came from my subconscious? Try as I might, I couldn't make myself spontaneously see someone.

I felt guilty, like I was mucking it up or short-circuiting the process by resisting. Like I thought I was too good for hypnosis. I didn't tell him I was struggling – instead, I tried to think of someone from my past I might plausibly feel upset towards. I didn't think I had many resentments, but I dutifully thought of someone and pictured them sitting there. Then I had to role-play myself and the other person, doing our voices out loud, tell them how they'd hurt me, and then reply in character as them. I was supposed to just 'become' them, and then Graham would address me with their name. I never felt I was doing anything but making it up to humour him. Maybe his previous clients had been able to let go and pass into this trance state where they channelled people from their past. Maybe I was blocking it by being uptight or sceptical. I played along to try to spare us both embarrassment.

I found much of it excruciating – when one conversation was done, he'd tell me to leave the imaginary room and come back in and see another person in the chair, and to repeat the process. What if someone I knew were to see me like this? Confessing these lingering resentments, this hurt, driving my fist into a cushion at his instruction to let out the anger. What if one of the people I was pretending to be found out I was role-playing as them? God, I'd cringe so hard I'd implode.

Most of this was stuff I'd never said out loud. I wasn't even sure how many of the feelings I was describing were true, or if I was just making up disclosures to please Graham so he'd be convinced I wasn't holding anything back and would stop asking me to see another person in the chair who I needed to speak with.

Finally, he told me I was going to leave the room and keep going down the hall, and the memories behind the doors were going to get younger and younger. He implied that there might even be memories from before I was born. Suddenly he told me I had to step into my first memory of anxiety.

'How old are you?' he said.

My mind was a blank. I had no idea what I was supposed to be imagining or what my earliest anxiety memory would be.

'Don't think,' he said rapidly, 'just answer.'

'Uh . . . uh . . .' I kept seeing myself in the garden of a pub in my hometown. I had this memory of being preschool age and wandering round the back of a Punch & Judy show to see behind the screen. Everything's blurry – it was from before I got my first pair of glasses. I'm just about to see what's inside the booth when I get squirted in the face with a green water pistol. Then the memory ends.

It wasn't particularly anxious.

'Don't think!' said Graham.

'Uh . . . two,' I said.

'Hello, little one,' Graham said, pitching his voice up a few semitones and cooing. 'Where are you?'

I started describing my parents' front room as I recalled it. I told him I was lying on the floor, looking up.

In the present, in the reclining chair, my heart was pounding. Any moment he would realise I wasn't really in a trance. That I was bluffing.

I told him I was scared and I didn't know why. After a few more questions, where I could only come up with vague answers, Graham suggested I come out of the memory and try to find an even earlier one. 'Don't think,' he said, and then, 'Hello, little one. Hello. How old are you?'

I told him I was only a few days old. As I spoke, the adult me was shaking and crying. I felt under such incredible pressure. I was confabulating fake intimate memories as a guy spoke to me in baby-talk. I was trying my best but I really felt like I was making it up, constructing a scene based on photos I'd seen of my mum in hospital just after either me or my brother had been born.

'What can you see?' he said.

I told Graham I could see the ceiling, and an adult I didn't recognise, but I couldn't see my mum. I didn't know where she'd gone. I was afraid, I said.

Eventually, to my relief, he instructed me to leave the memory behind, and then went through the process of bringing me out of hypnosis.

After the session, I was really shaken. Walking home the previous week, I'd felt light and relaxed. Now I felt almost . . . violated.

I don't think that's fair – Graham hadn't done anything malicious or deceptive – but it's how I felt. Like he had forced me into this embarrassing situation where I'd had no choice but to make stuff up – to invent a personal, primal trauma – rather than open my eyes and say, 'Look, sorry, it's not working.' At no point during our talks had Graham acknowledged there was a chance it might not work. He hadn't told me what to do if I felt trapped or stuck, except that I had to 'not think'.

'Don't think' is probably great advice for an improv actor – stop worrying about being original or funny, and just respond honestly in the moment – but less so if you're trying to dredge up real, auto-biographical information.

One recent study asked over 6,000 respondents to describe their earliest memory and the age it stemmed from. Nearly 40 per cent gave a memory from when they were two or younger. However, the authors claim that 'the overwhelming evidence and theory' shows that 'autobiographical memories do not emerge before . . . about 24 to 36 months'. Therefore nearly 40 per cent of respondents had first memories which were fictional. The authors suggest this is part of the constructed nature of memory, concluding, worryingly: 'All memories contain some degree of fiction.'[10]

Life admin meant I had to delay my next session with Graham by a couple of weeks. I wondered if I should go back. Or should I 'fess up and tell him I wasn't sure if the memory had been real? As far as he knew, I had genuinely recounted a 'lost' memory from when I was an infant. It wasn't his fault that I'd lied.

I agonised over it, worried about a confrontation, worried about letting him down, and kicked myself for trying hypnotherapy in the first place.

At the next session he asked how I'd been. I said our previous session had left me very unsettled, and that I'd had a few days of feeling really anxious. I stopped short of admitting I'd made the baby thing up – part of me clung to the possibility that maybe, yes, it was a real memory, and I had been shaken because revisiting it had been so emotional. Instead I said I wasn't sure what to make of it.

He said feeling unsettled was normal, and that I shouldn't worry too much. And that was it. I didn't bring it up again and he didn't mention it.

In our last two sessions he talked through panic attacks, and how thoughts like, *Oh no I'm having a heart attack,* or, *I'm going mad* triggered the fight, flight or freeze response. It was all stuff I knew, but it was nice to hear someone talk through it in a calm, friendly voice, making jokes. In the hypnosis sessions, he got me to imagine that the fear that comes with panic attacks was a big wave crashing through me. I had to try to feel its energy all through my body. He taught me some relaxation techniques, and had me imagine putting symbols in my safe place that would remind me of the things I'd learned.

During one talk, he mentioned that not everyone he'd seen had responded well – one or two people 'refused' to be hypnotised, or complied half-heartedly. He said that some people were negative and predicted failure, so they got it. 'Predict success,' he told me. I think he meant it as a boost, but I went away feeling even more under pressure, like if I failed it would be my fault. It also seemed to contradict his claim that he had a 100 per cent success rate. Perhaps he had meant with people who didn't drop out.

Maybe it sounds weird, but I was sad when our fourth session was finished. I wasn't used to therapy sessions that lasted over two hours. Everything had happened at a gentle pace. Aside from the regression, I'd found a lot of our time together pleasant and relaxing.

I knew that sometime soon I would have my next panic attack, and Graham's perfect record would come to an end. And I knew I wouldn't tell him because – despite my discomfort – I liked him, he'd been kind to me, and I didn't want to disappoint him.

XVIII.

RELIGION

Seeking certainty in gods, scriptures and meditation

A few years ago I visited the church that once held the cell of Julian of Norwich, Christian mystic and author of the earliest surviving book in English written by a woman, *Revelations of Divine Love*. Ecclesiastical history jaunts aren't my usual choice of leisure activity – my idea of culture is finding out the names of Pokémon in different languages. But a less intellectually impoverished friend was visiting and suggested we meet there.

St Julian's was built in the eleventh and twelfth centuries, and repaired and restored many times over the years before being destroyed in the Norwich Blitz of 1942. The rebuilt church contains a chapel in place of the anchorite cell that Julian of Norwich lived in. We think she lived between 1343 until some time after 1416. Her entry into the life of an anchorite would have involved a ceremony at the church, rather like a funeral, where psalms were sung before she was led into her cell, after which the door would have been sealed shut. She would have remained in the cell for the rest of her life.

At the age of thirty, Julian was stricken with an illness so grave that she assumed she was dying. She lay in bed for three days, the upper part of her body became numb, and her breath grew short. As a parish priest performed the last rites, she gazed at the crucifix he was holding. At that point, she would later write, the whole room became dark except for the crucifix, which began to bleed: 'Then I suddenly saw the red blood trickling down from under the crown of thorns, fresh and hot and very plentiful . . . I believed truly and strongly that it was he himself who showed me this, without any intermediary.'¹

What followed was a series of revelations in the form of visions, which she wrote down along with her understanding of their meaning. Julian of Norwich is a striking writer, partly because of the sensuous, quasi-erotic nature of her descriptions (the 'plentiful' blood, Jesus' drying flesh and parched lips) and partly because of the intense optimism of her interpretation of Christian faith. In her lifetime, the Black Death had swept through Norwich, killing – by some estimates – up to half the city's population. Regular existence was hard and uncertain, disease was rife, theft, arson and banditry plagued those outside big cities, and armed rebellions arose and were put down with equal violence.

Julian of Norwich writes not only about fear, pain and sorrow, but about an end to these things. She endures torment by a fiend, who jabbers and mocks her all night until sunrise, while she fixes her eyes on the cross and recites prayers. 'I thought this anxiety could not be compared to any other human anxiety,' she says, yet through her faith she survives this literal dark night of the soul.

Most famously, she wonders why God, in all His wisdom, allows sin to exist, to which Jesus replies: 'Sin is befitting, but all shall be well, and all shall be well, and all manner of things shall be well.' Even though she can't understand how all should be well when so many sinners, heathens and fallen angels are condemned to Hell, Jesus reassures her that 'what is impossible to you is not impossible to me. I shall keep my word in all things and I shall make all things well.' You can almost hear Jesus winking, like a mischievous uncle refusing to be drawn on the nature of the 'surprise' he's bringing you on his next visit. *Don't you worry, love. Yer old Uncle Jesus'll see you right.* His coyness is probably for the best, since Julian is veering thrillingly close to having Jesus endorse the heresy of universal reconciliation.

I stood alone in the little chapel that commemorates Julian of Norwich's cell, watching a candle's golden-white flame and thinking about what she once wrote. I wondered what it would feel like to truly believe that all shall be well. To feel it, deep in your soul.

All shall be well. Imagine.

———

I'd been thinking a lot about immuno-psychiatrist Dr Ruihua Hou's claim that one way to reduce inflammation was 'religion'. It had seemed like such an oddball answer. But, historically speaking, the assumptions of psychiatry – that terror might be instantiated in dysfunctional circuits of the brain, or be alleviated by a pill, or that recovery requires paying someone to sit and listen to you for an hour a week – seem pretty odd too.

Believing in a loving God who watches over you, or in a system of cosmic justice where kindness is always ultimately rewarded, must feel very comforting. I remembered Melvin Lerner's 'Just-World Hypothesis' – how he argued that most people can't believe in a universe that is random and unfair 'for the sake of their sanity'.

If you believed in eternal life, or a succession of lives through rebirth, wouldn't that free you from the fundamental threat behind almost all of our hardwired fears: death? Mightn't religion be the ultimate consolation? The truest balm for anxiety? You're safe. You're loved. You're indestructible. Everything has a purpose. Everything has meaning. It's all going to turn out all right in the end. Someone else, someone kind and supremely competent, is guiding this.

———

'Okay,' said Ruth, 'I'm going to start really small. It's not small for me.' She looked down and took a deep breath. 'I'm not sure if I can talk about it.'

Ruth had agreed to chat with me not as an expert on religion, though she has an MA in theology, nor about anxiety, but as 'a committed Christian with mental health issues'. I wanted to speak to someone who managed anxiety while having a faith in God. Someone with similar experiences to me, but a different way of relating to reality.

Six months before we talked, Ruth's parents were in South Africa working for a charity when they were in a serious car accident. Her mum was killed.

'My dad was on a ventilator. His bones crushed.' He had broken his left shoulder blade, his clavicle, and sixteen ribs. 'They didn't know what his brain state was going to be because they pulled him out of the water, not breathing.' Ruth and her brother flew to South Africa the next day, and her two sisters followed three days later.

From the moment she heard the news, Ruth was having regular panic attacks for at least a month – 'Really sitting on panic. And we had to do the most ridiculous things you could imagine, like telling our dad that Mum had died.' Two other passengers – their friends – were also killed, and Ruth and her siblings had to organise repatriating the bodies. 'We had to make a decision about cremating my mum before my dad was even conscious.'

Ruth grew up Christian, but she had always wondered if she was faking it. 'I didn't know how to know if I actually believed. Sometimes it seems like quite a credibility-stretching story to pin your life on.' Two thousand years ago, a man who claimed to be the son of God was nailed to a cross and came back to life. It's very specific, and – according to our current best medical understanding – impossible.

'In the middle of all that panic – all the adrenaline and I couldn't sleep – I had to be really grown-up. I had to be really grown-up for those two weeks.' Yet, in the midst of her family's nightmare, Ruth experienced something unexpected. 'I had this, like, exhilaration because I realised I really did believe it. And the sense of God's presence with me was . . . more real than I could have ever imagined.

'It didn't solve my anxiety in that time. Sorry . . . it's really hard to talk about it still. I don't think Christianity has any solutions for anxiety or depression. But my experience was of feeling held and cradled by this comforting presence who felt personal and— ' Ruth broke off, overcome with emotion.

Many of us have experienced hardships or traumas where it feels as if we've been thrown into a parallel universe. Things we took for granted are gone. Suddenly, we don't know if there's anything left we can trust. During those two panicked, grief-filled weeks in South Africa, that's the world Ruth found herself in. 'I thought, Okay, now you know in your head subjectively that everything can be shaken. But I discovered this unshakeable thing at the heart of it.'

I was shocked that what might seem like arbitrary, meaningless cruelty on the part of her creator affirmed her faith rather than destroying it. Why would God let such a terrible thing happen?

'I think, if you're going to think that, you should [think it] the first time you encounter suffering anywhere. Like, why are you the exception?' She brought up the gunmen who stormed a maternity ward in Kabul, killing mothers, children and unborn babies. 'One of those ladies had tried for a baby for seven years, and she got her son for four hours.'

Like many anxiety sufferers, I've often asked myself: *Why me?* As motivational speaker Les Brown once retorted: 'Why not you? Who would you suggest?'

Somehow, Ruth found aspects of her own tragedy to be grateful for – even her mum's death. 'She hated goodbyes more than anything, and she didn't have to say goodbye to a single person. So many people die from long drawn-out cancer battles, and that would have been torture for her, because she felt everyone's pain, not only her own.'

Psychologists call this effort to find alternative ways of thinking about an emotional event 'cognitive reappraisal'. We look at an experience – typically a negative one – and attempt to reframe it, for example considering what we might learn from it, unexpected positive outcomes that might arise from it, or ways in which some negative aspects might be temporary or less bad than they first appear.[2] Cognitive reappraisal doesn't mean denial, or nail-gunning a grin onto one's face – oh, I'm so *glad* I've been bereaved – but rather an attempt to regulate stress and painful emotions by balancing our awareness of downsides – which are typically obvious – with small mercies, moments of fortune, and things we are grateful for. Whereas trying to *suppress* negative emotions can be extremely taxing, and often results in a rebound effect where the buried feelings come back stronger, cognitive reappraisal allows for both negative and positive emotions to exist alongside one another.[3] That's the theory, anyway.

You might be tempted to dismiss this as thunderingly obvious to the point of banality. Cognitive reappraisal sounds suspiciously like looking on the bright side. No one's claiming it magically allows you to sidestep feeling the bad stuff, but when combined with the – in many ways much harder – practice of acceptance, willingly experiencing negative emotions without pushing them away, it predicts lower stress, less depression, and better outcomes for patients with chronic illnesses.[4]

It may be that a faith in a higher power encourages this kind of reappraisal. If you believe God loves you, when injury, suffering or death befalls you or your loved ones, that's going to create some serious cognitive dissonance. One strategy for reducing the gap between your belief – 'God loves me and is all-powerful' – and the event – 'My parent is terminally ill' – is to look for positives, or ways in which it could be worse, or small moments of unexpected grace.

Ruth told me she found it difficult to understand why her dad had survived. If a miracle could happen for him, why not her mum? 'But that doesn't in some ways trouble me, because how could I worship a God who I totally got? Then it would be like me, and I wouldn't worship myself.'

—

The psychologist Ken Pargament has researched what he calls 'religious coping methods'. He divides these into two forms: positive and negative. A positive type of religious cognitive appraisal is 'benevolent reappraisal' – reframing the stressful or painful event as potentially kind and beneficial, perhaps trying to see it as a lesson from God. Two negative equivalents are 'punishing reappraisal' and 'demonic reappraisal', looking for reasons why the event might be a punishment from God, or reframing the event as an act of malice by the Devil.

In a two-year study of elderly patients with chronic illnesses Pargament found that viewing stressors as punishments from God was associated with 'less independence in daily living, poorer cognitive functioning, poorer quality of life and more depressed mood'.[5] A previous study indicated that what he terms 'negative religious coping strategies' were associated with higher mortality amongst the elderly, a 22–33 per cent greater risk of dying once researchers had controlled for potential confounding variables.[6] People who blamed the Devil for their illness were more likely to die from it.

Ruth agreed that, without guidance, severe anxiety can interact with religion to create a feeling of conspiratorial mania. 'You're not just feeling the implications of your anxiety are going to hurt the people around you, you're also thinking there's some massive deity who's also really disappointed about this and maybe my eternity is in jeopardy too.'

One coping strategy I was surprised that Pargament listed as negative was 'pleading for direct intercession'. Praying for God's help seemed to me to be the classic religious activity. But Ruth saw prayer differently. 'I don't go to prayer thinking I have this third-party superpower,' she said. 'I feel like mostly things are left to run their course. It seems like the system is designed with laws that rarely get interrupted. A drunk driver gets in a car. The consequences of that play out. It's not like the hand of God reaches down and ensures he drives into a field and not into a kid.'

Ruth told me she's never really prayed for protection or anything like that. 'I feel, for me, prayer helps because of the sense that there's someone with a different, bigger perspective listening who cares about me, and who I think I trust, [who] is forming my character in a way that makes me more resilient and loving, and helping me to learn the lessons of the things that happen to me, so that I become closer with God.' She started laughing. 'Man, I'm sounding pious and awful, sorry. You know how you suddenly hover above yourself and you're like: who is this nun?'

Another aspect of faith – one that we saw before in the studies on inflammation – is the buffering effect of community. Pargament included 'seeking spiritual support' and 'seeking support from clergy or church members' as two of his positive religious coping methods.

'The church is a beautiful thing when it works well,' said Ruth. 'The care and the love that we have had as a family has been extraordinary. The way that we have had people gather around us. We were fed for months. All of our expenses in South Africa were covered. I came home to about a hundred and fifty cards. People popped round with stuff and hugs.'

After my grandmother's funeral, we had a very English wake, eating crisps and sausage rolls off white paper plates in a community hall. The vicar came round and talked to us in turn. I'd never met her before, but she chatted with me about my grandmother, and her life, and our memories. I remember thinking, *Wow, this is a real community*. Here was this person, going about, sincerely listening to people. Vicaring. I was suddenly conscious of the absence of that in my own life.

Ruth admitted that community can have a dark side too. Where there are shared values and acceptance there is also the power to ostracise, the pressure to conform, and human fallibility magnified. 'You can find Christians who think that if you have a faith in Jesus then you absolutely should not have anxiety or depression and it's a sign that you have weak faith, or you're ill-disciplined, or you're giving Christianity a bad name, or there's some kind of buried sin there, and if you can just find it and be sorry that'll cure you . . . I've encountered them and they were unhelpful and generally unpleasant people.'

Ruth told me that being a Christian hadn't cured her anxiety. It hadn't freed her from suffering. In many ways it forced her to make hard calls. But she thought it was worth it. 'The whole hideous experience [of the accident] has been an odd gift. Because you don't know until testing the strength of what you hold on to. I realise that actually I do believe. I don't understand the nuts and bolts, but I do believe in a life beyond.' She laughed. 'I feel like a bit of a nut. I'm quite a reasonable person – and I do believe there's going to be a physical life after death. That God will restore and redeem and make new the whole of creation, in a way that is suffering free.

'And I think I'm going to see my mum again. And I think all that was good and true about her will be there and recognisable, and all the things that were really difficult about her won't matter any more.'

———

I'm wary of anything that sounds too good to be true. Maybe that's anxiety all over. But I was wrongfooted by the ways in which Ruth said her faith challenged her. How it made some things harder. Yes, there were consolations, but it wasn't pure wishful thinking.

I wanted to learn more, so I spoke to the Reverend Dr Joanna Collicutt, a chartered clinical psychologist and specialist neuro-psychologist with a special interest in the meeting points between theology and psychology.

'Christianity and religions in general are not therapies,' she told me. 'It's easy to see them as that and those of us who are ministers and who are interested in the human condition would like in many ways to present them as that, because we'd get a lot more takers.'

Naively, I'd always thought that believing in God would obviate the need for therapy. You've got meaning, safety and ultimate refuge. God loves you, Jesus died for your sins and you can spend eternity in Heaven. If you accept that, the small neuroses of human existence should burn away like so much morning fog, shouldn't they? What's going on?

'I was a person who came to faith young, and thought it would solve all people's mental health problems. Then I became a clinical psychologist and found that the mental health hospitals were full of Christians. And that some of them had got there because of experiences in their churches.' Joanna said my question was one that had troubled her for some time. '[Christianity] ought to provide a simple answer of love, joy, peace and unconditional acceptance, and yet so many people find it very difficult to receive that.'

Joanna told me that in her preaching she often talks about faith as being not so much about believing, as accepting a gift and trusting that it's a gift. For people who have had chaotic childhoods, who have survived trauma, upheaval and abuse, who have developed a broken self-image, it can be harder to receive those gifts. We've learned not to trust the world. We don't think of ourselves as worthy of love. 'Though the research suggests when they do receive it, they receive it with a great deal more depth and joy because of deprivations they've had earlier.'

Yet the Christian message is not one of unalloyed comfort and relief from suffering. After all, its central image is a man with nails driven through his limbs, hanging from a cross. Joanna sees this duality – suffering and the promise of liberation from suffering – throughout the New Testament.

'One of the really interesting things in the gospel stories – and whether you believe in them historically or not is a secondary question in a way – the way they're constructed psychologically is that Jesus appears on the scene, he's baptised, and as he comes out of the water he hears this message: "You are my beloved son, and I am pleased with you." And that message, from a parent, of unconditional love, and that I love you, and you are pleasing in my sight, is the thing that we're all, I would say, longing for.'

In the baptism of Jesus, Joanna sees this moment where he's totally affirmed, totally accepted, perfectly set up to head out into the world. Yet instead he immediately heads into the desert to wrestle with demons. 'So you have the two sides: the kind of blissful sense of security and grounded self-worth, but the task of engaging with darkness. And I suppose in the Christian tradition that is the task that every one of us is invited to engage with. So the attractive bit is the blissful union, but there's always that second part as well.'

It's this second, darker part – the inevitability of suffering, temptation and fallibility – that Joanna believes makes Christianity tricky to consider in simple therapeutic terms. People with mental health issues often internalise highly destructive versions of religious teaching, incorporating it into negative life stories. 'There's a lot of material in our tradition that will feed guilt and worthlessness and fear of judgement after death or judgement in this life, or fear of exclusion.'

Indeed, one study found that women undergoing negative religious conflicts – such as feelings of guilt when their faith wavered – were significantly more likely to suffer from panic disorder.[7]

Joanna brought up some of Ken Pargament's research into two ways people use religion to make meaning. 'One is about conserving your worldview and your framework, and religion can be really helpful with that. And the other is about transforming it. Where it's broken apart and you're taken to somewhere you didn't know you were going to go. Which is a more rigorous and traumatic kind of experience but, at the end of the day, probably more enriching.'

What it notably *isn't* is calming. Sometimes, instead of making you feel safer, religious belief can challenge the reliability of all sorts of things you thought were permanent. It can turn your attention away from movie night to the inevitability of death. 'You can get studies which seem to imply that religion is not helping people,'

Joanna told me, 'because their levels of distress are high on questionnaire measures of anxiety and depression. But that can often be
a point on a journey where they are seeking some kind of meaning,
where if you go back some months later, you find that those distress
levels have fallen, but more importantly they've come to a new
understanding of themselves and the world.'

I stopped drinking in 2012. I wasn't an alcoholic, but my relationship with alcohol was unhealthy. I drank a lot, I drank to cope, and
I felt grim afterwards. I did many things while drunk I'm ashamed
of.

When I quit, my anxiety went up. Drinking may have been a
maladaptive coping strategy, but it was still a coping strategy. At
some level it worked – otherwise I wouldn't have done it. If you'd
taken simple measurements of my anxiety before and immediately
after I quit alcohol, you might conclude that giving up drink made
my mental health worse. Yet I think most people would see my
decision to quit as a positive, even necessary, step on the road to
recovery.

The same can be true of quitting a bad job or a relationship, of
leaving a city you hate, of finally facing up to financial problems or
addictions. Big life changes are disruptive. They can make things
worse before they make things better.

Joanna saw it as a finely balanced path. The *Spiritual Exercises
of Ignatius of Loyola* were composed in the early sixteenth century
and represent a kind of early journalling practice for Christians on
retreat, designed to be completed in four themed weeks. Once the
exercises had been completed, Ignatius proposed something called
the 'examen' as a way to continue to apply their lessons in everyday
life. 'What you do is, frequently, maybe every day, you start with a
prayer and you start with an intentional attitude of gratitude for life.
But then you go through your day and you look into your soul and
you identify what [Ignatius] calls consolations and desolations.
Which are things that have fed you during the day and have been

good for you – so it's not quite the same as things you've enjoyed – and things where you just think no, this dragged me down and diminished me. And you use that as a kind of means of being attentive to where you think God is leading you.'

The examen is close to classical CBT. You're reviewing your behaviour, honestly evaluating your feelings, good and bad, with the purpose of bringing yourself closer to the truth. But Ignatius was aware that, even with the best intentions, we can very easily deceive ourselves.

'So it's Ignatius in particular who introduces the idea of a spiritual director, or what is sometimes called a soul friend, who is precisely somebody who holds your hand through this.' Ignatius wrote using the vocabulary of demons and angels, but we can just as easily apply this wisdom to secular problems. 'It's easy to be deceived. The things that are most valuable to us are the things that we can most easily get wrong, oddly. Therefore we need trusted guides – in the form of an individual director, in some traditions, and in others in the form of a group who will help you reflect. So a bit like therapy again – an individual therapist and a group therapy.'

I told Joanna that, perversely, sometimes the moments I'd felt most hopeful on behalf of friends were times when they had felt most confused. When, instead of putting a brave face on it, they admitted: 'I don't know what to do next.'

'This is part of what Jesus means in our tradition when he says you need to become like a child. You have that openness to experience that you haven't had since you were a small child because you've had your world sorted out. So it's a potential window of opportunity and the question is: do you receive that as an opportunity or do you batten down the hatches and revert to the way you used to be?'

This is a bit like a term coined by psychologists Richard Tedeschi and Lawrence Calhoun, 'Posttraumatic growth', 'the experience of positive change that occurs as a result of the struggle with highly challenging life crises'.[8] It also reconnects with theories of why a mystical experience brought on by LSD or psilocybin might be transformative. A paper co-authored by Dr Robin Carhart-Harris, head of the Centre for Psychedelic Research at Imperial College London, hypothesises that acute stress can induce a serotonergic 'hyper-plastic state' that promotes 'deep learning'. The authors suggest psychedelics could be one way of inducing a crisis – what they term a 'pivotal mental state' – that makes psychological transformation more likely.[9]

Joanna worried that contemporary mental health discourse struggled to engage with the positive side to suffering. 'Sometimes we can pathologise distress too quickly. And some distress is good distress. The knack is knowing: when is this good pain, and when is it bad pain? When should I sit with it and listen to what it's telling me, and when do I need to take it as an alarm call, which is part of what mindfulness allows you to do?'

She told me that the Bible had a lot to say about anxiety and – to my surprise – panic. The most repeated command in the Bible is 'Do not fear' or 'Be not afraid.' Many people claim it appears in one version or another a suspiciously pleasing total of 365 times.

'I've never counted it,' said Joanna. 'I think the reason that it's said a lot is because life is frightening. People get frightened. This is not necessarily a pathological thing. We need to say it to each other quite a lot.

'If you look at the accounts of the death of Jesus, if you thought they were a fiction, they're almost designed to make you look in the face [of] the things that we're all really, really scared of. That is: great pain, social exclusion, abandonment – there's this cry from the cross, "Why have you forsaken me?"' The supreme anguish in Jesus' martyrdom is a moment of all-too-human fear.

As for panic, 'In Christianity, the recipe you are given for panic is love. There's this text you probably know, "Perfect love casts out fear," which is a key text people go round muttering to themselves – partly because it does the job, in that it's just very succinct.'

I was impressed – and a little intimidated – by the way in which Ruth and Joanna had talked about their faith, not as a bromide or a pleasing consolation, but as a torch. The catch was you had to use its light to venture deeper into the darkness.

For Joanna, it all came down to 'the Christian story which invites you to face the agony of it all, and ask: Is there something beyond this thing which scares us so much? Beyond mortality and annihilation?'

———

As much as I saw value in the ideas we'd discussed, I didn't believe in God. For many members of the Church of England this doesn't seem to be a dealbreaker, but for me it felt kind of central.

The closest I had come to religion was Buddhism. The first time I meditated, nearly twenty years ago, I sat in a room with a rope-mat floor, facing the wall, my legs crossed and my backside propped on a cushion. While people were sitting, the leader would periodically rise and whack meditators who were slouching with a long flat stick called a *keisaku* or *kyōsaku* – commonly translated as 'warning stick', 'awakening stick' or, in the latter case, 'encouragement stick'. (This sounds tantamount to abuse, but – at least in the tradition I practised in – it doesn't hurt.) I had found meditating much harder than I had expected, but it had also left me feeling quiet and centred.

So I decided to meet Sarvananda, an ordained member of the Triratna Buddhist Order who had been practising meditation for nearly forty years. At the Norwich Buddhist Centre, he made us both a cup of green tea and we went upstairs to the shrine room and sat in front of a big mural of the Buddha meditating.

Even here I was nervous. Sarvananda was friendly, giving unhurried answers in a soft Glaswegian accent, yet I felt terrified I might annoy or alienate him. I feel that way in a lot of social interactions – hypersensitive, as Kate Button suggested, to cues that the other person might be bored or displeased. I have this idea that, given their whole thing is compassion and equanimity, if you irritate a Buddhist you must be a dreadful person.

Like me, he had come to Buddhism in his early twenties, looking for something to deal with his anxiety and depression. 'I think one of the reasons I was anxious was because my mum was particularly anxious. Her parents were very, very anxious. Her father was in the First World War.' Sarvananda thought his grandfather passed down that war trauma to his mother, who passed it down to him.

I asked what he used to get anxious about.

'Primarily it was a fear of death. A fear of my own death, a fear of other people's death. An uncle died when I was about five, in a car crash, and that really made me aware of the fragility of life.'

In the classic Buddhist story, prince Siddhartha Gautama leaves his luxurious palace and sees for the first time a sick man, an elderly man, and a corpse. He realises, for all his wealth, he cannot escape these fates, and so renounces his royal life to seek an answer. Ultimately, after travelling and meditating, he achieves enlightenment while meditating under a bodhi tree, escaping the cycle of birth and death and becoming the Buddha, usually translated as the 'Awakened One'.

'According to the myth, it was old age, sickness and death that worried him, basically. What was the point of life in the face of the fact that the body decays and dies? That was his question, really.' Buddhism didn't offer easy reassurances. 'It was almost like they were saying well, yeah, things are really fragile. In this life you can't control certain events. But what you can do is work with your own mind and your own mental states.'

Sarvananda said the Buddha identified two qualities that one should cultivate through meditation: *samatha*, which roughly translates as 'calm' or 'tranquillity', and *vipassana*, which is often translated as 'concentration' or 'insight'. Becoming calmer makes it easier to concentrate, and becoming more focused makes it easier to quieten the mind and relax, but Sarvananda said they should be approached in a definite order. 'Samatha is to do with developing calmness and positive emotion. Vipassana comes second. Based on that calm and positive emotion, you then reflect on reality, or you try and understand things on a deeper level.

'A lot of it is just being aware of your thought processes. You're challenging your thoughts and things like that, thinking, "Well, is this true?" So there's quite a link between that kind of meditation and CBT.' The Dalai Lama, who rises at 3 a.m. and meditates for five hours every morning, often recommends a particular form of meditation called 'analytic meditation', which involves systematically calling to mind certain thoughts or ideas and investigating whether they are true. One might choose to reflect on the effects of anger, or ask, 'Who am I?' and deconstruct the various answers that arise.

With samatha, 'often it's coming back to your body, your physical experience. Not trying to push the thoughts away but trying to hold them with kindness.' Rather than deconstructing or challenging your thoughts, you're just noticing them, learning to recognise them as thoughts – a commentary on reality, rather than reality itself. 'You're really grounding yourself in the body and noticing the extent to which we identify with our thoughts, rather than seeing our thoughts as phenomena that arise, almost like clouds in the sky. We tend to stick to them and really identify with them and get into this loop of anxiety and fear.'

I was surprised when he told me that, while on retreat, meditating for long periods, he had experienced a great deal of fear. I'd always imagined a meditation retreat would be like a spa break.

'When you're on retreat you're away from all distractions, and you're just face to face with your mind. So in some ways, certain meditation practices heighten the fear because you're just much more aware of your mental habits.' TV, smartphones, work, socialising – all these things help us escape ourselves. When you're sat in a silent room for days, alone with your thoughts, you've got nowhere to hide.

On this particular retreat, he found himself gripped by a peculiar worry: *What if this fear goes for good?*

'I was terrified of that. I thought, well, that's interesting. Why am I so afraid of getting rid of fear? Obviously I've identified with it. In a strange way, the fear is reassuring because it's what I've identified with for so long. It's what I've based my character around.' A friend of his went through a similar thing working with hatred and irritability. As the feelings ebbed and faded, his friend felt something close to grief. 'He realised that part of him was really sad that this aspect of him was going to die.'

Sarvananda realised there was something comical about being afraid of losing your fear. But it was an important moment. He had been terrified so long it felt like part of who he was. Who would he be without his fear? 'The Buddha himself talked about fear. He experienced fear. There's this sutra, "The Discourse on Fear and Dread". In it, the Buddha talks about the fear that arises when one lodges in remote shrines in the forest:

> As I was staying there, brahman,
> either an animal came along,
> or a peacock broke off a twig,
> or the wind rustled the fallen leaves.
> It occurred to me:
> 'Surely this is that fear and dread coming.'

The Buddha says that, as fear and dread came upon him, he remained in whatever posture he was in until they passed. 'He just let it pass through him. Whatever he was doing, standing or lying down or walking, he continued to do it and tried not to react.'

For the Buddha, conquering fear required two things: leading an ethical life, free from greed, corruption, gossip, ambition, cruelty and laziness; and staying in place when fear arises – holding one's seat.

Sarvananda advised I try a combination of physical body work, like yoga, and meditation – especially 'metta' or loving-kindness meditation, where one works on feeling compassion towards all sentient beings, beginning, crucially, with oneself. 'Probably one of the most significant areas for me in lessening my anxiety is learning self-love and losing self-castigation, self-laceration.'

I expect self-castigation is a failed strategy for self-regulation. We want to protect ourselves from loss. What could be more motivating than yelling at ourselves? Surely the harsher we are, the better we'll listen. If I thought Suki was about to run into the path of a bus, I'd yell at the top of my voice.

For many of us, buses are coming at us from all directions. Relationship buses. Career buses. Parenthood buses. Political buses. We yell at ourselves – *Come on, you fucking idiot, move!* – because, unpleasant as it is, we think the alternative is worse. But the long-term costs of all this yelling are ruinous. Most of us accept this intellectually, yet we struggle to *believe* it. We're scared of easing off on ourselves. We can think of occasions in our past where we relaxed and something went wrong. We never give ourselves a chance to learn how to thrive under gentle encouragement, so we judge we can't do it.

One thing meditation may offer us is a chance, not to stop the yelling, but just to properly listen to it for the first time. We're so often caught up in either obeying the angry voice in our head or drowning it out – with alcohol, social media, chronic busy-ness – that when we're afraid, we don't act as the Buddha counselled: not reacting, but holding our position, and allowing the thoughts and feelings to pass through us.

Since I first tried meditation, interventions based on mindfulness have been heavily researched. Studies have found that mindfulness-based therapy can moderately improve anxiety symptoms,[10] and that mindfulness training may help people with GAD reduce the physiological symptoms of anxiety in stressful situations.[11] Some research suggests that mindfulness training leads to functional changes in hippocampal connectivity – which, as we've learned, is related to the recall of threatening memories – putting people in an optimal frame of mind for exposure therapy.[12] Mindfulness might be able to help people quieten down that threat response so they can willingly expose themselves to the stressful context or stimulus, and learn new, adaptive associations.

On the other hand, further studies suggest mindfulness training doesn't perform better than simply educating people about simple ways to manage stress,[13] which isn't to say that it has *no* effect, but that it's not more effective than existing options. Much of the research into mindfulness-based interventions suffers from poor study design – participants *know* they're meditating, which may leave them susceptible to expectation effects, and studies often don't record how well participants adhered to the programme. Did some meditate more than others, and did that affect outcomes? If people who didn't stick to the programme recovered just as well as those who did, that suggests that meditation wasn't the primary driver of recovery.[14]

A lot of mindfulness research is undertaken by enthusiastic meditators seeking to prove that meditation is an efficacious way of reducing anxiety, stress and depression. But much of the evidence is of ambiguous utility. Yes, studies of relatively small numbers of long-term meditators using electroencephalograms (EEGs) have found increased gamma-wave activity[15] compared to controls.[16] To which the obvious objection is: so fucking what? As the authors themselves admit, 'There is as of yet no clear understanding of the functional role of EEG gamma activity in the literature.'

Which isn't to say this area isn't worthy of research. Just that we don't yet know what it means, if anything. There's no special reason why voltage fluctuations in the brain should tell us anything pertinent about meditation's efficacy, and plenty of reasons to be cautious of interpreting notoriously noisy gamma band recordings in humans.[17] A lot of the experienced meditators studied by researchers are monks and nuns living in relative seclusion. Many aspects of their lives are radically different from the average person's, not just their practice of meditation.

It's hard to design a mindfulness study with a true 'placebo' condition, meaning a lot of the research lacks rigour. Attempts to get around this by showing changes in brain function and neuroanatomy are interesting, but when I mentioned them to Camilla Nord, she wasn't convinced: 'I'm familiar with those studies and if you want to have a structural endpoint to your study that's interesting. It's very, very cool that mindfulness causes structural changes.' But, she said, it wasn't exactly surprising. 'Any experience that you do again and again causes structural changes in your brain. If you want to show mindfulness impacts anxiety, measure anxiety.'

—

Speaking to Ruth, Joanna and Sarvananda, I found it helpful to hear how faith helped them navigate anxiety and panic – and how it didn't. In some ways, I was a little disappointed. I'd hoped they would tell me of this transformation, this moment of grace, where they exhaled and all fear, all dread, left them for ever.

For all my avowed commitment to evidence and rationalism, I was still clinging to that possibility. The belief in a transcendent moment, almost a death, where the fear would pass. Where I'd finally let go.

But the religion they were talking about wasn't a release. It wasn't an escape or a freedom. It was a turning towards. It was a being with. Very bad stuff was going to happen, and when it did you had a choice. You could resist. You could curse God. You could blame yourself.

Or you could accept it. You could sit with the beautiful disaster that is reality. And you could ask yourself: How can I use this to do good?

XIX.

IN THESE UNCERTAIN TIMES
Anxiety disorders and global catastrophe

It was February 1974, the sun was setting on Lubang Island in the Philippines, and Lieutenant Hiroo Onoda was creeping out of the jungle to pick jackfruit. He had been hiding in the same spot for three days, and his food supplies had run out. The jackfruit grove stood at the point where two rivers met, not far from a banana field. It was a good place to scavenge for food, but the island police knew that too.

Lieutenant Onoda had been trained in guerrilla warfare. He slept under the stars, brushed his teeth with palm-tree fibres, and kept his rifle from rusting by polishing it with palm oil. He was used to crawling into paddyfields, disguising his thefts by only taking a little unshelled rice from each husk. On this day, knowing that islanders might be searching for him, he waited until dusk, camouflaged his jacket and hat with leaves and twigs, and crept down the hill towards the trees.

As he approached the water, he noticed something large and white hanging from the branches. With a start, he realised it was a mosquito net. He was indignant. Someone was camping between him and his food. Reckoning that the net was only big enough for two, he resolved to rush the camp with a surprise attack. He could knock one of them out, then best the other in hand-to-hand combat. He cocked his rifle, pressed the knurled cap at the rear end of the bolt with his palm, and twisted it to the left, unlocking the safety.

As he approached, he came across a man building a fire beside the river. Onoda called out. Normally the islanders fled at his cries, but to his astonishment the young man saluted, calling back: 'I'm Japanese! I'm Japanese!'

Even more surprising was the young man's question a few moments later: 'Are you Onoda-san?'

Onoda was suspicious. There was something fishy about this long-haired boy. He had probably been sent by the enemy. Years ago the Americans had dropped leaflets across the island claiming the war was over. They had printed fake newspapers and broadcast tapes of real Japanese radio programmes, edited so as to discourage Japanese sympathisers. They had even gone so far as to send photos of his family, supposedly with news of how they were getting on, but the images were obviously doctored – the caption read 'Onoda-san's Family', but a neighbour unrelated to him was in the picture, and there was no reason to add *san* after his name, as anyone familiar with Japanese etiquette would have known.

Still, the young man did not appear to be armed. If this was a trap, it was a subtle one.

'Yes,' said Onoda, knowing there was little point in lying, 'I'm Onoda.'

'Really, Lieutenant Onoda?'

Onoda nodded.

The boy was wide-eyed and trembling. He wore a t-shirt, dark blue trousers, rubber sandals and thick woollen socks. This final clothing choice may have saved his life. Socks with sandals were so unlike anything the islanders ever wore, Onoda decided to wait before shooting him. It was just possible he really was Japanese.

In a stammering, high-pitched voice, the boy said: 'I know you've had a long, hard time. The war's over. Won't you come back to Japan with me?'

Onoda was filled with rage. 'No, I won't go back! For me, the war hasn't ended!'

'Why?'

'You wouldn't understand.'

How could he? The young man, whose name was Norio Suzuki, hadn't trained as a commando under Captain Shigetomi, who drilled his men constantly in suicide-attack manoeuvres, who was fond of slapping you in the face and calling you *baka* ('idiot'), whose favourite expression had been 'Better to sweat on the training ground than to bleed on the battleground.' This long-haired kid hadn't survived for nearly thirty years on an island less than half the size of the Isle of Wight, moving constantly, burying ammunition, enduring rats, rainy seasons and endless American attempts at deception, preparing for the inevitable Japanese counter-attack that would liberate him. He hadn't watched his two comrades, Shimada and Kozuka, get killed in shoot-outs with police.

Norio Suzuki was from a completely different world.

And here he was saying the war was over. Come out of the jungle. Lay down your rifle.

He might as well have plucked a fish from the river and told it to fly.[1]

—

Some of us have a hard time believing that the war is over.

Neuroscientist Alexander Shackman pointed me towards a 2015 meta-analysis of nearly a century of anxiety research, which found that people with anxiety disorders showed 'a small yet robust pattern of overgeneralization of the fear responses to safe cues'. The authors found it isn't that anxiety sufferers are more afraid in stressful situations, but we have a harder time learning that a situation is safe.[2] If we fear one thing, we generalise that fear to something similar more easily, we find it harder to suppress our feelings of fear, and it takes us longer to extinguish fears in safe situations.

This can be adaptive under certain circumstances. Neuroscientist Oli Robinson was involved in a study where participants had to choose between four competing slot machines – he and his fellow researchers found that anxious people were quicker to update their behaviour when a machine wasn't paying out compared to non-anxious people. Anxious people seemed to learn from negative outcomes quicker.[3] Psychologist Kate Button's work suggested anxious people are much better than non-anxious people at learning that people don't like them.

There are many environments in which updating your behaviour quickly in response to danger and spotting when someone is hostile are highly desirable. We wouldn't suggest a soldier unwilling to skip down a jungle trail twirling an umbrella and whistling had an anxiety disorder. In a theatre of war, we'd view such carefree behaviour as evidence of mental collapse.

When you ask someone with severe anxiety to give up the behaviours and feelings that have served them this far in life, what you're really asking is for them to adopt habits that, for years – perhaps their whole life – have seemed like insanity. You're asking them to lead with their chin. To step out of cover and expose themselves to snipers.

I thought of what Sarvananda had said about his terror of the fear leaving for good. That bizarre, almost comical sense of grief. When he said it, I didn't understand. I think I do now. I used to think anxiety was something apart from me. A diseased portion of flesh I could cut out. Here is me, my authentic self, and there, within the area marked out with dashes like a diagram showing cuts of beef on a cow, is anxiety. The mistake.

But so much is tangled up in that area I wanted to destroy. 'Interdigitated', as Alex Shackman might have put it. Anxiety saw the times I got hurt. The times people were cruel or heedless of my wellbeing. Anxiety noted each occasion down – where it happened, how, with whom – and more, it set about deducing what these events had in common, constructing models, calculating probabilities, weaving a great cat's cradle of red thread and push pins as it toiled to predict where the next catastrophe might take place.

Anxiety even stood vigil over me as I slept. Was I breathing? Like a mother, it watched the rise and fall of my chest, ready to wake me at the first sign of trouble.

Sure, it could be harsh. Draconian even. But it *cared*. Fundamentally, anxiety wanted me to be safe.

Woven through anxiety was the very thing I struggled with most. Love.

—

Three weeks after meeting Norio Suzuki, Hiroo Onoda finally surrendered to his superior officer, Major Taniguchi, who, for the past two decades, had been working as a bookseller. Even as Taniguchi gave the order to stand down, Onoda thought he might lean forward and whisper the 'real orders'.

When the secret message did not come, Lieutenant Onoda realised the truth. The war really was over.

We might imagine that release from a long, hard war would bring elation. Onoda's country was at peace and prosperous. Finally, he could return home.

He was devastated. For thirty years he had cared for his Arisaka Type 99 rifle 'like a baby'. And now he was learning that it was all for nothing.

Hiroo Onoda does not make for an endearing character: an unapologetic ethno-nationalist, it later emerged he had killed several islanders, a detail he omits from his autobiography (though he does describe robbing several at gunpoint). When he returned home, he donated money from well-wishers to the Yasukuni Shrine, a notorious war monument revered by Japanese nationalists and far right politicians the world over, which contains the tombs of fourteen Class-A war criminals.

352

So I hope you understand how disturbed I was when, reading about that moment when Hiroo Onoda emerged from the jungle to meet Norio Suzuki, I felt as if I understood him exactly. In fact, I've just realised what it made me think of.

This is going to sound weird – I guess because it is.

When my wife asked me to marry her, I had a panic attack. She had taken me to a really nice hotel, on a spa break. No one had ever done anything like that for me. I didn't expect her to propose. I'd been planning to ask her myself, though I kept delaying. I felt I'd never do it well enough. I kept constructing ever-more elaborate scenarios in my head, ones sufficiently grand and creative to show how much I loved her, then doubting my ability to pull them off. I was terrified of messing it up.

We were outside the hotel, having a drink together. Ducks glided across the millpond. The setting sun was golden on the water. And she asked me.

I know you've had a long, hard time. The war's over. Won't you come home?

———

When you ask an anxiety sufferer to give up their fear, what new reality are you offering in exchange?

Step out of the jungle. The fundamental assumptions upon which you have constructed your identity lie in ruins. The game you thought you were playing does not exist.

When Hiroo Onoda accepted that the war was over – that the war had, in fact, been over for several decades – it was a kind of death. It must have felt like stepping into a parallel universe. Reality becomes this improbable, ersatz confection that no longer conforms to your gut sense of what feels right or plausible. Everything feels slightly off. Unreal.

You stagger through it, waiting to wake up.

———

So many people blame themselves for horrendous suffering that was in no way their fault: physical or sexual abuse from a caregiver when they were children, for example, emotional neglect, bullying, bereavement. I asked a therapist who worked with trauma survivors why it's so common for people to add to their suffering with self-condemnation. Why on earth would you believe that such a thing was your fault – believe it so strongly that any attempt to convince you otherwise felt deeply threatening?

They said that sometimes the false belief protects you from a scarier one. If the trauma is your fault, it is under your control. If it is under your control, there are theoretical steps you can take to prevent it happening again.

But if it *isn't* your fault – if sometimes in life bad things happen to us that we do not deserve, that we can neither foresee nor prevent – then it could happen again. And there is nothing, no sequence of behaviours or thoughts, you can do to completely eliminate that possibility.

That's the reality we're being asked to embrace when we step out of the jungle. The home we're being asked to return to.

Hand back your rifle. The war is over.

———

By the start of 2020, something had started to shift.

Since my first hypnotherapy session with Graham, my panic attacks had stopped entirely. Given all my big talk about science, this was, at the very least, professionally inconvenient. I'd been grooming myself for the role of unflinching but sympathetic sceptic. Yet here I was. Panic-attack free for the first time in over a decade. When my mum found out I'd never live it down.

My anxiety seemed to have come right down too. I was letting things go more easily, not continually fretting about the future.

I had lost a bunch of weight and my running had come on so well I started training for my first marathon. I signed up for one-to-one boxing lessons. I told Dave, the gym-owner (a different Dave and a different gym), I wanted to learn how to get punched in the face.

I pushed myself to try new things. Lisa and I went to a trampoline park. When we arrived, I realised we were the only adults there not accompanying children. Immediately I became super-self-conscious. She told me not to be so silly.

In the end, we had a whale of a time.

One night our friend Molly came round for dinner. We hadn't seen her in a while, and I found myself telling her excitedly about all the stuff I'd been doing: how I had not one but two 'brain helmets' now – something normal, stable people say – how I didn't have panic attacks any more, and how my anxiety had come right down. 'I no longer qualify as having an anxiety disorder,' I announced. 'My anxiety is pretty much cured.'

Lisa gave me a sceptical look. Maybe I'd improved a bit, she said, but 'cured'? She thought I still overreacted to some things, that I still worried and fretted, and that certain social situations still set me off.

I felt a bit humiliated. Hadn't she seen how much progress I'd made? I'd done all this research, all this exercise, I'd come off my meds, I'd transformed my diet. I'd *worked* on myself. For six months I'd obsessively fought to defeat my anxiety. I was anxiety-free, or near enough. Now it was time to enjoy the fruits of a life without fear. Without stress.

I was no longer a coward.

A few days later I saw the news reports. The coronavirus pandemic had spread to Britain. Thousands upon thousands were going to die. If you went outdoors you were killing people. And the top-trending hashtag on Twitter: #UKLockdownNow.

Some habitual worriers report, in times of crisis, feeling oddly calm. Finally their inner world matches the outside world. Their fear is appropriate.

That's the funny thing about mental illness. It's contextual. Feeling anxious, feeling worried, feeling, in fact, *sick* with worry does not mean you have an anxiety disorder if there are bunnyquotes appropriate endbunnyquotes things to be anxious about.

As the UK and US entered lockdown, millions of people felt anxious.[4] One report published by a large American pharmacy management company found that, between mid-February and mid-March 2020, prescriptions for anti-anxiety medications fulfilled by their pharmacies increased by over a third.[5]

I had quit anxiety just as it went mainstream.

———

A box of Bibles with wipe-clean plastic covers outside somebody's house, with a cardboard sign that said: 'FREE STERILISED STUDY BIBLES. PLEASE TAKE ONE. ABSOLUTELY SAFE.' Rainbows chalked on the pavement, and written above them: 'ALL WILL BE WELL.' Julian of Norwich became an icon for the city during lockdown; a plague survivor who spent much of her life in self-isolation, yet somehow seemed to find reasons for hope.

In those first weeks, I barely slept. The ordinary acquired a febrile, delirious edge. Everything felt like an omen.

———

Sci-fi author Brian Aldiss coined the term 'cosy catastrophe' for a quintessentially British kind of disaster novel. Society collapses, most people die horribly, but the (invariably male) underachieving middle-class protagonist finds himself catapulted to the position of hero, lording it over the remnants with his pick of cars, houses and women. Aldiss was talking about novels like John Wyndham's *Day of the*

Triffids which present themselves as disaster narratives but secretly indulge a wish-fulfilment fantasy in which everyone above you in the social hierarchy has been killed off.

My childhood was the era of the four-minute warning, where the Cold War might at any moment erupt into a full thermonuclear exchange. I lost count of the number of 'child wanders through radioactive desolation' stories I was fed through books, radio and TV. The bombs, we all knew, would poison the water and block out the sun. They would create invisible zones of death where you would vomit, then your hair would fall out and your skin would slough off like a chrysalis. We were terrorised by dispatches from lost futures, dire warnings from chain-gangs of post-apocalyptic Marley's ghosts crackling with fallout.

When we find ourselves in uncharted territory, we fall back on stories. In big, scary moments, I've asked myself how people in books or TV shows handled this. We look to models for clues on how to behave.

It never occurred to me that my biggest asset as a writer – my imagination – might be my biggest liability.

In all the emails I was getting from various organisations, they kept calling lockdown 'unprecedented'. But it wasn't unprecedented to me. I had read the books. I had watched the movies. I *knew* where this was going.

I kept thinking to myself: in the first *Mad Max* the ice-cream shops were still open. He went on holiday. He had a job. Two films later they were trading animal pelts for non-irradiated water in a town run on murder and pig shit.

———

Unlike all those anxiety sufferers who said they had been expecting this – or something like it – who felt something close to relief now the rest of the world was taking on the burden of vigilance, I was completely blindsided. I had devoted half a year to slowly, slowly uncurling from my instinctive crouched, cowering position. For the first time since my childhood I had coaxed myself into dropping my guard. Into letting go of worry.

It was as if, after years of holding my breath, I finally exhaled. Then wham.

—

I spoke to Dr Adrian James, president of the Royal College of Psychiatrists, about the psychological impact of lockdown and the ongoing pandemic. I asked him if it's possible to have an anxiety disorder in the face of a global crisis. Both the DSM-5 and the ICD-11 specify that, in generalised anxiety disorder, the worry must be 'excessive'. Is anxiety under extreme circumstances 'excessive'?

'The fact that you've got an external threat doesn't mean you can't have pathological anxiety,' he said. 'I see it as being a combination of the degree of anxiety, the length of time in which it happens, the physiological effect on you, and its damaging effect to your mental functioning and to your everyday functioning.'

He talked about all the people who needed access to mental health services and no longer had it. 'We know that the earlier you treat mental illness, the better the outcome.' People were less likely to reach out for help, and when they did, they left it later, when they had got worse. He was particularly worried about young people, who were missing formative parts of growing up. 'My worry is, when it's all over, people will just say get on with it. Catch up. Do it twice as fast.' He said that, after the 1918 Spanish flu pandemic, the mental health impact took a while to unfold.

'This is, in my view, a perfect storm for there to be higher levels of anxiety, and higher levels of depression.'

I guess it's darkly hilarious. Man finds hope just in time for the apocalypse. In those first weeks, I struggled to see the funny side. I felt as if I were going mad. For a bit, I was. My thoughts became deeply paranoid – bordering at times on psychosis. People were clamouring for laws to restrict their own freedoms. What if it was all a trick? What if tanks started patrolling the streets? What if we were never allowed back out again?

My mood swung from sentimental, bleeding-heart sympathy to bitter, seething rage. Sometimes I couldn't bear to think of all the frightened, vulnerable people trapped in their homes. The whole human race – even politicians I didn't agree with – felt like my family. I wept because I couldn't protect them. At other times I found myself hating people for having the audacity to want to live. Why couldn't we all just go out and accept the inevitable? Let the virus sweep through us in a great biblical judgement. Anything but this horrible uncertainty.

The thought I kept having, over and over, was: *The world is ending. The world is ending.*

Compared to most people, we had it easy. But it wrecked me. I remembered how Ruth had said, after her parents' car crash, she suddenly found herself in a world where 'everything can be shaken.'

The superstitious child inside me – who once whispered 'and may I be damned if . . .' in his head a hundred times a day, who worried he had caused his granddad's heart attack by wishing they didn't have to go on holiday – watched the pandemic unfolding and thought: *I did this. This is my punishment.*

—

I never wanted to kill myself. But I didn't want to live.

That's a terrible thing for a father to think, I know. I was healthy, pain-free. I had a family who loved me. Wonderful friends. Years ahead of me.

But I felt like I couldn't go on. I wanted to be dead.

With a last push, I'd finally got myself to a point where I could cope with life. Then life – as if in response – had upped the difficulty level. I couldn't sleep. I couldn't concentrate. The slightest problem or bit of bad news would trigger waves of anxious rumination or hopeless collapse.

Basic coping strategies were suddenly off-limits: see your friends, do something new, get out of the house, *rest*. I knew – just *knew*, with utter certainty – that in the pressure-cooker of our home, with nowhere to escape to, Lisa and I would get divorced. I wouldn't be able to hold it together. I had no space. I would mess everything up and it wasn't fair, because I'd worked so hard. I'd done my best. But it hadn't been enough.

———

If anxiety is the high alert, the fire alarm, the desperate scrabbling flurry to anticipate and prevent the bad things, depression is the crash – the realisation that you're powerless. That every choice is wrong. That nothing you do can prevent the inevitable horror. That even choosing not to play is a losing move.

Depression sensitises you to anxiety. You've spent so long incapacitated that the smallest effort feels terrifying. You've no confidence. What if this attempt at recovery goes wrong? What if I make a mistake and trigger an avalanche of dark, depressive thoughts? You know how deep the pit is. How bad things can get. You become desperate to avoid failures that might nudge you into another spiral.

I called the Samaritans. I wasn't suicidal exactly, but I had no idea how I was going to get through the next hour, let alone the coming weeks and months. (I think if someone asks if you're suicidal and you have to specify 'Not exactly', you could probably use a chat.) I couldn't imagine talking was going to help – couldn't conceive of any plausible mechanism by which it might do so, but I didn't know what else to do.

After a short wait, a woman answered in a soft Yorkshire accent.

I found myself apologising for bothering them. Even in a crisis I felt terrifically embarrassed, worried I was taking this resource away from someone else who needed it, afraid in case the person scolded me for being self-obsessed or told me to hurry up.

But she was really kind. She said it was okay, and asked what I wanted to talk about.

I told her the whole story.

The darnedest bit was – 'This is going to sound silly,' I said – I was trying to write a book on anxiety. Finally, after all my research and experiments, I'd started improving. For the first time I'd really believed I was going to escape. Then the pandemic happened.

By the time I got to the end, I was sobbing.

'It sounds', she said very gently, 'like a lot of your anxiety is to do with control.'

I exhaled heavily.

'Yes,' I said. 'That's it. That's exactly it.'

———

Ex-FBI negotiator Chris Voss has said that, during hostage stand-offs, there was one phrase he was working towards – one phrase that, when he heard it, meant he'd won them over: 'That's right.'

If he could get the armed robber or terrorist to the point of saying 'That's right' – not 'You're right,' which implies compliance but not agreement – the whole tenor of the negotiation would change. The person felt understood.

It took me back to something the fantasy author Mike Shel once told me. I was chatting to him on my podcast when I found out he'd spent over two decades as a therapist specialising in anxiety. I asked him what he'd learned.

He said that when he started out he used to jump right in with explaining the fight, flight or freeze response and why we developed it from an evolutionary perspective. He'd explain what's going on in the body, then he'd go on to teach the cognitive model and some interventions. But he quickly realised that it wasn't enough.

What he needed to do first was *listen*. 'Until a person feels understood,' he said, 'all the information in the world, all the data, all the scientific understanding of the process and coping strategies are for naught. A person needs to feel that someone gets what they are struggling with.'

Saying all of it out loud to the person on the other end of the phone, the lengths I'd gone to . . . I sounded crazy. I'd devoted my entire life to mastering and eradicating fear. A normal person would have taken a week off and bought a foot spa.

I started laughing. A bit manically. Partly with relief.

Why did I do shit like this to myself? Why couldn't I just have a Garibaldi and go to bed?

As we continued to talk, I realised I was still clinging to the hope that human life is fixable. That there might be, somewhere out there, a correct, perfect sequence of moves which could keep out the grief, the loss, the possibility of rejection.

My whole quest to get rid of anxiety had been cooked up by my anxiety.

Anxiety's answer to anxiety: total control. Control of thoughts, control of neurochemistry, control of behaviour. Biopsychosocial totalitarianism. A police state of mind.

When everything is known perfectly, when every variable can be accounted for, when every threat can be predicted and averted, then we shall have peace.

—

I clung to my anxiety because letting go would mean accepting that I was not in control. That I could never be in control.

My choice was between a life of perpetual guerrilla warfare, or one where I admitted that the battle was unwinnable. All my striving, like Hiroo Onoda's thirty-year war, had been a tragic waste. The button wasn't wired to anything. To the extent I clung on to my fantasy of control, I would suffer. To the extent I could let it go, I would at least free up a bunch of mental energy I'd been wasting trying to steer the weather with my mind.

In the weeks and months that followed, what I would slowly come to understand was, this process of acceptance is never over. You don't check the box, take the pill, join the Facebook group and ping, your struggle's done. The comforting illusion of control, or the terrifying groundlessness of letting go? It's a choice we make every day.

—

There were many beautiful parts of lockdown. My wife drew a big chalk Snakes & Ladders board on the back patio and Suki and I threw dice, using ourselves as pieces. She and Suki dug up our front garden and planted tomatoes, butternut squash, peas and radishes. We climbed trees and skimmed stones across the river. At times, our family activities resembled a particularly on-the-nose satire of aspirational middle-class one-upmanship: Suki and I made our own hummus and pitta breads, and, under my supervision, she hand-roasted, ground and brewed her first batch of coffee.

Sometimes Suki and I went inside her little pop-up tent and read stories. Once it started raining and we zipped it up and sat on the cushions we'd brought out from the sofa and did *Where's Wally?* together, listening to the crackle of rain on polyester.

We found magical places near our house we'd never thought to visit. We walked amongst blue spruce and red maple, through showers of pink blossom, went on adventures in the woods where we found rabbits, squirrels and dormice, toadstools, giant plate fungi, rope swings and woodpeckers. I set up a couple of bird-feeders in our back garden, and some mornings Suki and I made a hide out of chairs and blankets and we watched great tits, sparrows and chaffinches eat breakfast, and listened to them sing. Suki would constantly find little treasures she wanted to bring home – acorns, oddly shaped pebbles, particularly good sticks. One time she made me fill my coat pocket with a mysterious, cloud-like substance that turned out to be wet dog hair.

I ignored the news, which led to some unusual situations. One Thursday I was on a run, listening to music. As I passed a garden, an older man emerged, smiling and applauding. I nodded and smiled back. His neighbour was out too, and as I passed she also gave me a round of good-natured applause. I waved. In the next garden a man was playing the violin. The next person had their eyes closed as they played a cello.

Glancing round the street I realised everyone was applauding and, for several seconds, I thought I was finally having a psychotic break. When I got home Lisa explained about clapping for the NHS.

I had good days, hard days and some really bad days.

When I felt low or anxious, I had nowhere to hide. Every emotion felt magnified. I phoned the Samaritans several times, each time thinking it was pointless, each time feeling ashamed for bothering them, each time feeling like a failure for not being able to cope. Each time, speaking to someone helped.

Actually, it helped more than almost anything else. Just connecting with someone kind. Talking. Properly talking, without holding back. Not having them jump in with their own stories or solutions or photocopied worksheets. Not feeling like I had to impress them. Not constantly checking the time or worrying I was boring or upsetting them or about how much it was costing me.

Being myself.

Being a coward.

—

Psychologist and founder of person-centred therapy Carl Rogers put it like this: 'The curious paradox is that when I accept myself as I am, then I change. I believe that I have learned this from my clients as well as within my own experience – that we cannot change, we cannot move away from what we are, until we thoroughly accept what we are. Then change seems to come about almost unnoticed.'[6]

I don't know if you've ever, after a long spell of putting a brave face on things, admitted to yourself you're having a shit time. Often, the relief is tremendous.

As James Baldwin put it: 'Not everything that is faced can be changed, but nothing can be changed until it is faced.'

XX.

THE MAGIC OF UNCERTAINTY

*The power of stories, and learning to be
comfortable when life is out of our control*

When I started my quest for a cure for anxiety, I thought that scientists had all the answers. I was shocked – and a little resentful – when they told me they didn't.

But this was never a claim they had made. It was *my* perception, *my* belief that science ought to be a realm of absolutes, and answers.

When I spoke to cardiologist Dr Rohin Francis, he described scientism as 'the elevation of science to a surrogate religion'. We treat anything that's 'peer-reviewed' as unimpeachable fact. Ironically, scientism often leads to bad science. The truth has no obligation to be simple, or pleasing. The truth need not be amenable to encapsulation in a slogan.

It's hard, when science is complicated and nuanced and a lot of the time concerned with probabilities rather than absolutes, for moderate voices not to get lost in a crowd of competing, attention-grabbing claims. Saying things like, 'It's complicated' or 'We don't know' or 'That seems to be one factor' invite accusations that your opinions are uninformed or woolly. 'The more sure you appear, the more people will listen to you,' said Rohin. 'That's how you get this evolution of initially quite sensible people coming out with complete crap after a few years.'

The largest, coldest buckets of water poured over my enthusiasm were provided by the researchers themselves. When I flagged areas where their discipline's current models are inadequate, they dealt with the point by conceding it. 'We don't know what we're doing, if we're being totally honest,' neuroscientist Dr Oli Robinson told me. 'We're going out and trying stuff and failing and not doing such a good job.' Neuroimaging, he said, had been around for twenty years or so. 'And the honest truth is, for mental health it hasn't led to any clear clinical outcomes.'

Researchers working with animals told me about the shortcomings of animal models. Psychiatrists highlighted the limitations of psychopharmacology and diagnostic labels. Psychologists like Dr Kate Button explained to me in great detail concepts like statistical power, and how study design inadequacies might mean that many, many psychological experiments reach misleading conclusions.

They weren't arguing that their fields are useless or defunct, but that the problems we're attempting to tackle (which include, but are not limited to: What is a thought? What is an emotion? How do we override responses that have ensured our survival for millions of years?) are terribly complex. That neuroscience hasn't put them to bed in a matter of decades – the blink of an eye in historical terms – should be neither surprising nor damning.

This is the difference between a scientist and a pundit: the willingness to say, 'I don't know.'

One definition of anxiety is an intolerance for uncertainty.

Science is the opposite. It's about the embracing of uncertainty. 'What about this?' 'Have you considered this?' 'What if we reframed the problem like this?' 'How can we be sure?' It crowbars open the obvious.

It's hard in the current climate – perhaps it always has been – to convey nuance. There are many commentators quick to take what we might call 'epistemic humility' as an admission of failure. In science we can never be 100 per cent certain. We work with the balance of probabilities. As George Box said, all models are wrong. Many people with their own agenda – those who are suspicious of publicly funded medicine, practitioners of alternative medicine, anti-vaxxers – jump on questions thrown up by a discipline's internal rigour as evidence of its invalidity, while never holding their own beliefs to the same evidential standard.

In my experience the more you learn the less certain you feel. I can't say my journey taught me humility, exactly, but I did start to get an appreciation of just how difficult the questions I was asking were. Moments of insight *do* exist, and progress *is* made (would you rather have a consultation with a psychiatrist from a hundred years ago, or from today?), but it's slow and granular and a community effort.

The fact was, I *had* got better. My panic attacks had stopped. I was calmer.

Anxiety is a kind of emotional fundamentalism. It craves hard answers. Research has shown that when we lack control we start perceiving patterns in random noise, seeing correlations in unrelated stock market data, seeing non-existent conspiracies, and developing superstitions.[1] From anxiety's point of view, it doesn't matter if the answers are wrong so long as our immediate need for certainty is gratified.

How do you beat anxiety? The truth is we do not know. Not in some absolute, one-size-fits-all way. No model covers every case. Anyone who tells you they *do* know a single, universal cause or solution is either lying, or unduly confident in their ability to achieve more than the combined efforts of every neuroscientist, psychologist, geneticist, microbiologist, sports scientist and priest on the planet.

We can answer in comparative terms. For example, I can tell you that, based on our current best understanding, evidence-based therapies like CBT and its more recent evolutions such as acceptance and commitment therapy (ACT) and elements of dialectical behaviour therapy (DBT) are more likely to help someone with an anxiety disorder than, say, essential oils or an exorcism. That doesn't mean that we can say absolutely that someone who undergoes a course of therapy with a skilled professional will see improvements. It doesn't mean that someone who visits a preacher who calls upon Jesus to purge the demon of anxiety from their soul *won't* see a remission of symptoms afterwards. It just means that, currently, the preponderance of evidence suggests the former course of action will work on more occasions than the latter.

That's not the sort of thing that fits in a tweet. It's not a good slogan and it doesn't roll off the tongue. But it's how science works. We incrementally zero in on best explanations for the available data, and when we need to solve problems we work with our best information at the time. We don't wait for perfection because we'll never achieve it.

Science tells stories, but holds them lightly. When a better story comes along we let the old one go.

—

Social psychologist James W. Pennebaker is the best-known researcher of how stories affect our wellbeing. Back in the eighties, as a new faculty member at Southern Methodist University in Dallas, Texas, he was looking at how we use physical symptoms as cues to decide how we're feeling: How do we know we're feeling hungry? How do we know we're feeling anxious? Towards the end of the project, he decided he ought to do a survey. He wanted to get a sense of what kinds of people get what kinds of symptoms.

He put together a 'ridiculously long' questionnaire. He asked about their diet. He asked about how they got on with their parents when they were children. Then one of the students helping him had an idea that would change everything.

The student suggested adding a single question: 'Did you ever have a traumatic sexual experience prior to the age of seventeen?'

He duly added it to the gigantic survey, which he passed out to about 800 students. 'And what I discovered is that one question about a traumatic sexual experience predicted health problems better than anything I had ever seen.'

He ended up working on a national sample of about 2,000 people, including a similar question. He forgets the numbers, 'but it was something like twenty-two per cent of women and eleven per cent of men' reported having had a traumatic experience prior to the age of seventeen. Those people were twice as likely to have been hospitalised in the past year for any cause, and they were more likely to have any kind of health problem, major or minor. It turned out the trauma didn't have to be sexual. It was any kind of upsetting experience that people kept secret.

Jamie came to wonder: What if he invited people into his lab and asked them to talk or write about these upheavals? Would putting the experience into words help?

With his colleague Sandra Beall, he divided student participants into four groups and asked them to write for fifteen minutes a day over four consecutive days.[2]

One group was asked to write about something neutral – for instance, describing the room they were in. The three other groups were asked to write about a traumatic experience.

One of these three groups was asked to just vent their emotions about the experience. The second was asked to stick to the facts, without expressing their emotions. And the final group was asked to write about a specific traumatic event *and* their emotions about that event, both at the time and now, looking back.

This last group was told to write 'continuously about the most upsetting or traumatic experience of your entire life' – something that 'has affected you very deeply'. They were told not to worry about spelling, punctuation and grammar. 'It is critical', their instructions continued, 'that you let yourself go and touch those deepest emotions and thoughts that you have. In other words, write about what happened and how you felt about it then, and how you feel about it now.' If they ran out of things to write, they should return to the beginning of the memory and start again, perhaps phrasing it differently.

During the experiment, some students wept as they wrote. One participant wrote about teaching her brother to sail. On his first solo voyage, he drowned. Another female subject recalled her parents asking her to clean her room when she was ten. She ignored them. That night, her grandmother came to visit, slipped on a toy, broke her hip, and died of complications during surgery a week later. A male subject wrote about his father taking him outside when he was nine to tell him that he and his mother were getting divorced 'because things haven't been the same since you and your sister were born'. Some reported dreaming about their writing over the four days.

Students in the other three groups – writing about trivial things, just venting emotions, or writing dispassionately about trauma – initially felt more positive about their writing than the fourth group, who all experienced a dip in mood.

But Pennebaker and Beall checked up on their participants after the study was finished, and made some startling discoveries. Four months later the students who had made those connections between specific events and their feelings reported, overall, significant improvements in mood. They were more positive, had more energy, and many felt they had resolved a difficult issue. Six months after the end of the study, Pennebaker and Beall discovered that those students' visits to the university health centre had dropped by 50 per cent.

The sample was small, so they conducted follow-up studies. In several they took blood samples. They discovered that participants who wrote about a traumatic event produced more white blood cells and showed an increased antibody response to the Epstein-Barr virus and hepatitis B vaccinations.[3]

Jamie was astonished. 'The question that I became obsessed with was: What is it about putting things into words that makes a difference?'

Since the eighties, there have been over a thousand studies on the effects and potential benefits of expressive writing. Researchers even found that people who write about a traumatic event in this way heal significantly faster from a 4mm punch biopsy wound than controls.[4]

At first, Jamie thought that the stress of holding on to hidden trauma made people sick. In line with Hans Selye's theory of general adaptation syndrome, where continual low-level anxiety eventually depletes the immune system and leaves people vulnerable to disease, he thought that maybe inhibition requires effort – effort that wears us out over time. In putting their experiences into words, participants released all that guilt and shame.

But he noticed some problems.

Firstly, it didn't seem to matter if someone was writing down a secret trauma or one they'd already shared. People who wrote about an experience they'd told others about seemed to benefit as much as people who wrote about an experience they'd kept secret.

Secondly, as his work became more widely known, people would approach him at parties and share horrible stories of traumatic experiences they'd been through. 'The people who would often do this had terrible health – then I'd see them at another party six months later and they'd come and tell me the exact same story.' Sharing their trauma didn't seem to have helped them at all. If anything, it seemed to be making them feel worse. 'It was a real puzzle.'

He went back to his research data and looked at who benefited from the exercise and who didn't. He noticed that if people came into his laboratory and had a story from day one, and they told it again and again over the following three days, they didn't benefit from writing. Conversely, people who at the beginning didn't have a very good or coherent story, but across the four days gradually put one together, showed clear health benefits.

It wasn't having a story that was good for you. It was the act of *constructing* one.

'This was such an insight for me. Sometimes we have stories, and they just don't work.' Yet, he said, we're so used to telling them, so sure of their meaning, we think, *By God, I'm going to stick with this story no matter what*. In psychology, telling yourself the same upsetting story over and over is called 'rumination', and it's associated with a vastly increased risk of depression. You keep bringing up the same negative emotions. You're stuck.

Jamie found that, to benefit from expressive writing, you have to not only return to your old experiences, but find something new in them. Tellingly, one marker of improvement was a shift from using mainly first-person pronouns – I, me, mine – to third-person pronouns – he, she, they. 'You have to change your perspective. You have to change your story.'

———

When I was twenty-five, I was trapped in a pub in my hometown by someone who wanted to beat me up. Two of his friends guarded the front door and fire exit so I couldn't escape. He sat down across from me at a table and two more guys sat either side of me. When I tried to stand they put their hands on my shoulders and shoved me back down into my seat. I remember I smiled at one of them, desperately trying to be friendly, and said, 'Hello. Who are you?'

He did not smile. 'I'm no one, mate.'

The guy sitting across the table frowned at me. 'You think you're better than me, don't you?'

I genuinely had no idea who he was, which he – of course – took as an insult. Apparently I was so aloof that remembering someone like him was beneath me.

No one intervened. I was pretty drunk, confused, and underneath it terrified. Coincidentally, one of the boys who used to bully me was in the pub – not involved in the incident, just watching. It was like I was back at school. I could barely form sentences. I felt powerless.

We went back and forth for a while, me being conciliatory,

putting myself down, apologising, begging for clemency basically. Eventually the guy let me get up to use the toilet. I hid in a locked cubicle, tried the tiny window. I wanted to phone my dad to come and rescue me, or the police, but I was afraid they wouldn't believe me, or I'd be too drunk to explain, or the men would follow me home. The main guy had described my house to make it clear he knew where I lived.

While I hid, a friend of mine tried to convince him that I was an idiot not worth bothering with. Eventually the guy lost interest, and I escaped.

Two days later I was in the freezer aisle at Waitrose – officially the centre of the middle-class universe and therefore the least threatening environment in existence – when my depth-perception went funny. Everything rippled and distorted. I felt like the walls were closing in. I had to get out.

I had just experienced my first panic attack.

I had one a few months later in Victoria station, and another on the night I moved into my flat in Cambridge. Over the next few years I went through several breakups, and a good friend took her own life. Panic attacks became a regular part of life, increasing in frequency from one every few months to several a week.

What's weird is, I'd forgotten when they had started. I never connected the incident in the pub with my first panic attack until I came to write this book. I never made the link when I'd find myself freezing in the kitchen when my wife came up behind me, when I'd stammer: 'I feel trapped.' Not even when, in the middle of a panic attack, I'd cover my head and cry: 'Please don't hit me.'

In looking back at that night, in turning it into a story, I created new connections. At some level I re-experienced it, like exposure therapy, but as an older, stronger observer, not a trapped, frightened victim. In writing it down, it was like I got to choose what lesson I took from it.

Did that encounter in the pub lead to my panic attacks? I'm not sure it matters. Having written it down, I felt lighter – as if all these years I'd been waiting for that punch to land.

——

Our ability to create stories might be humanity's key advantage. But, used unwisely, this ability breeds delusion.

A week or so after Christmas 2020 we had just put Suki to bed, when I came downstairs to find Lisa crying.

The tree lit the room a soft pulsing gold. It was 5 January. Tomorrow would be Twelfth Night, when we'd pack away the decorations for another year. The day after, it would be my fortieth birthday.

I asked her what was wrong.

'I feel like Christmas has gone so quickly,' she said. 'I feel like I didn't get enough out of it, and now it's over.'

It had been a rough year. Nothing in 2020 had turned out as we had imagined. It had been a reminder that the future we carry round in our heads – a future most of us think of as reality – is just another story.

Lisa and I comforted each other, then I went upstairs to write. I was reading my grandmother's account of her life, as told to my dad shortly before she died. There were hardly any dates in it – over seventy years had passed between the events and their retelling – but one stood out: 5 January 1945.

Exactly seventy-six years previously, my grandmother had stood gazing at the family Christmas tree, decorated in silver and white. The Christmas of 1944 had been one of the happiest of her life. Her father, who had been in Poland working with military transport, came home with a goose. The whole family was together. They were living in Kattowitz, in Upper Silesia. She had finished school, and was working as a stenographer for the Hitler Youth area command.

One night around Christmas, while she was at work, there was an air raid. Born with displaced hips, she walked with a limp. She had a special portable typewriter to take down into the shelter, but her department chief (being a fascist and all) ordered her to carry the heavy full-sized typewriter instead.

Rushing with the heavy typewriter, she lost her balance and fell, injuring herself. The doctor said she would need to travel to the hospital in Beuthen for a major operation. It would likely mean a stay of eight weeks.

Hence why, on 5 January, she had stopped to look at the Christmas tree one last time. She was leaving the next morning, and she expected not to return home for two months.

In fact, she would not return for fifty years.

While she was in Beuthen hospital, the war neared Kattowitz. Her family and co-workers were evacuated. She and the rest of the patients, on the other hand, were taken to a facility in more or less the opposite direction. She had no choice but to remain there. After her operation, she was in a lower body cast so heavy it broke her bed.

It wasn't until several months later, after the announcement of Hitler's death, that she signed discharge papers absolving the hospital of responsibility for releasing an underage girl, and set off across Germany alone, on crutches, in search of her family. Where trains were not running, she followed the tracks. She walked through the bombed-out ruins of Dresden. She faced that young Russian soldier guarding the bridge. In Rosenthal, she and her family were reunited.

Her co-workers, meanwhile, had been evacuated to Czechoslovakia. Had she stayed at home, she would have been expected to go with them, not her family. (Her father took no furniture and few belongings, because such behaviour was shamed as 'defeatist', i.e. treason. Everything they left behind was stolen, down to the lightbulbs.) After the war, Germans in Czechoslovakia were placed in internment camps and forcibly expelled. Many were executed, many died of starvation or disease, and thousands died by suicide. Some were transported to Soviet labour camps. Her co-workers were never heard of again.

Her boss's order to carry that heavy typewriter saved her life.

I never knew the circumstances that led to my grandmother's hospitalisation until the evening I found Lisa by our Christmas tree, crying.

And there I was reading about it, on the anniversary. Her grandson. The great-granddaughter she never knew asleep in the next room. (Later, when I talked about it with my dad, he reminded me Omi had died exactly eight years before – on the evening of 5 January 2013.)

I don't see the hand of fate in all this. Rather the ripples of a stochastic system. Echoes thrown up by randomness. Patterns in clouds.

My grandmother could never have predicted where her apparent piece of misfortune would lead her. Extrapolating lessons from experience is, as psychologists like to say, highly adaptive. But the very power of stories is what makes them so dangerous.

If we're not careful, we believe we have more control than we really do. We lose our trust in uncertainty. We think models are reality.

———

During the Christmas of 1944 that my grandmother recalled so fondly, Austrian physician Viktor E. Frankl was interned not so many miles away in a concentration camp. In the week between Christmas and New Year, the camp doctor told him that the death rate had increased dramatically. The doctor did not attribute these deaths to increased starvation or disease or harsher working conditions. Instead, he believed, 'the majority of these prisoners had lived in the naive hope they would be home again by Christmas'. When Christmas came and went, the story that had sustained them through months of brutal hardship was shattered. In the doctor's opinion, their powers of inner resistance simply collapsed.

This phenomenon is popularly known as the Stockdale Paradox. During the Vietnam War, Admiral Jim Stockdale was held as a prisoner of war in the Hoa Lo Prison – known by the ironic sobriquet 'the Hanoi Hilton' – for seven and a half years, during which he was beaten and tortured. When asked who had fared the worst under these conditions, he replied: 'That's easy – the optimists.' They were the ones, he said, who believed they would be free by Christmas. When Christmas came and went, they'd pin their hopes on Easter. Then Thanksgiving. Then Christmas again. With each disconfirmation, they lost a source of meaning and control. The story that had sustained them fell apart. 'And they died of a broken heart.'

Stockdale later claimed he had survived by stubbornly clinging to the belief that one day he would get out and come to regard his imprisonment not only as meaningful, but as 'the defining event of my life, which, in retrospect, I would not trade'. His 'paradox' is the necessity of accepting the gravity of one's predicament in order to find real, sustainable hope.

Similarly, Frankl believed finding the inner strength to persist under the terrible conditions of a concentration camp meant finding a powerful 'why'. 'Woe to him who saw no more sense in his life, no aim, no purpose, and therefore no point in carrying on. He was soon lost.'

Stockdale and Frankl were spinning their own stories – stories that, in several important senses, are false. Prisoners in the Hanoi Hilton did not die of broken hearts. They died of disease, abuse and starvation. So too for concentration camp victims.

Stockdale and Frankl may have constructed these narratives as a means of rationalising away their own guilt at surviving, to comfort themselves that there was at least some system in play, some *reason* that one person lived while another died. We cannot, for the sake of our sanity, believe in a schedule of random reinforcements.

Indeed, elsewhere in his account Frankl reflected: 'We who have come back, by the aid of many lucky chances or miracles – whatever one may choose to call them – we know: the best of us did not return.'

Hope, it seems, is necessary.

But it's not enough.

———

There's a moral hazard when we start talking about overcoming anxiety that we forget an anxious person does not exist in a vacuum. That they are not the subject of some hygienic, self-contained experiment, pulling levers, responding to ultimately meaningless cues in a laboratory. Some of the literature about Patient S.M. – the woman without an amygdala – comments on hardships she survived: death threats, attempted rape, attempted murder. It suggests she underwent these experiences because she was poor at gauging trustworthiness and detecting potential danger.

When I've spoken to or read papers by researchers who've worked with Patient S.M. directly, I've been struck by a sense of affection, even admiration, rarely found in academic work. John Wemmie spoke of her with tact and care.

But Patient S.M. did not get sexually assaulted or choked unconscious or held at gunpoint because of a deficiency in her brain. She suffered these assaults because men chose to inflict them on her. An average of 433,648 people are raped or sexually assaulted in the United States each year.[5] As far as we know, all of them have functioning amygdalae.

Some traumas, like those arising from accidents or natural disasters, are all but unavoidable. Others, such as domestic abuse, sexual violence, displacement due to conflict, and the horrors of war, arise from human choices. No model of treating anxiety disorders, especially PTSD, is complete unless it considers the conditions under which these disorders arose.

I know this seems obvious when stated bluntly – and perhaps a little sanctimonious – but it's easily forgotten when you immerse yourself in research about neural correlates of avoidant behaviours, or psychopharmacological interventions, or 'bad schemas'. I lost sight of it many times (and it is, of course, what Dr Lucy Johnstone told me).

We can get better at treating anxiety disorders of all kinds, but part of the solution has to be to create social conditions under which disordered anxiety is less likely to occur. Prominent books about mental health tend to be written by white, middle-class, cis, able-bodied authors (hi). This is part of a larger bias that bedevils all psychology: most of the samples on which we test our theories are too WEIRD – that is, they over-represent people from White, Educated, Industrialised, Rich and Democratic countries.[6] The 'classic' experiments, taught to psychology students as part of the discipline's storied history, tend to be on – and conducted by – white, middle-class westerners. Psychology's most common sampling method is known by the appropriate acronym SUCS: the Standard University Convenience Sample. That's when researchers recruit students on campus for their experiments – a cheap, convenient source of participants, but not representative of the world at large.

The majority of the research that's published – and therefore the majority of the advice that gets repackaged in lifestyle articles and communicated to the public – is by and for a very narrow audience. It assumes a shared set of challenges and values. We're stressed out because of a conflict with our supervisor. We're trying to juggle a career with raising a family. We're bummed out by the divisive nature of social media. What we need to do is book a mani-pedi, do some mindful stretching, and, ooh – maybe go down to four days a week and spend that time dead-heading the azaleas. Just stop working so hard guys, yeah? Quit your fast-paced city job and pursue your dream of artificially distressing old cabinets while kayaking at weekends.

All of which, if you're a single mother of three dealing with abusive neighbours and locked in a dispute with your landlord over rent arrears, deserves a two-word response. If you have a disability or you're caring for someone with a disability and you have your benefits slashed – or stopped altogether – that's an understandable source of anxiety. If you've been driven from your home by a conflict where both sides are armed with British-made weapons, it's not a case of Zoloft and yoga is it? It's not a fucking, 'Hmm, I wonder what consolations Spinoza might offer us' situation. If you're a teenager and your peers at school are carrying butterfly knives, we don't need to ask some senior neuroscientist what bits of your brain light up when you worry that pissing off the wrong person might earn you a blade in your kidney. We need to make you safe.

Much of what we talk about when we talk about anxiety are the downstream consequences of a problem that needs solving. Bulls are running amok in innumerable china shops, and instead of asking how they got in, our focus is on vase reconstruction – on developing better, stickier glue. As Dr Kate Button told me: 'Sometimes people are having genuine adverse reactions to properly shit stuff that's happened.' Creating a kinder, more equitable society, ceasing arms sales, welcoming refugees, protecting women from sexual harassment and assault, investing in public spaces, being responsible custodians of the natural world, valuing and promoting diversity so a multiplicity of people not only cope but thrive – these are all mental health issues.

So much of the conversation around anxiety presumes a safe home, food, protection from violence, a reasonable expectation that you can leave your house, go about your daily business, and return home without fear of assault, harassment or abuse. When the majority of the popular literature around mental health doesn't even acknowledge that, when it implicitly addresses an audience who are relatively privileged, it creates a false universality.

We're all in the same ocean. But only some of us have got boats.

The tragedy is that vulnerability and suffering are what connect us. They give us a common bond with every human on the planet. None of us escapes suffering and death, no matter how rich, thin, youthful, or amply proportioned in culturally preferred areas.

Buddhism has 'five remembrances' – facts that the Buddha recommended a person should reflect on frequently. The first three are: I am sure to become old. I am sure to become ill. I am sure to die. Their purpose is to help us overcome our conceit or false confidence – *mada* – to accept the reality of our predicament, so that, instead of looking for security in inherently insecure things like possessions, relationships, our looks, our health, we instead look further, deeper, for a refuge which does not change, which is not subject to death.

Everything is shakeable. That's the bad news.

———

Any of these stories – that anxiety is *just* a product of trauma, anxiety is *just* an expression of society's failings, *just* about illogical thinking, *just* about genetic vulnerabilities, or depleted neurotransmitters, or abnormal connectivity between brain regions – is destructive when taken alone and defended as an article of faith. When our world's been shaken, we're desperate for patterns.

Where trauma exists, we can help people work through it. Where oppression exists, we can push for change. Where people have absorbed unhealthy beliefs or ways of problem-solving we can teach them better strategies. Where someone could really use the support of an SSRI or SNRI, we can give them access to professionals who can offer informed choices. Where a friend really needs a sympathetic ear, and love, we can hold that space for them.

These interventions are not in competition. We need all of them.

When I read arguments over whether anxiety calls for individual or collective solutions, I feel like I'm watching two people have a brutal fist fight about whether Kermit is a muppet or a frog.

—

The word 'patient' – in the sense of someone who visits the doctor – has the same root as the adjective 'patient' – the Latin verb *pati*: to undergo, to suffer, to endure. *Pati* is where we get the term 'passion' from, as in Christ's Passion on the cross. Etymologically speaking, a patient is one who suffers, an object acted upon – first by the illness, then by their physician, then by medication. They are fundamentally passive, and their only responsibility lies in playing their role well.

The other polarity is an 'agent' – from the Latin verb *agere*, 'to do'. An agent is 'one who does'. They are not the object acted upon by external forces, but the subject, the origin of action. Psychotherapists in the Laingian antipsychiatry tradition assert that the so-called 'medical model' of mental illness casts us as passive victims, dependent upon the authority of doctors and psychiatrists to rescue us. In truth, they argue, we are always in control, though we may have learned to deny our power. Even our severe anxiety, our panic attacks, are purposeful assertions of our will – modes of expression we have, at some level, chosen. Once we acknowledge authorship of these decisions, trace their origins and get in touch with our true feelings, we can choose better.

In truth, we are both agent and patient. We act upon the world, and the world acts upon us. We don't get to decide if a global pandemic confines us to our houses, if the economy tanks, if someone we love falls ill or dies. We don't even get to choose our response – not really.

Steering our emotional responses is a skill, like catching a ball. We can't simply choose not to worry, not to feel hurt or upset, any more than I could choose to catch a lofted off drive one-handed while texting. Catching a ball is unquestionably a voluntary action, but it takes *practice*. That's where we have agency. Whether we work on developing our skill.

In weightlifting there's an expression: 'Training to failure'. It's where you lift a weight to the point where your muscles give out and you physically can't do another repetition. Much contemporary research suggests that training to failure is one of the best – if not *the* best – ways to stimulate muscle growth.[7] You don't 'choose to be stronger'. Neither do you passively accept your current limits. You do the thing until it's too hard, until you fail. Failing causes micro-tears in the muscles, which stimulate healing and growth.

The body, as Walter Cannon argued, wants to maintain homeo-stasis – a state of equilibrium where everything stays the same. Stress is anything which threatens that equilibrium. In his book *Peak*, psychologist Anders Ericsson gives the example of regular jogging leading to reduced oxygen levels in your leg muscles. Your body can't keep up with the demand, which stimulates the growth of new capillaries, which deliver more oxygen to the cells, re-establishing homeostasis.

But the stress has to be just right. Too little, and you won't disrupt homeostasis. Too much, and you might injure yourself and set your training back months. The same is true of developing skills. Early twentieth-century Soviet psychologist Lev Vgotsky called this sweet spot of growth the 'zone of proximal development'.

We know that by far the most successful intervention for anxiety is exposure. When I spoke to the psychologist Nicholas Walsh he likened anxiety to a pathogen that activates the immune system: if we're exposed to small, manageable amounts we develop antibodies – healthy, adaptive coping skills – that help protect us from it in future. This process is sometimes called 'stress inoculation'. 'If you're exposed to age-appropriate challenges when you're growing up,' he said, 'you develop a broader repertoire of strategies.'

Ericsson suggests an analogous process happens in the brain. When we practise a skill in that zone of proximal development –

hard enough to test us, but not so hard that it steamrollers us – connections between neurons grow and thicken. A substance called myelin grows round axons, acting as an insulating sheath that allows them to conduct electrical signals faster.

'I consider it a dangerous misconception of mental hygiene,' wrote Viktor Frankl, 'to assume that what man needs in the first place is equilibrium or, as it is called in biology, "homeostasis," i.e. a tension-less state. What man actually needs is not a tensionless state but rather the striving and struggling for some goal worthy of him. What he needs is not the discharge of tension at any cost, but the call of a potential meaning waiting to be fulfilled by him.'[8]

Resilience, meaning, ease – these aren't fixed traits you're either born with or you aren't. We cultivate them through habits of thought and specific behaviours – sometimes, perhaps, by rewriting our own stories. When we do, our neurobiology and physiology adapt to support us. But it takes time. It requires willingly submitting yourself to stress – stepping into that place of optimal tension that stimulates growth.

Maybe this is why anxiety, of all the problems humans face, has proven so fiendishly difficult to overcome. Getting better at dealing with anxiety asks us to judge the edges of our tolerance, then repeatedly expose ourselves to those unpleasant thoughts and feelings at the highest intensity we can manage.

Without discernment, this becomes martyrdom. Grinding stress wears us down and burns us out. Overwhelming terror reinforces our trauma. It's a hell of a task, finding the Goldilocks zone where the stressors are not too hard, not too soft, but just right. Unlike miles run or weights loaded onto a barbell, we don't have absolute control over the duration and intensity of stress we encounter. Sometimes life makes you bench press twice your bodyweight with no spotter, just because.

And sometimes, the above just isn't true. Sometimes you pop a pill and bing, you feel great. It's obvious not to be anxious. Sometimes it's about 'situation modification'. You move out of that dreadful flatshare. You bail on the job. A weight lifts from your shoulders and the anxiety recedes. There's not one Campbellian anxiety monomyth governing every situation.

But the flipside to that – the excellent news – is that many instances of anxiety share similar weaknesses. *All* instances of anxiety can be engaged with and improved. It's just that sometimes it takes time to find what works.

For me, the hardest part remains admitting that lack of control and trying to accept it. I wanted my life to be like *Sonic the Hedgehog 3 & Knuckles*: a series of themed challenges that gently ramp up in difficulty, with an epic final boss, a satisfying conclusion and an ending theme by Michael Jackson. Alas, pipes don't ask if your schedule's free before bursting. Global pandemics don't wait patiently backstage while you work through childhood traumas.

Our desire to construct stories, to find patterns in a world of astonishing – often beautiful – complexity, is strong. It may even be, as Jamie Pennebaker found, a vital component of our mental and physical health.

Letting go of stories may be more important still. We treat our memories like archive footage, not artful commentary assembled after the fact. Perhaps, in actively composing stories about our past, we're reminded that *all* our stories are constructed. Corrigible. Contingent. That we are the authors of our lives, and we get to choose what our experiences mean. If, later on, those meanings don't serve us, we can choose new ones. We don't have to settle on a single, pat answer.

We're much weirder, richer creatures than that.

———

Maybe the thing I've struggled with most, as a severe anxiety sufferer, is that balance between self-compassion and a belief in self-efficacy.

The thought was always: If I *do* have the power to change, why the hell don't I?

People would go: 'Hey, be kind to yourself. Stop beating yourself up.' It carries the implicit message: Stop expecting so much of yourself.

People told me not to be hard on myself but they never told me what to do instead. How to stop feeling uncomfortable, apprehensive, terrified. They never explained how I was supposed to navigate the week ahead, the dread and avoidance, the squandered opportunities, the arguments, the slow wasting disease of chronic anxiety.

What I've discovered is that the opposite of anxiety isn't comfort. It's curiosity. It's appetite. It's moving towards things that make you feel alive and embracing them, while doing your best to accept that things will go wrong. I can be terrified doing nothing, so I might as well get into some memorable scrapes.

And look at me. Surviving. Still moving. Coping with more than I ever thought possible. I still experience anxiety and discomfort, just like I still get achy legs from running. Instead of beating myself up, I recognise anxiety as evidence that I'm doing the work. That I'm exposing myself to challenges.

Perhaps as a result, I get less anxious less often. I recover faster. My panic attacks have completely stopped. At the time of writing, I haven't had one for over two years – a period which just happens to include the entirety of 2020, a twelve-month span of such monumental shitness that people spent it talking about 'going to work' with wistful nostalgia.

Was it the hypnosis? Was it the river swims? The exercise? The brain helmet? The mushroom gods? Was it the process of writing all this down – of making a story?

I don't know. And I'm comfortable with that.

———

Between comfort and anxiety, certainty and chaos, is a fertile zone where the two ecosystems meet – a place of wild, abundant growth that supports a far greater density and diversity of life than the two extremes that feed into it. We might call this zone 'possibility'.

It's not easy or safe. At times I struggle. But there are really, really good bits. It's worth it.

Cowardice has taught me so much. It reminds me that, underneath the gaudy ballgown of civilisation, I'm basically a macaque with an elaborate cover story. It shoves me towards empathy, vulnerability, kindness. It makes me ask for help.

I love my secret tail. But it's not the end of the story. We continue to evolve. Every day is a chance to take the next step, to stimulate our amazing capacity for growth by willingly moving towards uncertainty.

Bravery isn't a feeling. It's a direction.

APPENDIX

Here's what worked for me. It's just one data point. Human beings are gorgeously diverse. What didn't work for me might be just the ticket for you.

Don't think in absolutes. Be a good scientist. Try things. Observe the results. Don't let perfect be the enemy of a bit better. Some interventions take time to bed in – sometimes the vast ocean liner of the psyche turns slowly. Some offer rapid relief but don't last. These might be better to use when your anxiety is high and you want an escape.

Beware of dismissing something that doesn't cure you on its own. Imagine stepping outside on a snowy day in a coat, realising you're still cold, so coming back inside, taking the coat off, and putting on a scarf and gloves. You step outside and you're still cold. You might conclude that neither the coat nor the scarf and gloves were good at keeping you warm. But what you really needed to do was try them *together*.

The better evidenced a treatment, the better the odds you'll see some benefit, but there are no guarantees. What matters is what works for you. The only way you can find that out is by rolling up your sleeves and mucking in. May you have a beautiful adventure.

EXERCISE

A combination of HIIT (high-intensity interval training) and LISS (low intensity steady-state exercise, like walking and jogging), did wonders for my resilience and overall health, but remember: the only meaningfully 'best' exercise is the one you're most likely to do.

DIET

Cutting out sugary, caffeinated drinks, chocolate, sweets, crisps, and carby, fatty food like pizza massively reduced my blood-sugar-crash-related anxiety; eating heaps of fresh veg and fruit kept cravings manageable – the fibre fills you up, and helps regulate blood sugar, blood pressure, and inflammation. Using a calorie-counter app stopped losing weight becoming a psychological burden.

MEDITATION

Didn't do much for me, but if you try it, don't expect instant peace; it's closer to exercise, where the benefits build up slowly over time. Start with ten minutes once a day if you can manage it.

GETTING SHIT DONE

Tim Pychyl told me to ask: 'What's my next action?' Sometimes it's as simple as switching on my laptop or putting my trousers on; I try not to get caught up in worrying whether I can face doing the task – I just ask what the next tiny step I need to take to move myself towards it is.

COLD EXPOSURE

I love occasional cold showers as an emotional reset – they blast the panic out of me; I aim for three minutes. If you swim in open water, make sure it's safe and legal, take a friend, and never push yourself to stay in very cold water longer than a few minutes; consult your doctor if you have pre-existing conditions.

MEDICATION

Meds have sometimes done nothing for me, and sometimes made a colossal difference. SSRIs and SNRIs are the most common medications for anxiety disorders; speak to your GP if you want to know if they're suitable for you. It's okay to ask what the long-term plan is – how you'll monitor your progress, and how long the doctor imagines your course of treatment will be.

THERAPY

As with medication, my therapy experiences have been mixed; the key is to find a person and a style that you feel comfortable with. The NHS offers CBT for anxiety, or, if you can afford it, you can go private. Bibliotherapy is a well-evidenced anxiety treatment. Learning online or via a CBT workbook has been shown to be just as effective as face-to-face CBT, and there's no waiting list. If you need to talk to someone and you can't wait, *call the Samaritans* (116 123). It's made a huge difference to me in times of crisis.

HYPNOTHERAPY

Look, maybe it helped me, but I suspect it was the therapy part and the exposure aspect rather than any special hypnotic state that did the heavy lifting. If you want to try it, try to get a recommendation, and speak to the person beforehand to ask about their training and to check you feel comfortable with them.

JOURNALLING

For me, the best stress-relieving use of a journal has been a to-do list. It sounds too simple to work but it takes off a cognitive load. Writing about challenging memories, as in this book, has helped me deal with difficult feelings. If you want to attempt this, you might want to do it with support, even as part of a group, as the feelings it brings up can be challenging.

RELATIONSHIPS

The better I get at reaching out, the better I recover from anxiety. Resilience is a community trait, not just an individual one. The more I take on new roles – father, husband, friend, teacher, coward, naked stranger standing motionless on your front lawn at 2 a.m. – the more loosely I wear those identities. The looser I wear my identities, the less pressure I feel to defend them. Learning to listen to people, and to articulate what I'm feeling in the moment, has made much communication less stressful.

BREATHING

Wim Hof-style deep breathing exercises work well as an emotional circuit-breaker when I'm feeling panicky; otherwise I remember to slow things down when I feel that air hunger – six breaths a minute is a good rule of thumb.

SLEEP

Sleeping well helps my mood, but worrying if I'm getting enough stresses me out, which stops me falling asleep; I tried earplugs, weighted blankets, white noise, a screen watershed, etc. All of it made bedtime a bit of a production. Now I just think, *Fuck it, it doesn't matter* – I sleep more and better.

SOCIAL MEDIA

For me, heavy Twitter use is more a sign of growing anxiety than a cause; I periodically take a break. The mental health benefits are more to do with the fulfilling activities I have time for when I'm not wasting hours on digital arse-picking.

LOVE

Self-compassion is a muscle – I'm still working on getting shredded. In the meantime, I remind myself I don't owe anyone a certain level of mental health. I tell people I love them and I'm trying to be active in giving out sincere compliments and admiration. I take risks where I can, and open my heart, though it scares me. I'm going to feel anxious anyway, so I might as well leap out the plane and earn it.

SOME USEFUL CONTACTS

Anxiety UK: https://www.anxietyuk.org.uk/

NHS: The NHS website contains evidence-based self-help advice for generalised anxiety disorder, as well as guidance for when you should contact your GP. https://www.nhs.uk/mental-health/conditions/generalised-anxiety-disorder/self-help/

Samaritans: 116 123 (free 24-hour helpline), https://www.samaritans.org

Woebot: A free app developed by Stanford researchers that delivers CBT-based psychoeducation. https://woebothealth.com/try-woebot/

ACKNOWLEDGEMENTS

Creating this book would have been impossible without the generosity of everyone who gave me their time and expertise. Particular thanks to Adam Rutherford, Adrian James, Alexander Shackman, Alex Pike, Andrea Reinecke, Arne Dietrich, Bernard Rollin, Camilla Nord, Chi Amsterdam, Dave Thomas, Dawn Huebner, Jack El-Hai, Jamie Pennebaker, Joanna Collicutt, Joe LeDoux, John Spencer, John Wemmie, Kate Button, Lucy Johnstone, Mark Harper, Megan McConnell, Mike Shel, Nathaniel Daw, Nicholas Walsh, Oli Robinson, Rohin Francis, Ruihua Hou, Sarvananda, Simon Carding, Stefan Brugger, and the various people I spoke to anonymously or off the record, including many, many anxiety sufferers. I am sorry that I had to compress what was often hours of enlightening commentary to a few sentences, and for space reasons elide several contributions altogether.

More broadly I would like to thank the researchers across a diverse range of fields whose hard work comprised the 1000-plus papers I read on anxiety and adjacent topics.

Thank you to my agent, Sophie Lambert, for all her support and advice on shaping and refining the book and for her encouragement through a difficult writing process. Thank you to my editor, Jo Dingley at Canongate, for championing the book right from the start and for her brilliant feedback. Thank you to Hannah Knowles for taking on the project, giving incredibly helpful editorial advice and for helping me roll it over the line.

Most of all I want to thank my wife, Lisa Horton, who has continued to support and love me through some very challenging times. I love you so much.

Finally, thank you to my daughter Suki. You are vibrant and miraculous. I am so, so grateful to be your father.

NOTES

HOW TO READ THIS BOOK

1 *Enemies of Freedom: Understanding Right-wing Authoritarianism*, Altemeyer, 1988
2 A more honest alternative might be: 'This shit would never fly if I presented it to my colleagues at a conference.'

1. TAIL

1 'Human tails and pseudotails', Dao et al, 1984
2 'Generalization of Human Fear Acquisition and Extinction within a Novel Arbitrary Stimulus Category', Vervoort et al., 2014
3 'Observer's Reaction to the "Innocent Victim": Compassion or Rejection?', Lerner et al., 1966. The 72 participants were split across 6 conditions, meaning some had as few as 9 participants. Still, lots of studies have replicated these results and the effect remains robust across a range of cohorts.
4 'Behavioral Study of Obedience', Milgram, 1963. In which participants were instructed to administer electric shocks of increasing voltage to a fellow participant (really an actor) in an adjacent room. Two-thirds went all the way to lethal voltages, even when the other participant's screams had abruptly cut off. Some continued to comply while wracked with 'uncontrollable seizures' of nervous laughter.
5 *The Belief in a Just World: A Fundamental Delusion*, Lerner, 1980
6 'The Birth, Death and Resurrection of Avoidance: A Reconceptualization of a Troubled Paradigm', LeDoux et al., 2017

NOTES

2. SHIFT HAPPENS

1   Popularised by Walter B. Cannon's *Bodily Changes in Pain, Hunger, Fear and Rage*, 1915 (he coined the term in the *American Journal of Physiology* the year prior).

2   'Psychological Stress and the Human Immune System: A Meta-Analytic Study of 30 Years of Inquiry', Segerstrom et al., 2004. The headline conclusion is that the bigger and longer the stress, the worse the effect on your immune system. Long-term chronic stressors eventually result in 'global immunosuppression'. However, 'acute and time-limited' stressors result in a raised immune response – 'upregulated parameters of natural immunity' – preparing the body for, say, a bite or puncture wound that might leave the blood and skin vulnerable to infection.

3   This is a joke. Most psychological and neuroscientific models make tacit evolutionary claims, especially when they rely on animal models as part of their evidence base. The field has seen some very silly work published, but it's not intrinsically unscientific to attempt to reconcile neuropsychological phenomena with our best current understanding of how human beings came about. You are valid, evolutionary psychologists.

4   'Beyond Diathesis Stress: Differential Susceptibility to Environmental Influences', Belsky and Pluess, 2009

5   'Early School Outcomes for Children of Postpartum Depressed Mothers: Comparison with a Community Sample', Kersten-Alvarez, 2012

6   'The Impact of Various Parental Mental Disorders on Children's Diagnoses: A Systematic Review', Santvoort et al., 2015. 'Risk and Protective Factors for Children's and Adolescents' Mental Health: Results of the BELLA Study', Wille, 2008

7   'Impact of Maternal Mental Health on Pediatric Asthma Control', Ghaempanah et al., 2013

3. THE EXERCIST

1   *Bodily Changes In Pain, Hunger, Fear and Rage*, Cannon, 1915

2   Cannon acknowledged the possibility of freezing as a third reaction,

noting that major emotions like fear can, at times, have 'depressive rather than stimulating effects', lowering rather than raising blood pressure. He hypothesised that there might be a relationship between 'recognising the possibility of escape . . . and the degree of stimulating effect'. When it came to fear or rage, 'the effect may be paralyzing *until there is a definite deed to perform*.'

3   *Bodily Changes In Pain, Hunger, Fear and Rage*, 2nd edition, Cannon, 1920

4   The reason for these last changes is poorly understood. Some researchers speculate that decreased control by the prefrontal cortex means our ability to inhibit peeing or pooping is impaired – or, conversely, as some shy urinal-users discover, we can't pee even if we want to.

5   'pH of the Cytoplasm and Periplasm of Escherichia coli: Rapid Measurement by Green Fluorescent Protein Fluorimetry', Wilks et al., 2007

6   'Molecular Aspects of Bacterial pH Sensing and Homeostasis', Krulwich et al., 2011

7   'The Peripheral Sympathetic Nervous System: Its Role in Normal and Pathologic Anxiety', Hoehn-Saric et al., 1988

8   'The Role of the Hypothalamic-Pituitary-Adrenal Axis in Neuroendocrine Responses to Stress', Smith et al., 2006

9   'Stress and the General Adaptation Syndrome', Selye, 1950

10 'Plasticity of the Hippocampus: Adaptation to Chronic Stress and Allostatic Load', McEwen, 2006

11 Selye's reputation later suffered when he took up paid consulting work for the tobacco industry. Lawyers for the tobacco company Philip Morris paid Selye to write a paper arguing for 'the "stressful" effect on the US population of antismoking messages' and denying the likelihood of there being a mechanism by which smoking could cause heart disease. Many tobacco companies used his research as evidence that the rise in heart disease and cancer was down to many factors, including the stress of modern life – even the stigmatisation faced by smokers – and could not be conclusively linked to smoking. See 'The "Father of Stress" Meets "Big Tobacco": Hans Selye and the Tobacco Industry', Petticrew et al., 2011

12 'Stressed or Stressed Out: What Is the Difference?', McEwen, 2005

13 'The Physiological Effects of Shinrin-Yoku (Taking In the Forest Atmosphere or Forest Bathing): Evidence from Field Experiments in 24 Forests Across Japan', Park et al., 2009

14 'Shinrin-Yoku (Forest-Air Bathing and Walking) Effectively Decreases Blood Glucose Levels in Diabetic Patients', Ohtsuka et al., 1998

15 'A Comparative Study of the Physiological and Psychological Effects of Forest Bathing (Shinrin-Yoku) on Working Age People With and Without Depressive Tendencies', Furuyashiki et al., 2019

16 'Spending at Least 120 Minutes a Week in Nature Is Associated with Good Health and Wellbeing', White et al., 2019

17 'Effects of Physical Exercise on Anxiety, Depression and Sensitivity to Stress', Salmon, 2001

18 'Exercise for Anxiety Disorders: Systematic Review', Jayakody et al., 2013

19 'Exercise in the Treatment of Clinical Anxiety in General Practice – A Systematic Review and Meta-Analysis', Aylett et al., 2018

20 'A Meta-Analysis on the Anxiety-Reducing Effects of Acute and Chronic Exercise', Petruzzello et al., 1991. The quality of many of the studies in these three meta-analyses is poor: small sample sizes, no control group and possible experimenter bias. Even the authors' definition of aerobic exercise is vague – does walking count or not? Well, you don't know unless you measure participants' heart rate.

21 'Cardiorespiratory Fitness and Laboratory Stress: A Meta-Regression Analysis', Jackson et al., 2006

22 'Acute Stressors and Cortisol Responses: A Theoretical Integration and Synthesis of Laboratory Research', Dickerson et al., 2004

23 'Exercise Benefits Brain Function: The Monoamine Connection', Lin and Kuo, 2013

24 'Voluntary Exercise Improves Both Learning and Consolidation of Cued Conditioned Fear in C57 Mice', Falls et al., 2010

25 'Neurobiology of BDNF in Fear Memory, Sensitivity to Stress, and Stress-Related Disorders', Notaras et al., 2020. I'm using 'unlearning' loosely here. Current models suggest not that fear responses are 'unlearned' so much as superseded by new, stronger pathways; they

may atrophy, but the association remains, possibly to reactivate under conditions of extreme duress.

26 'Intense Exercise and Food Restriction Cause Similar Hypothalamic Neuropeptide Y Increases in Rats', Lewis et al., 1993

27 'Neuropeptide Y: A Stressful Review', Reichmann et al., 2016

28 'Endogenously Released Neuropeptide Y Suppresses Hippocampal Short-Term Facilitation and Is Impaired by Stress-Induced Anxiety', Li et al., 2017

29 'Low Baseline and Yohimbine-Stimulated Plasma Neuropeptide Y (NPY) Levels in Combat-Related PTSD', Rasmusson et al., 2000

30 'Voluntary Alcohol Consumption Is Controlled via the Neuropeptide Y Y1 Receptor', Thiele et al., 2002

31 'Exercise Offers Anxiolytic Potential: A Role for Stress and Brain Noradrenergic-Galaninergic Mechanisms', Sciolino and Holmes, 2012

32 'Functional Neuroanatomy of Altered States of Consciousness: The Transient Hypofrontality Hypothesis', Dietrich, 2003. I asked a few other neuroscientists what they thought about this theory, as the majority of scholarship on transient hypofrontality appears to have been authored by Arne himself (a bit of a red flag). The consensus was that, while not biologically implausible, we don't have enough evidence to know whether that's how the brain works. Since the burden of proof is on the theory (rather than on researchers to *disprove* it) our default assumption should be that it is false – a position we can update should new information come to light.

33 'Neural Correlates of Rumination in Depression', Cooney et al., 2010

34 'Effects of Exercise and Physical Activity on Anxiety', Anderson et al., 2013

4. EAT SHIT AND DIET

1 'A Review of Dietary and Microbial Connections to Depression, Anxiety and Stress', Taylor et al., 2018. This is a meta-analysis of previous dietary trials. Most of the research included relied on participants to fill in questionnaires about their food intake after the fact. As the authors admit, 'self-reported diet records may not accurately reflect the amount of food consumed by a participant', which is putting it mildly.

NOTES

2   'Effect of Vitamin D Supplement on Mood Status and Inflammation in Vitamin D Deficient Type 2 Diabetic Women With Anxiety: A Randomized Clinical Trial', Fazelian et al., 2019. This was a relatively small sample (51) of diabetic women with a marked deficiency in vitamin D. The authors cite several studies which found vitamin D had 'no therapeutic effects on anxiety and depression in healthy adults'. Vitamin D deficiency gets linked with all sorts of conditions, part of the problem being that it correlates strongly with inactivity and frailty.

3   'Peripheral Inflammatory Cytokines and Immune Balance in Generalised Anxiety Disorder: Case-Controlled Study', Hou et al., 2017

4   'Brain-Derived Neurotrophic Factor: A Bridge Between Inflammation and Neuroplasticity', Calabrese et al., 2014

5   'Immune System to Brain Signaling: Neuropsychopharmacological Implications', Capuron and Miller, 2011

6   'The Relationship Between Religious and Psychospiritual Measures and an Inflammation Marker (CRP) in Older Adults Experiencing Life Event Stress', Ironson et al., 2018

7   'Stress and Inflammation Among Older Adults: The Moderating Role of Religiosity', Tavares et al., 2019

8   'Postnatal Microbial Colonization Programs the Hypothalamic–Pituitary–Adrenal System for Stress Response in Mice', Sudo et al., 2004

9   'The Intestinal Microbiota Affect Central Levels of Brain-Derived Neurotropic Factor and Behavior in Mice', Bercik et al., 2011

10   'The Roles of Peripheral Serotonin in Metabolic Homeostasis', El-Merahbi et al., 2015

11   'Mouse Models for Human Intestinal Microbiota Research: A Critical Evaluation', Hugenholtz et al., 2017

12   'Why Can't Rodents Vomit? A Comparative Behavioral, Anatomical, and Physiological Study', Horn et al., 2013

13   *Ratting and Rabbiting for Amateur Gamekeepers*, Smith, 1979

14   Other studies with germ-free mice have had mixed results. Though the mice consistently pump out more hormones when placed under acute stress – like being trapped or forced to swim to avoid drowning – they also seem less cautious, readily venturing out and exploring an

402

open space in the so-called 'open field test'. Researchers label this readiness to explore an 'antianxiety-like' behaviour because, in the wild, wandering out into the open puts a mouse at risk of being caught by a predator.

15 'The Ascent of Mouse: Advances in Modelling Human Depression and Anxiety', Cryan and Holmes, 2005

16 'Grooming Analysis Algorithm for Neurobehavioural Stress Research', Kalueff et al., 2004

17 'Neurobiology of Rodent Self-Grooming and its Value for Translational Neuroscience', Kalueff et al., 2016

18 'The Mouse Forced Swim Test', Can et al., 2012

19 'Consumption of Fermented Milk Product with Probiotic Modulates Brain Activity', Tillisch et al., 2013

20 'Brain's "Fear Center" Skews Emotion in Anxious Kids', Digitale-Stanford, 2020, https://www.futurity.org/anxiety-children-regulate-emotions-2348282-2/

21 'Research Reveals How Magic Mushrooms Alter Connectivity in the Brain's Fear Center', Taub, 2020, https://www.iflscience.com/brain/research-reveals-magic-mushrooms-alter-connectivi-ty-brains-fear-center/

22 'Efficacy of Probiotics on Anxiety: A Meta-Analysis of Randomized Controlled Trials', Liu et al., 2018

23 'International Primate Neuroscience Research Regulation, Public Engagement and Transparency Opportunities', Mitchell et al., 2021

24 'Postnatal Microbial Colonization Programs the Hypothalamic–Pituitary–Adrenal System for Stress Response in Mice', Sudo et al., 2004

25 'Sensitization of Norepinephrine Activity Following Acute and Chronic Footshock', Irwin et al., 1986

26 'A New Assay of Thermal-Based Avoidance Test in Freely Moving Mice', Ding et al., 2005

27 'The Mouse Forced Swim Test', Can et al., 2012

28 'Effects of Single Cage Housing on Stress, Cognitive, and Seizure Parameters in the Rat and Mouse Pilocarpine Models of Epilepsy', Manouze et al., 2019. These were rodents of a phenotype prone to epileptic seizures, often used in epilepsy research.

29 *Animal Liberation: A New Ethics for Our Treatment of Animals*, Singer, 1975

30 'Crazy Like a Fox: Validity and Ethics of Animal Models of Human Psychiatric Disease', Rollin and Rollin, 2014; of course if we accept Box's maxim 'All models are wrong', it's just a question of *how* wrong.

31 'The Importance of Common Currency Tasks in Translational Psychiatry', Pike et al., 2021

32 'Systematic Review with Meta-analysis: The Efficacy of Faecal Microbiota Transplantation for the Treatment of Recurrent and Refractory Clostridium Difficile Infection', Quraishi et al., 2017

33 'Faecal Transplants: "My Dad's Poo Saved My Life"', Stevenson, 2016, https://www.dailytelegraph.com.au/lifestyle/health/body-soul-daily/faecal-transplants-can-restore-health--soon-we-might-be-popping-crapsules/news-story/7c91f28odcd8954do6d720acfbef8721

34 'Dietary Patterns and Depression Risk: A Meta-Analysis', Li et al., 2017

35 'Adherence to Mediterranean Dietary Pattern is Inversely Associated with Depression, Anxiety and Psychological Distress', Sadeghi et al., 2019

36 'Diet Quality and Depression Risk: A Systematic Review and Dose-Response Meta-Analysis of Prospective Studies', Molendijk et al., 2018

37 'Statins for Primary Prevention in People with a 10% 10-year Cardiovascular Risk: Too Much Medicine Too Soon?', Yerrakalva and Griffin, 2017. It's actually quite a bit more complicated than the authors of the Mediterranean diet study suggest; the NNT for statins depends on the risk score of the group receiving them; across all risk levels, 49 people need to take statins over 5 years to prevent 1 non-fatal cardiovascular disease event, 155 to prevent 1 stroke, and 138 to prevent 1 death. But if someone's already had CVD or they're in a high-risk group, the NNT drops way down.

5. TERRIFYING ABNORMAL DREAMS

1 *I Think You'll Find It's a Bit More Complicated Than That*, Goldacre, 2014

2 The adjective 'credible' is doing a lot of work in this sentence, admittedly. You can find outliers in psychiatry and psychology – like Lucy Johnstone – but it's disingenuous to characterise their opinions as the norm.

3 'The Expanded Biology of Serotonin', Berger et al., 2009

4 'Serotonin Synthesis and Reuptake in Social Anxiety Disorder: A Positron Emission Tomography Study', Frick et al., 2015; 18 is a tiny sample size, taken from participants over a decade. The authors admit that, while SAD is associated with increased serotonin transporter availability, it's frequently comorbid with major depressive disorder, which is associated with reduced serotonin transporter availability. They acknowledge 'a complex relationship' between the two, which is neurobiology-speak for 'who fucking knows?'

5 'The Role of Serotonin in the Regulation of Patience and Impulsivity', Miyazaki et al., 2012

6 'Serotonin and Brain Function: A Tale of Two Receptors', Carhart-Harris et al., 2017

7 'Serotonin-Prefrontal Cortical Circuitry in Anxiety and Depression Phenotypes: Pivotal Role of Pre- and Post-Synaptic 5-HT1A Receptor Expression', Albert et al., 2014

8 'Efficacy of Drug Treatments for Generalised Anxiety Disorder: Systematic Review and Meta-Analysis', Baldwin et al., 2011

9 'Evidence-Based Pharmacological Treatment of Anxiety Disorders, Post-Traumatic Stress Disorder and Obsessive-Compulsive Disorder: A Revision of the 2005 Guidelines from the British Association for Psychopharmacology', Baldwin et al., 2014

10 'Treatment of Generalized Anxiety Disorder with Citalopram', Varia et al., 2002. This study only had 13 participants and no control group, so it's not exactly conclusive evidence.

11 'Propranolol for the Treatment of Anxiety Disorders: Systematic Review and Meta-Analysis', Steenen et al., 2016

12 'Analgesic Effects of Branding in Treatment of Headaches', Branthwaite and Cooper, 1981

13 'Placebo Effect in the Treatment of Duodenal Ulcer', de Craen et al., 1999. Although the difference found between the two groups was

statistically significant, it was relatively small: 8 per cent who healed their ulcers versus 6 per cent.

14 'Demonstration to Medical Students of Placebo Responses and Non-Drug Factors', Blackwell et al., 1972

15 'Diagnosis Is Treatment', Brody and Waters, 1980

16 'Efficacy of Drug Treatments for Generalised Anxiety Disorder: Systematic Review and Meta-Analysis', Baldwin et al., 2011; 'A Meta-Analysis of the Efficacy of Psycho- and Pharmacotherapy in Panic Disorder With and Without Agoraphobia', Mitte, 2005. This meta-analysis looked at 124 studies and found that medication was more effective than a placebo, but that no particular drug class performed better than the others. It also found that CBT performed at least as well as medication.

17 'Comparative Efficacy and Acceptability of 21 Antidepressant Drugs for the Acute Treatment of Adults with Major Depressive Disorder: A Systematic Review and Network Meta-Analysis', Cipriani et al., 2018

18 'Putting the Efficacy of Psychiatric and General Medicine Medication Into Perspective: Review of Meta-Analyses', Leucht et al., 2012

19 'Dealing With Life's Challenges', NHS, https://www.nhs.uk/every-mind-matters/lifes-challenges/

20 'A Systematic Review into the Incidence, Severity and Duration of Antidepressant Withdrawal Effects: Are Guidelines Evidence-Based?', Davies and Read, 2018

21 'Selective Serotonin Reuptake Inhibitor "Discontinuation Syndrome" or Withdrawal', Massabki and Abi-Jaoude, 2020

22 'Antidepressant Discontinuation Syndrome', Warner et al., 2006

23 'Risk of Relapse After Antidepressant Discontinuation in Anxiety Disorders, Obsessive-Compulsive Disorder, and Post-Traumatic Stress Disorder: Systematic Review and Meta-Analysis of Relapse Prevention Trials', Batelaan et al., 2017

24 'Risk of Relapse After Antidepressant Discontinuation in Anxiety Disorders, Obsessive-Compulsive Disorder, and Post-Traumatic Stress Disorder: Systematic Review and Meta-Analysis of Relapse Prevention Trials', Batelaan et al., 2017

25 'Neural Regulation of Lacrimal Gland Secretory Processes: Relevance in Dry Eye Diseases', Dartt, 2009

26 'Withdrawal Symptoms after Selective Serotonin Reuptake Inhibitor Discontinuation: A Systematic Review', Fava et al., 2015

27 'MHRA Investigation into Glaxosmithkline/Seroxat', UK Medicines and Healthcare products Regulatory Agency, 2008, https://webarchive.nationalarchives.gov.uk/20141206221413/http://www.mhra.gov.uk/home/groups/es-policy/documents/websiteresources/con014155.pdf

28 'Pfizer Pays $2.3 Billion to Settle Marketing Case', New York Times, 2009, https://www.nytimes.com/2009/09/03/business/03health.html

29 'Say Om: How Mindfulness Meditation Became a $1 Billion Market', National, 2019, https://www.thenational.ae/business/technology/say-om-how-mindfulness-meditation-became-a-1-billion-market-1.853587

30 'Adding Psychotherapy to Antidepressant Medication in Depression and Anxiety Disorders: A Meta-Analysis', Cuijpers et al., 2014. The study did not find a significant improvement for generalised anxiety disorder, but the authors concluded there may have been too few studies in the sample to find an effect.

31 'Relative Effects of CBT and Pharmacotherapy in Depression versus Anxiety: Is Medication Somewhat Better for Depression, and CBT Somewhat Better for Anxiety?', Roshanaei-Moghaddam et al., 2011. The question mark in this title is a bit cheeky – if you read the study, the answer, from a statistical significance standpoint, is a clear no.

32 'Psychological Treatment of Generalized Anxiety Disorder: A Meta-Analysis', Cuijpers et al., 2014

33 'Hidden Waits "Leave Mental Health Patients in Limbo"', BBC News, 5 December 2019, https://www.bbc.co.uk/news/health-50658007

34 'Covid-19: Waiting Times in England Reach Record Highs', British Medical Journal, 2020, https://www.bmj.com/content/370/bmj.m3557

35 'Coronavirus (COVID-19) in Charts: What We Learned over the Past Month', UK Office for National Statistics, 1 March 2021,

https://www.ons.gov.uk/peoplepopulationandcommunity/healthand socialcare/conditionsanddiseases/articles/coronaviruscovid19incharts whatwelearnedoverthepastmonth/2021-03-01

36 *Talking Cures and Placebo Effects*, Jopling, 2008

37 At the time of writing, Psychiatry-UK quotes a fee of £360.00 for an online 'one hour assessment', payable in advance, with a further fee of £6 per minute if the meeting runs over. Private Psychiatry charges £350–£395 for a one-hour consultation. As far as I can tell, this is more or less the industry norm (and most private health-insurance policies don't cover psychiatric referrals as standard), but in any case, it was the only option offered to me when my GP referred me.

38 'Poverty, Stress, and Brain Development: New Directions for Prevention and Intervention', Blair and Raver, 2016

39 'Poverty, Social Inequality and Mental Health', Murali and Oyebode, 2004

40 'Do We Need to Challenge Thoughts in Cognitive Behavior Therapy?', Longmore and Worrell, 2006

41 'Efficacy of Drug Treatments for Generalised Anxiety Disorder: Systematic Review and Meta-Analysis', Baldwin et al., 2011

42 'Anxiety Disorders and GABA Neurotransmission: A Disturbance of Modulation', Nuss, 2015

43 'The Role of GABA in Anxiety Disorders', Bruce Lydiard, 2003

6. MODERN LIFE IS RUBBISH

1 This isn't true for the ICD-10 definition of generalised anxiety disorder, which simply says that the worry must be 'prominent' and 'about everyday events and problems'. This brings up the opposite issue – is it accurate to describe someone who worries a lot during a very stressful six months as having a 'mental disorder'?

2 *Man's Search for Meaning*, Frankl, 1946

3 M. Molly Backes, 6 September 2018, https://www.second-nature.com/blog/the-impossible-task

4 'Scaling-up Treatment of Depression and Anxiety: A Global Return on Investment Analysis', Chisholm et al., 2016

5 'The Epidemiology of Generalized Anxiety Disorder', Kessler et al., 2001

NOTES

6 'Prescription Cost Analysis', NHS Digital, 2019, https://digital.nhs. uk/data-and-information/publications/statistical/prescrip- tion-cost-analysis/2018

7 'Increasing Benzodiazepine Prescriptions and Overdose Mortality in the United States, 1996–2013', Bachhuber et al., 2016

8 'Mental Health of Children and Young People in England, 2017', https://digital.nhs.uk/data-and-information/publications/statistical/ mental-health-of-children-and-young-people-in-england/2017/2017. I have multiple issues with the study's methodology – too many to adequately summarise here. There's significant selection bias; one questionnaire used, the GHQ-12, a twelve-item screening test for minor psychiatric disorders, has an estimated false-positive rate of 30 per cent ('Factors Associated with Being a False Positive on the General Health Questionnaire', Bell et al., 2005). Many questions weren't even put to the child themselves but to parents, or sometimes teachers – and not always even the child's teacher, but heads of year. To borrow a term Dr Rohin Francis introduced me to, the whole study is a bit of a fishing expedition, and we should be very cautious about drawing big conclusions.

9 'Anxiety Disorders', Our World in Data, https://ourworldindata.org/ mental-health#anxiety-disorders. This data is drawn from the Institute for Health Metrics and Evaluation's 'Global Burden of Disease Study 2017'.

10 'Epidemiology of Anxiety Disorders in the 21st Century', Bandelow and Michaelis, 2015

11 'Anxiety Disorders', Our World in Data, https://ourworldindata.org/ mental-health#anxiety-disorders. This data is drawn from the Institute for Health Metrics and Evaluation's 'Global Burden of Disease Study 2017'.

12 'Death Squared: The Explosive Growth and Demise of a Mouse Population', Calhoun, 1973

13 *From Mice to Men*, Calhoun, 1973; money quote: 'That we are begin- ning to recognize the universality of mind, in mammals at least, is reflected in the article by Harry Harlow and his associates titled "Monkey Psychiatrists".' ('Monkey Psychiatrists', Suomi et al., 1972)

14 'Civilians in World War II and DSM-IV Mental Disorders: Results from the World Mental Health Survey Initiative', Frounfelker et al., 2017

15 *War Neuroses*, Grinker and Spiegel, 1945; quoted in 'War & Military Mental Health: The US Psychiatric Response in the 20th Century', Pols and Oak, 2007

16 'The Psychological Study of Anxiety in the Era of the Second World War', Shapira, 2013

17 'Incidence of Neurosis in England Under War Conditions', Lewis, 1942. This study relies on outpatient admissions in urban areas to make inferences, during a period when the cities in question were being bombed and significant sections of the population were off fighting or evacuated. It needs to be viewed in the context of likely sampling bias.

18 'The Stress of Life: A Modern Complaint?', Jackson, 2014

19 Quoted in *Stress, Shock, and Adaptation in the Twentieth Century*, eds Cantor and Ramsden, 2014

20 For far more on this than I have room for, I recommend the fastidious and eminently readable *Anxious Times: Medicine and Modernity in Nineteenth-Century Britain*, Bonea, Dickson, Shuttleworth and Wallis, 2019

21 'The Imperial Reserve: the Indian Corps on the Western Front, 1914–15', Greenhut, 1983

22 'Early Buddhism and the Urban Revolution', Gokhale, 1982

23 'Availability: A Heuristic for Judging Frequency and Probability', Tversky and Kahneman, 1973

24 'Poverty Raises Levels of the Stress Hormone Cortisol: Evidence from Weather Shocks in Kenya', Haushofer et al., 2012

25 'Poverty and Common Mental Disorders in Low and Middle Income Countries: A Systematic Review', Lund et al., 2010

26 'Global Extreme Poverty', Our World In Data, 2017, https://ourworldindata.org/extreme-poverty

27 *Religion and the Decline of Magic: Studies in Popular Beliefs in Sixteenth and Seventeenth Century England*, Thomas, 1971

28 *Germany: A New Social and Economic History, Vol. 1, 1450–1630*,

Scribner (ed.), quoted in *The Faithful Executioner: Life and Death in the Sixteenth Century*, Harrington, 2013

29 'Scaling-up Treatment of Depression and Anxiety: A Global Return on Investment Analysis', Chisholm et al., 2016

30 'The Looping Effects of Human Kinds', Hacking, 1995

31 'Mental Health Atlas 2017', World Health Organization, https://www.who.int/publications/i/item/9789241514019

32 'The History of Generalized Anxiety Disorder as a Diagnostic Category', Crocq, 2017

33 'Doctors "Too Reliant" on Depression Questionnaire Designed by Pfizer, Campaigners Warn', *Telegraph*, 21 May 2017, https://www.telegraph.co.uk/news/2017/05/21/
doctors-reliant-depressionquestionnaire-designed-bypfizer-campaigners/

34 'Using Generalized Anxiety Disorder-2 (GAD-2) and GAD-7 in a Primary Care Setting', Sapra et al., 2020

35 'Quick and Easy Self-Rating of Generalized Anxiety Disorder: Validity of the Dutch Web-based GAD-7, GAD-2 and GAD-SI', Donker et al., 2011; 'Mental Health, Risk Factors, and Social Media Use during the COVID-19 Epidemic and Cordon Sanitaire among the Community and Health Professionals in Wuhan, China: Cross-Sectional Survey', Ni et al., 2020

36 'Effects of Direct-to-Consumer Advertising on Patient Prescription Requests and Physician Prescribing: A Systematic Review of Psychiatry-relevant Studies', Becker et al., 2016

37 'Concept Creep: Psychology's Expanding Concepts of Harm and Pathology', Haslam, 2016

7. THIS IS FINE

1 'Group Inhibition of Bystander Intervention in Emergencies', Latané and Darley, 1968

2 'Between-subject Transfer of Emotional Information Evokes Specific Pattern of Amygdala Activation', Knapska et al., 2006

3 'Body Language in the Brain: Constructing Meaning from Expressive Movement', Tipper et al., 2015

4   See Chapter 11 for some reasons why the 'fearful faces protocol' may not be very reliable.

5   'Non-Conscious Recognition of Emotional Body Language', de Gelder and Hadjikhani, 2006

6   'Social Modeling of Eating: A Review of When and Why Social Influence Affects Food Intake and Choice', Cruwys et al., 2015. This report in the journal *Appetite* reviewed 69 studies on the effect of this social modelling on what and how much we eat, and found it to be a 'robust and profound phenomenon'.

7   'How Norms Work: Self-Identification, Attitude, and Self-Efficacy Mediate the Relation between Descriptive Social Norms and Vegetable Intake', Stok et al., 2014. This was a Dutch study about vegetable consumption which found that students who felt a 'strong connection' to their university were more likely to increase their vegetable consumption if they were told that students from their university ate 200g of vegetables a day.

8   'The Third-Person Effect in Communication', Phillips Davison, 1983

9   'Social Modeling of Eating: A Review of When and Why Social Influence Affects Food Intake and Choice', Cruwys et al., 2015

10   'Reinforcement Learning Signal Predicts Social Conformity', Klucharev et al., 2009. The study used two small samples of female students in their twenties, so we should be cautious before generalising the results.

11   'The Prevalence of PTSD and Major Depression in the Global Population of Adult War Survivors: A Meta-Analytically Informed Estimate in Absolute Numbers', Hoppen and Morina, 2019

12   'A Systematic Review of PTSD Prevalence and Trajectories in DSM-5 Defined Trauma Exposed Populations: Intentional and Non-Intentional Traumatic Events', Santiago et al., 2013

13   'Traumatic Events and Post-traumatic Stress Disorder in the Community: Prevalence, Risk Factors and Comorbidity', Perkonigg et al., 2000. 'Trauma' still lacks a universally accepted definition, so differences in results may largely be down to the severity and frequency of traumatic incidents.

8. THE ANXIETY GENE

1 'Crazy Like a Fox: Validity and Ethics of Animal Models of Human Psychiatric Disease', Rollin and Rollin, 2014

2 'Immobility in the Forced Swim Test Is Adaptive and Does Not Reflect Depression', Molendijk et al., 2015

3 'A Review and Meta-Analysis of the Genetic Epidemiology of Anxiety Disorders', Hettema et al., 2001

4 'Abnormal Behavior Associated with a Point Mutation in the Structural Gene for Monoamine Oxidase A', Brunner et al., 1993

5 In 1873 Galton wrote a lengthy article called 'Hereditary Improvement' in which he bemoaned racial degeneration in English factory towns, arguing that conditions of sickness, poverty and urban living favoured those able to withstand disease and poor food, rendering survivors 'more like the negro in the protrusion of the lower jaw'. He called for the cultivation of a 'gifted race' picked from the top quarter of English youth, a caste who would intermarry and ultimately displace their racial inferiors.

6 'Association of Anxiety-Related Traits with a Polymorphism in the Serotonin Transporter Gene Regulatory Region', Lesch et al., 1996

7 'Influence of Life Stress on Depression: Moderation by a Polymorphism in the 5-HTT Gene', Capsi et al., 2003

8 'A Novel Functional Polymorphism within the Promoter of the Serotonin Transporter Gene: Possible Role in Susceptibility to Affective Disorders', Collier et al., 1996

9 'The Serotonin Transporter Polymorphism, 5HTTLPR, Is Associated with a Faster Response Time to Sertraline in an Elderly Population with Major Depressive Disorder', Durham et al., 2003

10 'Neuroticism Is Not Associated with the Serotonin Transporter (5-HTTLPR) Polymorphism', Flory et al., 1999

11 'Differential Susceptibility in Youth: Evidence that 5-HTTLPR x Positive Parenting Is Associated with Positive Affect "For Better and Worse"', Hankin et al., 2011

12 'Collaborative Meta-Analysis Finds No Evidence of a Strong Interaction between Stress and 5-HTTLPR Genotype Contributing to the Development of Depression', Culverhouse et al., 2017

13 'Serotonin Transporter Gene Polymorphism (5-HTTLPR) and

Anxiety Reactivity in Daily Life: A Daily Process Approach to Gene-Environment Interaction', Gunthert et al., 2007

14   'Genome-Wide Association Analyses Identify 44 Risk Variants and Refine the Genetic Architecture of Major Depression', Wray et al., 2018. This study relied heavily on self-reporting, with over half the cases from users of DNA testing company 23andMe, so the accuracy of major depression diagnoses for a big chunk of the sample is, at the very least, a bit fuzzy.

9. AND IT FEELS LIKE HOME

1   'Relationship of Childhood Abuse and Household Dysfunction to Many of the Leading Causes of Death in Adults: the Adverse Childhood Experiences (ACE) Study', Felitti et al., 1998

2   'Relationship Between Multiple Forms of Childhood Maltreatment and Adult Mental Health in Community Respondents: Results from the Adverse Childhood Experiences Study', Edwards et al., 2003

3   'Rethinking Concepts and Categories for Understanding the Neurodevelopmental Effects of Childhood Adversity', Smith and Pollak, 2020

4   'Rethinking Concepts and Categories for Understanding the Neurodevelopmental Effects of Childhood Adversity', Smith and Pollak, 2020

5   'Critical Period for Acoustic Preference in Mice', Yang et al., 2012

6   'The Montreal Imaging Stress Task: Using Functional Imaging to Investigate the Effects of Perceiving and Processing Psychosocial Stress in the Human Brain', Dedovic et al., 2005

7   'Music Reveals Medial Prefrontal Cortex Sensitive Period in Childhood', Gabard-Durham et al., 2018

8   'A Review of Adversity, the Amygdala and the Hippocampus: A Consideration of Developmental Timing', Tottenham and Sheridan, 2010

9   *Origins of the Social Mind: Evolutionary Psychology and Child Development*, Ellis et al. (eds), 2005

10   'Differential Susceptibility of the Developing Brain to Contextual Adversity and Stress', Boyce, 2015

11   *Games People Play*, Berne, 1964

10. PIECE OF MIND

1   'A Tale of Survival from the World of Patient S.M.', Feinstein et al., in *Living without an Amygdala*, Amaral and Adolphs (eds), 2016

2   'A Tale of Survival from the World of Patient S.M.', Feinstein et al., in *Living without an Amygdala*, Amaral and Adolphs (eds), 2016

3   'Altered Experience of Emotion Following Bilateral Amygdala Damage', Tranel et al., 2006

4   From an interview with Paul Bucy, 8 April 1981, James W. Papez Oral History Collection

5   As trip reports go, the book is refreshingly dry. A typical account runs: 'Half an hour after taking the second dose vomiting occurred. Soon hereafter phenomena of the following kind could be observed with closed eyes: "Clouds from left to right through optical field. Tail of a pheasant (in centre of field) turns into bright yellow star; star into sparks. Moving scintillating screw; 'hundreds' of screws. A sequence of rapidly changing objects in agreeable colours. A rotating wheel (diameter about 1cm)."'

6   *Neuroscience*, Fifth Edition, Purves et al. (eds), 2011, p.653

7   'An Investigation into the Functions of the Occipital and Temporal Lobes of the Monkey's Brain', Brown and Sharpey-Schäfer, 1888

8   *Neuroscience*, Fifth Edition, Purves et al. (eds), 2011

9   Quoted in *Living without an Amygdala*, Amaral and Adolphs (eds), 2016

10 Quoted in *The Lobotomist*, Jack El-Hai, 2005

11 *Batman: Shadow of the Bat – The Last Arkham*, Grant, 1992

12 'Stereotaxic Amygdalotomy for Behavior Disorders', Narabayashi et al., 1963

13 'A Short History of the Lesion Technique for Probing Amygdala Function', Amaral, in *Living without an Amygdala*, Amaral and Adolphs (eds), 2016

14 'Bilateral Anterior Capsulotomy and Amygdalotomy for Mental Retardation with Psychiatric Symptoms and Aggression: A Case Report', Zhang et al., 2017

15 It's also possible to genetically engineer and breed mice which express DREADDs in target areas from birth: 'A Gαs DREADD Mouse for

Selective Modulation of cAMP Production in Striatopallidal Neurons', Farrell et al., 2013

16   'The Use of DREADDs to Deconstruct Behavior', Whissell et al., 2016

17   'Evidence in Primates Supporting the Use of Chemogenetics for the Treatment of Human Refractory Neuropsychiatric Disorders', Roseboom et al., 2021

18   'Green Fluorescent Protein as a Marker for Gene Expression', Chalfie et al., 1994

19   'Optogenetics: Turning the Microscope on Its Head', Cohen, 2016

20   'DREADDs: Use and Application in Behavioral Neuroscience', Smith et al., 2016

11. BRAIN STORM

1   *The Organization of Behavior,* Hebb, 1949

2   'Transcranial Direct Current Stimulation in Patients with Anxiety: Current Perspectives', Stein et al., 2020

3   Adverse events from tDCS include tingling/itching, tiredness, headache, nausea, and in rare cases insomnia. Currently there is no evidence of long-term neurological damage, though some people using homemade neurostimulation kits have given themselves nasty burns. 'Effects of Transcranial Direct Current Stimulation (tDCS) and Approach Bias Modification (ABM) Training on Food Cravings in People Taking Antipsychotic Medication', Grycuk et al., 2020

4   'Evidence from behavioural neuroscience strongly suggests that the unconditional (innate) capacity to experience fear, along with fear-typical patterns of autonomic and behavioural arousal, emerge from specific systems of the brain – the most prominent being a FEAR circuit, which courses between the amygdala and the central grey of the midbrain.' Panksepp, *Biological Psychiatry,* in *Principles of Medical Biology*, Bittar and Bittar (eds), 2000

5   Admittedly this example lands a little differently in Britain than America, where the only 'long, coiled' threat we're likely to tread on while walking in nature is a dog turd.

6   'Emotion, Memory and the Brain', LeDoux, 1994

7   'Equipotentiality of Thalamo-Amygdala and Thalamo-Cortico-

NOTES

Amygdala Circuits in Auditory Fear Conditioning', Romanski and LeDoux, 1992

8   *Emotional Intelligence: Why It Can Matter More than IQ*, Goleman, 1995

9   'Cognitive, Social, and Physiological Determinants of Emotional State', Schachter and Singer, 1962

10 'Cognitive Effects of False Heart-Rate Feedback', Valins, 1966

11 'Cognitive, Social, and Physiological Determinants of Emotional State', Schachter and Singer, 1962

12 'The Hippocampus and Amygdala Are Integrators of Neocortical Influence: A CorticoCortical Evoked Potential Study', Mégevand et al., 2017

13 'Hippocampal Involvement in Contextual Modulation of Fear Extinction', Ji and Maren, 2007

14 'The Dorsal Hippocampus Is Essential for Context Discrimination but Not for Contextual Conditioning', Frankland et al., 1998

15 'Is the Hippocampus Necessary for Contextual Fear Conditioning?', Gewirtz et al., 2000; 'Context Fear Learning in the Absence of the Hippocampus', Wiltgen et al., 2006

16 'Hippocampal Inactivation Disrupts Contextual Retrieval of Fear Memory after Extinction', Corcoran and Maren, 2001

17 'Surviving Threats: Neural Circuit and Computational Implications of a New Taxonomy of Defensive Behaviour', LeDoux and Daw, 2018

18 *Anxious: Using the Brain to Understand and Treat Fear and Anxiety*, LeDoux, 2015

19 'Diagnosing the Decline in Pharmaceutical R&D Efficiency', Scannell et al., 2012

20 Although, as neuroscientist Kay Tye has noted, 'Self-report is a behavioural output.'

21 'Language lateralization in healthy right-handers', Knecht et al., 2000

22 Joseph LeDoux, in *The Cognitive Neuroscience of Mind: A Tribute to Michael S. Gazzaniga*, Reuter-Lorenz et al. (eds), 2010

23 'Stress Reduction Correlates with Structural Changes in the Amygdala', Hölzel et al., 2009

24 'Dispositional Mindfulness Co-Varies with Smaller Amygdala and Caudate Volumes in Community Adults', Taren et al., 2013

25 'Smaller Amygdala Is Associated with Anxiety in Patients with Panic Disorder', Hayano et al., 2009

26 'Structural Evidence for Involvement of a Left Amygdala-Orbitofrontal Network in Subclinical Anxiety', Blackmon et al., 2011

27 'Amygdala Volume Changes with Posttraumatic Stress Disorder in a Large Case-Controlled Veteran Group', Morey et al., 2012

28 'A Tale of Survival from the World of Patient S.M.', Feinstein et al., in *Living without an Amygdala*, Amaral and Adolphs (eds), 2016

29 'Fear and Panic in Humans with Bilateral Amygdala Damage', Feinstein et al., 2013

30 'Attending to the World without an Amygdala', Todd et al., in *Living without an Amygdala*, Amaral and Adolphs (eds), 2016

31 'Lifetime Consequences of Early Amygdala Damage in Rhesus Monkeys', Bliss-Moreau et al., in *Living without an Amygdala*, Amaral and Adolphs (eds), 2016

12. PARANOID ANDROID

1 'Bonsai Trees in Your Head: How the Pavlovian System Sculpts Goal-Directed Choices by Pruning Decision Trees', Huys et al., 2012

2 'Dopamine Reward Prediction Error Coding', Schultz, 2016

3 'Structure and Function of Dopamine Receptors', Vallone et al., 2000

4 'From Prediction Error to Incentive Salience: Mesolimbic Computation of Reward Motivation', Berridge, 2012. This paper gives some good examples of how animals learn to associate stimuli with rewards.

5 'The Impact of Top-Down Factors on Threat Perception Biases in Health and Anxiety', Sussman et al., in *Cognitive Biases in Health and Psychiatric Disorders*, Aue and Okon-Singer (eds), 2020

6 'Social Inference and Social Anxiety: Evidence of a Fear-Congruent Self-Referential Learning Bias', Button et al., 2012

7 'Predicting Adolescent Cognitive and Self-Regulatory Competencies from Preschool Delay of Gratification: Identifying Diagnostic Conditions', Shoda et al., 1990

8   'Preschoolers' Delay of Gratification Predicts Their Body Mass 30 Years Later', Schlam et al., 2013

9   'Revisiting the Marshmallow Test: A Conceptual Replication Investigating Links Between Early Delay of Gratification and Later Outcomes', Watts et al., 2018

10   *The Marshmallow Test: Understanding Self-Control and How to Master It*, Mischel, 2015

11   'All for One and One for All: Mental Disorders in One Dimension', Caspi and Moffitt, 2018

12   'The Computational, Pharmacological, and Physiological Determinants of Sensory Learning under Uncertainty', Lawson et al., 2021

13   'Emotional Enhancement of Memory: How Norepinephrine Enables Synaptic Plasticity', Tully and Bolshakov, 2010

14   'Efficacy of Extended-Release Venlafaxine in Nondepressed Outpatients With Generalized Anxiety Disorder', Rickels et al., 2000

13. SAFETY

1   'Safety Behaviours Preserve Threat Beliefs: Protection from Extinction of Human Fear Conditioning by an Avoidance Response', Lovibond et al., 2009. There were a few extra pieces to the study – participants had a dial with which they could indicate how much they expected a shock, and the stimulus paired with a shock wasn't necessarily a blue square.

2   'The Effect of Attributional Processes Concerning Medication Taking on Return of Fear', Powers et al., 2008

3   '"If I Feel Anxious, There Must Be Danger": Ex-Consequentia Reasoning in Inferring Danger in Anxiety Disorders', Arntz et al., 1995. This is a very silly study where anxious and non-anxious participants were given scripts where they had to imagine themselves in certain situations. The result is something like creepy 'Choose Your Own Adventure' erotica, with scenarios like: 'You are in the elevator in the largest department store in Maastricht . . . You see two people faint: one falls into your arms. You smile. You've been interested in this person for quite some time and this seems to be a good opportunity.'

4   'The Effects of Safety Behavior Directed Towards a Safety Cue on Perceptions of Threat', Engelhard et al., 2015

5   *When Prophecy Fails: A Social and Psychological Study of a Modern Group That Predicted the Destruction of the World*, Festinger, Riecken and Schachter, 1956

6   'Obsessive-Compulsive Disorder Comorbidity: Clinical Assessment and Therapeutic Implications', Pallanti et al., 2011. This overview puts lifetime comorbidity of OCD and GAD at about 30 per cent; estimates for the comorbidity of OCD and panic disorder range from 13 per cent to a whopping 56 per cent.

7   'A Review of Obsessive-Compulsive Disorder in Children and Adolescents', Boileau, 2011

8   'Prevalence of Auditory Verbal Hallucinations in a General Population: A Group Comparison Study', Kråkvik et al., 2015

9   'Open-Label Placebos Reduce Test Anxiety and Improve Self-Management Skills: A Randomized-Controlled Trial', Schaefer et al., 2019

10   'Safety Behaviour: A Reconsideration', Rachman et al., 2008

11   'Anxiety Sensitivity, Its Stability and Longitudinal Association with Severity of Anxiety Symptoms', Hovenkamp-Hermelink et al., 2019

12   'Parent-Based Treatment as Efficacious as Cognitive-Behavioral Therapy for Childhood Anxiety: A Randomized Noninferiority Study of Supportive Parenting for Anxious Childhood Emotions', Lebowitz et al., 2020

13   'The Extrinsic Affective Simon Task', De Houwer, 2003

14   'Neurocognitive Processes in D-cycloserine Augmented Single-Session Exposure Therapy for Anxiety: A Randomized Placebo-Controlled Trial', Reinecke et al., 2020

15   'Changes in Automatic Threat Processing Precede and Predict Clinical Changes with Exposure-based Cognitive-behavior Therapy for Panic Disorder', Reinecke et al., 2013

16   'Early Effects of Exposure-based Cognitive Behaviour Therapy on the Neural Correlates of Anxiety', Reinecke et al., 2018

17   'Neurocognitive Processes in D-cycloserine Augmented Single-Session

Exposure Therapy for Anxiety: A Randomized Placebo-Controlled Trial', Reinecke et al., 2020

18 'The Structural and Functional Signature of Action Control', Schlüter et al., 2018

19 'The Loss of Glutamate-GABA Harmony in Anxiety Disorders', Wierońska et al., in *Anxiety Disorders*, Kalinin (ed.), 2011

20 'D-cycloserine for Treating Anxiety Disorders: Making Good Exposures Better and Bad Exposures Worse', Hofmann, 2014

21 'Augmentation of Cognitive and Behavioural Therapies (CBT) with D-cycloserine for Anxiety and Related Disorders', Ori et al., 2015

14. PSYCHEDELICS

1 This is part of the experimental protocol described in 'Pilot Study of Psilocybin Treatment for Anxiety in Patients With Advanced-Stage Cancer', Grob et al., 2011

2 'Antidepressants and the Placebo Effect', Kirsch, 2014

3 'Thirty Years of Psychedelic Research: The Spring Grove Experiment and Its Sequels', Yensen and Dryer, 1992

4 'Regulation of Human Research with LSD in the United States (1949–1987)', Bonson, 2018

5 'LSD in the Supportive Care of the Terminally Ill Cancer Patient', Kurland, 1985

6 'Rapid and Sustained Symptom Reduction Following Psilocybin Treatment for Anxiety and Depression in Patients with Life-Threatening Cancer: A Randomized Controlled Trial', Ross et al., 2016

7 'Psilocybin Produces Substantial and Sustained Decreases in Depression and Anxiety in Patients with Life-Threatening Cancer: A Randomized Double-Blind Trial', Griffiths et al., 2016

8 'Validation of the Revised Mystical Experience Questionnaire in Experimental Sessions with Psilocybin', Barrett et al., 2015

9 'Cognitive Consequences of Forced Compliance', Festinger and Carlsmith, 1959

10 'The Good-Subject Effect: Investigating Participant Demand Characteristics', Nichols and Maner, 2008

11 'Therapeutic Alliance and Outcome of Psychotherapy: Historical

Excursus, Measurements, and Prospects for Research', Ardito and Rabellino, 2011

12 'The Experimental Effects of Psilocybin on Symptoms of Anxiety and Depression: A Meta-Analysis', Goldberg et al., 2020

13 *War Neuroses*, Grinker and Spiegel, 1945, quoted in 'War & Military Mental Health: The US Psychiatric Response in the 20th Century', Pols and Oak, 2007

14 'The Therapeutic Potentials of Ayahuasca: Possible Effects against Various Diseases of Civilization', Frecska et al., 2016

15 'Neural Correlates of the Psychedelic State as Determined by fMRI Studies with Psilocybin', Carhart-Harris et al., 2011. This paper is mostly a collection of attempts to explain fMRI data through reverse inference – this bit of the brain showed activation, it also shows activation in studies looking at process X, therefore maybe what psilocybin does affects process X. Not that the generation of hypotheses isn't important, just that this is mostly interesting, informed spitballing rather than compelling evidence.

16 'Altered Default Mode Network Activity in Patient with Anxiety Disorders: An fMRI Study', Zhao et al., 2007

17 'The Default Mode Network In Late-Life Anxious Depression', Andreescu et al., 2011

18 'Meditation Experience Is Associated with Differences in Default Mode Network Activity and Connectivity', Brewer et al., 2011

19 'Psychological Treatments That Cause Harm', Lilienfeld, 2007

20 'The Tyranny of Structurelessness', Freeman, 1972

21 'Psychedelics Promote Structural and Functional Neural Plasticity', Ly et al., 2018

22 'Emotions and brain function are altered up to one month after a single high dose of psilocybin', Barrett et al., 2020. This was a tiny open-label trial of twelve 'healthy' volunteers – that is to say, people who didn't have anxiety disorders. So, suggestive that more research might be worthwhile, for sure, but not really proof of anything.

23 'Magic Truffles or Philosopher's Stones: A Legal Way to Sell Psilocybin?', Pellegrini et al., 2013

NOTES

15. THE WATER CURE

1 'Science and Statistics', Box, 1976

2 The example I've given above, taken from Belgian physician Joseph Guislain's *Traité sur l'aliénation mentale et sur les hospices de aliénés* ('Treatise on Mental Illness and Mental Hospitals') is based on a real design, but most asylums using cold-shock 'therapy' did so indoors, restraining the patient rather than constructing elaborate traps. After all, such a ruse would presumably work only once.

3 'Inside the Mind of the Ice Man', Wim Hof, Word Porn, https://www.youtube.com/watch?v=R_fqcruPL30

4 '"Brain over Body" – A Study on the Willful Regulation of Autonomic Function during Cold Exposure', Muzik et al., 2018

5 'Voluntary Activation of the Sympathetic Nervous System and Attenuation of the Innate Immune Response in Humans', Kox et al., 2014

6 'The Role of Outcome Expectancies for a Training Program Consisting of Meditation, Breathing Exercises, and Cold Exposure on the Response to Endotoxin Administration: A Proof-of-Principle Study', van Middendorp et al., 2016

7 'Hormesis Defined', Mattson, 2008

8 'Permanence of the Habituation of the Initial Responses to Cold-Water Immersion in Humans', Tipton et al., 2000

9 'Open Water Swimming as a Treatment for Major Depressive Disorder', van Tulleken et al., 2018

10 'Acute Anxiety Predicts Components of the Cold Shock Response on Cold Water Immersion: Toward an Integrated Psychophysiological Model of Acute Cold Water Survival', Barwood et al., 2018

11 According to www.nationalfirechiefs.org.uk/Be-Water-Aware there were 223 deaths from accidental drowning in the UK in 2019.

12 'Classical Diseases Revisited: Transient Global Amnesia', Owen et al., 2007

13 'The Moomins Discover the Island', Ep. 4, Moomin, Telecable Benelux BV, 1990

14 *Self-Efficacy: The Exercise of Control*, Bandura, 1997

16. BREATHING

1   *Feeling Good: The New Mood Therapy*, Burns, 1980

2   'Assessing Risk for Imminent Suicide', Galynker et al., 2014

3   'Neurocognitive and Somatic Components of Temperature Increases during g-Tummo Meditation: Legend and Reality', Kozhevnikov et al., 2013

4   'Prolonged Dry Apnoea: Effects on Brain Activity and Physiological Functions in Breath-Hold Divers and Non-Divers', Ratmanova et al., 2016

5   'Electroencephalographic Alpha Activity Modulations Induced by Breath-Holding in Apnoea Divers and Non-Divers', Steinberg et al., 2016

6   'Reactivity to a 35% CO_2 Challenge in Healthy First-Degree Relatives of Patients with Panic Disorder', van Beek et al., 2000

7   'Do Unexpected Panic Attacks Occur Spontaneously?', Meuret et al., 2011

8   'Testing the Suffocation False Alarm Theory of Panic Disorder', Klein, 1994; 'False Suffocation Alarms, Spontaneous Panics, and Related Conditions. An Integrative Hypothesis', Klein, 1993

9   'Hypoventilation Therapy Alleviates Panic by Repeated Induction of Dyspnea', Meuret et al., 2018

10 'The Physiological Effects of Slow Breathing in the Healthy Human', Russo et al., 2017

11 'Slow Breathing Reduces Chemoreflex Response to Hypoxia and Hypercapnia, and Increases Baroreflex Sensitivity', Bernardi et al., 2001

12 'Role of Chemoreceptors in Mediating Dyspnea', Buchanan and Richerson, 2009

13 'Neurobiology of Panic and pH Chemosensation in the Brain', Wemmie, 2011

14 'A Human Amygdala Site that Inhibits Respiration and Elicits Apnea in Pediatric Epilepsy', Rhone et al., 2020

15 'Breathing Inhibited When Seizures Spread to the Amygdala and upon Amygdala Stimulation', Dlouhy et al., 2015

16 'Fear and Panic in Humans with Bilateral Amygdala Damage', Feinstein et al., 2013

17 'Sequence of Information Processing for Emotions Based on the Anatomic Dialogue between Prefrontal Cortex and Amygdala', Ghashghaei et al., 2007

18 'Prefrontal Cortex and Executive Functions in Healthy Adults: A Meta-Analysis of Structural Neuroimaging Studies', Yuan and Raz, 2014

19 'Hypoventilation Therapy Alleviates Panic by Repeated Induction of Dyspnea', Meuret et al., 2018

20 '"Brain over Body" – A Study on the Willful Regulation of Autonomic Function during Cold Exposure', Muzik et al., 2018

17. HYPNOSIS

1 *Hysterical Disorders of Warfare*, Yealland, 1918

2 *Storm of Steel*, Jünger, trans. Creighton, 1929

3 'A Contribution to the Etiology of Shell Shock', Wiltshire, 1916

4 *A War of Nerves: Soldiers and Psychiatrists in the Twentieth Century*, Shephard, 2000

5 Gates v McKenna, England and Wales High Court (Queen's Bench Division, 14 August 1998)

6 'Hypnosis and Placebos: Response Expectancy as a Mediator of Suggestion Effects', Kirsch, 1999

7 'The Effectiveness of Hypnosis for the Treatment of Anxiety: A Systematic Review', Coelho et al., 2008

8 'Hypnosis as an Adjunct to Cognitive-Behavioral Psychotherapy: A Meta-Analysis', Kirsch et al., 1995

9 'Hypnosis as an Adjunct to Cognitive-Behavioral Psychotherapy for Obesity: A Meta-Analytic Reappraisal', Allison and Faith, 1996

10 'Fictional First Memories', Ahktar et al., 2018

18. RELIGION

1 *Revelations of Divine Love*, Julian of Norwich, trans. Spearing, 1998

2 'Seeing the Silver Lining: Cognitive Reappraisal Ability Moderates the Relationship Between Stress and Depressive Symptoms', Troy et al., 2010

NOTES

3 'Cognitive Reappraisal and Expressive Suppression Strategies Role in the Emotion Regulation: An Overview on their Modulatory Effects and Neural Correlates', Cutuli, 2014

4 'Cognitive Reappraisal and Acceptance: Effects on Emotion, Physiology, and Perceived Cognitive Costs', Troy et al., 2018

5 'Religious Coping Methods as Predictors of Psychological, Physical and Spiritual Outcomes among Medically Ill Elderly Patients: A Two-Year Longitudinal Study', Pargament et al., 2004; note 'associated with', not 'caused by'. The arrow of causality could point either way, or they could be downstream consequences of a third, unknown factor.

6 'Religious Struggle as a Predictor of Mortality Among Medically Ill Elderly Patients: A Two-Year Longitudinal Study', Pargament et al., 2001; the same caveats apply as with the previous study.

7 'Negative Religious Conflict as a Predictor of Panic Disorder', Trenholm et al., 1998

8 'Posttraumatic Growth: Conceptual Foundations and Empirical Evidence', Tedeschi and Calhoun, 2004

9 'Pivotal Mental States', Brouwer and Carhart-Harris, 2020. This paper proposes a model for psychological growth and suggests avenues for future research. It's tentative and hypothetical, which doesn't make it bad, but at most we might cautiously accept its framework as one possibility among many worthy of further investigation.

10 'The Effect of Mindfulness-Based Therapy on Anxiety and Depression: A Meta-Analytic Review', Hofmann et al., 2010

11 'The Effect of Mindfulness Meditation Training on Biological Acute Stress Responses in Generalized Anxiety Disorder', Hoge et al., 2018

12 'Hippocampal Circuits Underlie Improvements in Self-Reported Anxiety Following Mindfulness Training', Sevinc et al., 2020

13 'Randomized Controlled Trial of Mindfulness Meditation for Generalized Anxiety Disorder: Effects on Anxiety and Stress Reactivity', Hoge et al., 2013

14 'Does Mindfulness Meditation Improve Anxiety and Mood Symptoms? A Review of the Controlled Research', Toneatto and Nguyen, 2007

15 'Long-Term Meditators Self-Induce High-Amplitude Gamma Synchrony During Mental Practice', Lutz et al., 2004

16 'Increased Gamma Brainwave Amplitude Compared to Control in Three Different Meditation Traditions', Braboszcz et al., 2017

17 'In the Blink of an Eye: The Contribution of Microsaccadic Activity to the Induced Gamma Band Response', Schwartzman and Kranczioch, 2010

19. IN THESE UNCERTAIN TIMES

1 *No Surrender: My Thirty-Year War*, Onoda, 1974

2 'Updated Meta-Analysis of Classical Fear Conditioning in the Anxiety Disorders', Duits et al., 2015

3 'Altered Learning Under Uncertainty in Unmedicated Mood and Anxiety Disorders', Aylward et al., 2019

4 One study found that UK population-wide anxiety levels underwent a dip right at the start of lockdown, only to rebound as it progressed: 'Coronavirus and Anxiety, Great Britain: 3 April 2020 to 10 May 2020', UK Office for National Statistics, https://www.ons.gov.uk/peoplepop ulationandcommunity/wellbeing/articles/ coronavirusandanxie tygreatbritain/3april2020to10may2020

5 'America's State of Mind: US Trends in Medication Use for Depression, Anxiety and Insomnia', Express Scripts, 2020

6 *On Becoming a Person: A Therapist's View of Psychotherapy*, Rogers, 1961

20. THE MAGIC OF UNCERTAINTY

1 'Lacking Control Increases Illusory Pattern Perception', Whitson and Galinsky, 2008

2 'Confronting a Traumatic Event: Toward an Understanding of Inhibition and Disease', Pennebaker and Beall, 1986

3 'Writing About Emotional Experiences as a Therapeutic Process', Pennebaker, 1997

4 'The Effects of Expressive Writing Before or After Punch Biopsy on Wound Healing', Robinson et al., 2017

5 'National Crime Victimization Survey 2018', US Bureau of Justice Statistics, 2019

NOTES

6   'The Persistent Sampling Bias in Developmental Psychology: A Call to Action', Nielsen et al., 2017

7   *Current Diagnosis and Treatment: Physical Medicine and Rehabilitation*, Maitin, 2015

8   *Man's Search For Meaning*, Frankl, 1946